PUBLIC RECORD OFFICE HANDBOOKS
No 15 (Second Edition)

The Second World War

A Guide to Documents in the Public Record Office

John D Cantwell

London:HMSO

© *Crown copyright 1993*
Applications for reproduction should be made to HMSO

First edition Crown copyright 1972

ISBN 0 11 440254 X

British Library Cataloguing in Publication Data
A CIP catalogue record for this book
is available from the British Library

HMSO

HMSO publications are available from:

HMSO Publications Centre
(Mail, fax and telephone orders only)
PO Box 276, London, SW8 5DT
Telephone orders 071-873 9090
General enquiries 071-873 0011
(queuing system in operation for both numbers)
Fax orders 071-873 8200

HMSO Bookshops
49 High Holborn, London, WC1V 6HB
(counter service only)
071-873 0011 Fax 071-873 8200
258 Broad Street, Birmingham, B1 2HE
021-643 3740 Fax 021-643 6510
Southey House, 33 Wine Street, Bristol, BS1 2BQ
0272 264306 Fax 0272 294515
9-21 Princess Street, Manchester, M60 8AS
061-834 7201 Fax 061-833 0634
16 Arthur Street, Belfast, BT1 4GD
0232 238451 Fax 0232 235401
71 Lothian Road, Edinburgh, EH3 9AZ
031-228 4181 Fax 031-229 2734

HMSO's Accredited Agents
(see Yellow Pages)

and through good booksellers

Printed in the United Kingdom for HMSO
Dd294226 1/93 C25 G3397 10170

Preface

The preparation of the first edition of this *Guide* was the responsibility of Mr Lionel Bell, a principal assistant keeper of public records, with the assistance of Mr Michael Roper, keeper of public records from 1988 to 1992, and many other colleagues both within the Public Record Office and in other departments.

It was published in 1972 to coincide with the accelerated opening of Second World War records in that year. The present revision has been undertaken by Mr John Cantwell, an editor and former officer of this Department with the help of Ms Susan Healy and Dr Edward Higgs. It was seen through the press by Mr Melvyn Stainton and Miss Fiona Prothero.

Public Record Office
1992

Contents

Appendixes

Introduction

This *Guide* is a revised edition of the one prepared to accompany the general release of Second World War papers early in 1972. In addition to material received since that time it covers, unlike the original version, legal records and records of a number of smaller departments and certain royal commissions.

The record classes detailed have not been confined to records of the prosecution of the war but embrace to some extent records of activities arising from or affected by it, such as those of the British element of the Control Commission for Germany and the Allied Commission for Austria. Very many of the classes listed in this *Guide* also contain pre-war and post-war material. Information concerning covering dates and the number of pieces involved is to be found in the Public Record Office *Current Guide* Part 2. For a description of, and reference to, individual pieces readers should consult the class lists at the Public Record Office at Kew and Chancery Lane.

The Development of Administration

The Second World War, like the First, brought about an immense increase in the size of the government machine. The duties of existing departments were redistributed and new departments created. Internally departments were subjected to a succession of organizational changes as events found them wanting or circumstances altered. In general this flux seems to have lessened during 1943, though it never disappeared, and the administration settled down to a steady haul towards victory. In dealing with the administrative history of a period such as this it has not been possible, nor would it have been profitable, to pursue every minor variation in the distribution of duties among the divisions of a ministry. The evolutions of their internal structure have been described in broad terms, as much for the light this throws on the nature of their activities as for its own sake, and these descriptions are expected both to contribute towards comprehension of the records and to signpost the nature of the material to be found.

The enormous expansion of governmental control of many aspects of life, together with the growing strain on our resources as more and more of them were closely channelled into the war effort, meant that the interests of departments came to overlap and conflict to an extent that was largely unknown in the days of peace. The task of co-ordination in these areas of possible conflict was frequently given to ministerial and interdepartmental official committees which now appeared in large numbers. The key role of the War Cabinet and its secretariat, which serviced many of the official committees, needs no emphasis and is set out in the section concerning 'The Central Direction of the War', on pp 3-16 below.

As the tide of the conflict began to turn in favour of the allied forces, the attention given by home departments to domestic reconstruction is also noteworthy, and paved the way not only for such measures as the Education Act 1944 and the Family Allowances Act 1945, but also for much post-war legislation.

The Records

Certain distinctive features appear among the records of the Second World War because of this interlocking of the activities of separate departments. The records of some departments provide useful information on the activities of others, particularly where there is some kind of co-ordination through joint bodies. The war diaries transferred by the Army Department provide a number of examples of this kind, as do the files of the Foreign Office. Another aspect of shared interests is the prevalence of copies of documents passed for information. This leads to the creation of large numbers of information files distinct from the working files which are the usual tools and records of twentieth-century British administration. Telegrams played an especially large part in such distribution for information and their distribution lists are often longer than the messages. The problems of twentieth-century diplomatic may come to centre on distribution lists and the associated telegram prefix codes.

Public Access

Most of the records of the Second World War are open to public inspection. Where a record is not available either because it is subject to extended closure or because it is still held by the department concerned, a note appears in the appropriate list. Where an entire class is similarly or mainly affected that fact is noted in this *Guide*. The situation is not static and readers should contact the Search Department at the PRO at Kew for up-to-date information. At the time of writing further records of the Special Operations Executive (see pp 133-4) are being reviewed for possible release.

The Official Histories

As early as October 1939 departments were advised by the War Cabinet Office to take into consideration the preparation of official histories. The series of histories which have been published since the war have been invaluable in the preparation of this *Guide* and a list of them appears at Appendix C. The narratives which were written in connection with the histories appear among departmental records as well as those of the Historical Section of the Cabinet Office and they will be found to afford detailed introductions to many kinds of war-time activity, both civil and military.

Code Names and Abbreviations

There is a card index of code names in the Reference Room at the PRO at Kew giving details of associated records. Copies of Christopher Chart's *The Encyclopedia of Codenames of World War II* (Routledge & Kegan Paul Ltd, London, 1986) and *A Dictionary of Military and Technological Abbreviations and Acronyms* by Bernhard Pretz (Routledge & Kegan Paul Ltd, London, 1983) may be consulted at the Reference Desk at the PRO at Kew.

Wartime Legislation

For references to bill papers and other records concerning wartime Acts of Parliament, readers should consult the Legislation Index in the Reference Room at the PRO at Kew.

Central Direction of the War

War Cabinet 3 September 1939 - 10 May 1940

[Where no terminal date is given the minister remained a member of the War Cabinet until the end of the period.]

Name	Office held while in War Cabinet	Date in War Cabinet [1]
Neville Chamberlain, MP	prime minister and first lord of the Treasury	3 Sept 1939
Sir Samuel Hoare, MP	lord privy seal	3 Sept 1939 - 3 Apr 1940
Sir John Simon, MP	chancellor of the Exchequer	3 Sept 1939
Viscount Halifax	secretary of state for foreign affairs	3 Sept 1939
Winston S Churchill, MP	first lord of the Admiralty	3 Sept 1939
Sir Kingsley Wood, MP	secretary of state for air	3 Sept 1939 - 3 Apr 1940
Lord Chatfield	minister for co-ordination of defence	3 Sept 1939
Lord Hankey	minister without portfolio	3 Sept 1939 - 10 May 1940
Leslie Hore-Belisha, MP	secretary of state for war	3 Sept 1939 - 5 Jan 1940
Oliver Stanley, MP	secretary of state for war	5 Jan 1940

[For secretaries of the War Cabinet see foot of list for 1940 - 1945]

War Cabinet 11 May 1940 - 23 May 1945

[Where no terminal date is given the minister remained a member of the War Cabinet until the end of the period.]

Winston S Churchill, MP	prime minister and first lord of the Treasury, minister of defence	11 May 1940
Neville Chamberlain, MP	lord president	11 May 1940 - 3 Oct 1940

---

[1] Most of these ministers held office before the creation of the War Cabinet.

Sir John Anderson, MP	lord president	3 Oct 1940 - 24 Sept 1943
	chancellor of the Exchequer	24 Sept 1943
Clement R Attlee, MP	lord privy seal	11 May 1940 - 19 Feb 1942
	secretary of state for the dominions	19 Feb 1942 - 24 Sept 1943
	lord president	24 Sept 1943
Sir R Stafford Cripps, MP	lord privy seal	19 Feb 1942 - 22 Nov 1942
Sir Kingsley Wood, MP	chancellor of the Exchequer	3 Oct 1940 - 19 Feb 1942
Viscount Halifax	secretary of state for foreign affairs[1]	11 May 1940 - 22 Dec 1940
Anthony Eden, MP	secretary of state for foreign affairs	22 Dec 1940
Lord Beaverbrook	minister of aircraft production	2 Aug 1940 - 1 May 1941
	minister of state	1 May 1941 - 29 June 1941
	minister of supply	29 June 1941 - 4 Feb 1942
	minister of production	4 Feb 1942- 19 Feb 1942
Oliver Lyttelton, MP	minister of state	29 June 1941 - 19 Feb 1942
	minister of state (resident in Middle East)	19 Feb 1942 - 12 Mar 1942
	minister of production	12 Mar 1942
Herbert S Morrison,MP	secretary of state for the Home Department and minister of home security	22 Nov 1942
Ernest Bevin, MP	minister of labour and national service	3 Oct 1940
Richard G Casey	minister of state (resident in Middle East)	19 Mar 1942 - 23 Dec 1943
Arthur Greenwood, MP	minister without portfolio	11 May 1940 - 22 Feb 1942
Lord Woolton	minister of reconstruction	11 Nov 1943

[1] Thereafter ambassador to the United States of America but still regarded as a member of the War Cabinet.

Secretaries of the War Cabinet

[Unless otherwise stated the following served throughout]

Permanent secretary of the Cabinet Office and secretary of the War Cabinet
  Sir Edward E Bridges
Deputy secretary (civil)
  Sir Rupert B Howorth (until 17 March 1942)
  Norman C Brook (17 March 1942 - December 1943)
Under-secretary (civil)
  Jointly   (Sir J Gilbert Laithwaite (from December 1943)
                (W S Murray (from December 1943)
Deputy secretary (military)
  Maj-Gen Sir Hastings L Ismay
Senior assistant secretary (military)
  Lt-Col (later Brig and Maj-Gen) L C Hollis

The day war broke out the large peacetime Cabinet resigned and was replaced by a War Cabinet on the 1916 model whose members, apart from the prime minister, were the chancellor of the Exchequer, the minister for co-ordination of defence, the lord privy seal, the foreign secretary, the first lord of the Admiralty, the secretaries of state for war and air, and the minister without portfolio. At the same time the Committee of Imperial Defence, which had been responsible for the inter-war study of defence problems and had played an important part in co-ordinating the planning preparations for war, disappeared into the War Cabinet and its staff was transmuted into the military wing of the War Cabinet Secretariat. It was not to appear again as it had done after the first war.

The War Cabinet[1] met daily for most of the early period and was supported by an array of committees, both military and civil. The major feature on the military side was the Chiefs of Staff Committee which had been formed in 1923 as a sub-committee of the Committee of Imperial Defence to advise on defence policy as a whole in addition to the separate responsibilities of the chiefs of staff for the three Services. Interposed between them and the War Cabinet was the standing Ministerial Committee on Military Co-ordination containing the three Service ministers and the minister of supply under the initial chairmanship of the minister for co-ordination of defence. This Committee bore responsibility for advising the War Cabinet on the overall conduct of the war, but the system never settled down well and the chairmanship was later transferred for a short time to the first lord of the Admiralty and the prime minister. In April 1940 the deputy secretary (military) of the War Cabinet became also chief of staff to the first lord of the Admiralty in his capacity as chairman of the Military Co-ordination Committee and was appointed at the same time as the fourth member of the Chiefs of Staff Committee.

The subordinate staff of the Chiefs of Staff Committee was taken over directly from the Committee of Imperial Defence and consisted of a supporting Deputy Chiefs of Staff Committee together with Joint Planning and Joint Intelligence Committees. Various committees existed to deal with particular subjects such as the defence of vulnerable points, defence research and supply questions, and there was in addition an Anglo-French Liaison Section. Earlier a Joint Intelligence Sub-Committee of the Committee of Imperial Defence had collated intelligence on air warfare between 1937 and 1939, particularly in relation to the civil war in Spain.

On the civil side, although various matters had been investigated under the aegis of the Committee of Imperial Defence, there was no standing committee structure to be taken over though the need for co-ordination was, if anything, greater, for the ministers for the civil departments, unlike their

---

[1] This account is partly based on PRO Handbook No 17 *The Cabinet Office to 1945* (HMSO, 1975).

Service counterparts, were not members of the War Cabinet. Civil Defence, Home Policy, and Priority Committees of the War Cabinet were hastily established, followed shortly afterwards by an Economic Policy Committee (which was reinforced by a subordinate interdepartmental committee) and a Food Policy Committee. These War Cabinet committees were supported by a large number of sub-committees. At the highest level, co-ordination with France was to be ensured by the Supreme War Council, containing both prime ministers, other ministers as necessary, and all the chiefs of staff. It was strictly a co-ordinating body and executive authority was reserved to the individual governments. Meetings were held both in England and France.

The replacement of the Chamberlain government by the coalition under Churchill led initially to a reduction in the size of the War Cabinet. As the new prime minister was determined to grip more closely the conduct of operations, and shortly established machinery to enable him to do so, the presence of the service ministers in the War Cabinet was not necessary. Later in the year the chancellor of the Exchequer, who had been replaced in the War Cabinet by the lord president of the Council, was brought back and ministers of labour and aircraft production were added. It will be seen that many of the War Cabinet ministers had no immediate departmental responsibility, though all were given specific fields of activity, and it appears that they were appointed for their personal qualities rather than for the interests they represented. The questions brought before the War Cabinet were generally treated first in committee and as many matters as possible were determined there. Matters brought directly to the War Cabinet included major foreign policy questions and questions of a predominantly political character. Naturally, any matter of sufficiently high importance for which committee consideration was not appropriate might go straight to the War Cabinet. Strategic matters were less and less frequently referred to it as the war proceeded. Some persons who were not members of the War Cabinet were regularly present at its meetings and became known as the 'constant attenders'. They included the chiefs of staff and the three Service as well as other ministers, while further ministers were liable to be summoned for items in which they had an interest. War Cabinet papers were circulated to non-member ministers.

The general pattern of support for the War Cabinet consisted as before of layers of committees, both standing and *ad hoc*, both ministerial and official. Most of the important committees in the top layer were presided over by War Cabinet ministers and the decisions of such committees were therefore authoritative. Unlike most of the pre-war Cabinet committees these were standing bodies to which particular types of problem were regularly referred for solution and the efficiency of this regular machinery was much enhanced by the existence of the single Secretariat which serviced all committees and whose members constituted an invaluable network of liaison between them. Further co-ordination was achieved by the overlapping membership and chairmanship of the committees, and in some cases the Committee of Imperial Defence system was adopted whereby both ministers and officials might sit on one committee.

A major feature of the Churchill administration was the combination of the office of prime minister with that of minister of defence, though it may be regarded as a symbolic rather than a practical change. The office of minister of defence had not previously existed, disappeared for two years after the war, and had no defined scope. Its creation in 1940 made it possible to describe the military half of the War Cabinet Secretariat as the Office of the minister of defence and its head became his chief of staff. The papers at the highest level follow this division with the former prime minister's Private Office series being split into a 'confidential' part kept at No 10 and an 'operational' part kept close by the subterranean War Room. Most of the War Cabinet Office records are minutes, papers circulated to and reports of committees, but there are also series of registered files dealing with such matters as committee membership and structure together with other file series deriving from various individuals and organizations and these sometimes contain information of importance.

The Military Co-ordination Committee was replaced by a Defence Committee, presided over by the minister of defence, which worked in two panels called Operations and Supply. The former was attended by the Service ministers supported by the chiefs of staff and other ministers as necessary, the latter by the Supply ministers and Service representatives. But the Defence Committee cannot usefully be regarded in a formal light on the basis of membership and terms of reference. It was Churchill's instrument for waging the war, meeting when he wanted it and attended by those he summoned. The particular virtue of the Operations panel was that it provided regular direct contact between him and the chiefs of staff, who also continued to meet by themselves as the Chiefs of Staff Committee. As the war progressed, however, the Defence Committee (Operations) declined in importance as Churchill tended to work through staff meetings or conferences, whose records appear among those of the Chiefs of Staff Committee. The Defence Committee (Supply) also declined with the creation of a more elaborate machine for handling production and supply questions by a Ministry of Production (pp 135-9). The Deputy Chiefs of Staff Committee ceased to function, but from April 1940 there was a Vice-Chiefs Committee which took some of the load from their superiors.

Subordinate organizations for planning and intelligence were reorganized and expanded. The Joint Planning Staff, under the directors of plans of the three Services, was divided from September 1940 into sections for strategical, executive and future planning, and the existence of this structure at the centre made it possible to bring in and co-ordinate with military planning the work of several departments by means of the appointment of liaison officers. In 1942 a Committee of Principal Administrative Officers from the Services was formed to advise the chiefs of staff on administrative matters and in 1944 a Joint Administrative Planning Section was created in addition to advise the Joint Planning Staff and to report to the Principal Administrative Officers Committee. The Joint Intelligence Sub-Committee had as its chairman a representative of the Foreign Office and as well as the Service directors of intelligence it included a member from the Ministry of Economic Warfare. These five departments provided the Joint Intelligence Staff and associated with the Staff was an Intelligence Section (Operations) which furnished intelligence to commanders and planners, and the Inter-Service Security Board which was responsible, among other things, for code-names and security schemes for operations.

Mention should be made of the Home Defence Executive which was hastily established as France began to collapse in May 1940 and consisted of representatives of the Admiralty, Air Ministry, Ministry of Home Security and the main Royal Air Force metropolitan commands under the chairmanship of the commander-in-chief Home Forces. It considered all aspects of preparations against invasion but in the nature of things found itself unable to act in an executive fashion. Less than a month later, therefore, it was reorganized under the chairmanship of the chief civil staff officer to the commander-in-chief Home Forces and given co-ordinating functions, though retaining its old title until May 1941 when it became the Home Defence Committee. It was particularly concerned, as a link between the military and civil departments, with questions of joint interest such as civil defence, camouflage and the protection of vulnerable points. A parallel Home Defence (Security) Executive, which shared the staff of the Home Defence Executive, was established at the same time to consider the problems posed by possible 'fifth column' activities and to initiate action through departments. In the event it appears to have dealt with wider security aspects as well as with 'fifth column' activities.

In civil matters the counterpart of the Defence Committee was the Lord President's Committee. Its members, apart from the lord president, were at first only the lord privy seal, the minister without portfolio and the chancellor of the Exchequer, but the home secretary, who was also minister of home security, and the minister of supply were added later in the year. Its function was to ensure co-ordination of the Production Council (which replaced the ineffective Priority Committee) and

The illustration overleaf is taken from War Cabinet Registered File CAB 21/779.

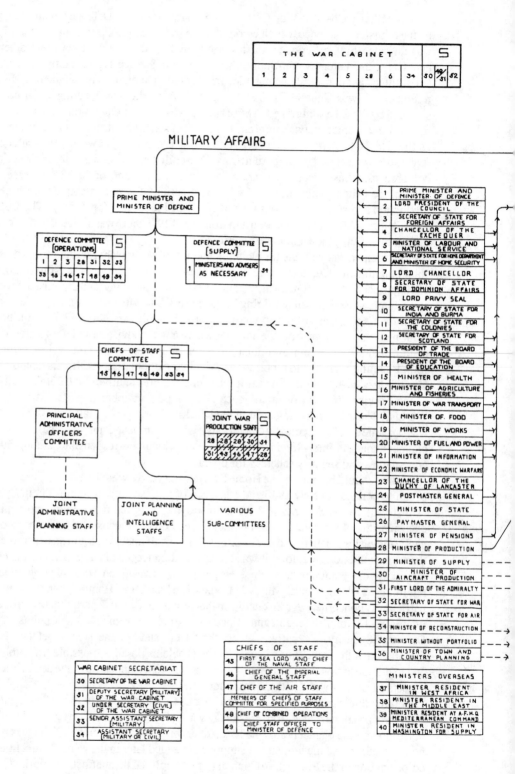

THE WAR CABINET | S

| 1 | 2 | 3 | 4 | 5 | 28 | 6 | 34 | 50 | 49/51 | 52 |

MILITARY AFFAIRS

PRIME MINISTER AND
MINISTER OF DEFENCE

DEFENCE COMMITTEE
[OPERATIONS] | S

| 1 | 2 | 3 | 28 | 31 | 32 | 33 |
| 33 | 45 | 46 | 47 | 48 | 49 | 54 |

DEFENCE COMMITTEE
[SUPPLY] | S

| MINISTERS AND ADVISERS AS NECESSARY | 54 |

CHIEFS OF STAFF
COMMITTEE | S

| 45 | 46 | 47 | 48 | 49 | 53 | 54 |

PRINCIPAL
ADMINISTRATIVE
OFFICERS
COMMITTEE

JOINT WAR
PRODUCTION STAFF | S

| 28 | 28 | 28 | 30 | 54 |
| 31 | 43 | 46 | 47 | 28 |

JOINT
ADMINISTRATIVE
PLANNING STAFF

JOINT PLANNING
AND
INTELLIGENCE
STAFFS

VARIOUS
SUB-COMMITTEES

1	PRIME MINISTER AND MINISTER OF DEFENCE
2	LORD PRESIDENT OF THE COUNCIL
3	SECRETARY OF STATE FOR FOREIGN AFFAIRS
4	CHANCELLOR OF THE EXCHEQUER
5	MINISTER OF LABOUR AND NATIONAL SERVICE
6	SECRETARY OF STATE FOR HOME DEPARTMENT AND MINISTER OF HOME SECURITY
7	LORD CHANCELLOR
8	SECRETARY OF STATE FOR DOMINION AFFAIRS
9	LORD PRIVY SEAL
10	SECRETARY OF STATE FOR INDIA AND BURMA
11	SECRETARY OF STATE FOR THE COLONIES
12	SECRETARY OF STATE FOR SCOTLAND
13	PRESIDENT OF THE BOARD OF TRADE
14	PRESIDENT OF THE BOARD OF EDUCATION
15	MINISTER OF HEALTH
16	MINISTER OF AGRICULTURE AND FISHERIES
17	MINISTER OF WAR TRANSPORT
18	MINISTER OF FOOD
19	MINISTER OF WORKS
20	MINISTER OF FUEL AND POWER
21	MINISTER OF INFORMATION
22	MINISTER OF ECONOMIC WARFARE
23	CHANCELLOR OF THE DUCHY OF LANCASTER
24	POSTMASTER GENERAL
25	MINISTER OF STATE
26	PAYMASTER GENERAL
27	MINISTER OF PENSIONS
28	MINISTER OF PRODUCTION
29	MINISTER OF SUPPLY
30	MINISTER OF AIRCRAFT PRODUCTION
31	FIRST LORD OF THE ADMIRALTY
32	SECRETARY OF STATE FOR WAR
33	SECRETARY OF STATE FOR AIR
34	MINISTER OF RECONSTRUCTION
35	MINISTER WITHOUT PORTFOLIO
36	MINISTER OF TOWN AND COUNTRY PLANNING

WAR CABINET SECRETARIAT

50	SECRETARY OF THE WAR CABINET
51	DEPUTY SECRETARY [MILITARY] OF THE WAR CABINET
52	UNDER SECRETARY [CIVIL] OF THE WAR CABINET
53	SENIOR ASSISTANT SECRETARY [MILITARY]
54	ASSISTANT SECRETARY [MILITARY OR CIVIL]

CHIEFS OF STAFF

45	FIRST SEA LORD AND CHIEF OF THE NAVAL STAFF
46	CHIEF OF THE IMPERIAL GENERAL STAFF
47	CHIEF OF THE AIR STAFF
	MEMBERS OF CHIEFS OF STAFF COMMITTEE FOR SPECIFIED PURPOSES
48	CHIEF OF COMBINED OPERATIONS
49	CHIEF STAFF OFFICER TO MINISTER OF DEFENCE

MINISTERS OVERSEAS

37	MINISTER RESIDENT IN WEST AFRICA
38	MINISTER RESIDENT IN THE MIDDLE EAST
39	MINISTER RESIDENT AT A.F.H.Q MEDITERRANEAN COMMAND
40	MINISTER RESIDENT IN WASHINGTON FOR SUPPLY

8

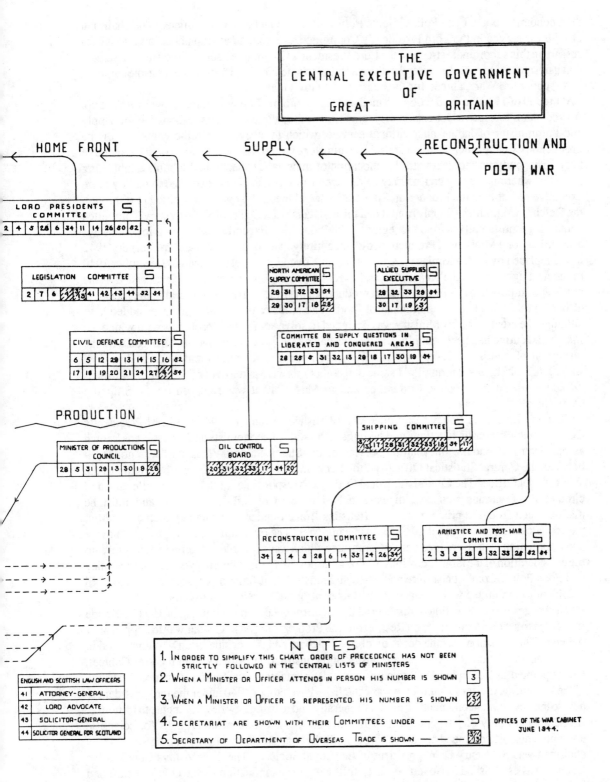

the Economic Policy, Food Policy, Home Policy and Civil Defence Committees. The chairmen of all these served in the Lord President's Committee. Although developments came to be necessary in this subordinate structure the Lord President's Committee itself fulfilled its role so well that it not merely survived to the end of the war but also extended its powers to become the supreme body, under the War Cabinet, for the control of all civil matters.

At the end of 1940 the Production Council and the Economic Policy Committee were wound up. A Production Executive was established, consisting of the three ministers responsible for supply and the minister of labour and national service, which took over the sub-committees of the Production Council other than Transport. The minister of war transport was added to the Executive later. This body was to deal with the allocation of materials, capacity and labour, establishing priorities where necessary and, as may be deduced from its name, was expected to deploy more executive power than the Production Council. War Cabinet policy was transmitted to it through the Defence Committee (Supply) and it had the assistance of a Central Joint Advisory Committee containing representatives from the regions. The Production Executive, which was in some ways a substitute for a Ministry of Production, did not entirely live up to its name and in February 1942 it was replaced by such a Ministry. An Import Executive was also established in December 1940 to secure a tight grip on the preparation and execution of import programmes. It consisted of the minister of supply, the minister of aircraft production, the first lord of the Admiralty, the president of the Board of Trade and the minister of food. The minister of war transport was added later although the creation of his Ministry was designed to solve some of the problems with which the Import Executive had been grappling, and at the end of 1941 the Executive was charged with the resolution of conflicts between United Kingdom import programmes and Middle East civil shipping requirements. During 1941 some of its functions were taken over by the prime minister's *ad hoc* Battle of the Atlantic Committee and in May 1942 it was replaced by the Shipping Committee.

When the Economic Policy Committee was abolished in January 1941 the Lord President's Committee took over its functions and with them the staff of economists and statisticians known as the Central Economic Information Service or the Stamp Survey. This staff was now split between the Central Statistical Office and the Economic Section, both of them belonging to the War Cabinet Office. The Central Statistical Office was responsible for the regular collection and circulation of various statistical digests, including some of military matters, and must be distinguished from the prime minister's Statistics Branch under Lindemann which carried out particular calculations as required by the prime minister. The Economic Section provided advice and information to the Lord President's Committee which was now able to extend its activities into the consideration of the larger questions of economic policy. In the following year the Home Policy and Food Policy Committees were abolished and most of their functions absorbed into the Lord President's Committee which thus tightened its control of home front activities.

The changes in the allocation of ministerial duties introduced at the beginning of 1941 had made it possible to set up a Committee on Reconstruction Problems to consider what was to happen after the war. This question was the occasion of much debate and its consideration was continued in various manifestations. Eventually a minister of reconstruction, with a seat in the War Cabinet, was appointed in November 1943 to co-ordinate departmental plans for the transitional period.

The Scientific Advisory Committee was established in October 1940 under the lord president to advise the government on scientific matters generally and to bring new developments to its notice. It had also the duty of advising the departments on the selection of individuals for scientific appointments. It continued to serve throughout the war and from the beginning of 1943 its chairman was Sir Henry Dale, president of the Royal Society. The Tube Alloys Consultative Council was established in November 1941 following the examination by the chiefs of staff and by a panel of the Scientific Advisory Committee of the utilization of the atomic energy of uranium.

It was responsible for the oversight of the arrangements for the making of the atomic bomb which were in the hands of the Department of Scientific and Industrial Research.

Just as many of the arrangements for the conduct of business at the highest level in Britain were shaped by the personality of the prime minister, his close relationship with the president of the United States gave a particular importance and style to dealings with that country, both through the impressive series of telegrams exchanged between them from the time Churchill took office and in the conferences they held, beginning in August 1941. At a lower level the lead given in this way was generally followed, and though there were instances of dispute and deadlock the records of all kinds of wartime organization afford physical evidence of the integration of British and American personnel serving in them. The conferences, which were held in every continent of the world except South America, were serviced on the British side by the War Cabinet Secretariat, as were some other international conferences and meetings, including those with Stalin. The conferences with the president were held to determine the major lines of strategy to be followed by the Allies and, consequent upon those decisions, the allocation of men, materials and transport to the various theatres.

The first conference after American entry into the war was responsible for the creation of the Combined Chiefs of Staff Committee, although it was not brought into formal existence until February 1942. The staffs had met as early as February 1941 but only now was it possible to create a standing committee on the lines of the British Chiefs of Staff Committee. The Combined Chiefs were based in Washington where the British chiefs were regularly represented by the head of the British Joint Staff Mission and the heads of the three Service delegations who constituted the Mission. The British chiefs of staff based in London took their place on the Combined Chiefs of Staff Committee at the international conferences and at Teheran, Yalta and Potsdam they were joined by the Russian chiefs of staff. The existence of the Combined Chiefs of Staff made it possible to place forces effectively under a commander of different nationality without breaking the chain of responsibility to their home government, for commanders were responsible to the Combined Chiefs and they in turn continued to remain responsible to their own governments. This responsibility was both advisory, in respect of the settlement between governments of the grand strategy, and executive, in respect of working out and issuing directives for the implementation of that strategy. The Combined Chiefs of Staff were equipped with a supporting organization of Combined Staff Planners, Combined Intelligence Committee and a Combined Staff Secretariat, together with a variety of committees on specific subjects. Their authority did not extend to operations controlled directly by the Admiralty and the Navy Department. These were primarily in the Atlantic.

The British Joint Staff Mission in Washington, to which reference has already been made, existed before December 1941 and thereafter was in close contact with the American chiefs of staff and their subordinates throughout the intervals between conferences. They provided the British element of the subordinate combined bodies and were served by a Secretariat modelled on the military wing of the War Cabinet Secretariat in London. Constant communication between London and Washington enabled them to link the widely separated chiefs of staff into an effective Combined Committee.

The system of supreme commanders[1] in operational theatres both depended on and did much to justify the Combined Chiefs of Staff Committee. The first of these was General Wavell in the doomed American-British-Dutch-Australian-Command in South-East Asia and the South-West Pacific, which had the distinguishing feature of the later and more successful commands in that it united not only forces of different nationalities but also of the different Services, which may be accounted more difficult. Problems were liable to occur in the relationship of Supreme Commands to forces and operations within their areas but outside their control, but it was, in general, a successful system which was capable of variation in its details according to the needs of each

[1] See also Admiralty, Air Ministry, War Office.

theatre. Orders were issued by the Combined Chiefs through the chiefs of staff of the appropriate Ally and in the case of the proposed invasion of Europe they appointed a chief of staff to the supreme commander to prepare plans well before his superior's appointment. The establishment of Combined Headquarters required very close working relationships with the Americans and a considerable interchange of official information between British and American officers. The latter were not given automatic access to British papers; but there was fairly free interchange on a 'need-to-know' basis. This close working relationship inevitably created a need for special measures to preserve the privacy of some purely national documents. For this purpose, from 1944 onwards British documents which it was necessary to keep from the Americans were marked 'Guard' in addition to their normal security classification, and their distribution was restricted.

Arrangements equally had to be made for the Allied control of civil or, more strictly, supply matters and it followed the pattern of the Combined Chiefs of Staff. Co-operation with the Americans was strikingly close even before they became involved in the fighting and this was particularly true in the economic sphere. After Pearl Harbour five boards were established, though not all at once, to deal with raw materials, shipping adjustment, production resources, munitions assignment and food. The British element on these boards was supplied by the staffs of the British Supply Council in North America and the specialist missions. The various British missions in Washington came gradually to co-operate with each other and eventually to establish a sort of Whitehall *in parvo* with the assistance of the embassy, though the missions naturally retained their separate allegiances to their parent departments in London. In 1944 a single secretariat was established on War Cabinet lines to serve both the civil and military organizations.

The British Supply Council existed to consider and co-ordinate the policies of the various missions concerned with supplies and the activities of the British representatives on the combined boards. It had been created as early as December 1940 and consisted of the heads of the separate missions, eventually Service as well as civil. It reported at first to the North American Supplies Committee of the War Cabinet in London, and when a minister resident (supply) was appointed to Washington in November 1942 to represent the minister of production he acted as chairman of the Council. The Council acquired its own secretariat which was gradually strengthened in 1942 and 1943 and in the following year was combined with the military secretariat already mentioned.

Meanwhile in London a need was felt to co-ordinate the various aspects of supplies from North America so that in October 1942 a Joint American Secretariat was established within the War Cabinet Secretariat. Half of its staff was supplied by the Ministry of Production to which the new secretariat was equally responsible. This body both acted as a channel between London and the British Supply Council and missions in Washington and provided liaison with the American Mission for Economic Affairs in London.

To oversee the provision of supplies to Russia after that country was brought into the war a Ministerial Allied Supplies Executive was established in October 1941. These supplies were regulated by four successive protocols outlining the British and American commitments to Russia, but additional supplies were demanded from time to time and it was the business of the Executive to determine questions of general priority and to seek the improvement of communications.

The appointment of resident ministers in various parts of the world may be seen both as an extension of central control by the War Cabinet, to which such ministers were responsible, and at the same time as a delegation of authority to a man on the spot, for these appointments were also intended to avoid the time-consuming referral of various types of question to London. The first two ministers were appointed in July 1941 to the Middle East and Singapore and three others were added in the following year in West Africa, Washington (for supply) and North West Africa. The Singapore appointment was inevitably shortlived and that in Cairo may be taken as the successful prototype, though none of the others had such a wide range of responsibilities.

The duties of the minister resident in the Middle East were deliberately described rather broadly in the first instance, and under the general head of representing the War Cabinet and carrying out its policy they were noted as being principally relieving commanders-in-chief of extraneous responsibilities such as relations with foreign governments, providing political guidance and settling promptly matters involving several authorities on the spot. The minister did not supersede the regular representatives of his majesty's government but co-ordinated the activities of a number of them. The first ministers of state in the Middle East were members of the War Cabinet but this did not become the general practice. The minister of state was chairman of the Middle East War Council consisting of HM ambassador in Cairo, the three commanders-in-chief and the intendant-general. Other ambassadors and governors attended when possible. Various sub-committees dealt with particular types of activity so that the whole system, with a small secretariat serving the minister, had a family resemblance to the War Cabinet Office in London. The Middle East Supply Centre, the work of the intendant-general in supplying the Armed Forces, the administration of enemy territory and propaganda were matters which particularly engaged the minister of state, but as far as possible he avoided executive duties and kept his staff small. An officer was placed in the War Cabinet Secretariat to serve as a channel for his communications with the prime minister, the War Cabinet and the Foreign Office.

The minister resident in West Africa was appointed in July 1942 to ensure the co-ordination of all services in the region. He was supported by a West Africa War Council and generally resembled his predecessor in the Middle East. The minister resident for supply in Washington, who was appointed in November, has already been mentioned. He was chairman of the British Supply Council and responsible to the minister of production for the work of the supply missions and the combined boards. The last to be appointed was the minister resident at Allied Force Headquarters North West Africa in December 1942(see pp 188-9). His duty was to provide, in conjunction with an equivalent American representative, a political element at Headquarters.

Detailed among the records below are a number of classes relating to the preparation of the Official War Histories by the Historical Section of the Cabinet Office, including its use of captured enemy documents. See also Appendix C.

The Records

CAB 21   Cabinet Office: Registered Files
         A selection of registered files on various matters dealt with by the War Cabinet. They include files relating to the machinery of the War Cabinet, its committees, and the establishment and work of the Secretariat. See also CAB 104.
CAB 44   Historical Section, Official War Histories, Narratives (Military) This class consists of draft chapters of the Official War Histories, some of them unpublished, and of similar compilations prepared by the Historical Section and others.
CAB 63   Hankey Papers
         Includes correspondence and papers of Lord Hankey relating to his work as a minister during the Second World War.
CAB 65   War Cabinet Minutes
         Minutes or conclusions of the War Cabinet, September 1939 to May 1945 (WM Series), and of the Cabinet, May to July 1945 (CM Series); also a subject index.
CAB 66   War Cabinet Memoranda WP and CP Series
CAB 67   War Cabinet Memoranda WP(G) Series
         The WP(G) series of memoranda was of a less secret nature than the WP and CP series (CAB 66) and was more widely distributed.
CAB 68   War Cabinet Memoranda WP(R) Series
         This series of memoranda consists of reports by various government departments to the War Cabinet.
CAB 69   War Cabinet Defence Committee (Operations)
         This class consists of the minutes and papers of the Committee and the secretary's file.
CAB 70   War Cabinet Defence Committee (Supply)
         The class consists of minutes and memoranda of the Committee and of its Sub-Committee on the Allocation of Small Arms Ammunition.

CAB 71   War Cabinet, Lord President's Committees
          This class consists of the minutes and papers of the Lord President's Committee, the Air Raid
          Shelter Policy Committee, the Service Travel Committee, the Committee on Emergency
          Legislation, the Industrial Sub-Committee and the Sub-Committees on Accommodation and the
          Supply of Books.
CAB 72   War Cabinet Committees on Economic Policy
          Minutes and papers of various committees and sub-committees on economic policy including
          those on Economic Warfare, Exports, Warehousing and Port Clearance.
CAB 73   War Cabinet Committees on Civil Defence
          Various committees and sub-committees on civil defence including Government Evacuation,
          Black-out Restrictions, Camouflage, Signposts, etc.
CAB 74   War Cabinet Ministerial Committee on Food Policy
CAB 75   War Cabinet Home Policy Committee
          Minutes of meetings and papers of the Home Policy Committee, 1939 to 1945, and of its sub-
          committees on Billeting and Office Accommodation, 1939 to 1940, Civil Liabilities, Rationing,
          Price Rises and Social Services, 1939, War Legislation, 1939 to 1940, Civil Liabilities, 1939 to
          1941, and Rent, Rates and Mortgages, 1940.
CAB 76   War Cabinet Committees on Imperial Communications and Censorship
CAB 77   War Cabinet Committees on Oil Policy
CAB 78   War Cabinet Committees, Miscellaneous and General Series
CAB 79   War Cabinet, Chiefs of Staff Committee, Minutes of Meetings
CAB 80   War Cabinet, Chiefs of Staff Committee, Memoranda
CAB 81   War Cabinet, Chiefs of Staff Committees and Sub-Committees
          Minutes and memoranda of various committees and sub-committees which were subordinated
          to the Chiefs of Staff Committee.
CAB 82   War Cabinet, Deputy Chiefs of Staff Committee and Sub-Committees
CAB 83   War Cabinet Ministerial Committee on Military Co-ordination
CAB 84   War Cabinet Joint Planning Committees
          See also CAB 119.
CAB 85   War Cabinet Anglo-French Committees
          Minutes of meetings, papers and files of the various Anglo-French liaison and co-ordinating
          committees and sub-committees on economic, military and post-war matters. See also CAB 99.
CAB 86   War Cabinet Committees on the Battle of the Atlantic and Anti-U-Boat Warfare
CAB 87   War Cabinet Committees on Reconstruction
          This class consists mainly of papers of committees relating to internal reconstruction problems
          but also includes those of the Committees on Supply Questions in Liberated and Conquered
          Areas. See also CAB 117.
CAB 88   War Cabinet: Combined Chiefs of Staff Committees and Sub-Committees
CAB 89   War Cabinet Survey of Economic and Financial Plans Committee
CAB 90   War Cabinet Scientific Advisory Committees
CAB 91   War Cabinet Committees on India
CAB 92   War Cabinet Committees on Supply, Production, Priority and Manpower
          See also CAB 109 and CAB 111.
CAB 93   War Cabinet Home Defence Committee
          Minutes and papers of the Home Defence Committee, 1940 to 1945, the Security Intelligence
          Centre, 1940, the Committee on Communism, 1941 to 1945, the Committee on Control at Ports,
          1941 to 1945, and minutes and papers of the Security Executive meetings and conferences, 1940
          to 1945. See also CAB 113 and CAB 114.
CAB 94   War Cabinet Overseas Defence Committee
CAB 95   War Cabinet Committees on the Middle East and Africa
CAB 96   War Cabinet Committees on the Far East
CAB 97   War Cabinet Shipping Committees
CAB 98   War Cabinet Miscellaneous Committees
          Minutes of meetings and papers of various committees and sub-committees whose terms of
          reference include civil, communications, economic, historical, military, political and security
          matters. The class also contains papers of the Tube Alloys Consultative Council.
CAB 99   War Cabinet: Commonwealth and International Conferences
          See also CAB 85.
CAB 100   War Cabinet Daily Situation Reports
          Reports left on the table in the Central War Room for the information of the War Cabinet.
CAB 101   Cabinet Office: Historical Section: Official War Histories (Second World War), Military
          A confidential set, with citations (not in the form of Public Record Office references) of original

sources omitted from the published version. The class also contains background papers, including drafts, concerning progress and publication. See also Appendix C.

CAB 102   Cabinet Office: Historical Section: Official War Histories (Second World War), Civil
The civil histories equivalent of CAB 101.

CAB 103   Historical Section: Registered Files
These files of the Historical Section of the Cabinet Office contain periodical progress reports, annual estimates and correspondence on various subjects.

CAB 104   Supplementary Registered Files
This class is supplementary to CAB 21. Some pieces retained by Cabinet Office.

CAB 105   War Cabinet Telegrams

CAB 106   Cabinet Office: Historical Section: Archivist and Librarian Files (A L Series)
Operational reports, despatches and other papers acquired for use in preparing Official War Histories. That part of the series dealing with enemy documents is held by the Imperial War Museum.

CAB 107   War Cabinet, Co-ordination of Departmental Action in the Event of War with Certain Countries
Minutes of meetings and memoranda. The countries concerned are France, Italy, Japan, Spain, Bulgaria, Hungary, Portugal, Roumania and Finland.

CAB 108   Central Statistical Office: Minutes and Memoranda
Statistics bearing on the development of the war effort in the United Kingdom, United States and other Allied countries.

CAB 109   London Munitions Assignment Board: Secretary's Files
For minutes and papers of the Board and its various committees see CAB 92.

CAB 110   Joint American Secretariat: Secretary's Files
These consist mainly of correspondence with the British Supply Organization in America, and include papers concerning Lend-Lease and supplies to liberated areas.

CAB 111   Allied Supplies Executive
This class contains the files of the Executive's Secretariat; they mainly cover the organization and procedure of the Executive, the allocation and transportation of supplies and exchange of technical information. Minutes of meetings and circulated papers of the Executive and its sub-committees are in CAB 92.

CAB 112   Vulnerable Points Adviser: Files
Retained by Cabinet Office.

CAB 113   Home Defence Executive: Secretary's Files
Retained by Cabinet Office. See also CAB 93.

CAB 114   Home Defence (Security) Executive: Secretary's Files
Retained by Cabinet Office. See also CAB 93.

CAB 115   Central Office for North American Supplies
Files arising mainly from British and Allied requirements for armaments and raw materials. The class also contains papers concerning relief supplies, particularly food, for other countries and territories. See also AVIA 38 and FO 115 (p 51 and p 87).

CAB 116   Departmental Security Officer: Files
Retained by Cabinet Office.

CAB 117   Reconstruction Secretariat Files
These files contain papers of the various official committees dealing with post-war reconstruction. See also CAB 87.

CAB 118   Various Ministers: Files
These papers were collected by Clement Attlee during his term of office as deputy prime minister. The files are mostly from the private offices of Neville Chamberlain, Sir John Anderson and Attlee himself during their periods of office as lord president.

CAB 119   Joint Planning Staff: Files
Correspondence and papers concerning memoranda for the Joint Planning Committees. See also CAB 84.

CAB 120   Minister of Defence: Secretariat Files
Files of the military secretariat of the Cabinet Office for the period that Churchill and Attlee successively combined the offices of prime minister and minister of defence. Include personal telegrams exchanged between Churchill and Presidents Roosevelt, Stalin and Inonu and Generalissimo Chiang Kai-Shek.

CAB 121   Cabinet Office: Special Secret Information Centre: Files

CAB 122   British Joint Staff Mission: Washington Office Files

CAB 123   Lord President of the Council: Secretariat Files

CAB 124   Minister of Reconstruction, Lord President of the Council and Minister for Science: Secretariat Files

CAB 125 Radio Board and Committees
Retained by Cabinet Office.
CAB 127 Private Collections: Ministers and Officials
Includes papers of General Ismay, Sir Stafford Cripps, Sir William Jowitt, Lord Cherwell, Hugh Dalton, Sir Henry Dale, Lord Beaverbrook and Sir Edward Bridges.
CAB 136 War Cabinet: Bacteriological Warfare Committees: Secretary's Files
Retained by Cabinet Office.
CAB 137 War Cabinet: Joint Technical Warfare Committee: Secretary's Files
Retained by Cabinet Office.
CAB 138 British Joint Staff Mission: Minutes and Memoranda
CAB 139 Central Statistical Office: Correspondence and Papers
CAB 140 Official Historians' Correspondence
CAB 141 Central Statistical Office: Selected Working Papers
CAB 142 United Nations Relief and Rehabilitation Administration: United Kingdom Delegation
CAB 146 Cabinet Office: Historical Section, Enemy Documents Section: Files and Papers
These include campaign narratives and information about enemy policies and operations taken from original sources by the Enemy Documents Section for the use of the official historians. The class contains correspondence files of the inter-departmental Joint Consultative Committee on Enemy Documents and correspondence with the Section's representative in Washington. German reports copied by the Section are now among other copies of captured enemy documents held by the Imperial War Museum.
CAB 150 Establishment Section: Files
CAB 154 London Controlling Section
Files of one of the agencies engaged in deception activities against the enemy. Retained by the Cabinet Office.
CAB 156 Cabinet Office: Cabinet War Rooms Collection
Retained by the Cabinet Office. Enquiries should be directed to the curator.
FO 660 War of 1939 to 1945: Ministers Resident, etc
This class contains the surviving records of: the political liaison officer with the United States Forces in Great Britain and North Africa, August 1942 to May 1943; the Office of the Minister Resident at Allied Force Headquarters in Algiers and Paris, 1943 to 1944; and the Office of the United Kingdom Representative with the French Committee of National Liberation at Algiers, 1943 to 1944.
FO 921 Minister of State, Cairo
Files of the office of the Minister of State Resident in Cairo.
PREM 1 Prime Minister's Office: Correspondence and Papers, 1916-1940
Miscellaneous papers of the Prime Minister's Office, arranged by subjects. The series is continued by PREM 3 and PREM 4.
PREM 2 Honours Lists and Papers
PREM 3 Operations Papers
Files of the Prime Minister's Office kept at the War Cabinet offices, dealing with defence and operational subjects.
PREM 4 Confidential Papers
Files of the Prime Minister's Office kept at No 10 Downing Street, dealing for the most part with civil and political matters.
PREM 7 Private Collections
Papers of Sir Desmond Morton, personal assistant to the prime minister, 1940 to 1945.
PREM 10 Private Office Diaries of War-time Visits by Prime Minister
Diaries compiled by the prime minister's private secretaries on his visits to USA and Canada and of meetings elsewhere with President Roosevelt, 1941 to 1945. There is also a diary of his visit to Italy in August 1944.
T 230 Economic Advisory Section: Files
Includes discussion papers of the Economic Section of the War Cabinet Secretariat.
T 273 Bridges Papers
Papers of Lord Bridges as secretary to the War Cabinet.

Admiralty

Admiralty Board

Name	Date of appointment
First lord of the Admiralty	
Winston S Churchill, MP	3 Sept 1939
Albert V Alexander, MP	12 May 1940
First sea lord and chief of naval staff	
Adm of the Fleet Sir A Dudley P R Pound	12 June 1939
Adm of the Fleet Sir Andrew B Cunningham	15 Oct 1943
Deputy first sea lord	
Adm Sir Charles E Kennedy-Purvis	29 July 1942
Second sea lord and chief of naval personnel	
Adm Sir Charles J C Little	30 Sept 1938
Vice-Adm [Sir] William J Whitworth	1 June 1941
Vice-Adm Sir Algernon U Willis	8 Mar 1944
Third sea lord and controller	
Rear-Adm [Sir] Bruce A Fraser	1 Mar 1939
Vice-Adm [Sir] W Frederick Wake-Walker	22 May 1942
Fourth sea lord and chief of supplies and transport	
Rear-Adm [Sir] Geoffrey S Arbuthnot	1 Oct 1937
Vice-Adm John H D Cunningham	1 Apr 1941
Rear-Adm Frank H Pegram	8 May 1943
Vice-Adm [Sir] Arthur F E Palliser	20 Mar 1944
Fifth sea lord and chief of naval air services [Title changed to fifth sea lord and chief of naval air equipment 14 January 1943, and to fifth sea lord(air) 1 May 1945]	
Vice-Adm the Hon Sir Alexander R M Ramsay	19 July 1938
Rear-Adm [Sir] A Lumley St G Lyster	14 Apr 1941 - 11 July 1942
(This office not on the Board 11 July 1942 - 14 January 1943)	
Rear-Adm [Sir] Denis W Boyd	14 Jan 1943
Rear-Adm [Sir] Thomas H Troubridge	1 May 1945
Deputy chief of naval staff (until 22 April 1940), vice-chief of naval staff (thereafter)	
Rear-Adm Tom S V Phillips	1 June 1939

Vice-Adm [Sir] Henry R Moore	21 Oct 1941
Rear-Adm Sir E Neville Syfret	7 June 1943

Assistant chief of naval staff (with responsibility for trade from 27 May 1940)

Rear-Adm [Sir] Harold M Burrough[1]	10 Jan 1939
Rear-Adm Henry R Moore	25 July 1940
Vice-Adm Edward L S King	21 Oct 1941
Rear-Adm John H Edelsten	7 Dec 1942 -
(Thereafter this office not on the Board)	30 Oct 1944

Assistant chief of naval staff (foreign)

Vice-Adm Sir Geoffrey Blake (retd)	8 Apr 1940
Rear-Adm Sir Henry Harwood Harwood	2 Dec 1940-
(Thereafter this office not on the Board)	8 Apr 1942

Assistant chief of naval staff (home)

Capt [Sir] Arthur J Power	27 May 1940 -
(Thereafter this office not on the Board)	28 May 1942

Assistant chief of naval staff (weapons)

Rear-Adm Rhoderick R McGrigor	9 Sept 1941
Rear-Adm Wilfrid R Patterson	8 Mar 1943 -
(Thereafter this office not on the Board)	February 1945

Parliamentary and financial secretary

Geoffrey Shakespeare, MP	28 May 1937
Sir Victor A G A Warrender	4 Apr 1940
(later Lord Bruntisfield)	
[9 February 1942 the two posts were divided and remained so until 4 August 1945]	
Parliamentary: Lord Bruntisfield	9 Feb 1942
Financial: G H Hall, MP	9 Feb 1942
James P L Thomas, MP	28 Sept 1943

Civil lord

Capt A U M Hudson, MP	15 July 1939
Capt Richard A Pilkington, MP	5 Mar 1942

Controller of merchant shipbuilding and repairs

Sir James Lithgow	1 Feb 1940

Permanent secretary

Sir R H Archibald Carter	23 July 1936
[Sir] Henry V Markham	5 Dec 1940

---

[1] Captain until 1 August 1939

Other offices

C-in-c Home Fleet
Adm Sir Charles M Forbes	12 Apr 1938
Vice-Adm [Sir] John C Tovey	2 Dec 1940
Vice-Adm Sir Bruce A Fraser	8 May 1943
Adm Sir Henry R Moore	14 June 1944

C-in-c Mediterranean Fleet
Adm Sir Andrew B Cunningham[1]	1 June 1939
Vice-Adm Sir Henry D Pridham-Wippell	1 Apr 1942
Rear-Adm Sir Henry Harwood Harwood	22 Apr 1942
Adm. of the Fleet Sir Andrew B Cunningham	20 Feb 1943
Adm Sir John H D Cunningham[2]	15 Oct 1943

C-in-c Eastern Fleet
Vice-Adm Sir Tom S V Phillips	Oct-Dec 1941
Vice-Adm Sir Geoffrey Layton	11 Dec 1941 - 5 Mar 1942
Adm Sir James F Somerville	5 Mar 1942
Adm Sir Bruce A Fraser	25 July 1944

[From 22 November 1944 merged in British Pacific fleet under Adm Fraser]

C-in-c Allied Naval Expeditionary Forces
Adm Sir Bertram H Ramsay	December 1943
Adm Sir Harold M Burrough	January 1945

Admiralty

At the beginning of the war the Board of Admiralty consisted of the first lord of the Admiralty, the first, second, third, fourth and fifth sea lords, the deputy chief of the naval staff, the assistant chief of the naval staff, the parliamentary and financial secretary, the civil lord and the permanent secretary. Each of these, apart from the first lord, was responsible for specific areas of Admiralty work which may be briefly described as follows. The first sea lord was chief of the naval staff and subordinate to him the deputy chief of the naval staff was responsible for policy and operations while the assistant chief of the naval staff dealt with trade protection. The second sea lord was responsible for personnel questions, the third sea lord as controller of the Navy was responsible for the construction of ships and their equipment and for armament stores, the fourth sea lord was responsible for provisioning, stores and pay, while the fifth sea lord was chief of the Naval Air Service. The civil lord was responsible for works and civilian labour while the parliamentary and financial secretary was responsible for contracts and carried out such other duties as were assigned to him from time to time by the first lord of the Admiralty. The permanent secretary was responsible for accounts, the organization of business and control of civilian staff of the Admiralty. While these duties were to a large extent identified with separate Admiralty departments, Board members might in some instances have over-lapping responsibilities inside departments.

During the first half of the war, as the number of elements in the Admiralty increased, particularly

---

[1] From 1 November 1942 until 20 February 1943 naval commander, expeditionary force
[2] From September 1943 c-in-c Allied Naval Expeditionary Force (Med)

divisions of staff, the membership of the Board was also increased, but this growth was later cut back. A controller of merchant shipbuilding and repairs was added to the Board in February 1940 when the Admiralty took over from the Ministry of Shipping the direction of these activities. An additional assistant chief of naval staff with the suffix (A) was added to the Board in April 1940 to have oversight of all activities in connection with foreign operations, and shortly afterwards the deputy chief of the naval staff became vice-chief of the naval staff in line with arrangements in the other services and took his place on the Vice-Chiefs of Staff Committee. By the autumn a third assistant chief of the naval staff was appointed to the Board and these assistants were now designated trade, foreign and home. In July 1941 an assistant chief of the naval staff (W) with responsibility for weapons and tactical developments joined the Board. These activities had in peacetime been the province of the assistant chief of the naval staff and had been neglected on account of the pressing operational duties of the assistant chief of naval staff (home). In February 1942 the post of parliamentary and financial secretary was split, with the parliamentary secretary dealing with personnel from the financial and political point of view and the financial secretary supervising contracts and contract labour. The removal of the assistant chiefs of the naval staff from the Board was determined on at this time to take effect as the current holders of the posts withdrew, and in April and May the assistant chiefs of the naval staff (foreign) and (home) were removed. The assistant chief of the naval staff for trade, now U-boat warfare and trade, was removed in October 1944 and the assistant chief of the naval staff (W) in February 1945. Meanwhile, however, in July 1942 a deputy first sea lord had been appointed to the Board.

The Board, as such, met only infrequently during the war but membership of it gave, as it had always done, great status. It was concerned on the whole with relatively long-term questions such as construction and matters of broad policy in such fields as pay and manning. The sea lords met from time to time as a separate body to prepare recommendations for the full Board on specifically naval matters, for example, promotions and inquiries into operations.

The operational control of naval activities was centralized in the naval staff of the Admiralty and it was the responsibility of the staff to ensure that information and communications facilities were available to make it possible to issue direct operational orders to vessels in any part of the world. The chief of naval staff bore this operational responsibility in addition to his duties as member of the Chiefs of Staff Committee and adviser to the minister of defence. Though almost all divisions of the naval staff played their part in operational control it was particularly the province of the Operations Division, which maintained plots of the movements and condition of all British warships. This division had been divided, shortly before the war, into Home and Foreign Sections each of which had its own director and, shortly afterwards, a deputy director also. Another deputy director was made responsible for mining operations and in 1941 a further deputy director was added for coastal work. The Operations Division provided daily summary reports of operations for the first lord and kept detailed records of the movements of all naval vessels. A Combined Operations Division was created in 1943.

The Plans Division of the Admiralty concerned itself with questions of strategy as well as operational plans and provided the naval part of the Joint Planning Staff (see p 7). There was a deputy director of plans in addition to the director and by 1943 a further deputy director (Q) had been appointed with responsibility for logistical planning. In the following year a separate Plans (Q) Division was created which concerned itself particularly with the organization of a fleet train to supply the British Fleet in its proposed operations against Japan in the Pacific. At its peak in 1943 there were as many as six assistant directors in the Plans Division.

The Naval Intelligence Division, which was responsible for collection, collation and distribution of information, was divided into Home and Foreign Sections in May 1940. There were then two deputy directors, of whom one was responsible for the Operational Intelligence Centre, and an assistant director of naval intelligence. The Operational Intelligence Centre, which had its counterparts in the overseas commands, tracked all movements of enemy ships and submarines which might affect operations, and had responsibility for the interception of enemy radio communications. From April 1940 it collaborated closely with the German Naval Section of the Division at the Government Code and Cypher School at Bletchley Park where intercepts were decrypted and translated, notably German signals and communications enciphered on the Enigma machine, the decrypts for which came to be known as ULTRA material from the middle of 1941. Additionally, the Centre was directly linked to the headquarters of the naval commands at home, the Coastal and Fighter Commands of the Royal Air Force and to the Area Command Headquarters which co-ordinated control of all three Services at the area level. By 1942 there were four assistant directors of naval intelligence. The Division had responsibilities in connection with censorship, representing the Admiralty on the Standing Interdepartmental Committee on Censorship, and at first for liaison with the Ministry of Information, but from January 1940 there was a separate Press Division under the deputy chief of the naval staff. The Intelligence Division retained for some time, however, an Information Section which produced and distributed periodic reports, including a daily summary of naval events. Naval reporting was one of the responsibilities of the Naval Control Service in ports around the world. The Intelligence Division was also responsible for the administration of the Interservice Topographical Department.

The Trade Division had been before the war a section of the Plans Division and was responsible for the protection of maritime trade and trooping by means of the organization of convoys and escorts and by the fitting of armaments in merchant vessels. Operating through officers of the Naval Control Service it concerned itself with such matters as the make-up of individual convoys and the methods of convoy signalling. It maintained plots showing the position of all convoys which could be compared with the information available in the adjacent Submarine Tracking Room of the Operational Intelligence Centre and kept detailed records of all merchantmen lost. The Division represented the Admiralty in the Ministry of War Transport's Diversion Room for the direction of inward convoys to ports.

The assistant chief of the naval staff (T) was responsible for the Trade Division, together with the related Divisions of Economic Warfare (except temporarily in 1941) and Anti-Submarine Warfare. The first of these had been created as a separate division just before the outbreak of war and the second shortly after it. The Division of Economic Warfare was responsible for the Contraband Control Service stationed in British-controlled ports around the world and for other means of applying economic pressure to the enemy. The threat posed by the submarine to our shipping led to a considerable augmentation of the naval staff. Three weeks after the war began an Anti-Submarine Warfare Division was formed from the Local Defence Division to be responsible for anti-submarine planning, operations and equipment. By 1943 this had been split into Anti-U-Boat and Anti-Submarine Warfare Divisions and an Anti-Submarine Materiel Department, the latter being placed in the controller's Department. The success of attack on U-boats was assessed by the U-Boat Assessment Committee and impetus was afforded from a high level by War Cabinet Committees on the Battle of the Atlantic (1941) and Anti-U-Boat Warfare (1942).

The Naval Air Division, with its responsibility for the policy and organization of the Fleet Air Arm, was generally subordinate to the fifth sea lord but was also a part of the naval staff under the first sea lord. Co-operation with the Air Ministry and the Royal Air Force was achieved in a number of ways. From 1940 a Coastal Command Liaison Section, later the Air Staff Liaison Section, was attached to the Operations Division, and in general the Operations Division dealt with the Air Ministry on immediate questions while the Naval Air Division did so on others. Overall operational control of Coastal Command was exercised by the Admiralty and at a lower level liaison was assured by the Area Command Headquarters. The fifth sea lord and the Naval Air Division represented the Admiralty on a joint committee with Coastal Command, while technical questions were settled directly between the appropriate departments. In July 1942 the Admiralty established an Air Co-operation Division to co-ordinate with the Air Ministry, but early in the following year both this and the Naval Air Division were replaced by a Naval Air Warfare and Flying Training Division and a Naval Air Organization Division.

The technical departments belonging to the fifth sea lord were the Air Materiel Department, responsible for design, production programmes for aircraft and for naval air bases, and the Aircraft Maintenance and Repair Department. When, in June 1940, the Ministry of Aircraft Production took over supply from the Air Ministry the needs of the Fleet Air Arm were eventually provided for by putting the director of air materiel on the Supply Board of the Ministry. In the spring of 1943 the Air Materiel Department was split into an Airfields and Carrier Requirements Department and an Air Equipment Department, and in the following year a Department of Naval Air Radio was added.

The Local Defence Division, like the Trade Division, was before the war a section of Plans Division. It was responsible for the naval defences in ports at home and abroad, including both anti-aircraft and seaward defences. The Mine-sweeping Division was separated from it shortly after the outbreak of war. The Training and Staff Duties Division was concerned with the principles of entry and training and, in particular, with gunnery and the preparation of textbooks. It included the Historical Section and, as well as supervising the preparation of separate war diaries by the Commands, compiled the naval war diary from information contributed by the other divisions. In 1941 a separate Gunnery and Anti-Aircraft Warfare Division was established. The Signal Department, like the Naval Air Division, had staff responsibilities but in 1944 a Signals Division of the staff was created to deal with communications separately from the production of communications equipment.

The responsibility of the second sea lord for the selection and appointment of executive officers in the Royal Navy was exercised through his naval assistant, with the help of assistants specializing in questions relating to officers of the Reserves and of the Fleet Air Arm. There was also an engineer rear-admiral for personnel duties. Questions of policy in relation to the supply of officers, such as the complements required for various duties, were also considered in this Department. The admiral commanding reserves had general supervision of the Coastguard Service from 1940, though the administration of this Service remained with the Ministry of Shipping (later War Transport), and immediate operational control was exercised by commanders-in-chief and flag officers around the country. The Department of Personal Services was responsible for complements, mobilization and welfare of ratings. In 1944 separate departments were added for manning, service conditions and welfare services. The medical director-general, the paymaster director-general, the adjutant-general Royal Marines and the director of the Women's Royal Naval Service were responsible for advising the second sea lord on the appropriate personnel questions, and other aspects of personnel duties were dealt with by departments for recruiting, physical training, education and combined operations.

The third sea lord as controller was responsible for the very large organization which existed to provide the Royal Navy with its ships and other equipment. Some of these departments were located at Bath. The overall design of ships and supervision of their building was in the hands of the Naval Construction Department, which was represented in all parts of the country by warship production superintendents charged with ensuring the progress of all work in their areas. Other departments specialized in the different types of equipment required. These included the Signal Department with its responsibility for design and development of communications methods and supervision of naval wireless stations which, as has been noted, was divided into the Radio Equipment Department and the Signals Division of the naval staff in 1944.

The third sea lord was also responsible for the Scientific Research and Experiment, Dockyard, Salvage and Boom Defence Departments, and for the Small Vessels Pool which co-ordinated the supply of such vessels for naval use. A Miscellaneous Weapons Development Department was established in March 1941, having begun in the previous year as the Department of the Inspector of Anti-Aircraft Weapons and Devices. During the course of the war further departments were added for unexploded bombs, wreck dispersal, net defence, de-magnetization, coastal forces materiel, combined operations materiel and anti-submarine materiel. Some research work was undertaken for the Admiralty by the National Physical Laboratory under the Department of Scientific and Industrial Research. The control of merchant shipbuilding and repair by the Admiralty, to which reference has already been made, brought the direction of all this industry under one roof.

The fourth sea lord supervised the activities of the Victualling Department and the Naval Stores Department which was responsible for the provision, storage and supply of all stores except armaments. The civil lord was responsible for the Department of the Civil Engineer-in-Chief, which handled naval works, while the parliamentary and financial secretary was initially responsible for the Department of the Director of Navy Contracts. This Department, together with a later established Department of the Director of Contracts (Merchant Shipbuilding), was transferred to the permanent secretary in October 1943 when similar arrangements were made in the other Service Departments. The parliamentary and financial secretary also supervised the handling of labour questions. This was for most of the war in the hands of branches of the Secretariat but from the spring of 1941 to the middle of the following year there was a Contract Labour Department to exercise control of shipyard labour.

The responsibility of the permanent secretary for the general conduct of Admiralty business, together with his financial responsibility as accounting officer, led to his Department including in its organization a number of branches which operated, as it were, in parallel with the other divisions and departments of the Admiralty for which they provided secretariat services. The Military Branch, for example, provided such services, including a Registry, for the naval staff, while the Air Branch provided a similar service in matters affecting the Fleet Air Arm. Among the other branches the Naval Branch was concerned with the conditions of service, complements and welfare of ratings and other ranks, the Naval Law Branch with discipline, including courts martial, and the Priority Branch represented the Admiralty in the Central Priority Organization (see p 149). Reference has already been made to the work of the Labour and Contract Labour Branches. Under the secretary the branches were supervised by a deputy secretary, an under-secretary and a number of principal assistant secretaries. During the rearmament period and the war a considerable degree of financial control was devolved by the Treasury to the Admiralty. Authorization of major expenditure was in the hands of the Treasury Inter-Service Committee, containing representatives of the Treasury and the Supply and Service Departments.

Correspondence in the Admiralty was traditionally filed on individual dockets which were marked with a running number and a prefix indicating the registry responsible for the docket, its distribution round the Admiralty and the despatch of communications. Several dockets on related subjects, or aspects of one subject, might come to be fastened together and a large collection of this kind and certain other files of specific kinds were known as 'cases'. As well as correspondence the material registered in dockets included, for example, reports of proceedings of individual ships, operations reports, reports of inquiries into ships lost and copies of documents from within commands such as general instructions to a fleet. Signals, which often required urgent distribution and action, were handled in a separate War Registry staffed both by civilians and naval signals staff but responsible to the secretary. Apart from the registered files departments maintained their own records, which were known as 'domestic', and some of the 'war history cases' are of this nature. Among the more important such papers were those kept for the first lord of the Admiralty and the first sea lord. War diaries were required to be kept on all stations at flag officer level. They generally consist of a narrative or chronological section supported by appendixes of documents.

The Royal Navy and Royal Marines

The right of the Admiralty to issue direct operational orders meant that, however great the desirability of leaving matters to the man on the spot, very detailed records had to be in Admiralty hands. The material available only from the commands, though some of it has been assigned to 'war history cases', is to that extent lessened in significance, but some account must nevertheless be given of the manner in which the units of the Royal Navy were organized and disposed.

The major part of the naval forces available in Home waters constituted the Home Fleet. There were in addition the Home naval commands of Portsmouth, Dover, Nore, Rosyth, Orkneys and Shetlands and Western Approaches, the latter of which was particularly concerned with Atlantic convoys. A separate command controlled submarines and a detached Force H was based at Gibraltar.

The foreign commands on the outbreak of war were North Atlantic, South Atlantic, America and West Indies (including the west coast of America), Mediterranean, East Indies and the China Station. When the Atlantic was divided into British and American strategic zones in 1942 the Eastern zone was sub-divided into Home, North Atlantic, West Africa and South Atlantic Stations. In the Mediterranean the seas west and North of Sicily were assigned to the naval commander Expeditionary Force appointed for the invasion of North West Africa in November 1942, and in February 1943 the waters around Sicily were added to this area to create a new Mediterranean Command, the eastern part becoming the Levant Command. The Levant Command was abolished and a single Mediterranean Command re-established at the end of 1943. The command arrangements for the invasion of North West Europe were similar, and an Allied naval commander Expeditionary Force had been appointed to begin planning as early as 1942. This was Sir Bertram Ramsay, who actually exercised command of operations in June 1944, though he had in the interval served as deputy and London liaison for the Allied naval commander Expeditionary Force for the invasion of North West Africa and as commander of the Eastern Task Force in the invasion of Sicily. Further east, following the Japanese successes of December 1941, the China Command disappeared and only the Eastern Fleet remained. This later came partially under the control of the supreme Allied commander South East Asia, an arrangement which led to some difficulties. Reference has already been made to the fleet train which was sent to Australia at the end of 1944 to supply the British ships operating in the Pacific.

Apart from their service in HM ships and in land operations under Army command the Royal Marines provided a Mobile Naval Base Defence Organization of coastal defence and anti-aircraft artillery, which could be rapidly put into operation at any port and was particularly intended for use overseas.

Naval Missions

In addition to the naval attachés appointed under the usual diplomatic system naval missions were despatched to North America and Russia. The British Admiralty Technical Mission was sent to Ottawa in June 1940 to seek supplies and investigate designs and repair facilities in North America. After the Lend-Lease system began operating in the summer of 1941 a British Admiralty delegation was sent to Washington. It consisted of the naval staff, which was attached to the Joint Staff Mission, the British Advisory Repair Mission, the British Admiralty supply representative and a civil secretariat. From the beginning of 1942 the delegation was organized into departments each of which represented the corresponding Admiralty Department and in 1943 a Naval Air Department was added. The naval mission in Moscow was particularly concerned with the organization for Arctic convoys to Murmansk and Archangel.

The Records

ADM 1   Admiralty and Secretariat Papers
The main series of papers concerning the administration of naval affairs. Large groups of papers which might have found their way into this class were sometimes made up into 'cases' and these will be found in ADM 116. Other papers of similar character which were assembled for Second World War historical purposes will be found in ADM 199. See also ADM 178.

ADM 4   Original Patents, Admiralty
Letters patent appointing the lords of the Admiralty.

ADM 53   Ships' Logs

ADM 64   Royal Marines General and General Standing Orders
Printed regulations regarding conditions of service, duties, uniform, and general organizational matters.

ADM 101   Medical Journals
Closed for 75 years.

ADM 104   Medical Departments: Service Registers and Registers of Deaths and Injuries
Include indexes and registers of reports of deaths.

ADM 116   Admiralty and Secretariat Cases
The nature of the papers in this class has been indicated in the note on ADM 1. See also ADM 178 and ADM 199.

ADM 136   Material Departments Ships' Books Series II
Reports and other papers giving the history of the maintenance of a ship (hull, machinery and armament) from construction to disposal. Ships' books in this class take the form of loose-leaf albums.

ADM 151   Nore Station Records, Correspondence

ADM 156   Courts Martial Records
Cases extracted from ADM 1, ADM 116 and ADM 167, including courts martial of Royal Marine officers and men. Closed for 75 or 100 years.

ADM 167   Board of Admiralty Minutes, Memoranda, etc
See also ADM 178.

ADM 169   Greenwich Hospital: Registered Files

ADM 171   Medal Rolls

ADM 173   Submarine Logs

ADM 175   Coastguard Records of Service
These relate to chief officers.

ADM 176   Material Departments Photographs of Ships
A complete set of photographs of HM ships which was formerly held by the Naval Construction Department. Other sets are held by the National Maritime Museum and the Imperial War Museum.

ADM 177   Navy Lists, Confidential Edition
The version not available to the public at time of issue, indicating where individual officers were serving, with the names of ships and establishments.

ADM 178   Admiralty and Secretariat Papers and Cases, Supplementary Series
Sensitive items concerning the administration of naval affairs, including papers extracted from ADM 1, ADM 116 and ADM 167. Most pieces closed for 100 years, but some may be seen by those who agree to specified restrictions on use.

ADM 179   Portsmouth Station Records, Correspondence
This class includes general orders and reports of actions and other papers concerning operations in the Channel.

ADM 182   Admiralty Fleet Orders
Printed confidential and routine orders issued to the Fleet, naval establishments and principal Admiralty overseers for information, guidance and necessary action.

ADM 183   Royal Marines, Chatham Division

ADM 184   Royal Marines, Plymouth Division

ADM 185   Royal Marines, Portsmouth Division

ADM 186   Publications
See also ADM 234, ADM 239 and ADM 264.

ADM 187   War of 1939 to 1945, Pink List
Printed sheets, issued at intervals of three to four days, showing the stations and voyages of HM and Allied ships.

ADM 189   Torpedo and Anti-Submarine School Reports

Annual reports of the School, together with other reports and papers dealing with mines and mine-sweeping, torpedoes and anti-submarine defences and weapons.

ADM 195   Civil Engineer-in-Chief Photographs
Photographs of works in dockyards, etc, in the United Kingdom and overseas.

ADM 196   Officers' Service Records Series III
These give dates of entry, down to 1922, and dates of discharge, down to 1954. They contain such information as dates of birth, rank, seniority, date of appointment, orders and commissions, awards, etc.

ADM 197   Admiralty Whitley Councils
Minutes of meetings.

ADM 198   Precedent and Procedure Books
These come from various branches and departments and include precedents, etc, concerning contracts, finance, victualling and honours.

ADM 199   War History Cases and Papers
Papers dealing with the administration of the Royal Navy and the planning and execution of naval operations, assembled by the Admiralty Historical Section. See also ADM 1.

ADM 201   Royal Marines: Royal Marine Office Correspondence and Papers
Includes lists of Royal Marines prisoners of war in Germany.

ADM 202   Royal Marines War Diaries
War diaries of the Royal Marine Division, Special Service and Commando Units, Mobile Naval Base Defence Organizations, etc, and despatches, letters and reports and files on operations. See also DEFE 2.

ADM 203   Royal Naval College, Correspondence and Papers
Includes lecture material relating to military and naval operations.

ADM 204   Admiralty Research Laboratory: Reports and Notes
Quarterly and half-yearly progress reports of the Laboratory and reports on particular experiments and investigations.

ADM 205   First Sea Lord Papers

ADM 207   Fleet Air Arm: Squadron Records
Daily accounts of their domestic and administrative activities. See also AIR 27.

ADM 208   Red List
Contains details of all minor war vessels in home waters, including vessels of Allied countries. Usually printed at weekly intervals from February 1940.

ADM 209   Blue List
Lists of ships under construction for the Royal and Dominion Navies. Printed at 1-3 monthly intervals from April 1940.

ADM 210   Green List
Weekly lists of landing ships, craft and barges in Home waters and foreign stations from August 1942, supplemented by a similar list of United States vessels from January 1944.

ADM 211   Office Memoranda

ADM 212   Admiralty Research Laboratory: Correspondence and Papers
Includes material relating to camouflage, degaussing torpedoes, underwater experiments and vision.

ADM 213   Admiralty Centre for Scientific Information and Liaison: Reports
A collection of reports from Admiralty research establishments, with some scientific reports from other sources of interest to the Royal Navy.

ADM 214   Civil Engineer in Chief: Papers

ADM 217   Station Records: Western Approaches
These consist mainly of convoy reports.

ADM 218   Royal Naval Scientific Service: A B Wood's Papers
Dr Wood was appointed superintendent of the Admiralty Research Laboratory in 1943, having previously served as chief scientist at HM Mining School.

ADM 219   Directorate of Naval Operational Studies: Reports
Reports on naval operations undertaken, and techniques employed, with conclusions as to their efficacy and possible future application.

ADM 220   Admiralty Surface Weapons Establishment
Reports of research into communications, radar missile control, electronic countermeasures and related fields.

ADM 223   Naval Intelligence Papers
Include 'ULTRA' material received from the Government Code and Cypher School, Bletchley Park. See also DEFE 3 and PRO 31/20 below.

ADM 226   Admiralty Experiment Works Reports
Reports on the design and performance of vessels.

ADM 227 Admiralty Engineering Laboratory
Reports and technical memos on the testing and development of engines and mechanical and electrical equipment and on chemicals and metals.
ADM 228 British Naval Commander in Chief, Germany: Papers
Files on the control and disposal of German shipping, stores and equipment, ports, and general and naval policy.
ADM 229 Department of the Director of Naval Construction: Unregistered Papers
Semi-official and private correspondence of Sir Stanley Goodall, director of naval construction, and a collection of notes and memoranda on official and professional subjects. See also ADM 281.
ADM 234 Navy Reference Books: BR Series
Non-confidential publications, including geographical handbooks prepared by the Naval Intelligence Division, battle summaries, damage reports and reports issued in the Interservices Information series. See also ADM 186 and ADM 239.
ADM 236 War of 1939-1945: Offices of Captains of Submarine Flotillas: Submarine War Patrol Reports and associated records
This collection is very incomplete. Some reports will also be found in ADM 199.
ADM 237 War of 1939-1945: Naval Staff: Operations Division; Convoy Records
Case files on individual convoys, including papers on their planning, composition, route, progress and fate.
ADM 238 Accounting Departments: Prize Branch Records
ADM 239 Navy Reference Books: CB Series
Publications graded 'Confidential' or above. See also ADM 186 and ADM 234.
ADM 243 Naval Staff Operations Division: Minelaying Operations
See also ADM 199.
ADM 244 Boom Defence Department: Photographs of Equipment
ADM 247 Admiralty Chemical Advisory Panel
ADM 248 Admiralty Chemical Department, Portsmouth: Reports
Reports of research into naval chemical and metallurgical problems.
ADM 249 Admiralty Corrosion Committee
Reports of research into corrosion and marine fouling.
ADM 250 Admiralty Craft Experimental Establishment
Extracts from German Hydrofoil Committee Reports, 1941 to 1945, and final report of the Motor Torpedo Boat Power Unit Committee.
ADM 253 Admiralty Mine Design Department and Admiralty Mining Establishment: Reports.
ADM 254 Central Metallurgical Laboratory
ADM 256 Naval Ordnance Department
ADM 259 Underwater Detection Establishment
This class includes a number of reports containing anti-submarine experiments and ASDIC research.
ADM 261 War of 1939 - 1945: Material used for Official Medical History
Closed for 75 years.
ADM 263 Admiralty Gunnery Establishment
See also ADM 294.
ADM 264 Air Publications (Naval)
ADM 265 Engineer-in-Chief: Unregistered Papers
ADM 267 Department of the Director of Naval Construction: Damage Reports and Damage Report Files
See also ADM 199.
ADM 277 Directorate of Miscellaneous Weapon Development
Reports and technical histories on the development and testing of weapons.
ADM 281 Department of the Director of Naval Construction: Reports
Includes reports on airflow, descent of funnel gas, etc, and exchange visits with French and USA naval officers. There is also a summary of damage by enemy action to steering gear, etc, on HM ships and a draft history of warship construction and conversion of auxiliary and amphibious vessels. See also ADM 229.
ADM 282 Directorate of Research Programmes and Planning: Reports
These arise from the post-war compilation of reports concerning Admiralty wartime research and development, including work done for the Admiralty by the Government Chemist.
ADM 283 Department of Scientific Research and Experiment: Reports
ADM 290 Torpedo Experimental Establishment: Reports and Technical Notes
ADM 292 Admiralty Underwater Weapons Department: Reports
Translations of German torpedo documents.

ADM 294   Admiralty Gunnery Establishment: Registered Files
           See also ADM 263.
ADM 298   Medical Research Council: Royal Naval Personnel Research Committee: Reports
ADM 315   Admiralty Experimental Diving Unit: Reports
           These reports include a number concerning diving suits, breathing apparatus, etc, dating from
           1942.
ADM 900   Specimens of Classes of Documents Destroyed
           These include flying log-books of Royal Air Force personnel serving with the Fleet Air Arm.
AIR 15   Coastal Command
           Files relating to organization, planning, exercises, tactics, protection of shipping, equipment,
           etc. See also AIR 24 for Operations Record Books.
AVIA 46   Ministry of Supply Files: Series 1 (Establishment)
           Include narratives and documents relating to Admiralty research establishments.
AVIA 53   Ministry of Supply Files: Series 6 (Contracts)
           Include papers concerning claims arising from wartime inventions for the Navy.
BT 164   Registrar General of Shipping and Seamen: Royal Naval Reserve: Representative Records of
           Service
           A volume recording awards, casualties, deaths, etc, of Royal Naval Reserve officers.
BT 166   Coastguard Service: Correspondence and Papers
BT 200   Norfolk Flax Limited
           These relate to the takeover by the Admiralty on behalf of the Ministry of Supply of the Norfolk
           Flax Station as a government establishment.
CAB 86   War Cabinet Committees on the Battle of the Atlantic and Anti-U-Boat Warfare.
CM 4   Directorate of Defence Services I (Army): Graves and Cemeteries Files
           These relate to the maintenance of UK graves and cemeteries at home and overseas. Some
           concern naval personnel.
DEFE 3   War of 1939-1945: Intelligence from Enemy Radio Communications
           These signals, known as ULTRA, consist of intercepts which were decrypted, translated and sent
           from the German Naval Section of the Admiralty's Naval Intelligence Division at Bletchley Park
           to the Division's Operational Intelligence Centre in the Admiralty; and intelligence summaries
           derived from such signals sent to the War Office, Air Ministry and overseas commands. See also
           ADM 223/36.
FO 963   Embassy and Consular Archives Egypt: Alexandria Naval Court Records
HMC 3   Evershed Papers
           This class includes a report on the internal organization of naval aviation.
MT 26   Board of Trade Marine Department: Local Marine Boards
           Includes a register of investigations, mainly by naval courts, of seamen charged with disciplinary
           offences.
PRO 31/20 ULTRA: Representatives with US Army Groups: Reports
           Copies of reports in the National Archives, Washington DC.
TS 32   Registered Files: Admiralty Series
           Case files of the Treasury solicitor arising from legal work carried out for the Admiralty.
WO 226   Committee on Detention Barracks
           Minutes, evidence, report, etc, of the Committee set up in 1943 to inquire into the treatment of
           men under sentence in naval and military detention barracks.
WO 252   Topographical and Economic Surveys
           Surveys, maps, plans, photographs, etc, of the Interservice Topographical Department which
           was administered by the Admiralty.
WO 257   War of 1939-1945: War Diaries: Ship Signal Sections
WORK 41   Maps and Plans: Naval Establishments
           Plans of dockyards, naval hospitals, workshops and magazines.

Ministry of Agriculture and Fisheries

Name	Date of appointment
Minister	
Col Sir Reginald Dorman-Smith, MP	29 Jan 1939

Robert Spear Hudson, MP	14 May 1940

Parliamentary secretary

Lord Denham	19 Sept 1939
Lord Moyne	15 May 1940
T Williams, MP	15 May 1940
Duke of Norfolk	8 Feb 1941

Permanent secretary

Sir Donald Ferguson	1 Sept 1936

Second secretary

D E Vandepeer (later Sir Donald Vandepeer)	27 Apr 1938

The circumstances of the war demanded, on the whole, an intensification of the activities of the Ministry of Agriculture and Fisheries rather than any abrupt change in them, although it did move into fresh fields in connection with labour supply, price control and the control of agricultural operations. The development of agriculture in England and Wales (Scotland being the responsibility of another Department) was of very great importance in view of the limitations imposed on imports. By the end of the war these were running at half their pre-war figure but by contrast net home production was up by a quarter in 1943 and grain production was doubled.

The Ministry was represented to the farmers by the 61 County War Agricultural Executive Committees consisting of farmers, landowners, workers' representatives and others locally interested in food production. Chairmen and executive officers of these organizations had been designated well in advance and thus when war was declared these committees were established and quickly began to operate in every county in the country. Sub-committees were established to deal with various technical aspects and District Committees to maintain even closer contact with the producers. The recommendations of these District Committees were forwarded to the Executive Committee who used the powers vested in them under the Cultivation of Lands Order to serve directions on the farmers concerned. Failure to comply with directions could and sometimes did result in Committees entering and carrying out work in default or taking possession of the land with a view to bringing it into cultivation either by farming direct through their machinery, cultivation and labour organization or by letting to approved farmers.

The execution of policy was thus firmly in local hands but its formulation was naturally in those of the Ministry in consultation with other departments. Links between the Ministry and the Committees were maintained by both its Local Organization Division and the chief agricultural adviser who had a staff of twelve liaison officers. These officers regularly attended the meetings of Executive Committees and met the minister and senior officials of the Ministry every month at Liaison Officers' Conferences. For the further guidance of Executive Committees circulars were issued covering such topics as the ploughing of grassland, the organization of work gangs, the planting of unfamiliar crops and the use of new types of machinery. Apart from the administrative divisions of the Ministry there were advisory and other associated committees such as the Publicity Advisory Committee, the Domestic Food Producers Council and the County Garden Produce Central Committee.

The programmes of production which constituted the policy behind the directions to Executive Committees were drawn up after consultation with the Ministries of Food and Shipping and with regard also to scientific advice about balanced diets. Their preparation involved the balancing of what was thought to be practicable in home production against estimates of the import situation a year later, together with calculations, for example, of the value of feeding-stuffs imports for home livestock against meat imports and of the increase in cereals for human consumption to be achieved by raising the extraction rate at flour mills to 85 per cent against the consequent decrease in feeding stuffs for animals. Increases in commercial production were supplemented by the efforts of domestic producers of vegetables, pigs and poultry, a campaign to which the Ministry devoted much attention.

Agriculture, like other industries, was severely affected by the progressive shortage of labour. At the beginning of the war the Women's Land Army was brought into existence to counteract some of the deficiencies in numbers caused by military service and a general drift from agriculture into other occupations. This drift led to a Restriction Order in June 1940 and in 1941 an Essential Work Order was made by the Ministry of Labour and National Service which in effect made unemployed agricultural workers into employees of the Executive Committees and prevented them from leaving that employment. The Executive Committees were encouraged to employ mobile labour gangs for drainage and other work, while for the harvest schoolboys' farming camps were organized. The Ministry also encouraged the more extensive use of machinery and this formed an appreciable part of its imports. An important aspect of the labour situation was the series of increases in the agricultural minimum wage that occurred during the war. This led to pressure for increases in the prices fixed by the Ministry and in conformity with the Government's general price policy subsidies were introduced at some points to hold the cost of living steady. Other financial measures were available to the Ministry to influence production, including grants for special purposes and special types of producers.

The wartime records of the Ministry are in most cases continuations of the pre-war classes.

The Records

MAF 32   National Farm Survey: Individual Farm Records
          Reports and returns on printed forms in respect of individual farms throughout the country made in connection with the National Farm Survey, 1941. Closed for 50 years. See also MAF 38 and MAF 73.
MAF 33   Agricultural Education and Research: Correspondence and Papers
MAF 36   Commercial Control: Correspondence and Papers
MAF 37   Crop Production: Correspondence and Papers
MAF 38   Statistics and Economics: Correspondence and Papers
          Memoranda and papers containing statistical information, including papers relating to the National Farm Survey, 1941; with policy and legislation files setting up the machinery for the collection of the information, and minutes, working papers, etc, of various statistical and economic committees. See also MAF 265.
MAF 39   Establishment and Finance: Correspondence and Papers
          Papers bearing on the history and organization of the Department and records of various departmental and other committees, including memoranda to County War Agricultural Executive Committees.
MAF 41   Fisheries Department: Correspondence and Papers
          See also MAF 71 and MAF 209.
MAF 43   Horticulture: Correspondence and Papers
MAF 44   Infestation Control: Correspondence and Papers
          Includes papers concerning Orders under Defence Regulations.
MAF 45   Information and Publicity: Correspondence and Papers
          Includes material concerning 'Growmore' and 'Dig for Victory' leaflets.
MAF 47   Labour and Wages: Correspondence and Papers
          Files dealing with labour recruitment and manpower policy, including the employment of school children and enemy prisoners of war, unemployment insurance, and agricultural wages. See also MAF 62 - MAF 64.
MAF 48   Land: Correspondence and Papers
          Some files concern land cultivation, restoration of defence works, etc, under wartime regulations.
MAF 49   Land Drainage and Water Supply: Correspondence and Papers

Files of correspondence dealing mainly with Drainage and Catchment Authorities, and papers concerning the administration of the several Land Drainage Acts and related questions, including drainage schemes of County War Agricultural Executive Committees.

MAF 51   Lime and Fertilizers: Correspondence and Papers
Papers relating to the measures taken before the Second World War to build up adequate supplies of fertilizers; encouragement given to farmers to improve the fertility of their land; and a scheme for State assistance in the erection of limestone grinding plant.

MAF 52   Livestock and Dairying: Correspondence and Papers

MAF 53   Secretariat and Parliamentary Branch: Correspondence and Papers
Includes material concerning wartime bills and debates relating to agricultural and food production matters.

MAF 54   Poultry and Small Livestock: Correspondence and Papers
Files relating to the Ministry's activities concerning goats, poultry and eggs, and rabbits.

MAF 55   Subsidies and Grants: Correspondence and Papers
Files relating to some of the measures taken for increasing food production and securing farmers against any substantial fall in prices, including acreage payments for potatoes, wheat and rye; barley, oats and rye subsidies; the marginal production scheme; and ploughing grants.

MAF 58   Agricultural Machinery: Correspondence and Papers
Papers showing the part played by the government in promoting the mechanization of the farming industry. The files preserved illustrate, among other things, the relevant legislation, the work of various administrative bodies set up to direct the supply and development of agricultural machinery, the control of imports and exports and some of the uses to which the machinery was put. There are also papers relating to the importation of machinery from the USA under the Lend-Lease Act.

MAF 59   Women's Land Army
Minutes of county committees, collections of photographs and recruiting posters, and selected files. See also MAF 900.

MAF 62   Agricultural Wages Board: Correspondence and Papers
See also MAF 47, MAF 63 and MAF 64

MAF 63   Agricultural Wages Board: Minutes
See also MAF 47, MAF 62 and MAF 64.

MAF 64   Agricultural Wages Committees
Minutes of meetings of District Committees and Permit Sub-Committees in England and Wales. See also MAF 47, MAF 62 and MAF 63.

MAF 65   Agricultural Returns: Parish Lists
Lists and names and addresses of the occupiers of agricultural holdings, their reference numbers and details of the amount of land worked, changes in ownership and size of holding. Access to these records is restricted by the Agriculture Act 1947. Sanction to inspect them must be obtained from the Ministry. MAF 65/81 is an alphabetical index of parish names keyed to parish numbers. The list of MAF 32, in alphabetical order, also serves as a key to parish numbers in this class.

MAF 68   Agricultural Returns: Parish Summaries
Summaries of annual returns of livestock and acreage in England and Wales given by proprietors on a voluntary basis. The original returns have been destroyed. Applications for use must be made to the officer in charge of the search rooms at the Public Record Office.

MAF 70   Welsh Department: Correspondence and Papers
Includes papers concerning the constitution of County War Agricultural Executive Committees in Wales.

MAF 71   Fisheries Department: Maps and Plans
See also MAF 41 and MAF 209.

MAF 73   National Farm Survey: Maps
Maps prepared in conjunction with the individual farm records of the National Farm Survey, 1941. See MAF 32.

MAF 77   Land Drainage and Water Supply: Maps and Plans

MAF 79   Animal Feeding Stuffs: Correspondence and Papers
This class deals with supplies and prices of feeding stuffs for livestock and the control of their distribution to farmers (including rationing in wartime) in collaboration with the Ministry of Food.

MAF 80   Agricultural Executive Committees: Minutes

MAF 82   Monthly Agricultural Reports
Summaries only.

MAF 89   General Division: Correspondence and Papers
These files relate mainly to war damage and war risks insurance.

MAF 107- Regional and Divisional Office Records
MAF 108,
MAF 110,
MAF 112,
MAF 146 -
MAF 147,
MAF 149,
MAF 157 -   These classes contain some material representative of
MAF 160,   the wartime activities of the Ministry in various
MAF 162 -   regions and localities.
MAF 163,
MAF 167 -
MAF 170,
MAF 173 -
MAF 177,
MAF 179 -
MAF 180
MAF 182
MAF 186   Registered Files: Manpower (MPB Series)
          Files of the Manpower and Wages Division. The class includes papers concerning the employ-
          ment of civil prisoners on agricultural work and minutes, etc, of the Women's Land Army
          Benevolent Fund.
MAF 197   Registered Files: Public Relations (PR Series)
          Include minutes, etc, of the Agricultural War Savings Advisory Committee and papers
          concerning 'Farm Sundays' in 1943 and 1944.
MAF 198   Registered Files: Further Education (FEM Series)
          These files include material relating to the retraining and provision of refresher courses in
          agricultural subjects for men and women released from war service.
MAF 200   Agricultural Research Council: Minutes and Papers
MAF 203   Registered Files: Milk Testing Service (MT Series)
MAF 209   Registered Files: Fisheries (FGB Series)
          See also MAF 41.
MAF 217   Information and Publicity: Leaflets, Photographic Prints and Posters
MAF 231   Registered Files: General Administration (GG Series)
          Include papers concerning the Councils of Agriculture for England and Wales.
MAF 232   Registered Files: Liaison with County Agricultural Executive Committees
          Minutes of the minister's meetings with wartime liaison officers.
MAF 234   Registered Files: Agricultural Housing and Buildings (AHB Series)
          Include papers concerning wartime emergency building for agricultural workers.
MAF 250   Ministry of Agriculture, Fisheries and Food: Registered Files: Defence and Emergency Services
          (DEF, DEF (M) and Z Series)
          Mainly minutes of meetings of heads of divisions to discuss organization of the Ministry.
MAF 265   Registered Files: Analysis of Agricultural Statistics (AAS Series)
          A few papers from 1941. For main series see MAF 38.
MAF 900   Specimens of Classes of Documents Destroyed
          Includes correspondence and papers selected to illustrate the day-to-day work of the Women's
          Land Army, 1939 to 1951.

Air Ministry

Air Council

Name	Date of appointment
Secretary of state for air	
Sir Kingsley Wood, MP	16 May 1938

Sir Samuel J G Hoare, MP   3 Apr 1940
Sir Archibald Sinclair, MP   11 May 1940

Parliamentary under-secretary of state for air
Capt H H Balfour, MP   16 May 1938
Lord Sherwood (House of Lords)   22 July 1941
Cdr R A Brabner, MP   22 Nov 1944
Maj The Hon Quintin Hogg, MP   13 Apr 1945

Chief of the air staff
Marshal of the Royal Air Force Sir Cyril   1 Sept 1937
L N Newall
Air Chief Marshal Sir Charles F A Portal   25 Oct 1940

Air member for personnel
Air Marshal C F A Portal   1 Feb 1939
Air Marshal E L Gossage, MP   3 Apr 1940
Air Marshal P Babbington   1 Dec 1940
Air Marshal Sir Bertine E Sutton   17 Aug 1942
Air Marshal Sir John C Slessor   5 Apr 1945

Air member for supply and organization
Air Marshal W L Welsh   1 Sept 1937
Air Chief Marshal Sir Christopher L Courtney   15 Jan 1940

Air member for training
Air Marshal A G R Garrod   8 July 1940
Air Marshal Sir Peter R M Drummond   27 Apr 1943

Air member for development and production
Air Chief Marshal Sir Wilfrid R Freeman   1 Aug 1938
(Appointment terminated with the formation of the
Ministry of Aircraft Production in May 1940)

Permanent under-secretary of state for air
Sir Arthur W Street   1 June 1939

Vice-chief of the air staff
Air Marshal Sir Richard E C Peirse   22 Apr 1940
Air Chief Marshal Sir Wilfrid R Freeman   5 Oct 1940
Air Vice-Marshal/Acting Air Marshal C E H   19 Oct 1942
Medhurst, MC [Acting Vice-Chief]
Air Marshal Sir Douglas C S Evill   21 Mar 1943

Operational Commands
[Air Officers Commanding-in-Chief]

Bomber Command
Air Chief Marshal Sir Edgar R Ludlow-Hewitt   12 Sept 1937

Air Marshal Sir Charles F A Portal	3 Apr 1940
Air Marshal Sir Richard E C Peirse	5 Oct 1940
Air Chief Marshal Sir Arthur T Harris	22 Feb 1942

Fighter Command

Air Chief Marshal Sir Hugh C T Dowding	14 July 1936
Air Marshal Sir W Sholto Douglas	25 Nov 1940
Air Marshal Sir Trafford L Leigh-Mallory	28 Nov 1942

Air Defence of Great Britain

Air Marshal Sir Roderic M Hill (Air Marshal Commanding)	15 Nov 1943

Fighter Command

Air Marshal Sir Roderic M Hill	15 Oct 1944
Air Marshal Sir James M Robb	14 May 1945

Coastal Command

Air Chief Marshal Sir Frederick W Bowhill	18 Aug 1937
Air Chief Marshal Sir Philip B Joubert de la Ferté	14 June 1941
Air Marshal Sir John C Slessor	5 Feb 1943
Air Chief Marshal Sir W Sholto Douglas	20 Jan 1944
Air Marshal Sir Leonard H Slater	30 June 1945

Transport Command

Air Chief Marshal Sir Frederick W Bowhill	25 Mar 1943
Air Marshal The Hon Sir Ralph A Cochrane	15 Feb 1945

Allied Expeditionary Force
[Air Commander-in-Chief]

Air Chief Marshal Sir Trafford L Leigh-Mallory	15 Nov 1943

Middle East Command

Air Chief Marshal Sir William G C Mitchell	1 Apr 1939
Air Chief Marshal Sir Arthur M Longmore	13 May 1940
Air Marshal [Sir] Arthur W Tedder	1 June 1941
Air Chief Marshal Sir W Sholto Douglas	11 Jan 1943
Air Marshal Sir Keith R Park	14 Jan 1944
Air Marshal Sir Charles E H Medhurst	8 Feb 1945

Mediterranean Air Command, later Mediterranean Allied Air Forces
[Air Commander-in-Chief]

Air Chief Marshal Sir Arthur W Tedder	17 Feb 1943

[Deputy Air Commander-in-Chief]

Air Marshal Sir John C Slessor	14 Jan 1944
Air Marshal Sir A Guy R Garrod	16 Mar 1945

Air Command South East Asia
[Allied Air Commander-in-Chief]
Air Chief Marshal Sir Richard E C Peirse   16 Nov 1943
Air Marshal Sir A Guy R Garrod   27 Nov 1944
Air Chief Marshal Sir Keith R Park   25 Feb 1945

Air Ministry

The basic pattern of the organization for the immediate direction of the British effort in the air was settled in 1936 and remained unchanged throughout the war, though there were far-reaching alterations in its application. At the centre the Air Ministry was responsible for all aspects of policy, while the Royal Air Force was organized in functional Commands in the United Kingdom and geographical Commands overseas which were responsible for the detailed conduct both of operations and administration. Within the Air Ministry business was conducted before the war on registered files controlled by a central registry but under the pressure of events the branches were forced to maintain in addition separate series of branch folders for their business and some of these survive in separate record classes for the secretary of state, the chief of air staff and the Directorates of Plans and Intelligence, as well as in the class of Unregistered Papers. Papers transmitted from one branch to another commonly had serial numbers marked on them by both branches, the series being distinguished by appropriate initials, and the original folder numbers may also be found. Some of the folders thus built up were for branch information only and used simply as works of reference, while others were used as files for the preparation of minutes and correspondence. Unlike registered files such folders would not normally go outside a branch into general Ministry circulation, separate papers being despatched instead. The papers have passed through the hands of the Air Historical Branch which was set up after the First World War. It received records from all parts of the Air Ministry and Royal Air Force, arranged them, gave reference numbers and prepared indexes. The present arrangement of the Second World War records is based where possible on the structure of the organization that existed when the records were created, but the lists which are the primary means of reference supply in some instances both the original and Air Historical Branch references of files.

The secretary of state for air, like the other Service ministers of the Second World War, was called upon to concern himself with what may be generally described as administrative matters rather than with the overall conduct of operations, for these were controlled by the machinery for central direction of the war under the minister of defence.

The Air Council, which consisted at the beginning of the war of the secretary of state, the parliamentary under-secretary, the chief of the air staff, the deputy chief of the air staff, the air members for personnel, supply and organization, and development and production, the permanent under-secretary, and the director-general of production, together with some additional members, was formally responsible, under the secretary of state, for all air matters. For the early part of the war it continued its pre-war practice of meeting as the Committee on Royal Air Force Expansion Measures and during this time it was able to get to grips to some extent with current problems, but thereafter was generally able to concern itself only with relatively long-term administrative policy. The investigation of night air defence carried out by a sub-committee of the Air Council under marshal of the Royal Air Force Sir John Salmond in September 1940 was something of an exception.

The chief of the air staff, as a member of the Chiefs of Staff Committee, had wider responsibilities in addition to his duties as principal adviser to the secretary of state in the direction of the Royal Air Force, and his responsibility for the overall operational command was in practice to the minister of defence. To assist him he had at the beginning of the war a deputy chief of the air staff and an assistant chief of the air staff. A vice-chief of the air staff was added on 22 April 1940, by which time there were two assistant chiefs, (General) and (Operational Requirements and Tactics). The continuing pressure of work led to a thorough re-examination of the structure and the revival in 1943 of the deputy post (which had been abolished) to supervise two assistant chiefs of the air staff who were then designated (Operations) and (General). Later that year the deputy chief took over from the parliamentary secretary to the Ministry of Supply responsibility for the co-ordination of intelligence and counter-measures against German rockets and flying bombs. Further assistant chiefs were in charge of Policy, Intelligence and Technical Requirements.

Below this level the Air Staff was generally organized in directorates, some of which were grouped into directorates-general and some of which were subdivided into deputy directorates. Their general responsibility was the assembly and study of information in their respective fields and, based upon this, the provision of advice to the chief of air staff and liaison between Commands and with other departments. Throughout the war new organs were developed and, less frequently, outmoded ones killed off. For Operations there was at the beginning of 1940 a director-general, soon to be replaced by an assistant chief of the air staff, controlling Directorates for Home, Overseas, Naval Co-operation and Military Co-operation, whose responsibility it was to provide information about current operations, including those of the other Services, to the chief of the air staff and to advise him on operational policy. Early in 1941 the Home Operations Directorate disappeared in favour of Bomber and Fighter, later Air Defence, Directorates, while by 1943 Naval Co-operation had become two Directorates for Anti-Ship and Anti-U-Boat Operations, only to merge into one Maritime Directorate in the following year. In 1944 also the Military Co-operation Directorate became the Tactical Directorate, and the Directorate of Overseas Operations was abolished. The Operations Duty Room enabled the activities of the branches to be co-ordinated to deal with urgent queries. The Directorate of Plans (from May 1942 under the assistant chief of air staff (Policy)) was responsible for the preparation of plans and directives to the Commands, for commenting on plans prepared outside the Ministry, for representation of the Ministry in the joint planning machinery in the United Kingdom and Washington, and for briefing the chief of air staff for his role in the Chiefs of Staff Committee. The War Room served the Air Staff by collecting information and preparing statistics. It must be distinguished from the War Group, a name given at one time to that part of the Staff most directly concerned with active operations. Signals began the war under a director reporting to the assistant chief of the air staff, acquired its own assistant chief (R), and later became a Directorate-General comprising Directorates of Signals, Radio Direction Finding (later Radar) and Telecommunications. Apart from its responsibility for development, technical planning and use of means of communication it was concerned in the prosecution of the radio war, involving both navigational and detection devices. In 1944 the Directorate of Staff Duties was revived with the new task of formulating staff doctrine and issuing air publications, and in the same year a director of navigation was appointed to control deputy directors of navigation, meteorology and flying control, that is, traffic and air safety measures.

The most considerable event in the administrative history of the Air Ministry in the Second World War was the transfer of its production functions to the Ministry of Aircraft Production, established under Lord Beaverbrook in 1940. This side of the work had been the province of the air member for development and production, with a director-general of production (who also had a seat on the Air Council) and a director-general of research and development as his immediate subordinates. Each of these had a number of directors reporting to him for various aspects of the work and the former had, in addition, two, later four, deputy directors-general to assist in co-ordination. This organization dealt with all aspects of the manufacture of aircraft, armaments, radio, radar and other equipment for the Royal Air Force from research, specification and planning through placing of orders, ensuring the provision of factories, industrial equipment and raw materials, to the inspection and storage of the finished products and their later repair. Associated with it was the powerful sub-committee of the Air Council concerned with Supply. The Ministry of Aircraft Production, brought into being by Order in Council on 17 May 1940, took over most of these functions together with the related parts of the permanent under-secretary's finance, establishment and secretariat duties.

From that time the Aeronautical Research Council advised the minister of aircraft production instead of the secretary of state for air. Those aspects of production which remained with the Air Ministry passed into the Department of the Air Member for Supply and Organization. Control of the Aircraft Torpedo Development Unit was transferred to the Ministry of Aircraft Production early in 1942. The relations between the Air Ministry and the new Department were outlined in an Agreement at ministerial level dated 3 August 1940, but details inevitably had to be worked out over a period and there were from time to time differences; for example, over the methods of calculating equipment requirements and allocating priorities. In this field the Air Ministry's Directorate-General of Equipment under the air member for supply and organization worked on the one hand in consultation with the similarly named division of the Ministry of Aircraft Production and on the other hand had representatives in the Commands at home and overseas. The Air Staff point of view was represented by the organization of the assistant chief of the air staff (Operational Requirements) which by 1944 consisted, under the general title of Technical Requirements, of the two Directorates of Operational and Armament Requirements, together with a Deputy Directorate of Photography. At a higher level there were at first regular meetings between the assistant chief of the air staff (Operational Requirements) and the director-general of research and development and then, after an interval, a Joint Development and Production Committee. Liaison was further reinforced by the transfer of individual officers between the two organizations. Research was also carried out for the Air Ministry by the Road Research Laboratory (see p 142).

The Department of the Air Member for Supply and Organization included besides the Directorate-General of Equipment, whose main business was the provisioning of the Royal Air Force with all its requirements, Directorates-General of Organization, Servicing and Maintenance, and Works. The overall structure of the Department in 1944 was much what it had been four years earlier, though the inevitable growth produced a great array of sub-divisions. The Directorate-General of Organization was responsible for the establishment work of the Royal Air Force. The Directorate-General of Servicing and Maintenance dealt through Maintenance Command with routine servicing of aircraft and allied equipment and with repairs that were not so extensive as to require return to the Ministry of Aircraft Production. The Directorate-General of Works oversaw the construction and maintenance of aerodromes, depots and other buildings.

At the beginning of the war the responsibilities of the air member for personnel included postings, discipline, manning, training, education, medical services, the Women's Auxiliary Air Force and religion, with appropriate Directorates. In July 1940 training and education passed to the air member for training, responsible for flying and ground training, educational services and the Air Training Corps. In the course of the war the Air Ministry Directorate of Training that had existed under the air member for personnel expanded into two directorates-general with six directorates.

Besides responsibility for the Meteorological Office the permanent under-secretary of state for air was also responsible for secretariat divisions located within the departments of other members of the Air Council, for the placing of contracts, the provision of capital finance to manufacturers, accountancy and public relations. As has already been mentioned the appropriate parts of this organization passed with the Department of the Air Member for Development and Production to the Ministry of Aircraft Production. During the rearmament period and the war a considerable degree of financial control was devolved by the Treasury to the Air Ministry. Authorization of major expenditure was in the hands of the Treasury Inter-Service Committee, containing representatives of the Treasury and the Supply and Service Departments.

The supervision by the Air Ministry of civil aviation in its Civil Aviation Department, under a director-general directly responsible to the secretary of state, was severely restricted in scope on the outbreak of war owing to military demands. In August 1940 the Air Transport Auxiliary, which was administered for the Air Ministry by the British Overseas Airways Corporation to provide mainly for the ferrying of aircraft from factories to the Royal Air Force, was transferred to the Ministry of Aircraft Production. The subsequent transfer of the overseas ferrying aspect of that work to Ferry Command and then to Transport Command is outlined below. In 1944 a committee under Lord Beaverbrook recommended the appointment of a minister of civil aviation at the head of a separate department with responsibility for the encouragement and development of British civil aviation. In October 1944 a minister of civil aviation was appointed to represent the United Kingdom at the international civil aviation conference at Chicago in November 1944. He exercised the powers of the secretary of state for air by arrangement, and was assisted by the Civil Aviation Department until April 1945 when a Ministry of Civil Aviation was established and took over the powers of the Air Ministry under the Air Navigation Acts and related legislation.

Reference has already been made to the radio war and the operations against German flying bombs and rockets. These were scientific applications of some magnitude and in general science played a considerable part in the British air war. The creation of a radar chain within a few years from the first demonstration of the principle in 1935 is a well-known achievement, which was controlled by the Directorate of Communications Development in the Department of the Air Member for Development and Production and was paralleled by the creation of an organization inside Fighter Command to enable its operations to be based on radar information. Later in the war senior staff of the Ministry of Aircraft Production were permitted to act also as advisers to the chief of the air staff, while within the Air Staff a Deputy Directorate of Intelligence (Science) was established. From 1944 there was an independent scientific adviser to the Air Ministry. Reference should also be made to the inception of operational research, the application of scientific standards to the study of operations and their effects, though the sections concerned with this development were located inside Bomber and Fighter Commands rather than in the Air Ministry itself.

The Commands

The typical headquarters arrangement in the major Commands was for the air officer commanding-in-chief to be supported on the operational side by a senior air staff officer and on the administrative, or housekeeping, side by an air officer in charge of administration. Other officers were responsible for specialized aspects of work and to some extent a Command Headquarters resembled a miniature Air Ministry in its autonomous handling of such subjects as intelligence, its detailed control of the organization of subordinate elements and its intimate dealings with external organizations. Air officers commanding might have informal contacts with the prime minister, the secretary of state and the chief of the air staff in addition to their formal communications with the Air Ministry, while the subordinate elements of a Command would also deal directly with the related branches of the Air Ministry. The papers of the Commands, and sometimes of their elements, survive as separate classes containing both registered files and unregistered folders.

Bomber Command's task was the strategic employment of air power based on the United Kingdom, and its headquarters were located at High Wycombe. It received its directives from the chief of the air staff after they had been settled by discussions in the Defence Committee, the Chiefs of Staff Committee, with the Ministry of Economic Warfare and with our Allies. The air officer commanding-in-chief played his part in such discussions.

Various devices were employed from time to time to facilitate the overall control of offensive air operations. For example, in June 1943 a Combined Operational Planning Committee was established to co-ordinate the operations of Bomber Command, Fighter Command and the United States 8th Air Force in, and in support of, strategic bombing. In the middle of 1944 a Joint 'Crossbow' Target Priorities Committee, consisting of Air Ministry and United States Army Air Force representatives, was established to decide the targets in the counter-offensive against German flying bombs and rockets. So that Bomber Command could take into account the needs of the battle in Europe it had a staff officer appointed to the Supreme Headquarters (Forward). The bomber squadrons comprising the Command were organized into Groups located in different parts of the United Kingdom.

The general structure of Fighter Command and the position of its air officer commanding-in-chief were similar to those already described for Bomber Command. Its primary responsibility was the defence of the United Kingdom against air attack but its first major encounter with the enemy was over Dunkirk. As the war progressed the Command was able from time to time to take a hand in offensive operations, until in November 1943, with the old title of Air Defence of Great Britain, it became for nearly a year part of the Allied Expeditionary Air Force for the invasion of Europe. In the primary defensive role Fighter Command Headquarters at Stanmore exercised operational control over the Army's Anti-Aircraft Command containing both guns and searchlights and over the Royal Air Force Balloon Command. For its operations it relied heavily on the information supplied by the radar chain and the Observer Corps (both of which were under its control) to Fighter Command Operations Room. Here it was compared with information about the state of the defensive forces so that the air officer commanding-in-chief could exercise minute by minute control of the broad aspects of the air battles. The Fighter Command War Room was a separate entity for the provision of longer-term information. The preliminary collation of information about enemy movements was carried out at first by a Filter Room in the Command and later by devolving this function to Filter Rooms in the Groups, each of which had their Operations Room. An appreciable part of Fighter Command business was the initiating and cancelling of air raid warnings. The giving of the actual warnings was carried out through the Ministry of Home Security on the receipt of instructions from Fighter Command. In 1941 the issue of warnings was transferred from Command to Group and it was finally taken over by the Ministry of Home Security in 1944. A level of command between Groups and squadrons was provided by sectors for each of which an operational airfield was the sector-station.

The role of Coastal Command, with headquarters at Northwood, was the exercise of air power over the waters round our coasts. In most respects — for example, in its relations with the Air Ministry, particularly with the Directorate of Naval Co-operation, and in its own organization into Groups — this Command resembled Bomber and Fighter Commands which had come into existence at the same time, but in one vital point it was quite different. Before the war it had been agreed that the primary role of the Command would be trade protection, reconnaissance and co-operation with the Royal Navy. In April 1941 Coastal Command passed under the operational control of the Admiralty, which thus bypassed the Air Ministry in stating the naval requirements to the Command. The Royal Naval Air Service had, of course, been transferred to the Admiralty in 1937. At a lower level liaison had always been close and before the war Coastal Command Groups had been arranged to coincide with the Naval Home Commands. Area Combined Headquarters in which all three Services were represented were established to exercise operational control at Group level and this arrangement continued under the new regime. In the course of the war the Command's 'Coastal' responsibilities were extended by the creation of Groups for Iceland, Gibraltar and the Azores. Its major tasks were escort and reconnaissance patrols, attacks on enemy submarines and surface vessels, mine-laying and air/sea rescue, in which it co-operated with Fighter Command as well as the Royal Navy. A Photographic Reconnaissance Unit and a Photographic Interpretation Unit, the forerunners of the Central Interpretation Unit, later the Allied Central Interpretation Unit, were established in the Command in 1940.

Balloon Command was responsible for the deployment of barrages of tethered balloons to assist in the protection of cities and key targets, such as docks, from air attacks. Operationally it came under the control of Fighter Command and its headquarters were with the latter's at Stanmore.

Maintenance Command carried out storage, servicing and repair functions for the Royal Air Force. Its headquarters were at Abingdon.

Training Command was established before the war to carry out both flying and ground training but the pressure caused by the need to expand soon brought about changes in this field. Under the Empire Air Training Scheme, signed in December 1939, arrangements were made for the common training of aircrew in the Dominions, by which the Royal Air Force not only provided aircraft and a nucleus of instructors to the Dominions but was able to have its own men trained there. While arrangements were thus made for the supply of basically trained aircrew it was found necessary to provide for their further training by the creation of Operational Training Units inside the Operational Commands, so that Training Command was responsible only for the flying training of aircrew. Further changes were made when in May 1940 the Command absorbed Reserve Command, which had previously been responsible for the Reserve squadrons, and was itself divided into separate Commands for Flying and Technical Training, both with headquarters at Reading.

The origins of Transport Command were in the need to deal with the delivery flights from the other side of the Atlantic. The control of these and other non-operational flights into and out of the United Kingdom was placed in October 1940 in the Overseas Air Movement Control Unit based at Gloucester under Maintenance Command. At this time the transatlantic ferrying of aircraft was in the hands of ATFERO, based in Canada and under the control of the Ministry of Aircraft Production. In the summer of 1941 this organization was taken over by the Air Ministry and became Ferry Command while the Overseas Air Movement Control Unit became No 44 Group in that Command. By 1943 it was agreed that responsibility for the various aspects of air transport then distributed among Ferry and other Commands should be centralized and Transport Command was formed on 25 March with a parallel Directorate of Air Transport Policy and Operations in the Air Ministry. Its headquarters were at Harrow and in addition to No 44 Group the remainder of the former Ferry Command became No 45 Group and No 216 Group was established at Cairo. Other Groups were added later, including No 46, which took part in the airborne operations in the campaign to liberate Europe. The determination of transport priorities by a Priority Board continued as before.

Upon the commencement of hostilities Royal Air Force detachments were sent to France consisting of an Air Component of the British Expeditionary Force to be employed in tactical co-operation with the Army and an Advanced Air Striking Force for strategic operations under Bomber Command. Co-ordination between these forces and the French was effected by Air Missions, but at the beginning of 1940 the two British elements were combined as British Air Forces France with a single headquarters which also conducted liaison with the French. This remained the organization until we were driven from Europe in the summer.

A small Royal Air Force detachment was created for the short-lived campaign in Norway under the title of Air Component North West Expeditionary Force.

After the forces of which the two last mentioned Royal Air Force detachments were part had been withdrawn it was decided to establish an Army Co-operation Command in the United Kingdom, and Air Marshal Barratt, who had commanded the British Air Forces France, became its air officer commanding-in-chief. The functions of this Command and the nature of its responsibilities to the Air Ministry on the one hand and the Army's General Headquarters on the other were a source of difficulty for some time. The original directive of 1940 envisaged these functions as being in the field of training rather than operations, and on the one hand barred Army Co-operation Command from advising General Headquarters in matters involving co-operation with Fighter and Bomber Commands and on the other placed the operational control of the Army Co-operation squadrons permanently allotted to the Army in No 71 Group rather than in Command Headquarters. No 70 Group carried out the aircrew and parachute training with which the Command was primarily concerned. In the summer of 1941 the Air Staff at General Headquarters became representative of the Command instead of the Air Ministry while No 71 Group was disbanded and replaced by six Army Co-operation Wings, one in each Army Command. A further Wing, No 38, was responsible for airborne operations and was closely involved in the creation of the Airborne Division. In 1943 the Command was disbanded and both its headquarters at Bracknell and its units were taken over for the Allied Expeditionary Air Force then being prepared for the invasion of Europe.

The Allied Expeditionary Air Force consisted of those Air Forces which were provided for the tactical support of the invasion and when the supreme commander had been appointed passed under his command. The strategic support provided by Bomber Command and the United States 8th Air Force and the co-operation afforded by Coastal Command were co-ordinated by the deputy supreme commander and these forces formed no part of the Allied Expeditionary Air Force. The headquarters of the Force were at Stanmore (formerly Fighter Command Headquarters) and the units composing the Air Defence of Great Britain were assigned to the Expeditionary Force. Along with them were the two Groups – No 38, formerly of Army Co-operation Command, and No 46, formerly of Transport Command – which were assigned to the airborne assault. To achieve maximum co-operation with the commander of the land forces the advanced headquarters of the Allied Expeditionary Air Force situated at Uxbridge, with the headquarters of No 11 Group Air Defence of Great Britain, had operational control of the Tactical Air Force consisting of 2nd Tactical Air Force (RAF) and 9th Air Force (USAAF). By October 1944 the Allied Forces were firmly established and the various headquarters were moving across the Channel. The headquarters of the Allied Expeditionary Air Force were thereupon dissolved and the command passed to Supreme Headquarters Allied Expeditionary Force, with Air Defence of Great Britain reverting, as a consequence, to Fighter Command.

At the beginning of the war the Royal Air Force in the region of the Middle East was organized into separate elements for the Middle East (headquarters in Cairo), Palestine and Transjordan, Iraq, Aden and Mediterranean, but with the commencement of hostilities against Italy in the summer of 1940 the air officer commanding-in-chief Middle East took operational command of all Royal Air Force Units in the whole area from East Africa to the Balkans and the Mediterranean to the Persian Gulf. This remained the overall position during more than two years of fighting in North Africa, but in 1941 the vigorous expansion of the Royal Air Force in an area which was not only far larger than the United Kingdom, but unprovided with the infrastructure available at home in the Air Ministry and Ministry of Aircraft Production, led to substantial changes in the organization. On the administrative side it was agreed after much debate that there should be a chief maintenance and supply officer supervising a Maintenance Group and responsible directly to the air officer commanding-in-chief and not to the air officer administration as was the conventional Royal Air Force practice. Subordinate operational commands were created from existing Groups for the local defence of Egypt (formerly No 202 Group) and operations in the Western Desert (formerly No 204 Group), but strategic bombing, naval co-operation and maintenance remained under the immediate control of headquarters. As the Allied Forces began to converge on Tunisia in early 1943 recasting of this structure became necessary in order to co-ordinate operations throughout the Mediterranean. The new organization had to take into account British responsibilities outside this immediate area and the differences in command structure between ourselves and the Americans. It was finally determined to create a Mediterranean Air Command subordinate for operations in North West Africa to the Allied commander-in-chief. The three elements in the Mediterranean Air Command established on 17 February 1943 were the Middle East Air Command, the Allied Air Forces North West Africa (with operational but not administrative control of the Desert Air Force) and the newly created Malta Air Command. The Mediterranean Air Command thus had wider responsibilities than the operations in North West Africa for which it was responsible to the Allied commander-in-chief. Within the North West African Air Forces there was the closest intermingling of British and American operational units in the strategic, coastal and tactical air forces. On 10 December 1943, with Allied Forces well established in Italy, the Mediterranean Air Command, which had absorbed the headquarters of North West African Air Forces, taking direct control of its component air forces, became Mediterranean Allied Air Forces and despite some difficulties retained operational control of the Middle East Command. This arrangement continued until the end of the war with occasional alterations in the subordinate commands as the course of events dictated, such as the creation of the Balkan Air Force and the establishment of an Air Force Headquarters Greece.

Further east there were, before the outbreak of war with Japan, Air Forces headquarters in India and Royal Air Force Headquarters Far East at Singapore. The former controlled the infant Indian Air Force as well as Royal Air Force units in India. The air officer commanding Far East was placed under the command of a new commander-in-chief of land and air forces in Malaya, Borneo, Burma and Hong Kong in October 1940, when an attempt was made to create a more effective organization for the control of operations to meet the growing threat from Japan. Included in this command were the British Air Forces in Ceylon, and during this last period of peace plans were made for co-ordination with Australian and Dutch Air Forces. After the Japanese attack much of this area was taken into the American-British-Dutch-Australian Command, but the whole of the structure was soon to be swept away and all Royal Air Force operations came to be based on India. From this time until November 1943 the India Command steadily developed its resources. Groups were based on Bangalore, Colombo and Peshawar, while at Calcutta, where there were two Groups, an Air Headquarters Bengal was established whence operations in Burma were controlled. The India Command was responsible in addition for the creation of a maintenance organization and the construction of a large number of airfields. Upon the creation of South East Asia Command in November 1943 the Air Command South East Asia took over the operational duties that had fallen to India, apart from the Royal Indian Air Force squadrons on the North West frontier, which were controlled by a new Air Headquarters India responsible to the Government of India. The use of Indian territory as a base and training area also fell to the new South East Asia Command. In the following months integration on the lines traced first by the American-British-Dutch-Australian Command and drawn out by the North West African Air Forces was achieved in South East Asia Command when the 10th USAAF was brought under the South East Asia Air Command as part of the subordinate Eastern Air Command for operations in Burma. The former Bengal Command was also included in Eastern Air Command. Though South East Asia Command Headquarters moved to Kandy in Ceylon in April 1944 the South East Asia Air Command remained for some time at Delhi. In December 1944 a Royal Air Force Headquarters Bengal-Burma was established to take over administrative duties in respect of the Royal Air Force element in Eastern Air Command. After the recapture of Rangoon in May 1945 the American Air Forces were withdrawn from South East Asia Command, and on 1 June Eastern Air Command was brought to an end. Headquarters Royal Air Force Burma was then established to command the Royal Air Force elements of the dissolved Command. This structure saw out the war.

Royal Air Force Delegation

The Royal Air Force Delegation to Washington was established before American entry into the war. It was part of the Joint Staff Mission in Washington and at the same time looked after the interests of the Air Ministry in the United States. Its duties included planning, supply, air routes and Royal Air Force training, and it was organized with a number of directorates on the model of the Air Ministry.

The Records

ADM 900 Specimens of Classes of Documents Destroyed
           These include flying log-books of Royal Air Force personnel serving with the Fleet Air Arm, 1939 to 1940.

| AIR 2 | Air Ministry, Registered Files |
| | Files of registered correspondence of the Air Ministry, covering the whole range of British air administration and related topics. Complementary unregistered papers are in AIR 20. |

AIR 2   Air Ministry, Registered Files
Files of registered correspondence of the Air Ministry, covering the whole range of British air administration and related topics. Complementary unregistered papers are in AIR 20.

AIR 4   Aircrews' Flying Log Books
A small representative selection of flying log-books, mainly of Royal Air Force aircrews, but including some log-books of Commonwealth and foreign personnel. See also ADM 900 and WO 900.

AIR 6   Records of Meetings of the Air Board and Air Council
Minutes of meetings of the Air Council, and memoranda, etc, submitted to the secretary of state's Progress Meetings on RAF Expansion Measures, 1935 to 1940.

AIR 8   Chief of the Air Staff
Records formerly held in the office of the chief of the air staff.

AIR 9   Director of Plans
Contains strategic and operational planning records, and includes operations record books of the Directorate of Plans.

AIR 10   Air Publications
A selection of administrative instructions, regulations and reports, and manuals of instruction for the use and servicing of aircraft and equipment.

AIR 13   Balloon Command
Files relating to organization, barrages, equipment, operations, etc, of Balloon Command. For operations record books see AIR 24.

AIR 14   Bomber Command
Files of Headquarters Bomber Command and associated units, relating to planning, carrying out, and reporting of operations, tactics, crews, equipment, etc The class also includes certain records of Groups, squadrons and RAF stations in the Command. In addition there are files concerning British prisoners of war and relations with Allied and United States Army and Air Forces. For operations record books see AIR 24, AIR 25, AIR 27 and AIR 28.

AIR 15   Coastal Command
Files relating to organization, planning, exercises, tactics, protection of shipping, equipment, anti-submarine operations and air/sea rescue operations, etc. For operations record books see AIR 24.

AIR 16   Fighter Command
Files, etc, of Headquarters Fighter Command relating to organization, defence schemes, trials, training, etc. For operations records books see AIR 24.

AIR 17   Maintenance Command
Files relate to the formation, organization and activities of Maintenance Command. For operations record books see AIR 24.

AIR 18   Judge Advocate General's Office, Courts Martial Proceedings
This class comprises proceedings of district, general and field general courts martial of officers and other ranks of the Royal Air Force. They are closed for 50 or 75 years.

AIR 19   Private Office Papers
This class includes papers of Sir Kingsley Wood and Sir Archibald Sinclair.

AIR 20   Unregistered Papers
Unregistered papers from many Air Ministry Branches and from the British Bombing Research Mission, the British Bombing Survey Unit, the Central Statistical Unit, the Empire Air Navigation School, GHQ Home Forces, the RAF Staff College, the Air Ministry War Room and various other commands in Britain and overseas. Also includes papers under the names of Air Chief Marshal Sir Robert Brooke-Popham, Sir Henry Tizard and Sir Harold Howitt.

AIR 21   Judge Advocate General's Office, Courts Martial Registers
Registers of charges giving the name and rank of each prisoner, place of trial, nature of the charge and sentence. This class is closed for 75 years.

AIR 22   Periodical Returns, Summaries and Bulletins
Information material provided to the Air Ministry War Room including daily summaries of operations of Commands; daily strength returns of established and operational squadrons and of available crews and aircraft; weekly reports on operations and intelligence; daily weather charts of North West Europe; daily secret bulletins of operations; weekly bulletins of information of interest to personnel, but not for release to the press, etc.

AIR 23   Overseas Commands
Includes records of Air Force Headquarters in Iraq and Aden and of Middle East and Far East Commands. For records of Air Forces in North West Europe see AIR 35 - AIR 37. For operations record books of the Command see AIR 24 - AIR 29.

AIR 24   Operations Record Books: Commands
AIR 25   Operations Record Books: Groups

AIR 26	Operations Record Books: Wings
AIR 27	Operations Record Books: Squadrons
AIR 28	Operations Record Books: RAF Stations
AIR 29	Operations Record Books: Miscellaneous Units
AIR 30	Submission Papers

Submissions to the sovereign for royal approval of appointments, promotions, awards and regulations.

| AIR 31 | Departmental Whitley Council Minutes |
| AIR 32 | Air Training Commands |

Files on the history of flying training, the medical aspects of Flying Training Command, training of special agents and for airborne operations.

AIR 33   RAF Inspectorate General

Reports of visits and on such matters as aerodrome defence, the Royal Australian Air Force and RAF organization; also papers of the Meteorological Services Committee and the Meteorological Policy Committee.

AIR 34   Central Interpretation Unit

Reports based on aerial photographic reconnaissance of the Unit, later the Allied Central Interpretation Unit, and of its predecessors the Photographic Development Unit and the Photographic Interpretation Unit. There are also reports of the Joint Allied Reconnaissance Intelligence Centre (UK), photographs from the Joint School of Photographic Interpretation and material from overseas centres relating particularly to operations of the Mediterranean Allied Air Forces.

AIR 35   British Air Forces in France

Records of the administration and operations of British Air Forces in France until and including evacuation in 1940.

AIR 36   Air Component North West Expeditionary Force (Norway)

Records relating to the organization of the Air component of the North West Expeditionary Force and its operations in Norway.

AIR 37   Allied Expeditionary Air Force and Second Tactical Air Force

Besides records of the Allied Expeditionary Air Force and its principal components, the Second Tactical Air Force RAF and the Ninth Air Force USAAF, the class includes files originating at Supreme Headquarters Allied Expeditionary Air Force.

AIR 38   Ferry and Transport Commands

The records include policy files, minutes of committee meetings, orders of battle and route books.

AIR 39   Army Co-operation Command

Files relating to organization, operations, etc, of Army Co-operation Command.

AIR 40   Directorate of Intelligence and other Intelligence Papers

Reports, narratives and surveys of enemy capabilities and reports of operations carried out against the enemy. A substantial number of files relate to the Air Forces and Commands of the United States Army Air Force. There are also records concerning the interrogation of enemy prisoners of war and reports of the Special Investigation Branch concerning the murder of 50 RAF officers at Sagan, Stalag Luft III camp.

AIR 41   Air Historical Branch: Narratives and Monographs

These historical studies, collected or written by staff of the branch, include monographs concerning balloon defences, flying training, international law of the air, photographic reconnaissance and the rise and fall of the German Air Force. The narratives cover most of the campaigns and theatres of the Second World War. The air defence of Great Britain and the Middle East campaigns are extensively described.

AIR 42   Combined Operational Planning Committee

The papers in this class relate mainly to the planning of action against specified targets. The Committee was staffed by RAF and USAAF personnel.

AIR 43   Judge Advocate General's Office, Courts Martial Charge Books

These contain out-letters of the Judge Advocate General's Office relating to the preparation of charges for trial by courts martial of Royal Air Force personnel. The class is closed for 75 years.

AIR 44   Judge Advocate General's Office, Courts Martial Minute Books

These contain the decisions and rulings of the Judge Advocate General. The class is closed for 75 years.

AIR 45   RAF Delegation, Washington

The files in this class relate to the allocation of aircraft, the training of RAF personnel in North America and liaison with the U.S Army and Navy Air Forces. They also include a series on air-sea rescue techniques and equipment.

AIR 46   Air Missions

Records of the Air Liaison Missions to Canada, South Africa and Egypt and of missions to the USSR. They cover the Empire Air Training Scheme, the training of the Royal Norwegian Air Force and some reports from the Military Mission to the USSR concerning prisoners of war and escapes from enemy occupied territory.

AIR 47   Operation Torch: Planning Papers
Records concerning the British air element in the allied invasion of North Africa in November, 1942.

AIR 48   United States Strategic Bombing Survey
Reports on the bombing offensive against Germany and Japan, including the effects of the atomic bombs at Hiroshima and Nagasaki.

AIR 49   History of RAF Medical Services
Most of the records comprise reports compiled for the Medical History of the War.

AIR 50   War of 1939-1945 Combat Reports
These were made by Allied air crew to their unit intelligence officers on returning from operations.

AIR 51   War of 1939-1945: Allied Forces HQ Files (Microfilm copies)
Retained by the Ministry of Defence.

AIR 52   US National Defense Research Committee
Reports received in accordance with wartime agreements for the exchange of scientific and technical information.

AIR 54   South Africa Air Force: Operations Record Books (Microfilm copies)

AIR 55   British Air Forces of Occupation
Papers relating to the British Air Forces of Occupation (Germany) and the Air Division Allied Commission Austria (British Element). Many of them relate to the Missing Research and Enquiry Service.

AIR 56   Headquarters No 90 (Signals) Group: Technical Drawings

AIR 57   Director General of Medical Services: Flying Personnel Research Committee

AIR 58   Director General of Medical Services: Institute of Aviation Medicine
Reports sent to the Institute by the USA Committee on Aviation Medicine.

AIR 62   Whittle Papers
Private papers and other records of Air Commodore Sir Frank Whittle relating to the development of the jet engine. See also AVIA 30.

AIR 64   Central Fighter Establishment
Papers from the inception of the Establishment in 1944 concerning trials, tests, etc, of fighter aircraft and equipment.

AIR 65   Air/Sea Warfare Development Unit Reports
Technical reports, etc, on trials of equipment and tactics.

AIR 66   Joint Air Transport Establishment: Reports
Reports of the Army Airborne Transport Development Centre relating mainly to the carriage of equipment.

AIR 67   Joint Air Transport Establishment: Drawings

AIR 71   Judge Advocate General's Office: Air Force Letter Books
These concern courts martial.

AIR 72   Air Ministry Orders
Printed routine orders.

AVIA 2   Air Ministry Civil Aviation Files
Files relating to all aspects of civil aviation business, created during the period when civil aviation was the responsibility of the Air Ministry. See also BT 217.

AVIA 8   Air Ministry: Inventions and Research and Development Files

AVIA 16   Aircraft Torpedo Development Unit Reports
Reports on trials of means of delivery of torpedoes and mines from aircraft.

AVIA 32   Aircraft Torpedo Development Unit: Files

AVIA 43   Personal Files
Closed for 50 or 75 years.

AVIA 46   Ministry of Supply Files: Series 1 (Establishment)
Include narratives and documents bearing upon wartime scientific research in the Air Ministry.

AVIA 53   Ministry of Supply Files: Series 6 (Contracts)
Include papers dealing with claims concerning wartime inventions for the Royal Air Force.

BJ 1   Kew Observatory: Correspondence and Papers
Include papers concerning measurements of the effects of bomb explosions, enemy meteorology and methods of testing clearance of barrage balloons from cloud.

BJ 5   Administrative Records
These relate to the entire range of the activities of the Meteorological Office during the war.

BT 217   Civil Aviation: R Series Files
          These contain some papers of the Civil Aviation Department of the Air Ministry. See also
          AVIA 2.
BT 218   Civil Aviation: Accidents Investigation Branch (AI Series Files)
          One of these files concerns liaison with the Royal Canadian Air Force.
DEFE 3   War of 1939-1945: Intelligence from Enemy Radio Communications
          These signals known as ULTRA consist of intercepts which were decrypted, translated and sent
          from the German Naval Section of the Admiralty's Naval Intelligence Division at Bletchley Park
          to the Division's Operational Intelligence Centre in the Admiralty; and intelligence summaries
          derived from such signals sent to the War Office, Air Ministry and overseas commands. See also
          ADM 223/36.
DSIR 22   Aeronautical Research Council: Minutes of Meetings
DSIR 23   Aeronautical Research Council: Reports and Papers
TS 28   Air Ministry (AM) Series Registered Files
          Case files of the Treasury Solicitor when handling legal business on behalf of the Air Ministry,
          mainly concerning patents of inventions.
WO 900   Specimens of Classes of Documents Destroyed
          These include flying log-books of Royal Air Force pilots serving with the Glider Pilot Regiment.
WORK 44   Maps and Plans: Air Force Establishments

Ministry of Aircraft Production

Name	Date of appointment
Minister	
Lord Beaverbrook	14 May 1940
J T C Moore-Brabazon, MP	1 May 1941
J J Llewellin, MP	22 Feb 1942
Sir Stafford Cripps, MP	22 Nov 1942
Parliamentary secretary	
J J Llewellin, MP	15 May 1940
Frederick Montague, MP	1 May 1941
Ben Smith, MP	4 Mar 1942
Alan T Lennox-Boyd, MP	11 Nov 1943
Permanent secretary	
Archibald Rowlands (later Sir Archibald Rowlands)	1940
Sir Harold R Scott	1943
Sir Frank Tribe	1945
Air member for development and production	
Air Marshal Sir Wilfrid Freeman	27 June 1938
Civil member for development and publication	
Cdr Sir Charles Craven	Apr 1940
Joint head of the Production Department and member of the minister's Advisory Council	
[Sir] Patrick Hennessy	May 1940 - Apr 1941

Controller-general of production

Cdr Sir Charles Craven	June 1941
[Sir] Alexander Dunbar	July 1942

Director-general of research and development

Air Vice-Marshal R M Hill	1940

Controller-general of research and development

Air Marshal [Sir] F J Linnell	June 1941
Air Marshal Sir Ralph Sorley	Apr 1943

Chief executive

Air Chief Marshal Sir Wilfrid Freeman	Oct 1942
Edwin Plowden	Jan 1945

The Ministry of Aircraft Production came into existence in May 1940 and was firmly based on the research and production elements of the Air Ministry which constituted the Department of the Air and Civil Members for Development and Production. The new Ministry was to be responsible for the production of aircraft, their armament and equipment and the control of repair and of research and development (including the Experimental Establishments). It exercised technical control of salvage units through No 43 Group Royal Air Force though administrative control remained with the Air Ministry. It was responsible for bringing aircraft into the Storage Units and putting them into operational condition, a duty which it performed through No 41 Group Royal Air Force. In these areas a formal division of responsibilities had to be agreed with the Air Ministry and in some respects discussions were still in progress in 1941. Relations with the Air Ministry, from the minister and secretary of state downwards, were generally close if not always close enough, and many Royal Air Force officers served in the Ministry of Aircraft Production, while Ministry of Aircraft Production officials were also placed for liaison purposes in Air Ministry directorates. From December 1941 to the appointment of a chief executive in October 1942 fortnightly meetings were held at a high level at which the Ministry of Aircraft Production and the Air Ministry jointly reviewed the pace of production and prospects of development. It was the importance of aircraft production which led the prime minister at a time of crisis to the creation of a separate Ministry and he continued thereafter to spur successive ministers with his enquiries. Although the Ministry of Aircraft Production consisted initially of segments taken whole from the Air Ministry the circumstances of its birth and the methods employed to galvanize production resulted in the organization being very fluid for the first three years of its existence. This was particularly the case at the highest levels where the distribution of duties and, consequently, of the responsibilities of large parts of the Ministry, was sometimes made to depend on the personalities available.

Upon the creation of the Ministry of Aircraft Production the air member for development and production lost his production responsibilities and was limited to research and development, repairs, factory defence and aircraft ferrying. Production was shared between the former civil member for development and production and Mr Patrick Hennessy, while the permanent secretary remained responsible for finance and establishments. In the course of 1940 duties at this level were redistributed from time to time and the lower echelons of the organization began to grow. By the end of the year production responsibilities were united under Mr Hennessy with subordinate directors-general for aircraft and engines. In May 1941 this post was given the title of controller-general. The permanent secretary now had control of aircraft distribution and of construction and regional services in addition to his former responsibilities, and the other officers reporting direct to the minister were the controller of research and development, the chief naval representative, the controller of telecommunications equipment and Sir Henry Tizard. The controller of North

American supplies and repair became independent of the controller-general later. Both the controller of research and development and Sir Henry Tizard sat also on the Air Council of the Air Ministry. The last major change was the introduction of a chief executive in October 1942 to whom the controller of research and development and the controller of communications equipment were now responsible, in addition to his supervision of the production activities of the controller-general. He had a joint interest with the permanent secretary in the controller of labour allocation and supply and the deputy controller of construction and regional services. The post of controller-general was allowed to lapse in June 1943 but the chief executive had the assistance of a deputy controller of production and later of an assistant chief executive.

Mention should be made of four bodies which played their part in the highest levels of the Ministry. The Air Supply Board began life as an Air Council Committee. Its particular concern was the consideration of production programmes and its approval was necessary for their financing. Its membership was broadly at the high levels discussed above or just beneath them and it survived all the changes that took place in these posts. The Aircraft Supply Council was brought into existence in the middle of 1941 and was responsible, under the minister, for the policy of the Ministry, though it was not a statutory body like the Air Council. It consisted of the minister's principal advisers and enabled them to discuss all the major issues affecting the Ministry. It could also be used as a channel of communication by the Air Ministry. During the period when the controller-general was in charge of production a Production Committee existed consisting of the director-general of aircraft production, the director-general of materials production, the director-general of production of aircraft equipment, the deputy director-general of engines production, the director of armament production and the deputy secretary. At the end of 1942 a Production Efficiency Board was established by the minister and this Board did much to introduce personnel management and motion study into the aircraft factories.

The production of the different elements that went to make up an aircraft were in the hands of production directorates or directorates-general of this kind. For the first half of the war provision of aircraft factories was controlled by the Ministry's Directorate-General of Aircraft Production Factories but in 1943 this responsibility was transferred to the Ministry of Works. The equipment side of production had also a spares and, consequently, a provisioning aspect in which connection liaison was maintained with the director-general of equipment in the Air Ministry. The difficulties of planning to meet equipment needs led to a succession of schemes and changes of organization in this part of the Ministry. The repair of aircraft too badly damaged to be handled by the Royal Air Force was the responsibility of a Directorate of the Ministry of Aircraft Production which controlled the Civilian Repair Organization with headquarters at Oxford.

Among the difficulties which led to disputes between the Ministry and the Air Ministry was that of preparing adequate plans and programmes, not only in the equipment field which has already been mentioned, but generally. In 1941 an investigation of statistics and plans was carried out. The former Directorate of Statistics had long lapsed and this activity was regarded as a function of the Production Committee but as a result of the enquiry a Deputy Directorate-General of Statistics and Programmes was created in September. The purpose of this was to calculate both requirements and production more finely so that they could be brought into balance in a programme or, rather, a set of co-ordinated programmes for aircraft, engines and equipment. The programmes had to take account of future types of aircraft and the rate at which these should replace obsolescent types in the factories.

Reference has already been made to the director-general of research and development and his control of the Experimental Establishments taken over from the Air Ministry. The title of this post was later changed to controller of research and development and in addition to the establishments he was responsible for various scientific and technical directorates at headquarters, including inspection, other than those devoted to communications. The Ministry concerned itself from the point of view of development with technical changes in air operations and provided the Air

Ministry and its Commands with the scientific advisers who carried out operational research. The control of this activity was a matter of contention with the Air Ministry that appears never to have been solved satisfactorily. Among the most important developments carried out under the Ministry of Aircraft Production was that of the jet engine, supervision of which was exercised from November 1941 through the Gas Turbine Collaboration Committee. All jet development work was eventually taken over by the Government. The importance of radar and allied equipment was such that it was in the hands of a separate controller of telecommunications equipment, later the controller of communications equipment, who was also responsible for a good deal of the equipment required for the Royal Navy and the Army. From October 1942 this post was combined with that of controller of communications in the Air Ministry, which had responsibility for the Signals Department. Control of the Aircraft Torpedo Development Unit was not transferred from the Air Ministry until 1942.

The responsibilities of the permanent secretary varied from time to time as has been seen but they always included finance which was particularly important since the Ministry was responsible for the provision of capital for factories. During the war a considerable degree of financial control was devolved by the Treasury to the Ministry. Authorization of major expenditure was in the hands of the Treasury Inter-Service Committee, containing representatives of the Treasury and the Supply and Service departments. The regional interests of the Ministry, that is, its share in the general regional system for the Supply Departments, in association with the Ministry of Supply and Ministry of Production, also came within the portfolio of the permanent secretary although at times this responsibility was shared with the production side.

Various external organizations were under the control, or partial control, of the Ministry of Aircraft Production. The Air Transport Auxiliary consisted of civilian pilots who were employed in ferrying aircraft produced in the United Kingdom, generally to Aircraft Storage Units, but also overseas. The Auxiliary was administered on behalf of the Ministry by the British Overseas Airways Corporation. The ferrying of aircraft across the Atlantic was in the hands of ATFERO under the Ministry until August 1941 when it was transferred to the Air Ministry as Ferry Command. Reference has already been made to Nos 41 and 43 Groups Royal Air Force.

Before the creation of the Ministry of Aircraft Production a mission, which worked in conjunction with the British Purchasing Mission (see pp 12, 151), had been sent to America to order aircraft. Lord Beaverbrook, the first minister of aircraft production, sent his personal representative to reinforce the mission and in November 1940 the British Air Commission was established in Washington independently of the British Purchasing Mission. Particularly after Pearl Harbour it acted as a channel for the pooling of technical information with the Americans.

The Ministry inherited the Central Registry system of the Air Ministry together with many of its files, prefixed B or SB. It then developed a system of file references consisting of the name of the division primarily responsible followed by a description of the subject and a serial number. Branch folders were also used and appear in some instances to have been placed on registered files after an interval. Other file series were created at out-stations such as the Experimental Establishments. Some Ministry of Aircraft Production files have found their way into Air Ministry registered files via the Air Historical Branch and, in general, the overlap of interests between the two Ministries makes it necessary to study the records of both for a number of questions.

In August 1945 a combined minister of aircraft production and minister of supply was appointed and on 1 April 1946 the Ministry of Aircraft Production was dissolved and its functions passed to the Ministry of Supply.

The Records

AVIA 1   Royal Aircraft Establishment Flight Log Books

These logs record particulars of all flights made from the Royal Aircraft Establishment aerodrome at Farnborough and include details of aircraft flown, names of pilots, duration of flights, etc

AVIA 6   Royal Aircraft Establishment Reports
Technical reports and notes from the Royal Aircraft Establishment, Farnborough.

AVIA 7   Royal Radar Establishment Files
These include files of the Telecommunications Research Establishment of the Ministry of Aircraft Production.

AVIA 8   Air Ministry: Inventions and Research and Development Files
Some files continued in use in the Ministry of Aircraft Production.

AVIA 9   Ministry of Aircraft Production: Private Office Papers
Unregistered papers of ministers and parliamentary secretaries.

AVIA 10   Ministry of Aircraft Production: Unregistered Papers
Records concerning contracts and finance, industry and labour production and supply, materials, armaments and bombs, radar and radio and research and development. In addition to some files on missions and visits, including the British Technical (Tizard) Mission to North America 1940 to 1941, other papers concern the Air Supply Board, the Aircraft Supply Council, the Air Council Committee on Supply and the 'Dam Busters' raid. The class includes papers of Sir Wilfrid Freeman and Sir Robert Watson-Watt. It also includes a collection of papers of A K (*later* Sir Alec) Cairncross relating mainly to aircraft production programmes.

AVIA 13   Royal Aircraft Establishment, Farnborough: Registered Files
Files relating to research and development.

AVIA 15   Ministry of Aircraft Production: Files
Files of the Ministry of Aircraft Production including papers taken over from the Air Ministry and a few papers added to the files by successor departments.

AVIA 16   Aircraft Torpedo Development Unit Reports
Reports on trials of means of delivery of torpedoes and mines from aircraft.

AVIA 18   Aeroplane and Armament Experimental Establishment: Reports
Reports of acceptance tests on aircraft, their armament and equipment.

AVIA 19   Marine Aircraft Experimental Establishment: Reports
Reports on research, acceptance tests and trials on marine aircraft and their equipment and armament and on air-sea rescue apparatus.

AVIA 20   Research and Development Establishment, Cardington: Reports
Reports of the Balloon Development Establishment.

AVIA 21   Airborne Forces Experimental Establishment: Reports
Reports on research and development of the means of transport and delivery of airborne forces and their equipment.

AVIA 24   Research and Development Establishment, Cardington: Drawings
This class contains drawings of various types of balloons and their constructional details made at the Balloon Development Establishment, Cardington.

AVIA 25   Research and Development Establishment, Cardington: Correspondence and Papers
Correspondence and papers of the Balloon Development Establishment.

AVIA 26   Royal Radar Establishment: Reports and Memoranda
This class contains the reports and memoranda of the Telecommunications Research Establishment of the Ministry of Aircraft Production.

AVIA 27   Air Transport Auxiliary
Records relating to the formation, recruitment, operations and winding up of the Auxiliary.

AVIA 28   National Gas Turbine Establishment: Reports
These include reports and papers of Power Jets Ltd. and Power Jets (Research and Development) Ltd.

AVIA 29   National Gas Turbine Establishment: Committee Records

AVIA 30   National Gas Turbine Establishment: Whittle Drawings
Drawings and negatives of various gas turbine aero engines and their components developed at Power Jets Ltd and its successors.

AVIA 31   Gas Turbine Collaboration Committee
Minutes and progress reports of the Committee and minutes of its various panels.

AVIA 32   Aircraft Torpedo Development Unit: Files
Records of the development of aerial torpedoes and mines and their means of carriage in, and delivery from, aircraft.

AVIA 33   Handbooks and Directories, etc

AVIA 34   Departmental Notices

AVIA 35   Civil Aviation Radio Advisory Committee: Correspondence and Papers

AVIA 36   Royal Radar Establishment: Journals

Journals of the former Telecommunications Research Establishment.

AVIA 38   North American Supplies
         Mainly files of the British Air Commission, the British Ministry of Supply Mission and the British Supply Council in the United States. See also CAB 115 and FO 115.

AVIA 39   Sub-Committee for Investigation of German Electronics and Signals Organization
         Reports and memoranda on German radar, communications and electronics work investigated by this inter-Service sub-committee of the Operations and Technical Radio Committee.

AVIA 43   Personal Files
         Closed for 50 or 75 years.

AVIA 44   Ministry of Supply and Ministry of Aircraft Production: Scientific and Technical Monographs
         These record the results of wartime research in the two ministries.

AVIA 46   Ministry of Supply Files: Series 1 (Establishment)
         Include narratives and documents relating to wartime events and developments in the Ministry of Aircraft Production.

AVIA 53   Ministry of Supply Files: Series 6 (Contracts)
         Include papers relating to claims concerning wartime inventions, such as jet engines.

AVIA 900 Specimens of Classes of Documents Destroyed
         Includes specimen requisitions of the British Air Commission for supplies from Canada and the USA.

DSIR 22   Aeronautical Research Council: Minutes of Meetings

DSIR 23   Aeronautical Research Council: Reports and Papers

SUPP 1   Logbooks of Aircraft, etc
         Technical logs and supplementary papers relating to the airframe and engine of the Gloster Whittle jet-propelled aircraft E.28/39 (the first jet-propelled aircraft to fly in this country). The documents are deposited on loan at the Science Museum, where the Gloster Whittle aircraft is on exhibition.

SUPP 9   Aircraft Data Sheets and Photographs
         Photographs and general data sheets of British and American aircraft.

Assistance Board

Name	Date of appointment
Chairman	
Lord Rushcliffe (as Sir Harold Betterton, chairman of Unemployment Assistance Board since June 1934)	1940
Lord Soulbury	1941
Secretary	
G T Reid	1938
G Stuart King	1944

The Board began the war as the Unemployment Assistance Board, a title which reflected its original purpose. It became the Assistance Board in 1940 when its responsibilities were extended to include the supplementing of old-age pensions, but by then it had already had imposed on it certain functions arising out of the war. The large number of the Board's local offices and their experience in providing relief to the public led to their use for assistance to persons in immediate need as a result of the war, mainly evacuees and refugees. Civilian casualties in bombing attacks received temporary support from the Board while their applications under the Personal Injuries (Emergency Provisions) Act were under consideration by the Ministry of Pensions. Similar arrangements were made in respect of war damage, since the Board was empowered to make small grants for the removal of furniture from damaged houses and advances on war damage payments for the replacement of furniture, tools, clothing and other personal property. The Assistance Board thus became part of the post-raid services and arrangements had to be made for the rapid opening of additional temporary offices in the aftermath of air attacks.

The Board also undertook investigations into the circumstances of individuals on behalf of the Service Departments and the Ministry of Pensions and issued utility furniture permits on behalf of the Board of Trade. After the war it was given special responsibilities under the Polish Resettlement Act 1947 in respect of those Poles who elected to remain in the United Kingdom.

The Records

AST 1   Assistance and Pensions: Representative Case Papers
          The class includes papers relating to wartime assistance and to grants to Polish and Jewish refugees. Closed for 75 years except to those who agree to specified restrictions on use for pieces over 30 years old.

AST 7   General Files
          General policy files relating to the whole range of duties of the Board. A few files relate to the wartime organization of the Board and to wartime agency duties carried out for other Departments.

AST 9   Establishment Files
          Files of the Establishment Division of the Unemployment Assistance Board and the Assistance Board concerning organization, staffing, conditions of service, premises, equipment, etc.

AST 10   Training
          Files concerning the fitting of unemployed persons for entry into, or return to, regular employment.

AST 11   Wartime Functions
          Papers relating to additional duties undertaken by the Unemployment Assistance and Assistance Boards during the Second World War, such as the granting of allowances to those evacuated under government schemes, to refugees (including alien refugees) and to those deprived by the war of their normal means of support; also papers relating to those functions, notably the making of advance payments of compensation for war damage, undertaken by the Board as agent for other departments.

AST 12   Board Papers
          Minutes of meetings, circulated memoranda, unpublished reports of the Unemployment Assistance Board and the Assistance Board; minutes of committees and conferences of regional officers; and reports of district officers.

AST 13   Codes of Instructions and Circulars
          Circulars and codes of instructions issued to local offices and local authority agencies of the Unemployment Assistance and Assistance Boards relating to unemployment assistance, non-contributory and supplementary pensions, special wartime assistance and services and work undertaken by these offices and agencies for other government departments.

AST 14   Solicitor's Files
          One file relating to the question whether a co-habitee is disqualified for an allowance under the Personal Injuries (Civilian) Scheme.

AST 18   Polish Resettlement
          Post-war papers dealing with the provision of accommodation, etc, under the Polish Resettlement Act 1947.

AST 22   Registered Files: Departmental Whitley Council (DWC Series)
          Include papers relating to civil defence and to provision of women visitors for survey of single mothers.

Charity Commission

Name	Date of appointment
Chief commissioner	
H D S Leake	1939
J C G Powell	1944

The Records

CHAR 3   Charity Commission: Secretariat: Registered Files
This class includes a few files concerning war charities legislation.

Civil Service Commission

Name	Date of appointment
First commissioner	
Sir (Alexander) Percival Waterfield	1939

The Records

CSC 5   Files: Series II
These include material concerning recruitment of demobilized servicemen, arrangements for prisoners-of-war, etc.

Colonial Office

Name	Date of appointment
Secretary of state	
Malcolm Macdonald, MP	16 May 1938
Lord Lloyd	12 May 1940
Lord Moyne	8 Feb 1941
Viscount Cranborne	22 Feb 1942
Oliver Stanley, MP	22 Nov 1942
Parliamentary under-secretary	
Marquis of Dufferin and Ava	28 May 1937
George H Hall, MP	15 May 1940
M Harold Macmillan, MP	4 Feb 1942
Duke of Devonshire	1 Jan 1943

Permanent under-secretary

Sir A C Cosmo Parkinson	Since May 1937
Sir George H Gater	1 Feb 1940

[seconded to Ministry of Home Security from May 1940 until April 1942, then resumed post in Colonial Office]

Sir A C Cosmo Parkinson

[acting, during Gater's secondment. Then attached for special duties in the colonies from April 1942 until retirement 21 December 1944]

The most significant feature in the development of the Colonial Office organization during the war was the growth in the number of 'subject' departments. These dealt with areas of activity common to all or to a number of Colonies, as opposed to the geographical departments dealing with all the business of the Colonies in a particular part of the world, and their growth had been foreshadowed in the inter-war years (see *The Records of the Colonial and Dominions Offices*, Public Record Office Handbooks, No 3). In 1940 the subject departments were Accounts, Appointments (dealing with recruitment to the Colonial Service), Colonial Development and Social Services, Colonial Service (dealing with the personnel questions of the Service), Defence (with a Military Staff attached), Economic, Establishment, and General, from which most of the subject departments had developed. Subjects which did not demand the creation of a separate department were dealt with by introducing advisers or Advisory Committees to the secretary of state for the Colonies.

In many respects the business of the Colonial Office, the oversight of the administration of the Colonies, was carried on as usual during the war and even the developments marked by changes in its organization were by no means wholly devoted to the pursuit of hostilities or dependent upon them. Certain co-ordinating functions, however, fell to be performed as a result of the war and the Office was concerned with such matters as the adoption of sedition laws and the imposition of censorship in the Colonies. It naturally continued to act as the channel of communications between government departments and the Colonies and was therefore involved, for example, in the working of the contraband control service in the Colonies, in recruitment both for the Armed Forces and for the munitions factories, and in the operation of the regulations for the custody of enemy property. This business was distributed among the appropriate subject departments. Control of the administration of the Colonial Forces passed to the War Office in 1940 but it continued to exercise that control through the existing Colonial Office machinery of the Military Staff.

In 1941 a Foreign Colonies Department was added to deal with business arising from French Colonies and occupied enemy Colonies. When in early 1942 the Japanese overran much Colonial territory in the Far East it became necessary to establish a Casualty Section to deal with enquiries about civilians and members of local Armed Forces. This later became the Prisoners of War, Internees, Enquiries and Casualties Department. By the end of that year a Public Relations Department had been established to deal, in conjunction with the Ministry of Information, with publicity both in and about the Colonies. The Economic Department first split off a separate Financial Adviser's Department dealing with questions of taxation, exchange control, war loans and war damage, and was itself divided in 1943 into Supplies and Production Departments, the whole constituting the Economic Division. The Supplies and Production Departments co-ordinated Colonial requirements, production and distribution and the former was represented in Washington by the British Colonies Supply Mission whose task was to assist in maintaining the flow to the Colonies of civil supplies from North America. The Financial Adviser's Department became later the Finance and Development Department. In August 1943 a Communications Department was created both to deal with transport questions such as civil aviation and shipping and to provide the communications facilities needed between the Office and the Colonies. In the same year the growing numbers and needs of Colonials in the United Kingdom led to the creation of a Welfare Department separate from the Colonial Development and Social Services Department

54

to provide hostels for them and generally look after their interests. The surviving Social Services Department continued to co-ordinate the handling of social questions in the Colonies. In 1944 the General Department which had been the precursor of many of the subject departments was abolished and the remains shared out among its offspring and the geographical departments. Defence, renamed Defence and General, took over general questions of international and imperial policy, many of them concerned with post-war planning, while other functions went to Establishment and Public Relations. At the beginning of 1945, as the prospect of liberating the Japanese-occupied Colonies grew nearer, a Far Eastern Economic Department was created out of the Eastern Department to plan the rehabilitation of those areas. To prepare for longer-term Colonial development a Research Department was established.

The arrangement of 'original correspondence' in the Colonial Office in series, each with its own register, has been described in *The Records of the Colonial and Dominions Offices*. The system continued during the war and new series were brought into existence as required. The series correspond broadly to the organization of the Office with a register for each Colony on the geographical side and separate registers for some of the subject departments. By this time the use of files rather than papers as the basic registry unit was general in the Colonial Office and registration continued to be controlled by a single Central Registry. File numbers were allocated in blocks to the registers and from the middle of the thirties it became the practice for registers to be allocated the same number in successive years. This naturally led to the use of a particular number year after year for a particular subject. Such repetition was generally maintained even among the stress and administrative changes brought about by the war though in areas of greatly increased activity this was not possible. Up to 1940 registers were usually made up yearly and the files were arranged similarly but thereafter some of the registers run for three years from 1941 to 1943 and again from 1944 to 1946. The general arrangement of the files follows this though in the nature of things many of the individual files cover single years. To accommodate the proliferation of subjects within this system sub-files were created and marked with letter and number suffixes. Space was allowed at the end of a block of file numbers for completely new subjects. To refer uniquely to a file it was necessary to add the year as a suffix.

Individual papers within the files were numbered and these numbers appear against their descriptions in the registers. No details of secret papers were entered in the registers though in some cases descriptions have been pinned to the register sheets at a later date. At the end of 1941 a Special Care Registry was opened to handle particularly secret papers as sub-files of the ordinary files.

The registers sometimes afford the main means of reference to Colonial Office correspondence since some lists show only the first and last file numbers in each box. Within the box a list of file titles will be found pasted to the lid but these lists omit files which were classified secret.

Classes of Acts, Sessional Papers, Government Gazettes and Blue Books of Statistics for the individual Colonies continue during the war but are not included in the following list.

The Records
[For key to geographical classes see Appendix A (1)]

CO 23   Bahamas Original Correspondence
CO 28   Barbados Original Correspondence
CO 37   Bermuda Original Correspondence
CO 54   Ceylon Original Correspondence
CO 67   Cyprus Original Correspondence
CO 78   Falkland Islands Original Correspondence
CO 83   Fiji Original Correspondence
CO 87   Gambia Original Correspondence
CO 91   Gibraltar Original Correspondence

CO 96	Gold Coast Original Correspondence
CO 111	British Guiana Original Correspondence
CO 123	British Honduras Original Correspondence
CO 129	Hong Kong Original Correspondence
CO 137	Jamaica Original Correspondence
CO 152	Leeward Islands Original Correspondence
CO 158	Malta Original Correspondence
CO 167	Mauritius Original Correspondence
CO 225	Western Pacific Original Correspondence
CO 247	St. Helena Original Correspondence
	Includes Ascension.
CO 267	Sierra Leone Original Correspondence
CO 273	Straits Settlements Original Correspondence
CO 295	Trinidad Original Correspondence
	Includes Tobago.
CO 318	West Indies Original Correspondence
CO 321	Windward Islands Original Correspondence
CO 323	Colonies, General: Original Correspondence
	Correspondence relating to the Colonies generally, mainly from the General Department. See also CO 378 and CO 537.
CO 333	Bahamas Registers of Correspondence
CO 334	Bermuda Registers of Correspondence
CO 337	Ceylon Registers of Correspondence
CO 339	Falkland Islands Register of Correspondence
CO 341	Gambia Registers of Correspondence
CO 342	Gibraltar Registers of Correspondence
CO 343	Gold Coast Registers of Correspondence
CO 345	British Guiana Registers of Correspondence
CO 348	British Honduras Registers of Correspondence
CO 349	Hong Kong Registers of Correspondence
CO 351	Jamaica Registers of Correspondence
CO 354	Leeward Islands Registers of Correspondence
CO 355	Malta Registers of Correspondence
CO 356	Mauritius Registers of Correspondence
CO 366	St. Helena Registers of Correspondence
CO 368	Sierra Leone Registers of Correspondence
CO 372	Trinidad Registers of Correspondence
CO 375	West Indies Registers of Correspondence
CO 376	Windward Islands Registers of Correspondence
CO 378	Colonies, General: Registers of Correspondence
	These relate to CO 323.
CO 419	Fiji Registers of Correspondence
CO 426	Straits Settlements Registers of Correspondence
CO 448	Honours: Original Correspondence
CO 492	Western Pacific Registers of Correspondence
CO 512	Cyprus Registers of Correspondence
CO 525	Nyasaland Original Correspondence
CO 530	Seychelles Original Correspondence
CO 531	British North Borneo Original Correspondence
CO 533	Kenya Original Correspondence
CO 535	Somaliland Original Correspondence
CO 536	Uganda Original Correspondence
CO 537	Colonies, General: Supplementary Original Correspondence
	Mainly post-war secret despatches and telegrams withheld from the various classes of original correspondence when they were bound up, but since declassified. There are, however, a small number of files concerning the History of the War, reparations, prisoners-of-war, etc.
CO 554	West Africa Original Correspondence
CO 555	West Africa Registers of Correspondence
CO 565	Barbados Registers of Correspondence
CO 583	Nigeria Original Correspondence
CO 618	Zanzibar Original Correspondence
CO 628	Kenya Registers of Correspondence
CO 682	Uganda Registers of Correspondence

CO 691	Tanganyika Original Correspondence
CO 703	Nyasaland Registers of Correspondence
CO 712	Seychelles Registers of Correspondence
CO 713	Somaliland Registers of Correspondence
CO 717	Federated Malay States Original Correspondence
CO 725	Aden Original Correspondence
CO 728	Honours: Registers of Correspondence
CO 732	Middle East Original Correspondence
CO 733	Palestine Original Correspondence
CO 746	Tanganyika Registers of Correspondence
CO 763	Nigeria Registers of Correspondence
CO 772	Zanzibar Registers of Correspondence
CO 773	Aden Registers of Correspondence
CO 777	British North Borneo Registers of Correspondence
CO 786	Federated Malay States Registers of Correspondence
CO 788	Middle East Registers of Correspondence
CO 793	Palestine Registers of Correspondence
CO 795	Northern Rhodesia Original Correspondence
CO 796	Northern Rhodesia Registers of Correspondence
CO 820	Military: Original Correspondence
CO 822	East Africa Original Correspondence
CO 825	Eastern Original Correspondence
CO 831	Transjordan Original Correspondence
	For records of the Residency at Amman see FO 816.
CO 847	Africa Original Correspondence
CO 850	Colonial Office: Personnel: Original Correspondence
	Records of the Personnel Division, etc. see also CO 877.
CO 852	Economic: Original Correspondence
	Records of Economic Departments.
CO 854	Colonies, General: Circular Despatches
	For indexes see CO 949.
CO 859	Social Service: Original Correspondence
	Files of the Social Service Department concerning labour conditions, nutrition, public health, education, housing, etc.
CO 865	Far Eastern Reconstruction: Original Correspondence
CO 866	Establishment: Original Correspondence
	Records of the establishment officer and Establishment Department.
CO 867	Establishment: Registers of Correspondence
CO 869	East Africa Registers of Correspondence
CO 870	Transjordan Registers of Correspondence
CO 871	Military: Registers of Correspondence
CO 872	Eastern Registers of Correspondence
CO 874	British North Borneo Company Papers
	Reports of the governor, etc; correspondence and papers relating to the production of rubber, oil, timber and minerals, food supplies, immigration and labour, disturbances, staff matters, prize jurisdiction, wartime activities, relations with Japan, the Japanese occupation and British re-occupation.
CO 875	Public Relations and Information: Original Correspondence
	Records of the Information Department.
CO 876	Welfare and Students: Original Correspondence
	Records of the Welfare and Students Departments.
CO 877	Appointments: Original Correspondence
	Records of the Personnel Division, etc, relating to appointments.
CO 878	Establishment: Miscellanea
	Includes a series of establishment notices.
CO 879	Confidential Print Africa
CO 882	Confidential Print Eastern
CO 884	Confidential Print West Indies
CO 885	Confidential Print Miscellaneous
CO 888	Colonial Labour Advisory Committee
	Papers and minutes of the Colonial Labour Committee to 1941, and the Colonial Labour Advisory Committee from 1942.
CO 917	Africa Registers of Correspondence

CO 918	Appointments: Registers of Correspondence
CO 919	Personnel: Registers of Correspondence
CO 920	Economic: Registers of Correspondence
CO 926	Mediterranean Original Correspondence
CO 927	Research Department: Original Correspondence
CO 935	Confidential Print Middle East
CO 936	Colonial Office: International Relations: Original Correspondence
	Records of the International Relations Department
CO 937	Communications: Original Correspondence
	Records of the Communications Department.
CO 949	Colonies, General: Indexes to Circular Despatches
	Indexes to circular despatches in CO 854.
CO 962	East Africa Conference of Governors
CO 965	Social Services: Registers of Correspondence
CO 967	Private Office Papers
CO 968	Defence: Original Correspondence
CO 969	Prize Courts: Original Correspondence
CO 970	Colonial Development Advisory Committee
CO 971	West Indies, United States Bases: Original Correspondence
CO 972	West Indies, United States Bases: Registers of Correspondence
CO 973	Communications: Registers of Correspondence
CO 974	Defence: Registers of Correspondence
CO 975	Far Eastern Reconstruction: Registers of Correspondence
CO 976	Research Department: Registers of Correspondence
CO 977	Welfare and Students: Registers of Correspondence
CO 978	Public Relations and Information: Registers of Correspondence
CO 980	Prisoners of War and Civilian Internees Department
	These relate to enemy aliens who were prisoners of war or civilian internees in the colonies, and to British subjects held as prisoners of war or internees by the enemy both in Europe and the Far East. See also CO 1012.
CO 981	Welfare and Students: Selected Personal Files
	These files deal with the welfare, education and training of colonial nationals in the United Kingdom.
CO 988	Prize Court: Registers of Correspondence
CO 990	Colonial Economic Advisory Committee: Minutes and Papers
CO 992	North Borneo, Brunei and Sarawak Registers of Correspondence
CO 997	Colonial Social Welfare Advisory Committee: Minutes and Papers
CO 1008	Far Eastern Economic and Supplies Committee: Minutes and Papers
CO 1012	Prisoners of War and Civilian Internees: Registers of Correspondence
	For correspondence see CO 980.
CO 1043	British West Indies: Governor's Office: Registered Files
	Retained by Foreign and Commonwealth Office.
CO 1044	Palestine: Custodian of Enemy Property: Registered Files
FO 816	Embassy and Consular Archives Jordan: Correspondence
	Files of the Residency at Amman.
RG 33	Miscellaneous Foreign Registers and Returns
	Includes two volumes noting deaths from enemy action in the Far East, 1941 to 1945.

Combined Operations Headquarters

Name	Date of appointment
Director	
Lt-Gen. Alan G B Bourne	June - Aug 1941
Adm of the Fleet Sir Roger J B Keyes	Aug - Oct 1941
Adviser	
Cmdre Lord Louis Mountbatten	Oct 1941 - Mar 1942

Chief

Vice-Adm Lord Louis Mountbatten	Mar 1942
Maj-Gen R E Laycock	Oct 1943

As early as June 1940 a small organization was established to take command of raiding operations against the Continent and to provide advice on combined operations. It was this that became Combined Operations Headquarters, staffed by all three Services yet distinct and independent from all of them. This unusual status led to considerable difficulties for there was much disagreement about where the responsibilities of Combined Operations Headquarters ended and those of the conventional organizations began. In March 1941 a fresh directive for Combined Operations was issued in which the emphasis was laid on training in irregular warfare and the landing of troops, the development of techniques, the initiation of operations and the giving of advice to the Chiefs of Staff Committee. Combined Operations Headquarters had command of raiding forces such as commandos except when they were employed as part of larger operations. The head of Combined Operations Headquarters, who was first director of, later adviser on, and then chief of combined operations, sat with the Chiefs of Staff Committee when combined operations were under discussion and from March 1942 sat as a member of the Committee for major issues. The Headquarters was responsible for the initial planning of raids and for the Combined Training Centres in which the techniques developed by it were passed on and practical trials could be made of the great variety of special equipment developed for carrying out opposed landings. In particular it became responsible for the advance preparations of facilities for the invasion of Europe. Provision of much of the equipment was arranged in the Admiralty, which had general control of shipbuilding, through its Department of Combined Operations Materiel or Department of Naval Equipment (Combined Operations), and some of the research was carried out by the National Physical Laboratory under the Department of Scientific and Industrial Research. Supply to the eventual users was the responsibility of Combined Operations Headquarters. Personnel were similarly provided through the Department of Combined Operations Personnel of the Admiralty and Combined Operations Headquarters saw to their training and allocated them to particular duties. From 1942 the Headquarters contained also American staff. The possibility of doing away with Combined Operations Headquarters and transferring responsibilities to a Combined Operations Staff directly responsible to the Chiefs of Staff Committee was discussed and rejected in 1943, though some operational functions were handed over to the Admiralty.

In March 1942 the chief of combined operations was given the rank of vice-admiral and equivalent ranks in the other Services. He had a major-general as vice-chief, an air vice-marshal as deputy chief and a commodore as assistant chief, who were responsible individually for their own Service staffs, while a chief of staff was responsible for inter-Service matters. At the beginning of 1944, following the discussion on the future of Combined Operations Headquarters, the structure was changed from separate Service staffs to one of fused functional groups, which continued to be supervised by an executive consisting of the chief of staff and the three Service advisers to the chief of combined operations. These advisers were also individually responsible for separate functional groups. Internal administration, including the handling of papers, was the responsibility of the secretary. The papers reflect the responsibility of Combined Operations Headquarters not only for the development of technical aspects of combined operations and for controlling raids but also for advising on major operations at the highest level.

Combined Operations Headquarters was represented in the Joint Staff Mission at Washington and much information was exchanged in this way with the United States of America.

In the Middle East a Directorate of Combined Operations was established as early as December 1940, which both operated a Combined Training Centre and worked on plans for opposed landings. In India a Directorate of Combined Operations, reporting to the chiefs of staff, was responsible for advising planners and commanders, for the combined training of all forces in India earmarked for such operations and for much experimental work in the development of equipment. In September 1944 it was settled that such overseas directorates should be regarded as representatives of the chief of combined operations while remaining under the command of local commanders-in-chief.

The Records

DEFE 2   Combined Operations Headquarters Records
The records include war diaries; operations files, arranged mainly in alphabetical order of operational code-names, and a number of associated charts, maps, drawings and photographs; miscellaneous files covering administration, planning, training, armament, etc; some files concerning Admiralty Landing Bases and an incomplete set of representative bulletins of the USA chief of combined operations from 1944. DEFE 2/1373 is an index of persons mentioned in the series of miscellaneous files.

Control Commission for Germany and Allied Commission for Austria

Name	Date of appointment
Chancellor of the Duchy of Lancaster and minister for Germany and Austria J B Hynd, MP	1945

Administrative arrangements for the post-war government of Germany were worked out by the British, Americans and Russians in a European Advisory Commission, which met from December 1943 until September 1945. After the disarmament, demilitarization and denazification of Germany it was the intention to reconstruct the country on a democratic basis, and the principles upon which this was to be done were laid down in the Potsdam Agreement of August 1945.

To co-ordinate action an Allied Control Authority was established in Berlin and Germany was split into British, American, Russian and French zones, under the control of the respective commanders-in-chief of the occupying armies. In the British zone a Control Commission operated under the control of the deputy military governor. A similar division into four zones took place in Berlin which, because it fell in the Russian zone, was the centre of much tension between 1948 to 1949, when the Russians blockaded rail and road communications between Berlin and the West and the Western Powers resorted to an air lift to transport food, coal and other essential materials to their sectors.

The seriousness of the underlying political differences between the Western Powers and Russia, which had given rise to the Berlin blockade, had already manifested itself in the complete failure of the Allied Control Authority to operate effectively over the four zones for which it was nominally responsible. In 1946 the British and Americans agreed to form what came to be known as a 'Bizone' by putting their zones together for economic purposes. In 1948 they were joined by the French, and so 'Bizonia' was converted to 'Trizonia'. In 1949 a Federal Government was formed in Western Germany although the direction of foreign affairs and related matters was reserved to the Western Allies under the Occupation Statute. These modifications of the occupation were effected by the formation of an Allied High Commission in place of the former military governments. Under the Bonn Conventions of 1952 the first steps were taken to abolish the Allied High Commission, and eventually led to Western Germany becoming fully independent in 1955 and joining the North Atlantic Treaty Organization (NATO).

In Austria, political differences between the Western Powers and the Russians also militated against a common solution, but the situation there was not quite so acute because although Austria, like Germany, was split into four zones it was allowed to have a provisional government of its own almost from the outset of the occupation. That government had as its main aim the negotiation of a final peace settlement, but it was not until 1955 that an Austrian State Treaty was signed and the occupation troops of all four powers were withdrawn.

The British elements of the control authorities in Germany and Austria were organized on functional and regional lines. The classes of records detailed below correspond mainly to the divisions or regions by which they were created. Besides those covering the usual domestic activities governing the running of the economy, there are others concerning broader issues, such as reparations, prisoners of war, displaced persons and the recruitment of key German scientific and technical personnel.

As regards overall control from London reference should be made to the Foreign Office sub-section concerning the Control Office for Germany and Austria (p 86).

The Records

(1) Germany

ADM 228   British Naval Commander in Chief, Germany: Papers
           Files on the control and disposal of German shipping, stores and equipment, ports, and general and naval policy.
AIR 55   British Air Forces of Occupation
           Papers relating to the British Air Forces of Occupation (Germany) and the Air Division, Allied Commission for Austria (British Element). Many relate to the Missing Research and Enquiry Service.
FO 934   Potsdam Conference 1945: United Kingdom Delegates Archives
FO 937   Control Office: Legal
           This class includes papers of the Rear Headquarters of the Legal Division of the British element of the Control Commission for Germany. See also FO 1060.
FO 1005   Control Commission for Germany(British Element): Records Library
           Record set of minutes, papers etc, including a number of the Allied Control Authority, the Allied High Commission and various bipartite (British/American) and tripartite (British/American/French) bodies.
FO 1006   Control Commission for Germany(British Element): Schleswig-Holstein Region
           This class includes Kreis reports, monthly economic reports, British residents' monthly reports, and files concerning land tax legislation, local government policy etc, political parties and refugees. The records are arranged under the following headings: Administration Group; Economic Group; Finance; General; Government Group; Historical Material; Land Commission; Political; Prisoners of War and Displaced Persons.
FO 1010   Control Commission for Germany(British Element): Lower Saxony Region
           These records are grouped under the headings of Internal Affairs and Communications, Military Government, Political and Public Safety, and include papers concerning conferences, education in the Hanover Region, labour, transport and the Belsen war memorial.
FO 1012   Control Commission for Germany(British Element): Berlin
           This class, which includes some papers concerning the Berlin airlift is arranged under the headings of Administration Group; Displaced Persons; Economic Group; Finance; General; Government Group; Legal; Public Safety and Transport.
FO 1013   Control Commission for Germany(British Element): North Rhine-Westphalia Region
           Most of these records are grouped under the headings of Administration, Economic, General and Government. Among other papers are files concerning disarmament, education, finance, foreign interests and claims, industry (mainly relating to I G Farbenindustrie), prisoners of war and displaced persons, public health, religious affairs, reparations and transport.

FO 1014   Control Commission for Germany(British Element): Hansestadt Hamburg
These records are grouped mainly under the headings of General, Government and Economic. There are also papers of the Maintenance Branch and of Kreis resident officers, Hamburg, and a number of files concerning industry, commerce, food, agriculture and forestry, public utilities and transport.

FO 1023   Control Commission for Germany(British Element): Allied General Secretariat.
Meeting papers and other papers of the Allied High Commission and its council. Related papers of the UK High Commissioner in Germany are in FO 1008.

FO 1024   Control Commission for Germany(British Element): Allied National Prison Werl: General and Prisoners Files
These mainly concern convicted war criminals.

FO 1025   Control Commission for Germany(British Element): Bipartite Control Office: Secretariat
These mainly deal with economic and financial matters.

FO 1026   Control Commission for Germany(British Element): Bipartite Control Office: Transport Group
These files deal with international and internal transport. See also FO 1058 and FO 1069.

FO 1027   Control Commission for Germany(British Element): Bipartite Economic Control Group

FO 1028   Control Commission for Germany(British Element): Coal Control

FO 1029   Control Commission for Germany(British Element): Combined Steel Group

FO 1030   Control Commission for Germany(British Element): HQ SHAEF, Special Echelon and Military Government HQ
Private Office files including those of the Military Governor and the High Commissioner. For SHAEF pre-occupation papers see WO 219.

FO 1031   Control Commission for Germany(British Element): Headquarters
T Force and Field Information Agency
The papers in this class relate particularly to reparations and the recruitment of key German scientific and technical personnel. See also FO 1078.

FO 1032   Control Commission for Germany(British Element): Planning Staff, Military Sections and Headquarters Secretariat

FO 1033   Control Commission for Germany(British Element): Governmental Sub-Commission
These files relate mainly to constitutional and administrative matters, and the handover of responsibility for governmental administration to the Germans, including denazification policy and the organization of elections.

FO 1034   Control Commission for Germany(British Element): Economic Sub-Commission

FO 1035   Control Commission for Germany(British Element): Office of the Chief Administrative Officer

FO 1036   Control Commission for Germany(British Element): Office of the Economic Adviser

FO 1037   Control Commission for Germany (British Element): Zonal Advisory Council: British Liaison Staff

FO 1038   Control Commission for Germany(British Element): Military Divisions

FO 1039   Control Commission for Germany(British Element): Economic Divisions

FO 1046   Control Commission for Germany(British Element): Finance Division

FO 1047   Control Commission for Germany(British Element): Intelligence Division: Censorship Branch
Retained by Department.

FO 1049   Control Commission for Germany(British Element): Political Division

FO 1050   Control Commission for Germany(British Element): Internal Affairs and Communications Division

FO 1051   Control Commission for Germany(British Element): Manpower Division

FO 1052   Control Commission for Germany(British Element): Prisoners of War and Displaced Persons Division

FO 1056   Control Commission for Germany(British Element): Public Relations and Information Services Control Group

FO 1057   Control Commission for Germany(British Element): Reparations, Deliveries and Restitutions Division

FO 1058   Control Commission for Germany(British Element): Transport Division
See also FO 1026 and FO 1069.

FO 1060   Control Commission for Germany(British Element): Legal Division
These include some papers concerning the prosecution of war criminals. For records of the Division's Rear Headquarters see FO 937.

FO 1061   Control Commission for Germany (British Element): Civil Aviation Board

FO 1062   Control Commission for Germany (British Element): Disarmament Branch

FO 1063   Control Commission for Germany (British Element): Allied Liaison Branch

FO 1064   Control Commission for Germany (British Element): Industry Division: Mandatory Requirements Office

Policy and procedure files concerning demands on the German economy of the armed forces and other mandatory consumers.

FO 1065   Control Commission for Germany (British Element): Establishment, Organization and Personnel Branches

FO 1066   Control Commission for Germany (British Element): British Zone Petroleum Co-ordinating Authority

FO 1067   Control Commission for Germany (British Element): Maintenance Directorate

FO 1068   Control Commission for Germany (British Element): Welfare Service Directorate

FO 1069   Control Commission for Germany (British Element): Road Transport Directorate
See also FO 1026 and FO 1058.

FO 1070   Control Commission for Germany (British Element): Zonal Statistical Organization

FO 1071   Control Commission for Germany: Combined Travel Board and Zonal Travel Directorate and Bureaux

FO 1072   Control Commission for Germany (British Element): CCG College
Files of the college at Brunswick where staff of the CCG (BE) were trained.

FO 1073   Control Commission for Germany (British Element): Frontier Control and Inspection Services

FO 1074   Control Commission for Germany (British Element): Military Security Board
This class relates to demilitarization, scientific research and the control and reconstruction of industry. See also BT 211.

FO 1075   Control Commission for Germany(British Element): Joint Export and Import Agency

FO 1076   Control Commission for Germany (British Element): Lt Col J L Prescott's Post War Diaries
From May 1945 until March 1946 Prescott served with the Economic Division of the Allied Commission for Austria, and from then until April 1948 with the Control Commission for Germany, including service as the first British secretary of the Anglo-American Bipartite Board from September 1946.

FO 1077   Control Commission for Germany (British Element): Army Air Transport Organization: Operation 'Plainfare' (Berlin Air Lift)
See also FO 1012.

FO 1078   Control Commission for Germany (British Element): Reich Ministry for War Production: Papers
Field Information Agency Technical (FIAT) reports of interrogation of Albert Speer and other civilian personalities, intelligence reports, Ministerial Collecting Centre reports, Speer Ministry documents and papers, largely concerned with German economic administration and politics.

FO 1079   European Advisory Commission
Minutes of meetings, circulated papers and general and secretariat files.

FO 1082   Control Commission for Germany (British Element): Historical and Reference Material
Includes a glossary of abbreviations and code names, Who's Who in the British Zone 1946, a Ministry of Economic Warfare handbook on occupied France, and a study of German Air Force organization, 1935-1945.

PRO 30/90 Meekings Papers
C A F Meekings, a later assistant keeper of records, was archive officer to the British element of the Control Commission for Germany. Other papers on German archives will be found among the Jenkinson Papers in PRO 30/75.

(2) Austria

AIR 55   British Air Forces of Occupation
Papers relating to the British Air Forces of Occupation (Germany) and the Air Division, Allied Commission for Austria (British Element). Many relate to the Missing Research and Enquiry Service.

FO 1007   Allied Commission for Austria (British Element): Library Material
Papers circulated by British, Allied and Anglo/US organizations and subsequently deposited in the library of the Allied Council for Austria (British Element).

FO 1020   Allied Commission for Austria (British Element): Headquarters and Regional Files
These records cover a wide range of administrative matters dealt with in the British zone. They include papers of the Military and Air Divisions and files of the Economic, Education, Finance, Internal Affairs, Legal, Political, Prisoners of War and Displaced Persons, Reparations and Social Administration Divisions. In addition to a 'Top Secret' series of files and records concerning the Monuments, Fine Arts and Archives Branch, the class includes Carinthia (Karnten) Zonal records and civil liaison files relating to Vienna and Styria (Steiermark). There

are also some records of the commander-in-chief's office concerning Operation Freeborn (the occupation of Austria) and three files regarding a Ministry of Labour Mission 1948-1949.

FO 1076   Control Commission for Germany (British Element): Lt Col J L Prescott's Post War Diaries From May 1945 until March 1946 Prescott served with the Economic Division of the Allied Commission for Austria, and from then until April 1948 with the Control Commission for Germany, including service as the first British secretary of the Anglo-American Bipartite Board from September 1946.

Courts of Law and Administrative Tribunals

Name	Date of appointment
Lord Chancellor[1]	
Viscount Caldecote	1 Sept 1939
Viscount Simon	12 May 1940
Lord Chief Justice	
Viscount Hewart	1922
Viscount Caldecote	1940

The Records

Administrative Tribunals

BF 1   Pensions Appeal Tribunals: Registers of Cases
These relate to appeals against decisions on entitlement to, or assessment of, war disability pensions. Papers concerning further appeals to the High Court are in J 96. See also PIN 40.
BF 2   Pensions Appeal Tribunals: Case Files
Closed for 75 years.
BF 3   Pensions Appeal Tribunals: Correspondence and Papers
J 101   Shipping Claims Tribunal
These records concern compensation claims arising from the requisition, etc, of vessels under the Compensation (Defence) Act 1939.
LAB 3   Arbitration Tribunals
Files concerning awards made by the Industrial Court, the National Arbitration Tribunal and the Railway Staff National Tribunal. Also includes correspondence and papers of the Tramways Tribunal, 1924 to 1945, and lists of members of the Coal Mines National Industrial Board.
LT 1   War Damage (Valuation Appeals) Panel: Case Files
Registers are in LT 2. For War Damage Commission records see separate section (p 176-8).
LT 6   General Claims: Files
Claims for payment under the Compensation (Defence) Act 1939 and later Acts arising from the requisitioning of land, buildings, goods, etc. For registers see LT 7.

Admiralty and Prize Courts

ADM 238   Accounting Departments: Prize Branch Records
Admiralty records relating to prize administration.
CO 969   Prize Courts: Original Correspondence
Colonial Office records relating to prize administration.
CO 988   Prize Court: Registers of Correspondence
FO 963   Embassy and Consular Archives Egypt: Alexandria Naval Court Records
HCA 2   Instance and Prize Courts Accounts

---

[1] For records of the Lord Chancellor's Department see separate section.

Awards arising from collision between HMS *Curacoa* and the Cunard White Star *Queen Mary* in the Atlantic in 1942.

HCA 20   Admiralty Court Instance Papers, Series V

HCA 27   Admiralty Court Instance Minute Books
These contain brief notes to all the proceedings in a case. Indexes are in HCA 56.

HCA 52   Admiralty Court Instance Miscellaneous Correspondence and Papers

HCA 54   Admiralty Court Reference Books Registrars' Reports

HCA 57   Minute Books (Prize)
These contain details of progress of prize court cases.

HCA 59   Commissions
Issued in connection with setting up of prize courts at home and abroad.

HCA 60   Appeals Records: Minute Books
Registers of appeals to the Court of Appeal.

HCA 61   Registrars' Miscellaneous Files

HCA 62   Admiralty Marshal's Office
Warrants for the arrest of ships.

LCO 2   Registered Files
These are files of the Lord Chancellor's Department. A few relate to prize business: there are also some establishment papers in LCO 4.

MT 26   Board of Trade Marine Department: Local Marine Boards
Includes a register of investigations, mainly by naval courts, of seamen charged with disciplinary offences.

TS 13   Queen's Proctor: Prize and Prize Bounty Cases, Decrees and Affidavits
Papers of the Treasury solicitor and HM procurator general.

Assize Courts

ASSI 26   Assizes: Western Circuit: Criminal Depositions and Case Papers
The class includes depositions concerning a case under the Official Secrets Act.

ASSI 52   Assizes: Northern Circuit: Criminal Depositions and Case Papers
Include papers concerning possession of secret documents, evasion of military service and offences under rationing orders.

ASSI 65   Assizes: North and South Wales Circuit, Chester and North Wales Division: Criminal Depositions
One piece concerns a prosecution for sabotage.

ASSI 72   Assizes: North and South Wales Circuit, South Wales Division: Criminal Depositions
Include papers concerning an attempt to cause disaffection and sabotage.

Central Criminal Court

CRIM 1   Central Criminal Court Depositions
The class includes papers in the trial of William Joyce ('Lord Haw Haw') for treason. Appeal papers are in J 82.

Courts Martial

ADM 156 Courts Martial Records
These relate to Royal Navy and Royal Marines personnel. Closed for 75 or 100 years.

AIR 18   Judge Advocate General's Office: Courts Martial Proceedings
These records and those in the AIR classes below relate to Royal Air Force personnel. Closed for 50 or 75 years.

AIR 21   Judge Advocate General's Office: Courts Martial Registers
These give the name and rank of the accused, place of trial, nature of charge and sentence. Closed for 75 years.

AIR 43   Judge Advocate General's Office: Courts Martial Charge Books
Closed for 75 years.

AIR 44   Judge Advocate General's Office: Courts Martial Minute Books
Closed for 75 years.

AIR 71   Judge Advocate General's Office: Air Force Letter Books

WO 71   Judge Advocate General's Office: Courts Martial Proceedings

These records and those in the WO classes below relate to Army personnel. Closed for 50 or 75 years.

WO 81   Judge Advocate General's Office: Letter Books
Closed for 75 years.

WO 82   Judge Advocate General's Office: Day Books
Closed for 75 years.

WO 83   Judge Advocate General's Office: Minute Books
These contain the decisions and rulings of the Judge Advocate General. Closed for 75 years.

WO 84   Judge Advocate General's Office: Charge Books
Closed for 75 years.

WO 86   Judge Advocate General's Office: District Courts Martial
Registers giving name, rank and regiment of prisoners, place of trial, nature of charge and sentence. Closed for 75 years.

WO 88   Judge Advocate General's Office: District Courts Martial, India
Similar register to those in WO 86. Closed for 75 years.

WO 90   Judge Advocate General's Office: General Courts Martial Abroad
Similar registers to those in WO 86. Closed for 75 years.

WO 92   Judge Advocate General's Office: General Courts Martial Registers
Closed for 75 years.

WO 93   Judge Advocate General's Office: Miscellaneous Records
WO 213   Judge Advocate General's Office: Field General Courts Martial and Military Courts Registers
These give the name, rank and regiment of each prisoner, place of trial, nature of the charge and sentence. Closed for 75 years.

Supreme Court of Judicature

J 53   Supreme Court of Judicature: High Court of Justice, Chancery Division: Petitions
Include a few for payment out of funds in court under the Trading with the Enemy Act 1939.

J 82   Court of Criminal Appeal: Case Papers
Includes the case of William Joyce ('Lord Haw Haw'); depositions are in CRIM 1.

J 86   Principal Probate Registry: Correspondence and Papers
This class includes material regarding evacuation of the Registry from London, problems concerning servicemen's wills, divorce procedure in cases involving prisoners of war, etc.

J 96   Appeals from Pensions Appeal Tribunals: Application Papers
These concern claims for pensions arising from death or injury as a result of the war and are subject to extended closure. Pensions Appeal Tribunals records are in BF 1-3.

J 141   Supreme Court of Judicature: Central Office Files
Include papers concerning work under the Liabilities (War Time Adjustment) Act 1941 and wartime emergency plans, etc.

War Crimes

[The classes listed below relate exclusively or mainly to war crimes. For war crimes records generally see Appendix B]

FO 1019   War Crimes Trials Nuremberg: Correspondence and Papers
Records of the Court Contact Committee and the British War Crimes Executive.

FO 1024   Control Commission for Germany (British Element): Allied National Prison Werl: General and Prisoners Files
These relate mainly to convicted war criminals.

TS 26   Treasury Solicitor and HM Procurator General: War Crimes Papers
Correspondence and papers of the Treasury Solicitor's War Crimes Branch, including lists of war criminals, copies of charges, reports of SHAEF courts of enquiry and papers of the United Nations War Crimes Commission and its British National Office.

WO 235   Judge Advocate General's Office: War of 1939-1945: War Crimes Papers
Includes case files of war crimes trials before British military courts in Europe and the Far East, and a register of convicted war criminals.

WO 238   Judge Advocate General's Office: Sound Recordings: Trial of Field Marshal von Manstein
Von Manstein was accused of committing war crimes in Poland and Russia between 1939 and 1944. No equipment survives upon which these sound recordings can presently be played.

WO 309   War of 1939-1945: HQ BAOR: War Crimes Group (NWE) Files

Policy and case files dealing mainly with war crimes in North West Europe, and some CROWCASS (Central Registry of War Criminals and Security Suspects) lists.

WO 310   War of 1939-1945: Rear HQ British Troops Austria: War Crimes Group (SEE): Case Files

WO 311   War of 1939-1945: Military Deputy, Judge Advocate General: War Crimes Files
Files dealing with the investigation and prosecution of alleged war criminals for offences in all theatres of the war, including some CROWCASS lists. Indexes are in WO 353 and WO 356.

WO 325   War of 1939-1945: War Crimes, South East Asia: Files
Files on investigations into incidents, and conditions in POW camps.

WO 331   War of 1939-1945: HQ Allied Land Forces Norway : War Crimes Investigation Branch Files
Policy and case files, and nominal rolls of prisoners in Jessheim camp.

WO 353   War of 1939-1945: Military Deputy Judge Advocate General: War Crimes, Europe: Card Indexes
Indexes serving as a means of reference to files in WO 311.

WO 354   War of 1939-1945: Judge Advocate General: War Crimes, Europe: Card Indexes

WO 355   War of 1939-1945: War Crimes, Europe: Card index of persons passed to or wanted by various allied authorities
Closed for 75 years.

WO 356   War of 1939-1945: Military Deputy Judge Advocate General: War Crimes, South East Asia: Card Indexes
Indexes serving as a means of reference to files in WO 311.

WO 357   War of 1939-1945: War Crimes, South East Asia: Record Cards.
Assorted indexes covering the investigation, prosecution and imprisonment of war criminals. In general they do not serve as a means of reference to files in other classes.

Crown Agents for the Colonies

Name	Date of appointment
Chief clerk	
H K Purcell	1933

The Records

CAOG 9   Finance Files
Files arising from measures to help the war effort.

Commissioners of Crown Lands

Name	Date of appointment
Permanent commissioner and secretary	
C L Stocks	1934
O S Cleverly	1941

The Records

CRES 35   Registered Files, Estates
A few span the wartime period.

CRES 36 Registered Files, Establishment, Finance and General
         Include a few papers concerning wartime agriculture.
CRES 37 Crown Estate Office: Foreshores: Registered Files
         These concern foreshores fronting on crown property.
CRES 46 Windsor Estate Office: Correspondence and Papers
         This class includes some papers regarding military training areas.

Board of Customs and Excise

Name	Date of appointment
Chairman	
Sir (George) Evelyn C Pemberton Murray	1934
Sir (Crawfurd) Wilfrid Griffin Eady	1941
Sir (Richard Henry) Archibald Carter	1942

The Records

CUST 44 Annual Reports
CUST 106 War Registry: Registered Files
CUST 115 Exchange Control: Registered Files
         See also T 231.

Dominions Office

Name	Date of appointment
Secretary of state	
Anthony Eden, MP	3 Sept 1939
Viscount Caldecote	14 May 1940
Viscount Cranborne	3 Oct 1940
Clement R Attlee, MP	19 Feb 1942
Viscount Cranborne	24 Sept 1943
Parliamentary under-secretary	
Marquis of Hartington, MP	4 Mar 1936
(later Duke of Devonshire)	
Geoffrey Shakespeare, MP	15 May 1940
P V Emrys-Evans, MP	4 Mar 1942
Permanent under-secretary	
Sir E John Harding	24 Jan 1930
Sir A C Cosmo Parkinson	1 Feb 1940

until May 1940
[when he returned to Colonial Office]
Sir Eric G Machtig   1 Feb 1940

Although a separate Dominions Office had been established in 1925 it continued to share the Colonial Office building and some of its common services. Close co-operation between the two Offices continued during the war. The Dominions Office remained responsible for the United Kingdom government's business with the governments of the Dominions and of Eire and in many ways the content of this work was not altered by the war. It was largely diplomatic in character though there were also administrative tasks to be performed in different ways in respect of Newfoundland, Southern Rhodesia and the High Commission Territories of Bechuanaland, Basutoland and Swaziland. A good deal of the work arose in connection with the armed forces of the Dominions for there were many legal questions arising from their presence not only in the United Kingdom under the Visiting Forces Act but elsewhere in the Empire. The Office also co-ordinated information about casualties. It looked after the interests of the Dominions in such questions as the allocation of shipping and circulated much information about the course of the war to the Dominions governments through the British high commissioners. Information was also provided to the Dominions high commissioners in London. Important and urgent questions were thrashed out by the exchange of telegrams at prime ministerial level whereas the longer-term discussion of post-war political problems was channelled through the Office. The Office also played a leading role in the Children's Overseas Reception Board which was set up in 1940 in response to offers of hospitality from the Dominions and the United States arising from the menace to the United Kingdom from enemy action.

The internal organization of the Office during these years was in purely 'subject' departments apart from some questions connected with the administrative work mentioned above and with Eire. There is one major series of correspondence which covers this period in two chronological blocks 1937 - 1942 and 1943 - 1946. In both of these there are subject sub-divisions indicated by alphabetical prefixes to the file or paper references which consist of main numbers for particular subjects or activities within the sub-divisions and sub-numbers for aspects of those subjects or activities. Both files and single paper units were in use during the war and the letter W was added to the existing alphabetical prefixes of sub-divisions to indicate those matters which were thought to have wartime content. Completely new prefixes were also brought into use and the W prefix cannot in practice be relied upon either inclusively or exclusively. A major change in procedure occurred at the end of 1942 when the registers, hitherto the major means of reference, were discontinued. Nevertheless papers may still be found numbered serially within files. Lists of file titles are available for the second block of correspondence. Additionally, records of the British Phosphate Commissioners responsible for the administration of the Island of Nauru and Ocean Island in the Western Pacific were deposited with the United Kingdom government in 1982 and are recorded in the list below.

Classes of Acts, Sessional Papers and Government Gazettes for the Dominions continue during the war but are not included in the following list.

The Records

DO 3   Dominions Register of Correspondence
DO 35   Dominions Office and Commonwealth Relations Office: Original Correspondence
          This class contains the main series of Office files to which reference is made above.
DO 114   Confidential Print Dominions
DO 115   Confidential Print Dominions (Australian)

DO 116   Confidential Print Dominions (South African)
DO 118   Agreements, Treaties and Miscellaneous Documents
DO 119   Governor of Cape Colony and High Commissioner for South Africa and Territories Archives: Correspondence
DO 121   Private Office Papers
This class includes the exchange of personal telegrams in 1944 between Field Marshal Smuts and Churchill on the conduct of the war and private papers of Sir Eric Machtig, permanent under-secretary from 1940.
DO 126   High Commission and Consular Archives, Australia: Correspondence
DO 127   High Commission and Consular Archives, Canada: Correspondence
DO 130   United Kingdom Representative to Eire: Archives, Correspondence
DO 131   Children's Overseas Reception Board
In addition to general administrative and establishment files, the class includes a small selection of case files of children sent overseas and their escorts, registers of child applicants, and a history of the Board.
DO 140   British Phosphate Commissioners
Records of the commissioners responsible for the administration of the Island of Nauru and Ocean Island, which were occupied by the Japanese in 1942.

Ministry of Economic Warfare

Name	Date of appointment
Minister	
Ronald H Cross, MP	3 Sept 1939
Hugh Dalton, MP	15 May 1940
Viscount Wolmer (later Earl of Selborne)	22 Feb 1942
Director-general	
Sir Frederick W Leith-Ross	1939
Earl of Drogheda	April 1942
Parliamentary secretary	
Dingle M Foot, MP	17 May 1940

It had been agreed before the war that the conduct of all operations of economic warfare should be in the hands of a single, independent Ministry which was accordingly established on 3rd September 1939. Much of the planning which enabled this step to be taken had been carried out in the Co-ordination Section of the Foreign Office and the new Ministry inherited a great deal of information accumulated by the Industrial Intelligence Centre. The Ministry was organized at first into four departments for Plans, Foreign Relations, Prize and Intelligence. The Plans Department soon disappeared, while the work of the Foreign Relations and Prize Departments was distributed after the summer of 1940 to three Contraband and Neutral Trade Departments. These, together with the Records and Statistics, Establishments, and Legal Departments were placed under a director and were afterwards known as the General Branch. Press and Enemy Transactions Departments were added later, while the Records and Statistics Department, by then known as Information and Procurement, was largely transferred to the Enemy Branch. This was the later designation of the other group of departments in the Ministry which was also controlled by a director and carried out intelligence functions. The work of the two directors was at first co-ordinated by a director-general but he later took over the direction of General Branch, and Enemy Branch was directed by the deputy director-general. Co-operation with the French in the first nine months of the war was mainly achieved through the French Economic Warfare Mission in London.

The first step in operations was to establish the blockade of Germany. Contraband-control bases were set up to which all vessels intercepted by the Royal Navy were sent for examination to determine whether the cargo might constitute prize. The evidence collected at these bases was sent to the Ministry for assessment by the Contraband Committee which included at various times representatives of the Admiralty, the Board of Trade, the Ministry of Supply, the Procurator-General's Department of the Treasury Solicitor, the *Ministére du Blocus*, the Foreign Office and the Colonial Office. To avoid delays at the control bases the navicert system devised in the First World War was reinstituted in December 1939. Exporters from a foreign country could submit information in advance to the British Mission in that country which could then issue a navicert, *ie* a certificate of destination for specified cargo, which would speed these goods through contraband control. The Mission issued the navicert either on its own responsibility or after reference to the Ministry. Where all the cargo in a ship was covered by navicerts the ship could be given a navicert of its own. After the fall of France when the rigour of the blockade was greatly increased the navicert procedure was made compulsory and all unnaviderted cargo was liable to be regarded as destined for the enemy. All applications were now referred to the Ministry. At the same time the ship warrant scheme was introduced in conjunction with the Ministry of Shipping (see pp 163-4), whereby only those neutral shipowners who had given satisfactory undertakings as to the employment of their vessels would be given access to British insurance, stores, repairs and other facilities.

Further measures were taken to restrict the flow of goods into Germany by means of control at source. Exports from the Commonwealth and Empire were subjected to licensing control from early in the war and in January 1940 the United Kingdom Commercial Corporation was established to make pre-emptive purchases of strategic goods to prevent them falling into enemy hands and this practice was greatly extended from the summer of 1940. In 1941 agreement was reached with the United States of America on joint pre-emptive measures against Japan as well as Germany. The United Kingdom Commercial Corporation later extended its activities in the Middle East, where, for example, it represented the Ministry of Economic Warfare in the Middle East Supply Centre Executive Committee (see p 169) and operated transport facilities in Persia. It also handled supplies for Russia and dealt with the purchase and sale of goods from neutral countries, particularly Turkey, Spain and Portugal.

In the case of some neutral countries it was possible to negotiate a War Trade Agreement by which the neutral would undertake to limit the sale of specified goods to Germany in exchange for an undertaking by the United Kingdom to facilitate its imports. In other cases to prevent re-export to Germany by neutral countries their imports were subjected to a compulsory rationing scheme introduced at the same time as the other stricter controls. The imposition of all these blockade measures led to pressures arising from allegations of deprivation of the inhabitants of enemy-occupied territories as a result of which the Ministry eventually became concerned in relief shipments by the Red Cross.

Enemy exports were placed under an embargo from November 1939. Cargoes from neutral or allied countries could be provided by British Missions abroad with passes or certificates of origin in much the same way as navicerts were issued and an Enemy Exports Committee, which included representatives of the Foreign Office, Admiralty, Board of Trade, the Colonial Office, the Ministry of Shipping, the Procurator-General's Department and the *Ministére du Blocus*, sat at the Ministry to consider particular cases. Copies of these certificates were sent to the Ministry from April 1940.

The Intelligence Division was at first responsible for the collation and interpretation of all kinds of economically important information, much of which was made available to the Ministry in connection with the operations already described. For example, copies of ships' manifests were supplied to Contraband Control and copies of navicerts and certificates of origin were transmitted by British Missions abroad. A section of the Division was responsible for collecting evidence about firms and individuals suspected to have dealings with the enemy with a view to their being placed on the Statutory List or Black List. British firms were prohibited by the Trading with the Enemy Act operated by the Board of Trade and the Treasury from dealing with such firms and the lists were also used as evidence by the Contraband and Enemy Exports Committees and in connection with the issue of navicerts, certificates of origin and ship warrants. The placing of names on the lists was under the control of the Black List Committee which included representatives of the Admiralty, the Ministry of Shipping and, later on, of the United States of America. These aspects of 'blockade intelligence' later became the responsibility of Records and Statistics Department in the General Branch of the Ministry while the Enemy Branch concentrated on 'economic warfare intelligence' about commodities and shipping and also dealt with the financial side of economic warfare. Enemy Branch circulated monthly reports on the economic situation in German Europe. At the beginning of 1941 the Branch was organized in four departments corresponding with these four activities and in the course of that year a Services Liaison Department was added, although it disappeared in 1942 when it was replaced by an Objectives Department. In that year the Commodities Department was abolished and the Financial Transactions Department and most of the Shipping Department were transferred to the General Branch while, on the other hand, most of Information and Procurement was transferred from General Branch to Enemy Branch. These changes were designed to transform Enemy Branch into a purely intelligence organization and in this connection the former Enemy and Occupied Territories Department became four Enemy Resources Departments. In 1943 the Objectives Department was also split, one of the new departments continuing to provide operational intelligence while the other contributed information to handbooks about European territories likely to be occupied by Allied Forces. In 1944 a Shipping Department was split off from the Objectives Department and yet another department was created for post-hostilities work. In April of that year the Enemy Branch was transferred to the administrative control of the Foreign Office under the title of Economic Advisory Branch. After the German surrender the Ministry was wound up and an Economic Warfare Department established within the Foreign Office.

The development of contacts between the Enemy Branch and the Armed Services, first in the Joint Intelligence Committee (see p 7) and then with the Services individually, is but one example of the close relations of the Ministry of Economic Warfare with other departments. The Foreign Office, which was one of its parents, was always closely concerned with economic warfare questions and particularly with their political aspects. It was the recipient of frequent complaints from neutral countries about the application of economic controls and advised on the limits to which such controls could prudently be extended. Its missions abroad carried out economic warfare functions and it provided the Ministry with much of its communications system. Much information about economic warfare can therefore be found in the records of the Foreign Office and of the embassies and consulates, such as Trieste. Pre-emptive purchases when also required for supply were carried out by the Board of Trade, the Ministry of Food or the Ministry of Supply as appropriate. The Economic Warfare Division of the Admiralty operated the Contraband Control Service, while the Treasury and the Board of Trade were jointly responsible for the Trading with the Enemy Branch. These two departments were also naturally concerned with the financial and commercial repercussions of economic warfare activities.

The Ministry played a leading part in the Economic and Industrial Planning Staff, an interdepartmental body set up early in 1944 to study the economic aspects of plans for liberated or occupied territories in Europe. After the end of the war in Europe its brief was extended to the Far East. In October 1945 work in respect of Germany and Austria was passed to the newly-established Control Office for those countries (see p 86).

The Ministry was represented in a number of foreign countries by Co-ordinating Centres whose function it was to accumulate information about suspect firms and individuals in those countries but its representation in the United States of America by the War Trade Department in the embassy was by far the most important part of its overseas organization both before and after American entry into the war. In the spring of 1941 one of its two directors was sent to Washington to take charge of the Department and to deal with the American Government at a high level. Following American entry into the war the issue of navicerts by the War Trade Department was replaced by the issue of export licences by the United States Government from April 1942.

The Records

BT 192   United Kingdom Commercial Corporation and English and Scottish Commercial Corporation Papers
Many concern supplies to Russia. See also T 263.

FO 837   Ministry of Economic Warfare
Policy files, progress reports, war trade lists, enemy shipping intelligence, committee papers, etc, arising from contraband control and associated work of the Ministry. There are also reports and surveys regarding industrial targets in German towns and cities. The class includes material, much of it post-war, concerning enemy property, relief programmes and reparations. The later files are those of the Ministry's successor, the Foreign Office, including a number concerning operations under the safehaven programme.

FO 935   Control Office: Intelligence Objectives Sub-Committee
Files mainly of the Ministry of Economic Warfare and the Economic Warfare Department of the Foreign Office relating to the work of the Combined Intelligence Objectives Sub-Committee and the British Intelligence Objectives Sub-Committee in obtaining and disseminating technical and political intelligence of urgent military importance. German documents, evaluation reports, etc, collected by these Sub-Committees are held by the Imperial War Museum.

FO 942   Control Office: Economic and Industrial Planning Staff
Although the bulk of this class concerns Austria and Germany, there are also files on Allied control in Bulgaria, Hungary and Roumania, on peace treaty negotiations with Italy and on broad questions of restitution, reparations, etc, affecting other European countries.

FO 952   Embassy and Consular Archives Norway: Various Consulates' Records captured by the Germans
Include instructions from the Ministry to consulates on trade controls.

MT 71   Goeland Company Records
Papers arising from the activities of this government-owned company in its efforts to reduce the benefits derived by Germany from Danube shipping.

T 188   Leith-Ross Papers
Papers of Sir Frederick Leith-Ross, director-general of the Ministry, 1939 to 1942.

Education and Arts Departments

Name	Date of appointment
President of the Board of Education	
Earl de la Warr	27 Oct 1938
H Ramsbotham, MP	3 Apr 1940
(later Viscount Soulbury)	
R A Butler, MP	20 July 1941
(became minister of education on 3 August 1944)	
Parliamentary secretary	
Kenneth M Lindsay, MP	28 May 1937

J Chuter Ede, MP   15 May 1940

Permanent secretary
Sir Maurice Holmes   1937

Deputy secretary
Sir Edward Howarth   1937
R S Wood   1940
(later Sir Robert Wood)
W C Cleary   1945

The title of 'Board of Education' was changed to that of 'Ministry of Education' by the Education Act of 1944 but for the sake of simplicity 'Board' is here used throughout.

The major wartime function of the Board, and one for which a new Division was created within it, was evacuation. In this field it operated in conjunction with the Ministry of Health and was, of course, particularly concerned with school children, on whom the official evacuation scheme centred. Various provisions to deal with problems arising from evacuation were made by local education authorities under the guidance of the Board. These included additional communal feeding for school children, extension of school health measures where existing provisions in reception areas were inadequate to deal with the influx of evacuees, and nursery centres for younger children. Where accommodation was not available makeshift classes were conducted for small groups of children in private houses.

The Board was also concerned with the use of school buildings by the Armed Forces and others for war purposes, air raid precautions in schools and the conscription of educational staff. Educational institutions were used to assist in the training of members of the Women's Services and to provide instruction for women generally in dealing with wartime problems, *eg* in first-aid or overcoming shortages of domestic goods. It also assumed responsibility for youth welfare services on the dissolution of the National Fitness Council in October 1939.

Through its Department of Intelligence and Public Relations the Board participated in the work of national and international educational reconstruction. Besides fostering Anglo-American and Anglo-French co-operation it worked closely with other government departments, particularly the Foreign Office and Colonial Office, and the British Council. It was also involved in the Conference of Allied Ministers of Education which led to the establishment of UNESCO.

Among records detailed below are some of the Council for the Encouragement of Music and the Arts (the later Arts Council) and a few of the University Grants Committee. There are also some concerning the Victoria and Albert Museum.

The Records

ED 10   General Education, General Files
          General files concerned with the administration of the Education Acts embracing educational matters common to, or not peculiar to, elementary or secondary education. Second World War files reflect the impact of the war upon education in the field of air raid precautions, evacuation, manpower problems, wartime restriction of supplies and emergency legislation. They also contain a history of education in wartime and papers dealing with post-war reconstruction of the education system.

ED 11   Elementary Education, General Files
          Papers concerned with general subjects relating to elementary education. The class includes papers relating to arrangements for the education of foreign refugee children, evacuation and reception, modifications to the educational system in respect of the employment of children, school attendance, curricula and re-arrangement of holidays during the Second World War.

ED 12   Secondary Education, General Files

Papers relating to general subjects concerned with secondary education. Papers of the Second World War relate to fees and special places provided for evacuees; grants to children of Service men; staffing problems; the modification of examinations and academic certificates; the training of school-leavers for employment; and the expansion of cadet corps.

ED 22   Inspectorate Memoranda

This class includes circulars and memoranda relating to evacuation, air raid precautions, nursery centres, war savings and training for war industries.

ED 23   Department of Education and Science and predecessors: Establishment Files

Files relating to the organization and management of the Board (and Ministry) of Education and of the museums and other institutions under its control. Some of the files relate to evacuation and other wartime matters which affected the running of the Board and the museums.

ED 31   Bill Files

Many of these relate to the 1943 Education Bill.

ED 34   Ministry of Education and Department of Education and Science: Parliamentary Questions and Answers: Papers

Briefs, etc, from December 1944.

ED 35   Secondary Education, Institution Files

Include material concerning applications to the General Nursing Council for approval of pre-nursing courses; the building of new or extended school canteens to meet wartime needs; and records relating to special problems arising from evacuation.

ED 42   External Relations: Conference of Allied Ministers of Education: Papers

Selected reports, minutes, agenda, memoranda and correspondence. See also BW 74 (under Foreign Office section p 87), ED 121 and FO 924.

ED 46   Further Education: General Files

These files are mainly concerned with the policy and administration of schemes relating to the provision of further education, including juvenile unemployment centres, by local education authorities under the Education Acts 1918 and 1921. Papers of the Second World War deal with the training of ex-servicemen and prisoners of war, modifications in the award of academic certificates, and planning for post-war reconstruction of the educational system.

ED 50   Special Services, General Files

Files concerned with the provision and administration of special educational facilities for mentally and physically handicapped children and with the organization and administration of the School Meals and School Health Services. Evacuation and other wartime problems placed special strain upon the School Health Service and the School Meals Service, which is reflected in some of the files. See also ED 123.

ED 51   Further Education: Local Education Authority Files

Some files contain papers regarding wartime food education schemes.

ED 66   Board of Education and successors: Nursery Education: Local Education Files

Include material concerning the provision of nursery schools for women war-workers.

ED 84   Victoria and Albert Museum

There are a number of files in this class concerning air raid precautions.

ED 86   Teachers: General Files

These are concerned mainly with the drafting and revision of the Training of Teachers Regulations; the supply of trained teachers and the provision of training colleges; and the introduction of building grants in aid of the establishment of training colleges. Papers of interest for the wartime period relate to the evacuation of training colleges, the wartime training of teachers, including servicemen and prisoners of war, and the recruitment of ex-servicemen as physical training instructors.

ED 100   Accountant General's Department, General Finance Files

These are concerned with general financial policy and administration of grants to local education authorities. The few papers of the Second World War relate to such special measures as the apportionment of evacuation expenditure, use of school buildings for wartime purposes, emergency building labour, and victory celebrations.

ED 102   Nursery Education, General Files

Policy files which include drafts of regulations, circulars, letters and administrative memoranda, papers referred for legal decisions, correspondence with other Departments on matters of common policy, etc. Complementary papers will be found in ED 50. Some files relate to the provision of wartime nurseries.

ED 121   Education Department and successors: External Relations: General Files

Files of the Department of Intelligence and Public Relations including papers relating to the British Council, broadcasting and educational reconstruction, and Control Commission education services in post-war Germany. There are also some papers concerning the Central Council for Health Education and the Conference of Allied Ministers of Education. See also ED 42.

ED 123	Special Services: Local Education Authority: School Meals Service: Files See also ED 50.
ED 124	Further Education: Youth Welfare: General Files This class includes minutes and papers of the National Youth Committee, 1939 to 1942, and its successor the Youth Advisory Council.
ED 128	Polish Resettlement Act 1947, Education of Poles in Great Britain Includes a few files of the wartime period taken over by the Committee for the Education of Poles in Great Britain. See also WO 315. Post-war files dealing with the administration of the Act are in AST 18.
ED 131	Teachers' Superannuation: General Files General correspondence and papers relating to the administration of the legislation on teachers' pensions. Some files relate to measures taken during both world wars to safeguard the pensions of teachers who were transferred to essential non-teaching work or who served in the Armed Forces or ancillary services.
ED 134	War of 1939-1945, Miscellaneous General Local Education Authority Files
ED 136	Private Office Papers Series II Includes papers concerning war emergency measures and precautions, youth registration, army education, post-war education and 1944 Education Act bill papers.
ED 138	History of Education in the War 1939-1945: Drafts, etc Material assembled for a proposed official history, but which was abandoned after the death in 1965 of the editor, Dr Sophia Weitzman.
ED 142	Circulars and Administrative Memoranda
ED 143	Emergency Recruitment and Training of Teachers
EL 1	Council for the Encouragement of Music and the Arts: Minutes and Papers
EL 2	Council for the Encouragement of Music and the Arts: Correspondence: Central Includes files concerning factory concerts.
EL 3	Council for the Encouragement of Music and the Arts: Correspondence: Regional
UGC 5	University Grants Committee: Miscellanea This material relates to the organization, etc, of universities during wartime.

Ministry of Food

Name	Date of appointment
Minister	
William S Morrison, MP	8 Sept 1939
Lord Woolton	3 Apr 1940
J J Llewellin, MP	11 Nov 1943
Parliamentary secretary	
A T Lennox-Boyd, MP	11 Oct 1939
R Boothby, MP	15 May 1940
G Lloyd George, MP	22 Oct 1940
W Mabane, MP	3 June 1942
Secretary	
Sir Henry L French	1 Dec 1939
Commercial secretary	
J F (later Sir John) Bodinnar	1941
Second secretary	
E Twentyman	1941
J P R Maud (acting)	1943

Deputy secretary

Sir Quintin Hill	28 Sept 1939
Sir Russell Scott	1 Dec 1939
S W Hood	1 Nov 1940
P J Wheeldon (acting)	1 Dec 1941
H Broadly	1941
J P R Maud	1941
M I Hutton	1944
G R P Wall	1944

Financial secretary

Sir Harry Peat	12 Oct 1939

Planning for food control in the event of war was entrusted in 1936 to the Food (Defence Plans) Department of the Board of Trade and by the outbreak of war the machinery of control both in respect of commodities and local organization was largely ready. Two sets of ration books had been printed. In September 1939 this department became the independent Ministry of Food with its own minister, subject to the broad direction of the Food Policy Committee of the War Cabinet. This direction was later taken over by the Lord President's Committee. The responsibility of the Ministry for food supply was shared in respect of home production with the Ministry of Agriculture and Fisheries and the planning of such production had to be negotiated, often with difficulty, between them.

The minister kept in touch with his senior officers by means of his Office Council. Here inter-divisional questions could be thrashed out and its minutes were circulated in the upper levels of the Ministry. The need for co-ordination became even more pronounced after a large part of the Ministry was evacuated to Colwyn Bay and elsewhere in June 1940.

The supply side of the Ministry consisted of commodity divisions which drew heavily for staff on the private trade and in some cases had previously been government sponsored trade organizations. The Cereals Control Board, for example, became the Cereals Division of the Ministry in the summer of 1940. Purchases from overseas which were proposed by the commodity divisions had to be approved by the Ministry's Overseas Purchases Board, or by its Standing Committee, which was thus able to consider the overall programme, particularly in the light of available shipping and foreign currency. It was replaced in the summer of 1941 by the Food Supply Board which considered food supplies from all sources. Its sub-committees were Imports, Home Agricultural Supplies, Home Manufactured Supplies, and Consumption Plans. In two cases importing companies were formed, namely the Meat Importers' National [Defence] Association Ltd and the Bacon Importers' National [Defence] Association Ltd. Other divisions of the Ministry dealt with rationing policy and the control of the Ministry's local offices, while the Economics Division was responsible for the preparation of programmes, such as those for overseas purchase, and the study of particular problems affecting more than one commodity division. Further co-ordination within the Ministry was provided by committees such as the Margins Committee which dealt with the profits allowed to traders in controlled foods and the Orders Committee to which all proposed Statutory Regulations and Orders had to be submitted.

During the second half of 1940 the general organization of the Ministry came under examination and it was decided to group the commodity divisions into one Supply Department and to group the other divisions into a Divisional and Local Services Department, except for the Economics Division which became the basis of a new General Department. Each of these departments was at first to be under the control of a deputy secretary reporting to the permanent secretary who retained directly under his hand the Finance, Legal and Establishments Divisions. The position was slightly altered in early 1941 by the introduction of a second secretary controlling the General

Department directly and the Supply Department via a deputy secretary, and the final pattern at this level was reached in the summer of that year when a commercial secretary was appointed to be directly responsible to the minister for the work of the Supply Department, while the permanent secretary continued in charge of the other two.

Within the new Supply Department a Central Division was created to deal with questions affecting more than one commodity division, such as Processing or Distribution, and Service Divisions such as Transport, Warehousing, and Cold Stores, initially with Divisional and Local Services Department, were soon transferred to the Supply Department. In 1941 the full control by trade directors of their commodity divisions was explicitly recognized and the role of officers attached to the divisions, *eg* by the financial secretary, became more advisory.

The work of the commodity divisions in ensuring food supplies was conducted as far as possible through the normal trade channels and the advice of the trade was made available to the divisions through such bodies as the Retail Meat Trade Consultative Conference and the Egg Products Advisory Committee. The Ministry also had an extensive area organization to represent it at the points where food was imported or produced. In some cases, as with fatstock and cereals, the Ministry became the major or sole importer and purchaser of home produce, existing stocks being requisitioned on the introduction of such schemes. Some purchases abroad were made in conjunction with the United Kingdom Commercial Corporation (see p 71). The prices of almost all foods were fixed by the Ministry and in the case of milk and some others it introduced a subsidy to hold the price down. Each of the divisions prepared emergency plans, including dispersal of stocks and preparations for decentralization of powers, although the overall responsibility for emergency schemes rested with the Divisional and Local Services Department.

The main business of the Divisional and Local Services Department was those matters such as rationing, distribution and transport which were controlled through the Ministry's network of Divisional and Local Food Offices. This network consisted of some 1,500 Local Food Offices supervised by 18 Divisional Food Offices grouped under 5 Chief Divisional Food Offices. They were all controlled for establishment by the Divisional and Local Organization Division and advised as to their functions by the other divisions of the Divisional and Local Services Department at Headquarters. The Local Food Offices were responsible for a multiplicity of contacts with the citizen, especially after their fusion with the local National Registration Offices (see p 98) at the end of 1942, which was the final step taken to meet the difficulties of co-ordinating the issue of ration books with the registration of the population by the General Register Office. They were also responsible for contacts with retailers and served as the channel for their demands which was essential if allocations of supplies were to be correctly distributed to honour the ration. The Divisional Food Offices in addition to their supervisory function formed part of the Regional system for emergencies under the Ministry of Home Security. The provision of accommodation for food stocks known as 'buffer depots', whether to support the normal distributive services or to supersede these services in emergency, was the responsibility of the divisional food officers co-ordinated by the Warehousing Division and Emergency Services Division. They began by requisitioning suitable property, but from 1941 buildings began to be specially erected for the purpose.

The general organization of rationing, including the preparation of books and planning their distribution by local offices, was in the hands of the Rationing Division, though the determination of the amount of the ration was a matter of policy to be settled at the highest level. The registered rationing system by which consumers were tied to retailers, who then received their supplies on the basis of the number of their registrations, was supplemented at the end of 1941 by the points rationing scheme under which consumers were able to exchange coupons for certain varieties of goods at any shop they chose and a Points Rationing Division was created to administer the scheme. The final degree of control was the licensing of retail and catering establishments which provided a framework for rationing and for the control of foods subject to distribution schemes. In each local authority area a Food Control Committee, containing representatives of the public and of retailers, was established at the beginning of the war and on their recommendation licences were issued by the food executive officers who were responsible for the administration of the local Food Offices. Licences could be revoked where the Ministry's regulations were breached and the Committees could also undertake prosecutions though these were more generally undertaken by the divisional food officers. Oversight of these activities was exercised by the Licensing and Enforcement Divisions.

At the end of 1941 a Welfare Foods scheme was begun to carry out the special distribution of certain essential foods such as eggs, cod-liver oil, concentrated orange juice and milk, the supplies of which would not permit a guaranteed ration to all members of the community. The main recipients were young children and expectant and nursing mothers and the scheme was controlled by the Welfare Foods Division with the help of the Scientific Adviser's Division in the General Department. Another aspect of consumption which closely concerned the Ministry was the actual preparation and provision of meals, at first in emergencies caused by bombing raids and then as communal feeding for the sake of economy. The Wartime Meals Division encouraged local authorities to establish British Restaurants for the use of the public and the Ministry provided the necessary capital in the form of a loan. Industrial canteens were also encouraged for similar reasons and because they provided a way of meeting demands for special treatment for heavy workers.

In addition to the Economics Division the General Department took over the direction of Statistics, Public Relations, and Scientific Advice. It was intended to act as a focus for the examination of all questions of general policy and particularly to ensure timely consideration of long-term difficulties. It contained divisions for Import Plans, later Import and Utilization Plans, External Relations, Supply Plans, Distribution Plans and Post War, later Reconstruction, Plans. It acted as the point of contact for the British Food Missions abroad and was responsible for advising on policy in international matters such as the conclusion of a wheat agreement with the major exporters aimed at stabilizing the market and the signing of long-term contracts for bulk purchase running into the post-war period. As early as 1942 Peace Food Plans were under discussion as it became clear that the wartime shortages would continue into the peace period, along with the control of consumption, home production, imports and prices that they entailed. In relief questions the Ministry of Food acted as an agent of the Relief Department of the Foreign Office and co-operated with the Civil Affairs authorities in the Army through the War Office. It was represented on the North African Economic Board and undertook commitments to Supreme Allied Headquarters for supplies to liberated areas in Europe.

The scientific adviser to the Ministry of Food was appointed in February 1940 shortly before the War Cabinet's Scientific Food Committee came into being. The latter body concerned itself with the basic elements of nutrition but never succeeded in directing the Ministry's policy into concentration solely on a nutritional target. Through the Adviser's Division, however, nutritional requirements were taken into account in the planning of production and import programmes and in communal feeding. The Division both co-ordinated scientific inquiries within the Ministry and acted as a liaison with research institutions under the Department of Scientific and Industrial Research. As well as the general nutritional situation which it investigated, for example, by means of calculating the vitamin content of actual British Restaurant meals and by the Body-Weight Survey of a sample of the population, the Division was concerned with special diets and technological questions, such as methods for drying meat and eggs, and with food standards and labelling.

Upon the passing of the Lend-Lease Act early in 1941 a British Food Mission was established in Washington to provide liaison between the Ministry and the American authorities in securing our food requirements. The procurement and shipment of Lend-Lease foodstuffs was placed in the hands of an Anglo-American Food Committee with an operating sub-committee. In the following summer it was this, in effect, that became the Combined Food Board on the lines of the other combined Anglo-American bodies (see p 12). Apart from providing representation on the Combined Board the Mission dealt with the Office of Lend-Lease Administration, the Department of Agriculture and the Combined Production and Resources Board (for agricultural machinery). The food requirements of all parts of the Empire as well as those of the civilian population and Armed Forces of the United Kingdom had to be channelled through the British Food Mission for allocation by the Combined Food Board and as well as its contacts with the General Department the Mission was in regular touch with the minister. For almost all the war it was involved in discussions on wheat which arose initially from the possibility that this commodity might once more be over-produced in the post-war period. By the summer of 1942 these discussions had led to the establishment of an International Wheat Council in Washington. In the following year an International Food Conference was held at Hot Springs to discuss international arrangements for the post-war period: from this derived eventually the Food and Agriculture Organization. Perhaps the heaviest burden that fell on the British Food Mission came during the later part of the war when the shipping shortage, transport difficulties in the United States and relief demands imposed the most stringent limitations on imports to the United Kingdom and a searching review of the British foodstock position had to be made to satisfy the Americans. Food imports eventually dropped to half their pre-war size. Early in 1945 the prospect of shortages led the minister of food to visit Washington to settle with the United States government the problems of allocation that had not proved soluble by the Combined Food Board.

A branch of the Washington Mission was established at Ottawa in February 1942, to deal with supplies to the United Kingdom procured with the financial assistance of the Canadian government. A further Mission represented the Ministry in Australia and others were established in the liberated areas. When the Combined Food Board was set up a need was felt for a clearing house to co-ordinate Empire requirements and production and the London Food Committee, later the London Food Council, was established to this end. The Dominions, the Ministry and other departments were represented on it.

The Ministry began its existence with a Central Registry system which took over the files of the Food (Defence Plans) Department. The move of part of the Ministry to Colwyn Bay and the proliferation of divisions made the continuance of this system impracticable and a number of separate registries was established. They created their own file series but those Central Registry files on which action had been completed before this time remained separate. Other such files were re-registered in the new series. The present arrangement of these series in classes does not, however, reflect the distribution of the related functions during the war for the Ministry continued to evolve in the post-war period and the structure as it existed at the beginning of 1947 has been used as the basis of classification. The major difference between this and the wartime structure is the disappearance of the General Department whose duties were distributed mainly to the Supply Secretariat and the Services Secretariat. Some of the common service activities carried out in the Supply Department during the war will be found in the records of the Services Department.

The Records

MAF 67   Food Control Committees: Selected Minutes
Records illustrating all aspects of the Committees' work in England, Scotland, Wales and Northern Ireland.

MAF 72   Board of Trade Food (Defence Plans) Department (1936 to 1939)
Files dealing with plans to procure, control and distribute food in wartime, and the co-ordination of food supply policy. The class includes some later papers of the Ministry of Food and records of the Overseas Purchases Board. See also MAF 74.

MAF 74   Ministry of Food Central Registry: Correspondence and Papers
Correspondence and papers first opened in the Ministry's Central Registry prior to the

decentralization of the registration system from 1940 onwards, and records of the Food (Defence Plans) Department of the Board of Trade.

MAF 75   Ministry of Food: Permanent Record of Operations (1939 to 1954)
This collection records the main functions and activities of most of the divisions of the Ministry of Food during the period of control. Two pieces are microfiche copies of the rest of the class.

MAF 83   Ministry of Food: Supply Department: Supply Secretariat
Files originating in branches once part of the Economics Division and its successors the General Department and the Supply Secretariat. They concern food production, supply and distribution policy at home and overseas.

MAF 84   Ministry of Food: Supply Department: Cereals Group
Files of the divisions responsible for the procurement, distribution and processing of cereals and cereal products.

MAF 85   Ministry of Food: Supply Department: Dairy Produce and Fats Group
Files of the divisions responsible for the procurement, distribution and processing of dairy produce and fats.

MAF 86   Ministry of Food: Supply Department: Fish and Vegetables Group
Files of the divisions responsible for the movement, distribution and processing of fish and vegetables.

MAF 87   Ministry of Food: Supply Department: Groceries and Sundries Group
These are files of the control divisions responsible for the procurement, distribution, processing, and, sometimes, wholesale and retail price control of confectionery, cocoa, coffee, tea, sugar and starch.

MAF 88   Ministry of Food: Supply Department: Meat and Livestock Group
Files of the divisions responsible for trading activities and a wide range of control over home killed and imported meat.

MAF 97   Ministry of Food: Establishment Department: British Food Mission, Washington
From 1942 these are files of the British Food Mission for North America. For records of the Ottawa Office see MAF 104.

MAF 98   Ministry of Food: Scientific Adviser's Division
These files deal particularly with nutritional policy and surveys.

MAF 99   Ministry of Food: Services Department: Distribution Group
Many of the files in this class concern emergency services, rationing, transport and communal feeding arrangements.

MAF 100 Ministry of Food: Services Department: Regional Administration Group
Records relating to the general administrative control of the regional and local offices, enforcement work and liaison with local Food Control Committees.

MAF 101 Ministry of Food: Services Department: Food Standards Group
This class includes papers concerning food standards and labelling, and the allocation and distribution of welfare foods.

MAF 102 Ministry of Food: Services Department: Public Relations Group
Papers concerning food advice booklets, leaflets, broadcasts, etc. Also contains press notices and minister's press conference reports.

MAF 103 Ministry of Food: Services Department: Services Secretariat
General policy papers concerning food consumption, distribution and export.

MAF 104 Ministry of Food: Establishment Department: British Food Mission, Ottawa
This class includes a few wartime papers of the Ottawa Office when part of the British Food Mission in Washington (see MAF 97).

MAF 127 Ministry of Food: Establishment Department
MAF 128 Ministry of Food: Senior Officers' Papers
MAF 129 Ministry of Food: Finance Secretariat
MAF 138 Ministry of Food: Finance Department
MAF 150 Ministry of Food: Legal Department Registered Files (L Series)
MAF 151 Ministry of Food: Committees
Unregistered papers of committees set up under wartime regulations.

MAF 152 Ministry of Food: War History Papers
MAF 153 Ministry of Food: Miscellanea
Authorities to act under wartime regulations, signed instruments of appointments and terms of reference to members of Food Control Committees.

MAF 154 Ministry of Food: Orders Committee
Papers arising out of the Committee's supervision and co-ordination of the exercise by the Ministry of statutory control of commodities.

MAF 156 Ministry of Food and Ministry of Agriculture, Fisheries and Food: Statistics and Intelligence Division: Correspondence and Reports

MAF 223 Ministry of Food: Publications
MAF 286 Ministry of Food: Ministers' Office Papers
             Most of these files contain prime minister's correspondence.
MAF 900 Specimens of Classes of Documents Destroyed
             Includes correspondence and papers selected to illustrate the day-to-day work of the Ministry of Food.
MH 110   Ministry of Agriculture, Fisheries and Food: Welfare Food Files
             These concern distribution outlets and financial accounts.

Foreign Office

Name	Date of appointment
Secretary of state for foreign affairs	
Viscount Halifax	1 Mar 1938
R Anthony Eden, MP	23 Dec 1940
Chief diplomatic adviser	
Sir Robert G Vansittart	1 Jan 1938 - 25 June 1941
Parliamentary under-secretary	
R A Butler, MP	26 Feb 1938
Richard K Law, MP	21 July 1941
George H Hall, MP	28 Sept 1943
Additional parliamentary under-secretary	
Harcourt Johnstone, MP	17 May 1940
Permanent under-secretary	
Sir Alexander M G Cadogan	1 Jan 1938
Ambassadors	
To USA	
Marquis of Lothian	29 Aug 1939
Viscount Halifax	24 Jan 1941
To France	
Sir Eric C E Phipps	24 Apr 1937
Sir Ronald H Campbell	1 Nov 1939 - 24 June 1940
[24 June 1940 - 22 October 1944 Mission withdrawn]	
Alfred Duff Cooper, MP	28 Oct 1944
To USSR	
Sir William Seeds	19 Jan 1939
Sir R Stafford Cripps, MP	12 June 1940
Sir Archibald J K C Kerr	4 Feb 1942
(later Lord Inverchapel)	

To China
Sir Archibald J K C Kerr   1 Feb 1938
Sir Horace James Seymour   7 Feb 1942

The pursuit of policy by other means from September 1939 inevitably lessened the importance of many of the traditional activities of the Foreign Office, yet at the same time it created new prospects in international relations to which the Office devoted much attention from an early stage in the war. Such prospects appeared mainly in connection with post-war planning in which the most important aspects were the World Security Organization which was discussed at Dumbarton Oaks and developed into the United Nations Organization, the European Advisory Commission which prepared for the occupation of Germany and Austria, and general questions of reconstruction including relief and the re-establishment of civil government in the liberated areas. The future economic and financial structure of the world was being discussed by the Office at least as early as 1941. On the other hand, while political considerations, in the diplomatic sense of that word, often had to take second place to military requirements it was the responsibility of the Office to see that such considerations were not completely overlooked in strategical discussions.

During the war the organization of the Foreign Office remained basically the same as before (see *The Records of the Foreign Office 1782 to 1939*, Public Record Office Handbooks No 13), but there were numerous detailed changes. Among the 'country' departments a Co-ordination Section had been set up inside the Western Department in May 1938 to deal with war emergency work in liaison with the Committee of Imperial Defence and soon combined this work with economic relations. For a brief period after the outbreak of hostilities there was a Co-ordination Section in the Central Department but thereafter Co-ordination was the responsibility of Western Department, which shortly lost its remaining countries to Central Department and, as it now dealt purely with subjects, was renamed General Department. Its files, however, retained the W prefix in references to papers. As a consequence of its 'country' work Central Department (prefix C) was charged in 1940 with the co-ordination of dealings with the Allied governments in London, their domestic problems and the administration of agreements concerning their Armed Forces, but this work was later transferred to the General Department. The 'war aims' aspect of post-war planning and questions relating to war crimes also fell at first to Central Department but were later handled by Economic and Reconstruction Department and its successors. A French Department (prefix Z) was established in 1941 to handle negotiations with the Free French and all matters relating to France and the French Empire, and in the same year the American Department was divided into North and South American Departments, though the A prefix was retained for some time, AN and AS appearing later. In the last year of the war a German Department (prefix C) was established, replacing the Central Department. Other countries dealt with by the Central Department and the French Department were transferred to a revived Western Department (prefix Z).

Filed among the records of the General Department are those of a separate department, Dominions Intelligence, which originally concerned itself with the collection of information from the Dominions and circulation to them and had been in the Treaty Department before the war. During the course of the war the Dominions Intelligence Department became responsible for providing Foreign Office representation on the Joint Intelligence Committee (see p 7), thus ensuring a political element in the deliberations of that body. This duty was transferred in 1943 to a Services Liaison Department so that the Dominions Intelligence Department could concentrate on its Dominions work. Some of the activities of the General Department later developed sufficiently to justify the creation of separate departments, notably the Economic and Reconstruction Department from which further fission occurred, and the Refugee Department (prefix WR) which handled many individual cases as well as general questions respecting refugees. The other duties of the General Department included Allied Administrative Affairs (formerly with Central Department as noted above), Censorship, Commercial Aviation (a responsibility shared with the

Air Ministry) and Shipping. The Economic and Reconstruction Department (prefix U) came into existence in 1942. It included from the beginning of 1943 the Foreign Research and Press Service which had previously been housed at Oxford and administered by the Royal Institute of International Affairs under a Foreign Office grant. In April 1943 the Foreign Research and Press Service was amalgamated with the Weekly Intelligence Summary Section of the Political Intelligence Department to form the Foreign Office Research Department. The Political Intelligence Department had some links with the Political Warfare Executive (pp 132-5) to which it provided cover and with which it shared accommodation in Woburn Abbey. When the Political Warfare Executive was wound up after the end of the war with Germany, certain of its work, including that of its Prisoner of War Division, passed to the Political Intelligence Department. In 1946 the Political Intelligence Department was itself wound up, and its German and Austrian work was passed to the Control Office to which reference is made below. At the same time its research and intelligence work on other areas became the responsibility of the Foreign Office Research Department and Library. The Economic and Reconstruction Department was concerned with such matters as plans for the disarmament of Germany, civil affairs with the War Office, the preparation of food stocks for post-war relief, future commercial policy and the creation of the United Nations Relief and Rehabilitation Administration. In many of these activities it dealt with the Office of the Minister of Reconstruction in the War Cabinet Office. The responsibilities of the Board of Trade's Relief Department were transferred to the Foreign Office in September 1943 but the requirements and supplies aspects were hived off to the Ministry of Production at the end of the year, leaving the Foreign Office with relief personnel and policy. By 1945 the unmanageable expansion of all these activities had led to the creation of separate Departments for Economic Relations (prefix UE), Reconstruction (prefix U) and Relief (prefix UR).

The other departments of the Office continued much as they had done. In addition to the Consular Department a new Consular (War), later Prisoners of War, Department (prefix KW) was created. Some of the functions of the News Department were transferred to the Ministry of Information. A British Council Section established as part of the Library in 1941 became an enlarged and separate Cultural Relations Department in 1944.

The overlapping of Foreign Office areas of activity with those of other departments of state has already been noticed in a number of instances. Reference should also be made in this connection to the Ministry of Economic Warfare (pp 70-73) with whose activities the Office was particularly concerned. In 1944 administrative control of the Enemy Branch of the Ministry of Economic Warfare was taken over by the Foreign Office for whom the branch was to appreciate economic questions relevant to political problems in enemy held areas without abandoning its responsibilities to the Ministry. After the German surrender the Ministry was wound up and an Economic Warfare Department was established within the Foreign Office to take over its residual functions. Consequently, the Foreign Office took over the main responsibility for the campaign against German external assets, known as the safehaven programme, including tracing and restoring loot, such as works of art; preventing the escape of war criminals and their assets; and taking steps against the resurgence of Nazi Germany in neutral countries and under neutral cloaks by the settlement of technicians and the establishment of funds as a basis for industrial rearmament. In addition to such overlapping interests the Office provided communications facilities for all the civil departments with business to conduct abroad, and the handling of telegrams for these departments, together with the circulation to them of Foreign Office telegrams, constituted a large part of the duties of the Communications Department (prefix Y). In highly technical matters the Office served mainly as a post office, but in many others it was able to make a political contribution to discussions.

In principle the system for handling papers within the Foreign Office remained what it had been before the war (see *The Records of the Foreign Office 1782 to 1939*). Each paper received an alpha-numerical reference which both indicated the department to which it belonged and the country or the section of the department concerned, and identified it uniquely among the records of that department. The papers were grouped by the Registry into files and for each paper a précis jacket was prepared which took its place in the Registry while the paper was in circulation. The pressure of business on this elaborate system, in which in theory written action on a paper could not take place in a department until the process of registration was complete and the paper enclosed in a docket sheet, though in practice they were often seen and action begun by departments before registration, led to considerable difficulties. Even greater problems were caused by the heavy increase in the number of Green papers, *ie* those of special secrecy and other categories, which could not be handled in the Registry. In the first part of the war Green papers were kept by the departments and a guarded account of each of them supplied to the Registry on the basis of which it allotted references (suffixed G), prepared précis jackets and assigned them to files. In due course, after they had lost their need for special handling, the papers were sent to the Library, there to be united with the files to which they had originally been assigned and indexed (for the first time) in a Green Index separate from the Main Index, which would normally have been printed by this stage. In January 1941 a Green Registry was opened to hold these papers instead of the departments. It received references for individual papers from the Registry in the same way as before, though the Green Registry used no country numbers, and also attempted to maintain the Green parts of files constructed by Registry. Registry continued to hold the précis jackets but there were difficulties in keeping the numbers in step. The Green Registry also attempted to keep an index, small parts of which for 1941, were later incorporated by the Library in its Green Index. The Green Registry's card index 1942-1945 survives separately. At the final processing of papers in the Library, in some cases the Green papers were not forthcoming to replace their précis jackets either because of loss or destruction or because they were assigned to different files as a result of a closer examination of their contents. Where précis jackets are now found in files it may be possible to trace the papers by judicious use of the Green Index.

In the majority of cases British Missions around the world were situated as before and their records continued during the war in the same series, though their content naturally reflects the changed circumstances and, sometimes, considerable changes in the activities of the Mission. The Washington Embassy was particularly important both before American entry into the war, when our diplomatic relations with the United States of America were of the highest importance, and after that event, when many aspects of the war were the concern of combined bodies in Washington or necessitated visits there from London, for the Embassy was able to play a considerable co-ordinating and advisory role by virtue of its thorough knowledge of the local circumstances (see p 12).

The recognition of General De Gaulle in June 1940 as the leader of the Free French led to the appointment of a liaison staff and the chief liaison officer was given head of mission status at the beginning of 1941. With the transfer of recognition to the Free French National Committee, later the French Committee of National Liberation, in September 1941 the Mission acquired a somewhat more formal character and after the Committee had moved to Algiers in 1943 the minister resident at Allied Force Headquarters was appointed HM representative to it. Apart from political questions the minister resident was concerned with 'civil affairs' in the liberated areas and with the various bodies dealing with the economic rehabilitation of North Africa. At the beginning of 1944 a separate representative was appointed who became ambassador in Paris when the Embassy re-opened in the autumn. Another Mission was sent to Syria, part of the old French Empire, where it concerned itself particularly with agricultural questions in conjunction with the Middle East Supply Centre under the Ministry of War Transport. The appointment of ministers resident is discussed elsewhere in connection with the Central Direction of the War (pp 12-13). Those appointed to the Middle East and Allied Force Headquarters had some functions of a diplomatic character and were therefore served by Foreign Office staff. Planning for the British elements of the Control Commission for Germany and the Allied Commission for Austria (pp 60-64) was carried out by the Foreign and War Offices under the general supervision of the Post-Hostilities

Planning Committee, a sub-committee of the Chiefs of Staff Committee, and in accordance with agreements made in the European Advisory Commission. The Enemy Branch of the Ministry of Economic Warfare, to which reference has been made above, was also concerned in this planning.

As a consequence of the capture by the Allies of many thousands of files from enemy archives a considerable number were sent to Britain and the United States for scrutiny and research. Many were filmed and a number from the German Foreign Ministry will be found under GFM references among the records detailed below. Some photocopies of captured Italian documents are also in GFM 36.

Control Office for Germany and Austria

After much discussion it was agreed that when the British elements of the Control Commission for Germany and the Allied Commission for Austria went overseas the War Office should become responsible for their administration from London. A Control Commission London Bureau was established by the War Office Directorate of Civil Affairs for that purpose in June 1945, but it soon became clear that matters concerning the occupation ranged well beyond the military sphere. Accordingly, a Control Office for Germany and Austria, with the chancellor of the Duchy of Lancaster as its ministerial head, became responsible for the entire work in October 1945 taking over the appropriate parts of the War Office Directorate of Civil Affairs and the Economic and Industrial Planning Staff of the Foreign Office. It also took over the German and Austrian work of the Foreign Office Political Intelligence Department when that Department was wound up in 1946, involving in particular, information services and the screening and reeducation of German prisoners of War.

In April 1946 certain staff of the Control Office's German Economic Department, who were responsible for briefing industrialists and similar experts being sent to Germany to collect industrial intelligence, were brought together in a Central Briefing Unit and transferred to the German Division of the Board of Trade (see pp 159-60), where they worked alongside War Office staff attached to the British Intelligence Objectives Sub-Committee (BIOS). In the following month the German Economic Department's Foreign Documents Unit, whose main job was to translate and prepare abstracts of German documents for the information of British industry, was similarly transferred. Responsibility for the residual work of the British War Crimes Executive, arising from the proceedings of the International Military Tribunal at Nuremburg, passed to the Control Office in January 1947.

In April 1947 the Control Office ceased to exist as an independent unit and was incorporated in the Foreign Office to form part of a new German Section. Ministerial responsibility then passed to the foreign secretary, assisted by the chancellor of the Duchy of Lancaster as minister of state.

The Records

[*For key to country classes see Appendix A(2)*]

BW 1- BW 4, BW 84	British Council: Registered Files: General and Subject Series
BW 5- BW 66 BW 88, BW 93, BW 105	British Council: Registered Files: Country Series Headquarters files relating to British Council activities in various coun- tries, and correspondence with its overseas representatives.
BW 67, BW 70-	British Council: Various Committees Mainly minutes and papers.

BW 71,	
BW 77-	
BW 81,	
BW 89	
BW 68	British Council: Governing Board and Executive Committee: Minutes and Papers
BW 69	British Council: Executive Committee and Finance and Agenda Committee: Minutes and Papers
BW 74	Conference of Allied Ministers of Education: Minutes and Papers
	See also ED 42, ED 121 and FO 924.
BW 75-	British Council: Secretariat: Various Records
BW 76	Bulletins, instructions, etc. For photographic collection see INF 11.
BW 82	
BW 110	
BW 108	British Council: National Hearths: Correspondence and Papers
	Surviving files of the Resident foreigners section covering the Netherlands, Polish and Yugoslav homes, which were established in London for war refugees from Western Europe and members of Allied Forces.
CAB 142	United Nations Relief and Rehabilitation Administration: United Kingdom Delegation
	Minutes of meetings and papers of the UK Delegation, and similar material from the British Commonwealth delegations and from the UNRRA Council and its committees.
FO 93	Protocols of Treaties
	Arranged by countries or geographical areas.
FO 94	Ratifications of Treaties
	Arranged similarly to the protocols in FO 93.
FO 96	Miscellanea Series II
	Include some cigarette cards of Nazi personalities and functions received from the British Embassy in Chile, and some German identity documents issued to Channel Islanders.
FO 111	Embassy and Consular Archives Algiers: Correspondence, Series I
FO 115	Embassy and Consular Archives United States of America: Correspondence
	This class includes a large number of files concerning North American supplies. See also AVIA 38 and CAB 115.
FO 118	Embassy and Consular Archives Argentine Republic: Correspondence
FO 123	Embassy and Consular Archives Belgium: Correspondence
FO 128	Embassy and Consular Archives Brazil: Correspondence
FO 132	Embassy and Consular Archives Chile: Correspondence
FO 135	Embassy and Consular Archives Colombia: Correspondence
FO 141	Embassy and Consular Archives Egypt: Correspondence
	Material for the period 1930 to 1941 has not survived.
FO 146	Embassy and Consular Archives France: Correspondence
	Two files were raised in 1946 and concern war crimes.
FO 160	Embassy and Consular Archives Libya (Tripoli): Letter Books and Correspondence
FO 170	Embassy and Consular Archives Italy: Correspondence
FO 173	Embassy and Consular Archives: Portugal, Lisbon
FO 174	Embassy and Consular Archives: Morocco, Tangier
	Correspondence of the consulate general and legation.
FO 177	Embassy and Consular Archives Peru: Correspondence
FO 179	Embassy and Consular Archives Portugal: Correspondence
FO 181	Embassy and Consular Archives Russia: Correspondence
FO 185	Embassy and Consular Archives Spain: Correspondence
FO 188	Embassy and Consular Archives Sweden: Correspondence
	Some correspondence for 1939 and 1940 was destroyed in 1940 under the threat of enemy invasion.
FO 195	Embassy and Consular Archives Turkey: Correspondence
FO 198	Embassy and Consular Archives Turkey: Miscellanea
	Case papers.
FO 204	Embassy and Consular Archives Mexico: Correspondence (Series II)
FO 211	Embassy and Consular Archives Denmark: Correspondence
FO 226	Embassy and Consular Archives Turkey: Beirut Correspondence, etc
	Includes files of the Beirut legation, 1942 to 1945, and two files of the Spears Mission, 1942. See also FO 922 and WO 202.
FO 233	Embassy and Consular Archives China: Miscellanea
	Includes claims arising from Sino-Japanese hostilities, 1927 to 1940.
FO 238	Embassy and Consular Archives Holland and Netherlands: Correspondence
	The archives for 1939 have not survived.

FO 242	Embassy and Consular Archives Netherlands: Amsterdam Correspondence
FO 248	Embassy and Consular Archives Iran (Persia): Correspondence
FO 252	Embassy and Consular Archives Guatemala: Correspondence
	The minister of the legation at Guatemala was set in authority over the consular officers in Nicaragua, Salvador and Honduras, and copies of the more important telegrams, despatches, etc, sent and received by those officers are to be found among the correspondence in this class.
FO 262	Embassy and Consular Archives Japan: Correspondence
	Post-war files concerning Japanese war criminals.
FO 286	Embassy and Consular Archives Greece: Correspondence
	Correspondence for the period 1938 to 1941 has not survived.
FO 288	Embassy and Consular Archives Panama: Correspondence
FO 321	Embassy and Consular Archives Denmark: Reykjavik
	Iceland, although an independent kingdom, continued to have the same sovereign as Denmark and diplomatic relations continued to be conducted through Copenhagen until 1940. Then following the German invasion of Denmark and the British occupation of Iceland, a legation was established at Reykjavik. Iceland became fully independent in 1944.
FO 332	Embassy and Consular Archives Spain: Seville
FO 337	Embassy and Consular Archives Norway: Correspondence
FO 345	Embassy and Consular Archives Japan: Miscellaneous
FO 366	Chief Clerk's Department Archives
	Correspondence, etc, of the Chief Clerk's Department
FO 369	General Correspondence (after 1906): Consular
	Correspondence, etc, of the Consular Department.
FO 370	General Correspondence: Library
	Correspondence, etc, of the Library. See also FO 924.
FO 371	Foreign Office: General Correspondence: Political
	Correspondence, etc, of the Political Departments, the main series of FO papers.
FO 372	General Correspondence (after 1906): Treaty
	Correspondence, etc, of the Treaty Department
FO 380	Embassy and Consular Archives Vatican: Correspondence
FO 388	Embassy and Consular Archives Bulgaria: Correspondence
FO 395	General Correspondence after 1906: News
	Correspondence, etc, of the News Department.
FO 401	Confidential Print Abyssinia (Ethiopia)
	See also FO 403.
FO 402	Confidential Print Afghanistan
	See also FO 406.
FO 403	Confidential Print Africa
	Correspondence relating to the countries of Africa, including Madagascar, Algeria, Tunisia, Morocco, Suez Canal and Egypt, and Abyssinia.
FO 404	Confidential Print Central Europe
	Correspondence relating to Austria, Czechoslovakia, Hungary, Germany and Poland, 1942 to 1946.
FO 406	Confidential Print Eastern Affairs
	Correspondence relating to Arabia, Iraq, Palestine, Syria and Lebanon; also to Persia and Afghanistan, 1942 to 1946.
FO 407	Confidential Print Egypt and the Sudan
	See also FO 403.
FO 408	Confidential Print Germany
	Including correspondence relating to Austria, 1938 to 1941. See also FO 404.
FO 409	Indexes (Printed Series) to General Correspondence
	The class also includes separate indexes to Green papers, originally classified as confidential or secret, but now in their normal place in the General Correspondence.
FO 411	Confidential Print League of Nations
FO 413	Confidential Print Morocco and North West Africa
	See also FO 403.
FO 414	Confidential Print North America
	Correspondence relating to the United States and Canada. See also FO 461.
FO 416	Confidential Print Persia (Iran)
	See also FO 406.
FO 417	Confidential Print Poland
	This series contains, in addition, correspondence relating to Czechoslovakia and Hungary, 1939 to 1941. See also FO 404.

FO 418	Confidential Print Russia and Soviet Union
	See also FO 490.
FO 419	Confidential Print Scandinavia and the Baltic States
	Correspondence relating to Estonia, Finland, Latvia, Lithuania, Denmark, Iceland, Norway and Sweden. See also FO 490.
FO 420	Confidential Print America, South and Central
	Correspondence relating to the countries of South and Central America and to Mexico. See also FO 461.
FO 421	Confidential Print South-East Europe
	Correspondence relating to Albania, Bulgaria, Greece, Roumania, Yugoslavia, Italy and the Vatican, and Turkey.
FO 423	Confidential Print Suez Canal
	See also FO 403.
FO 424	Confidential Print Turkey
	See also FO 421.
FO 425	Confidential Print Western Europe
	Correspondence relating to Gibraltar, Portugal, Spain and Switzerland; also to Belgium, France, Luxembourg and the Netherlands, 1942 to 1946.
FO 432	Confidential Print France
	This series contains, in addition, correspondence relating to Belgium, Luxembourg and the Netherlands. See also FO 425.
FO 434	Confidential Print Southern Europe
	Correspondence relating to Albania, Bulgaria, Greece, Italy, Roumania, the Vatican and Yugoslavia. See also FO 421.
FO 436	Confidential Print Far Eastern Affairs
	Correspondence relating to China, Japan, Nepal, Siam and South East Asia.
FO 438	Confidential Print War, General
FO 443	Embassy and Consular Archives Morocco: Rabat Correspondence
FO 446	Embassy and Consular Archives Argentine Republic: Buenos Aires
FO 447	Embassy and Consular Archives Russia: Moscow Correspondence
FO 448	Embassy and Consular Archives Russia: Moscow Registers of Correspondence
FO 458	Embassy and Consular Archives Liberia: Correspondence
FO 461	Confidential Print America
	Correspondence relating to the United States, Canada and the countries of South and Central America. See also FO 414 and FO 420.
FO 475	Confidential Print General Affairs
FO 490	Confidential Print Northern Affairs
	Correspondence relating to the Baltic States, Denmark, Finland, Iceland, Norway, Russia and Sweden. See also FO 418 and FO 419.
FO 505	Embassy and Consular Archives Uruguay: Correspondence
FO 511	Embassy and Consular Archives Finland: Correspondence
FO 536	Embassy and Consular Archives Yugoslavia: Correspondence
	During the Second World War the embassy was withdrawn to London in 1941, transferred to Cairo in 1943, re-transferred to London in 1944 and returned to Belgrade in 1944. Its archives for the period 1920 to 1940 have been destroyed.
FO 561	Embassy and Consular Archives France: Paris Correspondence and Letter Books
FO 593	Embassy and Consular Archives Italy: Trieste Registers of Correspondence
	Registers of correspondence with the Ministry of Economic Warfare for the first half of 1940.
FO 606	Embassy and Consular Archives Belgium: Antwerp Letter Books and Correspondence
FO 610	Passport Registers
FO 612	Passport Office: Correspondence
FO 624	Embassy and Consular Archives Iraq: Correspondence
FO 628	Embassy and Consular Archives Thailand (Siam): Correspondence
	Post-war files concerning war claims and history of the construction by the Japanese of the Siam-Burma railway.
FO 641	Embassy and Consular Archives Portugal: Oporto Correspondence
FO 643	Embassy and Consular Archives Burma: Correspondence
	Records of the Burma Secretariat (in exile in India until October 1945, and afterwards stationed in Rangoon) inherited by HM embassy in Rangoon under an agreement between the Foreign Office and the Burma Office, London.
FO 649	Embassy and Consular Archives Denmark: Thorshavn Correspondence
FO 660	War of 1939 to 1945: Ministers Resident, etc
	This class contains the surviving records of: the political liaison officer with the United States

Forces in Great Britain and North Africa, August 1942 to May 1943; the Office of the Minister Resident at Allied Force Headquarters in Algiers and Paris, 1943 to 1944; and the Office of the United Kingdom Representative with the French Committee of National Liberation at Algiers, 1943 to 1944. See also FO 892, FO 921 and FO 922.

FO 671	Embassy and Consular Archives China: Shanghai Correspondence, etc
FO 676	Embassy and Consular Archives China: Correspondence, Series II

Files of the legation at Peking, the embassy at Nanking, the embassy at Shanghai to 1940, and the embassy at Chungking.

FO 684	Embassy and Consular Archives France: Damascus
FO 688	Embassy and Consular Archives Poland: Correspondence

Correspondence of the British embassy to the Polish Government in the United Kingdom, 1940 to 1946. The 1939 files were destroyed in Warsaw in that year.

FO 698	Embassy and Consular Archives France: Marseilles
FO 700	Embassy and Consular Archives United States of America: Various Consulates

Includes two files concerning British war brides and one about the presentation of badges, etc, by the Royal Navy to American cities and towns in commemoration of Lend-Lease destroyers.

FO 708	Embassy and Consular Archives France: Pondicherry
FO 710	Embassy and Consular Archives France: Tananarive (Antananarivo)
FO 722	Embassy and Consular Archives Lithuania: Kovno and Memel

Registers of births and deaths at Kovno to 1940.

FO 723	Embassy and Consular Archives Mexico: Mexico City
FO 743	Embassy and Consular Archives Brazil: Rio de Janeiro
FO 748	Embassy and Consular Archives Sweden: Stockholm

These relate mainly to births, marriages and deaths.

FO 749	Embassy and Consular Archives Denmark: Copenhagen
FO 753	Embassy and Consular Archives Finland: Helsinki (Helsingfors)
FO 762	Embassy and Consular Archives Italy: Genoa
FO 766	Embassy and Consular Archives Nepal: Correspondence
FO 770	Embassy and Consular Archives Roumania: Correspondence
FO 773	Embassy and Consular Archives Spain: Vigo
FO 778	Embassy and Consular Archives Switzerland: Geneva
FO 784	Embassy and Consular Archives Turkey: Indexes to Correspondence
FO 794	Private Office Individual Files

Selected files of correspondence, etc, relating to ambassadors and senior diplomats.

FO 799	Embassy and Consular Archives Iran (Persia): Isfahan
FO 800	Private Collections: Ministers and Officials: Various

Private Office papers of the secretary of state; papers of under-secretaries; and private papers of senior diplomats and other officials and individuals connected with foreign affairs.

FO 817	Embassy and Consular Archives Czechoslovakia: Correspondence

Correspondence with the Czechoslovakian Government in exile in London.

FO 818	Embassy and Consular Archives Sweden: Gothenburg Correspondence
FO 835	Embassy and Consular Archives Morocco: Casablanca Correspondence, etc
FO 836	Embassy and Consular Archives Morocco: Marrakesh Correspondence
FO 837	Ministry of Economic Warfare

Policy files, progress reports, war trade lists, enemy shipping intelligence, committee papers, etc, arising from contraband control and associated work of the Ministry. There are also reports and surveys regarding industrial targets in German towns and cities. The class includes material, much of it post-war, concerning enemy property, relief programmes and reparations. The later files are those of the Ministry's successor, the Foreign Office, including a number concerning operations under the safehaven programme.

FO 838	Embassy and Consular Archives Iraq: Amara
FO 847	Embassy and Consular Archives Egypt: Alexandria Consular Court Records

Includes papers concerning inquests on a number of servicemen.

FO 850	General Correspondence after 1906: Communications

Records of the Communications Department of the Foreign Office, relating to king's messengers, etc.

FO 854	Embassy and Consular Archives Colombia: Bogota
FO 859	Embassy and Consular Archives France: Brazzaville
FO 867	Anglo-Egyptian Sudan

Minutes of proceedings of the Governor-General's Committee.

FO 889	Embassy and Consular Archives Spain: Valencia
FO 891	Embassy and Consular Archives Egypt: Alexandria
FO 892	British Mission to the French National Committee

The papers in the class deal with such topics as diplomatic privilege, recruitment into the Free French Forces, Lend-Lease supplies from America, imports of manufactured goods and foodstuffs, operational control of French ships based in United Kingdom ports, training and operational use of the Free French Air Force, etc. See also FO 660.

FO 908 Embassy and Consular Archives Japan: Yokohama

FO 912 Embassy and Consular Archives France: Douala
One file concerning the Free French Movement from the consulate-general.

FO 916 War of 1939 to 1945: Consular (War) Department: Prisoners of War and Internees
Reports from various sources on prisoners of war and internment camps, etc, in enemy and enemy-occupied countries and on the treatment of British subjects both military and civilian. Other matters dealt with include welfare, exchanges, repatriations, escapes, deaths, etc. Later reports are in WO 224.

FO 921 Minister of State, Cairo
Files of the Office of the minister of state resident in Cairo.

FO 922 Middle East Supply Centre
Files relate to various aspects of the centre's work, including the director-general's office, the Spears Mission to Syria and Lebanon (see also FO 226 and WO 202), agriculture, transport, industrial production, etc.

FO 924 General Correspondence after 1906: Cultural Relations
Many relate to the British Council in continuation of files in FO 370. Records of the Council itself are in BW classes above.

FO 927 Embassy and Consular Archives Spain: Malaga

FO 934 Potsdam Conference 1945: United Kingdom Delegates Archives

FO 935 Control Office: Intelligence Objectives Sub-Committees
Files mainly of the Ministry of Economic Warfare and the Economic Warfare Department of the Foreign Office relating to the work of the Combined Intelligence Objectives Sub-Committee and the British Intelligence Objectives Sub-Committee in obtaining and disseminating technical and political intelligence of urgent military importance. German documents, evaluation reports, etc, collected by these Sub-Committees are held by the Imperial War Museum.

FO 936 Control Office: Establishments
Files of the Establishment and Organization Department of the Control Office for Germany and Austria, later transferred to the German Section of the Foreign Office.

FO 937 Control Office: Legal
Many of these are records of the Rear Headquarters of the Legal Division of the British element of the Control Commission for Germany.

FO 938 Control Office: Private Office Papers
In addition to papers of the chancellor of the Duchy of Lancaster and senior staff of the Control Office the class also includes material from the Foreign Office German Section.

FO 939 Control Office: Prisoners of War
Files relating to treatment of prisoners of war under British control not only in the United Kingdom, but in the Middle East and elsewhere.

FO 940 Control Office: Travel
Much of the class is arranged under the heading of movements of fiancées and distressed relatives, compassionate visitors and displaced persons holding Ministry of Labour permits out of Germany.

FO 941 Control Office: Central Secretariat
Papers in this class reflect work on policy and administration carried out both by the Central Secretariat of the Control Office for Germany and Austria and, after reorganization in April 1947, by the Foreign Office German Section. There is considerable overlap between the subject-matter of files in this class, which were not entered in the Foreign Office Annual Index, and files of the German Section in FO 371, which were. In many cases, files in this class continue in FO 371.

FO 942 Control Office: Economic and Industrial Planning Staff
Although the bulk of this class concerns Austria and Germany, there are also files on Allied control in Bulgaria, Hungary and Roumania, on peace treaty negotiations with Italy and on broad questions of restitution, reparations, etc, affecting other European countries.

FO 943 Control Office: Economic
Files in this class relate to all economic aspects of British, and later to some extent of Anglo-US bizonal, control in Germany, including policy on agriculture, food, industry, refugees, relief, reparations and international trade. A few early files in the class originated with the Economic and Industrial Planning Staff. Most are those successively of the Control Office for Germany and Austria and the Foreign Office German Section.

FO 944 Control Office: Finance
Records of the Finance Division of the Control Office for Germany and Austria and of the

German Section of the Foreign Office. They relate to a very wide range of matters affecting currency provisions and all financial aspects of control.

FO 945 Control Office: General Department
This class reflects the broad scope of the General Department which dealt with most matters arising from control in Germany and Austria except for the purely economic and financial. A large section relates to displaced persons. There is also a quantity of former War Office files which the Control Office re-registered, and these include a series of 'US post-defeat directives'.

FO 946 Control Office: Information Services
These files reflect the public relations work undertaken by the Control Office, including the production of exhibitions, films and publications, relations with the press and one file of minutes of the Overseas Information Committee of the Cabinet, 1946-47.

FO 950 General Correspondence: Claims
Files of the Claims Department concerning war compensation claims by British nationals against foreign governments.

FO 952 Embassy and Consular Archives Norway: Various Consulates' Records Captured by the Germans
One file relates to the 'Altmark' incident.

FO 954 Avon Papers
Photographic copies of private office papers of Anthony Eden, later earl of Avon, as foreign secretary from 1936 to 1938 and from 1940 to 1945. The originals together with personal and private papers, are deposited in Birmingham University Library.

FO 962 Embassy and Consular Archives Iceland: Correspondence
FO 963 Embassy and Consular Archives Egypt: Alexandria Naval Court Records
FO 969 Embassy and Consular Archives France: New Caledonia, Noumea
FO 970 Embassy and Consular Archives Italy: Naples
FO 981 Embassy and Consular Archives Morocco: Fez
FO 984 Embassy and Consular Archives Abyssinia (Ethiopia): Correspondence
FO 995 Embassy and Consular Archives Italy: Rome
FO 996 Embassy and Consular Archives Greece: Salonika

FO 1004 Foreign Compensation Commission
Records regarding war compensation for loss of British property, rights and interests.

FO 1011 Loraine Papers (formerly PRO 30/73)
Personal and official papers of Sir Percy Loraine, mainly concerning Italian affairs.

FO 1015 Foreign Office Administration of African Territories
This class relates to the administration of the former Italian colonies in Africa. From 1941 until 1949 the papers are those of the War Office.

FO 1019 War Crimes Trials Nuremberg: Correspondence and Papers
Records of the Court Contact Committee and the British War Crimes Executive.

FO 1055 French Welfare 1940-1945
Papers dealing with the welfare of French nationals after the fall of France.

FO 1079 European Advisory Commission
Records of the Commission established in 1943 by the governments of the UK, USA and USSR.

FO 1093 Foreign Office: Rudolf Hess: Miscellaneous Unregistered Papers

GFM 1 Repertoria, etc
Film copies of lists of captured records of the German Foreign Ministry.

GFM 3 Official Projects (GWDP), Project K
Produced by the German War Documents Project set up by the British and American governments (and subsequently joined by the French) to film, study and publish German Foreign Ministry files for the period 1918 to 1944.

GFM 4 Official Projects (GWDP), Project L
Produced by the German War Documents Project.

GFM 5 Official Projects (GWDP), Project M
Produced by the German War Documents Project.

GFM 19 Miscellaneous

GFM 23 Commonwealth National Library, Canberra, and Mitchell Library, Sydney, Selection (CNLC and MLS)

GFM 30 Official Projects (GWDP), Project C
Produced by the Foreign Office/State Department Document Unit. It includes some documents of the Reich Chancellery at Heidelberg.

GFM 36 The Italian Collection (Captured Italian Records): Photocopies

T 188 Leith-Ross Papers
Papers of Sir Frederick Leith-Ross relating mainly to international economic affairs and post-war relief in Europe.

Forestry Commission

Name	Date of appointment
Chairman	
Sir Roy Lister Robinson	1932
Secretary	
A G Herbert	c 1925

The Records

AVIA 46   Ministry of Supply Files: Series 1 (Establishment)
          This class includes narratives and documents relating to wartime timber control.

F 1   Minutes

F 18   Forestry Commission: Head Office Headquarters: Registered Files
          Policy files of the Commission's Headquarters, which include material relating to transfers of functions from other departments, organization and establishment, acquisitions of land, the work of various committees and conferences relating to forestry, unemployment relief schemes, forest and estate management, finance, grants and private forestry.

F 19   Forestry Commission: Assistant Commissioner for England and Wales, and English Directorate: Correspondence and Papers
          Files containing papers relating to research, legislation, forest preservation, forest parks, transfer of crown lands, establishment and staffing matters, etc.

F 21   Research Division Correspondence and Papers

F 22   Census of Woodlands, Reports and Data
          These relate to the 1942 survey for Dorset and Cardiganshire.

F 23   Census of Woodlands, Maps
          These supplement material in F 22.

F 27   Meetings of Divisional Officers and Conservators, Minutes

F 32   Secretariat: Law Files
          Includes bill papers for Forestry Act 1945.

F 34   Commissioners' Reports
          Of the reports for the years 1939 to 1945 only the report for 1945 was published.

F 35   Reports from Conservancies
          These cover the years 1941 to 1942.

MAF 50   Legal Department: Papers
          These concern case work undertaken for the Commission by the Treasury solicitor and include papers arising from the requisitioning by the military authorities of leased properties.

Registry of Friendly Societies

Name	Date of appointment
Chief registrar and industrial assurance commissioner	
Sir John Fox	1937

The Records

FS 23   Subject and Policy Files
         These relate mainly to the operation of Societies in wartime conditions.

Ministry of Fuel and Power

BOARD OF TRADE
(until 11 June 1942)

Name	*Date of appointment*
President	
Oliver Stanley, MP	28 May 1937
Sir Andrew Duncan, MP	5 Jan 1940
Oliver Lyttelton, MP	3 Oct 1940
Sir Andrew Duncan, MP	29 June 1941
J J Llewellin (later Lord Llewellin), MP	4 Feb 1942
Hugh Dalton, MP	22 Feb 1942
Secretary for mines	
Geoffrey Lloyd, MP	21 Apr 1939
David R Grenfell, MP	15 May 1940
Secretary for petroleum	
Geoffrey Lloyd, MP	17 May 1940
Under-secretary for mines	
Sir Alfred E Faulkner	1927
Sir Alfred Hurst	1940
Director-general, Petroleum Department	
Sir Cecil H Kisch	1939
Chairman of the Petroleum Board	
Sir Andrew Agnew	22 Sept 1938

MINISTRY OF FUEL AND POWER
(from 11 June 1942)

Minister	
Gwilym Lloyd George, MP	3 June 1942
Joint parliamentary secretaries	
Geoffrey Lloyd, MP (secretary for petroleum)	3 June 1942
Tom Smith, MP (secretary for coal)	3 June 1942

Controller-general

Lord Hyndley   June 1942
Sir Hubert S Houldsworth   1944

The Ministry of Fuel and Power came into existence in June 1942 mainly as a result of difficulties experienced with coal supplies which led the government to the view that a closer control required to be exercised. Since it had become apparent that in conditions of total war the overlapping sources of energy required a single direction the opportunity was taken to endow the new Ministry with responsibility for all of them. These responsibilities had previously been exercised by independent departments of the Board of Trade although from the autumn of 1941 fuel and power controllers had co-ordinated the activities of the departmental representatives in the regions. The Ministry was consequently organized into three major Divisions, namely Coal, Petroleum, and Gas and Electricity.

The Coal Division had previously been the Mines Department of the Board of Trade where it had its own ministerial head, the secretary for mines. At the beginning of the war the Department had put into action the planned organization for coal control consisting of coal supplies officers in the coalfields, divisional coal officers in the Civil Defence Regions to deal with distribution and rationing, and coal export officers in the coal-shipping districts. Severe difficulties were experienced in distribution in the first winter of the war, largely due to lack of shipping, and in the autumn of 1940 a Lord President's Coal Committee was established to grip the problem of the coming winter. At a lower level a House Coal Distribution (Emergency) Scheme was established to provide liaison between the Department and the distributive trade, principally by means of house coal officers selected from the trade to co-operate with the divisional coal officers.

On the production side co-operation between the Department and the mines was strengthened from April 1940 by the establishment of Coal Production Committees which contained representatives of the owners and the unions and whose coal production advisers dealt with district and pit production committees in the pursuit of increased output. In May 1941 an Essential Work Order issued by the Ministry of Labour and National Service was applied to the mines and prevented miners from leaving their employment, while a little later the Registration of Miners Scheme was introduced in an attempt to counteract further wastage of labour in the pits. In the following year, however, it was apparent that output continued to fall while demand was expected to grow and reorganization of the industry under government control was determined upon. This form of control left the ownership of the mines untouched while the government directed their operations as necessary, for example by concentrating production in the more easily worked pits. This was done through new regional controllers, each supervising directors for production, labour and services. The divisional coal officers, but not the coal supplies officers and coal export officers, were absorbed into the new system. The organization was headed by a controller-general and there were subordinate directors for production, labour and services, together with another for finance. The Coal Production Council was replaced by a National Coal Board with Regional Boards. Economy in consumption was promoted by the Fuel Efficiency Branch, by the continued restriction of supplies to householders and by the extension of the practice of calculating and imposing programmes for large consumers of coal. In the following year labour began to be directed into the pits and from the end of 1943 arrangements were made to group pits under group production directors responsible to the regional controllers. Control of the industry was maintained in this form until it was nationalized after the war under another National Coal Board.

The Petroleum Division also began the war in the Mines Department of the Board of Trade but from May 1940 became a separate department with its own minister entitled secretary for petroleum. The industry was organized through the Petroleum Board which purchased supplies and managed their import and distribution in the United Kingdom. Broad questions of policy were the province of the Oil Control Board, a War Cabinet body under the chairmanship of the secretary for petroleum on which official users were represented. It concerned itself with such matters as the world-wide stocks situation, requirements and tanker distribution. The Petroleum Department equally concerned itself with the oil situation in detail in all parts of the world and particularly with the supplies available to Germany about which it provided information to the War Cabinet Committee on Preventing Oil Supplies to Germany.

Within this country the Petroleum Department had responsibility for motor fuel rationing and exercised it directly through its divisional petroleum officers in respect of private and agricultural vehicles, while the rationing scheme for goods and public service vehicles was in the hands of the Ministry of Transport, later the Ministry of War Transport. When the Petroleum Department became the Petroleum Division of the Ministry of Fuel and Power its minister continued as the secretary for petroleum and as chairman of the Oil Control Board. Relations with the United States played an increasingly important part in the business of the Division, which was represented by a Mission in Washington and in 1944 assisted in the negotiations undertaken there respecting the future of the oil industry.

Attached to the Petroleum Division, as to its predecessors, was the Petroleum Warfare Department. Among the best known of its activities was the PLUTO scheme, which involved the planning and installation, in conjunction with the Royal Navy and the Army, of a number of pipelines across the Channel to supply the invading armies of 1944.

The Gas and Electricity Division of the Ministry also derived immediately from the Board of Trade which had, however, acquired its responsibility for electricity from the Ministry of Transport as recently as September 1941.

The Records

BX 5   Coal Industry Social Welfare Organization: Annual Reports
          Report on miners' welfare in wartime.
COAL 4   Coal Mines Act 1930: Central Coal Mines Scheme 1930 and District Coal Mines Scheme: Records
          There are a few files in this class concerning the War Emergency Assistance Scheme.
COAL 11   Mining Association of Great Britain
          These records mainly relate to wage arbitration and awards and conditions of work in the coal mining industry. See also LAB 3.
COAL 20   Coal Utilization Council
COAL 42   Memoranda of Agreements
          These relate to national agreements concerning wages and conditions of employment in the coal mining industry.
HMC 3   Evershed Papers
          These include Evershed's papers as chairman of the North Midlands coal-producing region.
POWE 3   Solid Fuel Control and Rationing (1939 to 1958) Representative Papers
          A representative collection of documents from three regions (Northern, Wales and the London Regional Group) illustrating the working of the various systems of control and rationing.
POWE 8   Safety and Health Division and Inspectorate of Mines and Quarries
          Includes papers concerning a report for the Lord President's Committee on the state of health of coal miners.
POWE 10   Establishments Division: Correspondence and Papers
          Until 1942 these are mainly records of the Establishment Division of the Mines Department, and subsequently of the Establishments Division of the Ministry of Fuel and Power. Included in the class are certain Board of Trade papers relating to the coal, gas, petroleum and electricity industries.
POWE 11   Electricity Commission: Minutes
          The last volume is an index to the minutes (not complete). See also POWE 12.
POWE 12   Electricity Commission: Correspondence and Papers
          Correspondence and papers of the Commission respecting the supply, transmission and distribution of electricity. The papers include some relating to wartime emergency measures and

the defence of generating stations. See also POWE 11, POWE 13 and POWE 14. Some Ministry of Fuel and Power papers are included in this class.

POWE 13 Ministry of Transport: Electricity Correspondence and Papers
The records in this class originated largely in the Ministry of Transport, but there are a few wartime papers of the Ministry of Fuel and Power. See also POWE 11, POWE 12 and POWE 14.

POWE 14 Electricity Division: Correspondence and Papers
Files relating to administration and legislation, electric lighting companies, distribution charges, metering, overhead lines, power stations and generating plant. Wartime papers include some relating to control of electricity charges. Some earlier files of the Board of Trade, the Ministry of Transport and the Electricity Commission are included in this class. See also POWE 11-13.

POWE 16 Coal Division: Early Correspondence and Papers
Files selected from a number of defunct registered series and certain groups of unregistered papers to illustrate various aspects of coal mining. They contain papers and correspondence relating to production, marketing, manpower, subsidence, drainage and war emergency measures; also included are a few files dealing with metalliferous mining. The records are mainly of the Mines Department, with some later ones of the Ministry of Fuel and Power and the National Coal Board (1942 to 1945). Similar subjects are developed on files in POWE 17-22.

POWE 17 Coal Division: Emergency Services: Correspondence and Papers
Files relating to the price, control, supply, demand and distribution of coal, coke, anthracite, etc, during the Second World War. Until 1942 these are records of the Mines Department. See also POWE 16.

POWE 18 Coal Division: Fuel and Lighting: Correspondence and Papers
Files relating to local fuel overseers, rationing and control of supplies and miners' concessionary coal. Until 1942 these are records of the Mines Department. See also POWE 16.

POWE 19 Coal Division: House Coal: Correspondence and Papers
Files relating to the rationing, stockpiling and distribution of house coal. Until 1942 these are records of the Mines Department. See also POWE 16.

POWE 20 Coal Division: Labour and Labour Relations: Correspondence and Papers
The class includes files on the employment of women and children, absenteeism, strikes, wages and conditions of work, holidays, non-union workers in mines, clerical staffs, pit-head baths, and wartime emergency measures. Also contained are some papers relating to metalliferous and other mining. These are files of the Mines Department until 1942, thereafter of the Ministry of Fuel and Power. See also LAB 3 and POWE 16.

POWE 21 Coal Division: Mines Department War Book and Associated Matters: Correspondence and Papers
Files relating to the control of supplies of coal and coal products, including correspondence with Divisional Coal Offices and circulars of divisional coal officers and coal supplies officers. Until 1942 they are records of the Mines Department. See also POWE 16.

POWE 22 Coal Division: Production: Correspondence and Papers
The class includes files concerned with administration and legislation, coal and mineral rights, finance, other fuels, labour relations, mechanization, metalliferous mining, subsidence and drainage schemes. Papers of wartime interest include some dealing with the development of coal production, allocation of manpower and the planning of post-war reconstruction of the mining industry. These are records of the Mines Department until 1942 and thereafter of the Ministry of Fuel and Power. See also POWE 16.

POWE 25 Chief Scientist's Division: Correspondence and Papers
These are mainly files of the Chief Scientist's Division of the Ministry of Fuel and Power, with some earlier records of the Mines Department. They also include records of various wartime fuel efficiency and other committees, representative files relating to the Regional Fuel Efficiency and Government Loan Scheme and to wartime control of fuel industries, and records of the Safety in Mines Research Establishment.

POWE 26 'A' Files
Correspondence and papers relating to various subjects including: emergency arrangements, mineral transport, metalliferous mining, mining royalties, wartime controls of the mining industry and various bills and Departmental committees. Until 1942 they are records of the Mines Department and subsequently of the Ministry of Fuel and Power.

POWE 28 Statistics and General Division: Correspondence and Papers
The papers in this class, which have been arranged chronologically, include wartime papers on fuel and power planning, intelligence and statistics and Departmental committee reports and Parliamentary papers relative to the Coal Industry Nationalization Bill 1945. See also POWE 16-22. They consist of records of the Planning Division and the Statistics Division of the Ministry of Fuel and Power.

POWE 29 Gas Division: Registered Files
   The class includes files relating to gas standards, and papers of the Gas Industry Committee and the Heyworth Committee of Enquiry into the Gas Industry, 1944 to 1945. Before 1942 these files are records of the Board of Trade.
POWE 33 Petroleum: Correspondence and Papers
   Much of this class is concerned with wartime controls, including defence measures and post-war rationing. It includes some records of the Oil Control Board. See also POWE 34.
POWE 34 Petroleum Division: Miscellaneous Oil Control Board Papers
   See also CAB 77 and POWE 33.
POWE 45 Petroleum Warfare Division Files
   Deal mainly with the PLUTO scheme for the underwater transport of oil in connection with the Allied invasion of Europe in 1944.
SUPP 15 Flame Warfare Committees: Minutes and Reports
   These are records of the Petroleum Warfare Department.
SUPP 18 Joint Industrial Council: Minutes
   Minutes of meetings from its inception in 1941.

General Register Office

Name	Date of appointment
Registrar general	
Sir Sylvanus P Vivian	1921

The registrar general was responsible for the National Registration system under which all civilians were centrally registered and issued with corresponding identity cards. These had to be produced on demand to the police, members of the Armed Forces on duty and national registration officers, and later came to be used for other purposes such as the issue of ration books. Special cards were issued to those who required to enter protected places and areas.

The Register was based initially on an enumeration carried out on 29 September 1939 using the machinery which had been devised for the Census in 1941 which, but for the war, would have been carried out. Transcripts of the enumerators' schedules were centralized at Southport and this Central Register was kept up to date by the entry of births, deaths, changes of address and recruitment into the Armed Forces. The original schedules were transferred to local Food Offices under the Ministry of Food where they were used in connection with the issue of ration books. National Registration Offices in each district were responsible for passing fresh information to the Central Register and for maintaining accurate local Maintenance Registers with the help of information received from Southport. National Registration records were used to assist the Ministry of Labour and National Service in carrying out registration for National Service and other employment.

The national registration officer was usually the clerk of the local authority and served also as food executive officer. The local Food Offices and National Registration Offices had in general terms a common interest in maintaining an accurate record of persons in their area, but their objects and detailed requirements differed sufficiently to create difficulties in co-ordination even after the local offices were combined early in 1943. Henceforward rationing and registration operations were conducted under one roof, and in that year the opportunity was taken to issue a fresh set of identity cards at the same time as the new ration books.

As mentioned above the decennial census scheduled for 1941 was not taken. There is, therefore, a 30-year gap in the series between 1921 and 1951 because the 1931 returns were lost by fire in 1942.

RG 20	Establishments and Accounts: Correspondence and Papers
	Include material concerning the evacuation of staff and records.
RG 26	Population and Medical Statistics: Correspondence and Papers
	This class includes records relating to civilian deaths due to war operations, sample survey of sickness 1943 to 1945, etc.
RG 28	National Registration: Correspondence and Papers
	Records arising from the administration of the National Registration Act 1939.
RG 33	Miscellaneous Foreign Registers and Returns
	Includes two volumes noting deaths from enemy action in the Far East, 1941 to 1945.
RG 41	Circulars
RG 50	Registrar General: Private Office Papers
	One file containing correspondence with Ministry of Health about wartime provisions for creation of new ministries and decentralization.
RG 900	Specimens of Documents Destroyed
	This class contains specimen National Identity Cards.

Government Actuary's Department

Name	Date of appointment
Government actuary	
Sir George Selby Washington Epps	1936
Percy Norman Harvey	1944

The Records

ACT 1	Correspondence and Papers
	Includes files concerning the reconstruction of social insurance under the Beveridge Report. There are also some papers concerning equal pay, London air raids, population trends and the post-war Civil Service.

Government Chemist's Department

Name	Date of appointment
Government chemist	
Sir John Jacob Fox	1936 - 1944
George Macdonald Bennett	1945

The Records

DSIR 26	Laboratory of the Government Chemist: Correspondence and Papers
	See also ADM 282 under the section for the Admiralty.

Ministry of Health

Name	Date of appointment
Minister	
Walter E Elliot, MP	16 May 1938
Malcolm MacDonald, MP	13 May 1940
Ernest Brown, MP	8 Feb 1941
Henry U Willink, MP	11 Nov 1943
Parliamentary secretary	
Florence Horsbrugh, MP	14 July 1939
Permanent secretary	
Sir George Chrystal	1935
Sir John Maude	1940
Deputy secretary	
J Maude	1934
A N Rucker	1940
(later Sir Arthur Rucker)[1]	
J C Wrigley	1941
(later Sir John Wrigley)	
Chief medical officer for Ministry of Health and Board of Education	
Sir Arthur S MacNalty	1935
Sir William Jameson	1940

When the Second World War began the Ministry of Health was responsible for housing and planning policy and the oversight of local authorities as well as for health questions, and its wartime functions were based on all these interests. In Wales many of these matters were discharged on the minister's behalf by a Welsh Board of Health. The Ministry's main wartime duties were in connection with evacuation, care of the homeless, air raid shelters and emergency medical services. In association with the Board of Education it also worked closely with the Central Council for Health Education.

To prepare for evacuation a new division had been established in the Ministry in 1938 when this responsibility was transferred from the Air Raid Precautions Department of the Home Office. Plans were made for the evacuation of school children and mothers with younger children from areas thought to be liable to air attack, while the local authorities in the reception areas surveyed the available accommodation and arranged for the billeting of the majority of evacuees in private houses. Billeting allowances were paid to these householders and recovered, so far as possible, from parents. In the event smaller numbers came forward for evacuation in September 1939 than had been expected and in the absence of air attack many of these returned home. In the following year, however, many children were evacuated by the Ministry both from potential invasion areas and from targets for air attack. Free travel and billeting allowances were extended to mothers with children making their own arrangements for accommodation in reception areas. From January

[1] Secretary in Office of Minister of State, Cairo.

1941 some former reception areas were closed to evacuees by Lodging Restriction Orders made by the minister of health primarily in order to keep accommodation available for war workers. From this time also the Ministry's billeting powers were employed for those engaged on work of national importance. To supplement billets for evacuees hostels were provided and used generally for children whose accommodation in billets had, for one reason or another, proved difficult. In principle the local authorities in reception areas were not to be put to any extra expense on account of evacuees. The children's 'home' authorities remained liable for expenditure that would have been incurred in peacetime and were duly charged by the reception authorities, while the Exchequer was responsible for expenditure arising directly from the war. These financial questions involved the Ministry closely in the detailed operation of the scheme. The number of evacuees declined after heavy raiding came to an end but rose sharply again with the flying bomb and rocket attacks of 1944. The Ministry was responsible towards the end of the war for the return of the few remaining evacuees to their homes.

The task of providing for those made homeless by bombing was placed initially upon the Poor Law Authorities and handled centrally by the Ministry's Poor Law Division. The scale of help that could be afforded in this way was, however, too limited to deal with the consequences of heavy bombing and in November 1940 the financing of rest centres and provision of other services for the homeless was taken over by the Exchequer. The great quantities of equipment such as beds and blankets required for the centres and other emergency services under the control of the Ministry led to the creation of a Supply Division in 1941. A special commissioner was appointed by the government in September 1940 to co-ordinate services for the homeless in the London Region. In connection also with its general responsibility for housing the Ministry of Health was interested in the repair of war-damaged houses and the requisitioning of empty property into which the homeless could be transferred from the rest centres. In November 1940 rehousing the homeless was declared to be a civil defence function and at the local level control could by exercised by air raid precautions controllers. With the encouragement of the Ministry, welfare officers were appointed who operated not only in the rest centres but also in the reception areas for evacuees. Administrative centres were established in which the homeless could find representatives of various local offices under one roof as well as information centres where they could find answers to their questions.

The Ministry was responsible for sanitation, equipment, ventilation and order in public shelters. To carry out these functions it appointed officers to the Regional Commissioners' Organization under the Ministry of Home Security. In conjunction with the minister of home security the minister of health appointed a commissioner to be responsible for shelters in the London Region.

Elaborate plans were made before the war to deal with the very large numbers that were expected to be injured or suffer mental illness in time of war. The organization, which was known as Emergency Medical Services, was headed by a director-general. It employed doctors both full-time and part-time and was thus able to deploy them wherever required. A major part of the Service was the national hospital service by means of which all hospitals in the country, while retaining their autonomy, pooled their facilities under the general control of the Ministry, which also undertook the building of hutted hospitals and conversion of other buildings to auxiliary hospitals. In collaboration with the General Nursing Council much attention was given to the training and recruitment of nurses. Midwifery matters were handled in consultation with the Central Midwives Board.

Supervision on behalf of the Ministry was exercised through representatives at the Civil Defence Regional level, except in London where a more elaborate control of hospitals was exercised directly by the Ministry. Much of the staff of these organizations was brought in from the medical profession. The Ministry was responsible for the general supervision of the first-aid parties, the first-aid posts and the ambulances, but the immediate control of these services was in the hands of the local authorities. It was also responsible for purchasing the great variety of equipment needed for all the branches of the emergency service and it carried out these purchases through the medical supplies branch of the London County Council, the Office of Works, the General Post Office and other agencies. In November 1941 this duty was transferred to the Medical Supplies Directorate of the Ministry of Supply.

In addition to the functions already described the Ministry was concerned with the allocation of labour in the fields for which it was responsible, such as house-building, and for such other extensions of its peacetime duties as ensuring the supply of water and sewage services under war conditions and the burial of those killed in air raids.

In 1942 the planning functions of the Ministry of Health were transferred to the Ministry of Works and Planning and in the following year they passed to the Ministry of Town and Country Planning. Its responsibilities for health insurance were transferred to the Ministry of National Insurance in 1945.

The Records

AST 11 Wartime Functions
        This class contains a few files of the Ministry of Health relating to the planning of measures for the prevention and relief of wartime distress.
BD 11   Local Authority Files (LA Series)
        These concern Welsh local authorities. A few of them relate to civil defence, etc, measures during the wartime period. They were taken over from the Ministry of Health by the Welsh Board of Health in 1940.
DT 2   General Nursing Council for England and Wales: Constitution: Correspondence and Papers. Papers relating to the Nurses Act 1943.
DT 4   General Nursing Council for England and Wales: Constitution: Uniforms and Badges
DT 5   General Nursing Council for England and Wales: Council and Committees: Minutes
DT 6   General Nursing Council for England and Wales: Council and Committees: Proceedings
DT 7   General Nursing Council for England and Wales: Council and Committees: Election Papers
DT 8   General Nursing Council for England and Wales: Council and Committees: Standing Orders and Precedents
DT 9   General Nursing Council for England and Wales: Council and Committees: Seal and Seal Books
DT 10   General Nursing Council for England and Wales: Registration: The Register of Nurses
DT 11   General Nursing Council for England and Wales: Registration: The Roll of Nurses
DT 13   General Nursing Council for England and Wales: Registration: Correspondence and Papers One piece concerns war casualties 1942 to 1945.
DT 14   General Nursing Council for England and Wales: Registration: Statistics
DT 15   General Nursing Council for England and Wales: Registrar: Circulars, Reports and Publications
DT 16   General Nursing Council for England and Wales: Registrar: Correspondence and Papers, General
DT 20   General Nursing Council for England and Wales: Registrar: Correspondence and Papers, Council and Statutory Members
DT 21   General Nursing Council for England and Wales: Registrar: Property: Plans, Inventories, Valuations and Papers
DT 26   General Nursing Council for England and Wales: Examinations: Final, Intermediate and Preliminary Examination Papers
DT 27   General Nursing Council for England and Wales: Examinations: Preliminary and Intermediate Examinations, Results Lists
DT 28   General Nursing Council for England and Wales: Examinations: Final Examination, Pass and Fail Lists
DT 33   General Nursing Council for England and Wales: Education: Hospital Inspectors' Reports and Papers
DT 35   General Nursing Council for England and Wales: Education: Nurse Training Schools: Correspondence and Papers, Parts I and II
DT 38   General Nursing Council for England and Wales: Education: Syllabus and Schemes for Nurse Education and Training in Approved Hospitals
        For correspondence concerning pre-nursing courses in schools see also ED 35.
DT 39   General Nursing Council for England and Wales: Personnel: Correspondence and Papers

DT 40	General Nursing Council for England and Wales: Solicitor
DT 47	General Nursing Council for England and Wales: Finance: Accounts, Correspondence and Papers
DT 48	General Nursing Council for England and Wales: Council and Committee Minutes (Microfilm Duplicates)
DV 1	Central Midwives Board: Minutes
DV 3	Central Midwives Board: Rules of Conduct
DV 5	Central Midwives Board: Penal Case Files
DV 6	Central Midwives Board: Policy and General Files
DV 10	Central Midwives Board: Board Members: Correspondence and Papers
DV 11	Central Midwives Board: Secretariat: Correspondence and Papers
HLG 7	Special Wartime Functions

Files of general correspondence and papers and other records relating to certain wartime functions of the Ministry of Health. These included duties in connection with civil defence, manpower, war damage, evacuation and billeting, care of children and the homeless, accommodation for emergency hospitals, children's homes and maternity homes, emergency water supplies, and related financial matters. The files include some of the London regional organization. Files of other regional organizations have largely been destroyed. Files from the same series retained by the Ministry of Health after 1951 will be found in MH 76. See also HLG 900.

HLG 27	Royal Commission on the Distribution of the Industrial Population, 1937 to 1940

This Commission was appointed in 1937 under the chairmanship of Sir Montague Barlow (later known as Sir Anderson Montague-Barlow), to investigate the problems of distribution of the industrial population and to propose remedies. This set of the Commission's numbered papers is incomplete, and it is uncertain whether the papers were contemporaneously weeded or were destroyed by enemy action. Ministry of Health files relating to the Commission are in HLG 52/1004-1006.

HLG 29	Public Health and Local Government Legislation: Bill Papers
HLG 31	Housing Notes and Instructions
HLG 36	Central Housing Advisory Committee: Minutes and Papers

Files of Departmental correspondence and papers relating to the constitution and operation of the Committee and its sub-committees, copies of minutes and papers of the Committee and bound volumes of its signed minutes.

HLG 37	Central Housing Advisory Committee: Reports of Sub-Committees

Departmental files containing minutes, papers and minutes of evidence and reports of the various sub-committees, together with related correspondence.

HLG 40	Rural Housing and Tied Houses

This class includes some files concerning the emergency scheme to provide cottages in rural areas to meet the needs of wartime agriculture.

HLG 41	Rent Control

Includes papers of the Ridley Committee 1944.

HLG 43	Local Authorities Areas, Boundaries and Status: Correspondence and Papers

Papers concerning Sir William Jowitt's study of post-war problems relating to central and local government will be found in this class.

HLG 50	Water and Sewerage: Correspondence and Papers
HLG 51	Local Government Services: Correspondence and Papers
HLG 52	Local Government Administration and Finance: General Policy and Procedure

There are a number of files concerning the possible breakdown of essential services owing to financial difficulties.

HLG 54	Bill Papers: Local Authorities
HLG 55	Air Pollution and Smoke Abatement: Correspondence and Papers

Some papers deal with the question of smoke prevention in relation to post-war reconstruction.

HLG 56	Rating and Valuation: Correspondence and Papers

A number of files concern the problem of rating properties vacated or damaged on account of the war.

HLG 57	Local Authorities Audit Files: 97000 and LA Series.

This class includes a few files dealing with audit difficulties arising from the war such as the destruction of documents owing to enemy action, scope of emergency expenditure, etc.

HLG 68	100,000 Series Files

This class contains files of the Ministry of Health originally registered in a confidential series (indicated by the distinctive reference 100,000). The papers cover a wide variety of subjects relating to functions later exercised by the Ministry of Housing and Local Government and to special wartime functions. The list contains a subject index. Further files from this series will be found in MH 79 and PIN 8/85-167.

HLG 94   Inter-departmental Committee on House Construction
The class consists of minutes of meetings, reports, circulated papers and suggestions from various bodies and members of the public.

HLG 101 Housing Files: 92000 Series
Includes files relating to emergency housing and provision of post-war housing.

HLG 102 Ministry of Health and Ministry of Housing and Local Government: Miscellaneous Files (99000 Series)
Includes files on the government evacuation scheme, the distribution of industry and the release of requisitioned property.

HLG 104 Planning and Development: 99200 Series
This class contains a Ministry of Health file regarding an Interdepartmental Committee on factory development set up in 1944 on the suggestion of Ernest Bevin, as minister of labour and national service.

HLG 105 Central Valuation Committee Correspondence and Papers

HLG 108 Ministry of Housing and Local Government: Public Health Administration Files
Mainly concerning publicity, particularly in relation to evacuation. They come from the 93000 series files of the Ministry of Health.

HLG 110 Office Machinery and Procedure Files (96203-96219 Series)
This series includes a few papers concerning wartime publications and draft annual reports of the Ministry of Health. See MH 132.

HLG 117 Housing Files, 'H' Series: Policy Files

HLG 900 Specimens of Classes of Documents Destroyed
This class includes material concerning the government evacuation scheme, civilian war dead and war damage.

MH 10   Circular Letters
Circulars issued by the Ministry of Health, including those relating to emergency wartime services. The class includes registers of circulars to 1951, and indexes to 1946. Volumes 18-84 contain subject indexes to their contents.

MH 53   Public Health and Poor Law Services, Local Government Administration and Finance, General Files
This class contains a few files relating to air raid precautions duties of sanitary inspectors.

MH 55   Ministry of Health: Public Health Services: Registered Files
General subject files relating to the administrative side of public health, and services supplied for the public health under the auspices of the Ministry of Health. A few files relate to the wartime civil nursing reserve and recruitment and training of nurses, provision of nurseries, and other emergency health and social questions.

MH 56   Foods
Includes papers concerning wartime diet and nutrition.

MH 57   Public Assistance
Includes papers concerning chargeability of relief afforded to evacuees and to maintenance of refugees from overseas.

MH 58   General Health Questions
Subject files of correspondence concerning general health questions including papers relating to medical manpower and other implications of the Military Training Act 1939 and to social services in war factory areas.

MH 71   Various Committees
Papers of the Medical Advisory Committee including some arising from meetings with the minister and minutes, etc, of the Advisory Sub-Committee on Venereal Diseases.

MH 76   Emergency Medical Services
This class comprises registered files of the Emergency Medical Services with particular reference to the war of 1939-1945. The subjects covered include hospitals and first-aid posts, personnel, supplies, equipment and specialized services. The class also contains Departmental files of correspondence relating to evacuation, refugees, rest centres and the planning of measures for the prevention and relief of wartime distress. Papers on these and related subjects will also be found on the series of confidential files in MH 79 and HLG 68.

MH 77   National Health Service: Post-War Planning and National Health Service Act 1946
Ministry of Health files relating to a preliminary survey of hospitals (1940 onwards) and the early planning of post-war health policy, including discussions with the medical profession and other bodies.

MH 78   Establishment and Organization Files
This class contains files relating to the organization of the Ministry of Health, and subordinate

departments, including the Welsh Board of Health, the Board of Control, the Government Lymph Establishment and the General Register Office. The papers also relate to establishment matters generally. See also MH 96.

MH 79   100,000 Series Files

This class contains files from the Ministry of Health's 100,000 series of confidential files. Many of the files relate to the planning and operation of wartime medical services, but there are also files relating to various aspects of health, public assistance, health insurance and pensions administration, and to the organization of home and overseas information services, 1945-1951. Other files in the same series were transferred to the Ministry of Housing and Local Government in 1951 (see HLG 68) and to the Ministry of National Insurance (see PIN 8/85-167); the latter were re-registered in a NI 99 series.

MH 80   Bill Papers

Mainly concerning the introduction of a National Health Service.

MH 82   Central Council for Health Education

Minutes of meetings and circulated papers. See also ED 121.

MH 96   Welsh Board of Health: Registered Files

Includes many files concerning emergency wartime services in Wales. See also BD 11 and MH 78 above.

MH 101   War Diaries

This class consists mainly of reports, circulars and diaries of events.

MH 107   Personal Files

These relate to senior officers and include a few relating to the wartime period.

MH 122   Children and Old People

This class contains a few papers concerning the arrangements for the future care of orphans and other homeless and unaccompanied children on the termination of the government evacuation scheme.

MH 130   Social Welfare

Two files, one concerning policy and the other the international exchange of social workers and administrators.

MH 132   Annual Reports

See also HLG 110.

MH 900   Specimens of Classes of Documents Destroyed

Includes forms concerning infectious and venereal diseases.

PIN 3   National Insurance, Pensions and Unemployment Insurance Acts, Bill Papers

PIN 4   Pensions and Insurance

Files of the Ministry of Health continued in the Ministry of National Insurance relating to the administration of national health insurance, contributory old-age, widows' and orphans' pensions and national insurance. A few files relate to the administration of, and appeals under, the non-contributory old-age pensions scheme. The class contains papers relating to the implementation of the proposals of the Beveridge Committee and the planning of the Ministry of National Insurance.

PIN 8   Social Insurance and Allied Services (Beveridge Report)

The second part of this class (PIN 8/85-167) contains files of the Ministry of Health later transferred to the Ministry of National Insurance. They include papers reflecting both the direct responsibility of the Department in the field of social insurance and allied services and Departmental representation on the Beveridge Committee, the Phillips Committee, which considered the implications of the Beveridge Report, and the central staff responsible for implementing those proposals which had been accepted. Papers of the Phillips Committee are in PIN 8/115-116; minutes and memoranda of the Beveridge Committee are in CAB 87/76-82.

Home Office

Name	Date of appointment
Secretary of state	
Sir John Anderson, MP	3 Sept 1939
Herbert S Morrison, MP	3 Oct 1940

Parliamentary under-secretary

Osbert Peake, MP	21 Apr 1939
Earl of Munster	31 Oct 1944

Permanent under-secretary of state

Sir Alexander Maxwell	26 Jan 1938

Deputy under-secretary of state

Sir Wilfred Eady	26 Jan 1938
F A Newsam	16 Apr 1941
(later Sir Frank Newsam)	

When in September 1939 the Home Office handed over its Air Raid Precautions Department to the new Ministry of Home Security it retained its normal administrative control of the police and fire services as well as its other peacetime duties. Both services became subject to an Order in June 1940 which compelled policemen and firemen to continue in these services and men were later allowed to volunteer for them as an alternative to military service. In April 1941 conscripts under the National Service Act became liable to be directed for service in the Auxiliary Fire Service or the Police War Reserve.

Recruitment of auxiliary police in the Police War Reserve began before the war. Apart from this addition to their strength no major changes were made to the organization of the police forces during the war and their oversight by the Home Office continued on routine lines. The police retained their responsibility for the security of the country, including arrests made on the instruction of the home secretary under Defence Regulation 18B. The other duties of the police included the sounding of air raid warnings, enforcement of lighting restrictions and assistance with civil defence. Many policemen were appointed as incidents officers to exercise general control at the scene of an attack and a number of chief constables were air raid precautions controllers.

In August 1940 the Home Office took over from the War Office administrative responsibility for internment camps for civilian enemy aliens. In April 1941 it assumed also financial responsibility for these camps and the internees.

The organization by local authorities of the Auxiliary Fire Services which formed part of the Civil Defence Services was strongly encouraged by the Home Office before the war and through its Fire Brigades Division it authorized grants and supplied equipment on loan for this purpose. The Division was organized in a number of branches and had, in addition, an Inspectorate. In May 1941 when the National Fire Service was established the Fire Brigades Division became the Fire Service Department. In addition to the Inspectorate there was now also a professional Fire Staff concerned with training, techniques and the work of the Home Office Fire Control. This had been brought into existence early in the war to control inter-regional assistance and operated by means of its links with the Regional Offices which were in turn in touch with the separate Fire Brigades. The existence of the Brigades and their distinction from the Auxiliary Fire Service was brought to an end between May and August 1941 when all the existing forces were combined into one National Fire Service. This was organized into Fire Forces under fire force commanders and within each region there was a chief regional fire officer. In England and Wales 1,443 Brigades were replaced by 32 Fire Forces. Fire force commanders were responsible for the deployment of men and equipment in their Fire Areas and regional commissioners for their movement between Areas, while the Fire Control Room continued to direct inter-regional reinforcements. The Fire Service Department was now able in its control of a single service to issue detailed instructions on such questions as fire fighting tactics or conditions of service in a manner which resembled the centralized administration of the Armed Forces. Uniformity was reinforced by the establishment by chief regional fire officers and fire force commanders of their own Inspectorate. To assist him the home secretary established a Fire Service Council, including the parliamentary secretaries and the secretary of the Ministry of Home Security as well as the senior Fire Service Department staff. The Council was concerned with broad questions of policy in such fields as manpower and organization.

The control of the sale of alcohol did not pose the same problem as in the First World War, but in addition to its oversight of the licensing laws the Home Office continued its supervision of the State Management Districts in Carlisle and in Scotland, which had been established in 1916 to manage licensed premises in certain areas of munitions production. Inevitably, the war increased the work of the Office's Explosives Inspectorate, and there was also some increase in the work of its Children's Department, which besides sharing certain child care responsibilities with other departments, notably the Ministry of Health, had particular responsibility for remand homes, approved schools and adoption procedures. On the other hand the administration of the Factories Acts and control of the Factories Inspectorate passed to the Ministry of Labour and National Service in June 1940.

The Records

BN 28	Home Office: Children's Department: Case Papers and Administrative School Records Closed for 75 years. See also MH 102 and MH 109 below.
EF 2	Explosives Inspectorate: Reports and Papers
EF 3	Explosives Inspectorate: Circulars
EF 5	Explosives Inspectorate: General Correspondence and Papers
HO 45	Home Office: Registered Papers This is the main class of general correspondence of the Home Office. Papers of wartime interest relate to police and fire service functions, including emergency duties carried out on behalf of the Ministry of Home Security, and general duties in relation to internment of civilian enemy aliens, Channel Islands occupation, N. Ireland and civil defence. See also HO 144 and HO 326.
HO 46	Home Office: Daily Registers of Correspondence Daily subject registers of correspondence received in the Home Office and largely to be found in HO 45 and HO 144.
HO 144	Home Office: Registered Papers, Supplementary Papers on criminal and certain other subjects separated from related files in HO 45 because of their sensitivity at the time of transfer. See also HO 326.
HO 158	Home Office: Circulars Circulars on various special wartime and normal peacetime subjects to police and local authorities. For air raid circulars see HO 208.
HO 185	Ministry of Munitions and Home Office: Central Control Board (Liquor Traffic) and State Management Districts: Central Office Records
HO 187	Fire Brigades Division and Fire Service Department Files arising from the administration of the Fire Brigades Act 1938 and the Fire Services (Emergency Provisions) Act 1941.
HO 190	Ministry of Munitions and Home Office: Central Control Board (Liquor Traffic) and State Management Districts: Carlisle Office Records
HO 194	Ministry of Home Security and Home Office: Finance Divisions: Civil Defence Grants: Registered Files After May 1945 these are Home Office files relating to wartime grants to local authorities for civil defence expenditure.
HO 208	Home Office and Ministry of Home Security: Air Raid Precautions and Home Security Circulars
HO 213	Home Office: Aliens Department: General (GEN) Files and Aliens' Naturalization and Nationality (ALN and NTY Symbol Series) Files
HO 214	Internees: Personal Files Chiefly enemy or neutral aliens but include a few of British subjects detained under Defence Regulation 18B.
HO 215	Internment: General Files The class includes reports by the International Red Cross or the protecting power on conditions in British internment camps, and in enemy internment or prisoner of war camps.

HO 250	Home Office: Inter-departmental Committee on Civil Defence Gallantry Awards: Minutes and Recommendations
HO 283	Home Office: Defence Regulation 18B, Advisory Committee Papers
	Includes papers concerning the internment of Sir Oswald Mosley.
HO 294	Czechoslovak Refugee Trust: Records
	See also T 210.
HO 312	Home Office: Civil Defence Circulars
	Continuation of Ministry of Home Security classes HO 204 and HO 208.
HO 326	Home Office: Long Papers
	These papers were too large or bulky to be kept with their parent files in HO 45 or HO 144. One file concerns the victory celebrations and parade in 1946.
HO 329	Home Office: Statistical Branch: Files (R Series) and Registers
	A few files, etc, concerning judicial, criminal and licensing statistics.
HO 333	Home Office and Ministry of Home Security: Internal Notices
HO 334	Home Office: Immigration and Nationality Department: Duplicate Certificates of Naturalization, Declarations of British Nationality and Declarations of Alienage
HO 341	Home Office: Communications (COM Symbol Series) Files
	Mainly concern wartime communications arrangements in the police and civil defence services. Related material is in MEPO 2.
LAB 14	Safety, Health and Welfare: General
	Files relating to the administration of factory inspection.
LAB 15	HM Factory Inspectorate
	Inspectorial staff conferences, monthly circulars, arrangement of districts, etc.
LAB 59	Home Office: Explosives Inspectorate: Annual Reports
MH 102	Home Office: Children's Department: Six Figure Series Files
	General policy files covering many aspects of the detention and care of children, and adoption arrangements. See also BN 28 above.
MH 109	Home Office: Children's Department: Circulars
PIN 11	Workmen's Compensation Bill Papers
PIN 12	Home Office and Ministry of National Insurance and Successors: Workmen's Compensation Correspondence and Papers

Ministry of Home Security

Name	Date of appointment
Minister	
Sir John Anderson, MP	3 Oct 1939
Herbert S Morrison, MP	3 Oct 1940
Parliamentary secretary	
A T Lennox-Boyd, MP	6 Sept 1939
W Mabane, MP	24 Oct 1939
Ellen C Wilkinson, MP	3 Oct 1940
Secretary	
Sir Thomas Gardiner	September 1939
Sir George Gater	May 1940
Sir Harold Scott	Apr 1942
Sir William B Brown	November 1943
Joint secretary	
Sir George Gater	September 1939

Deputy secretary

H R Scott	1 May 1940
T H Sheepshanks	13 Apr 1942
O C Allen (under-secretary acting as deputy secretary)	23 Sept 1944

The Air Raid Precautions Department, which was the forerunner of the Ministry of Home Security, was established as part of the Home Office in 1935. Its function was to advise local authorities in the preparation of schemes for the protection of the citizen against all forms of air attack. Air raid precautions of this kind formed only a part of civil defensive activities and in October 1938 the lord privy seal was made responsible for co-ordinating all activities in this field carried out by government departments. He was given direct control of the Air Raid Precautions Department and of the emergency measures of the Fire Brigades Division as well as his own small co-ordinating staff. The system of regional commissioners created for civil emergencies had been redesigned to take over the reins of government in areas which became cut off from the centre and this organization came to acquire also co-ordinating functions in civil defence. The responsibilities of the Air Raid Precautions Department for design, supply and financing of equipment and shelters brought about a rapid growth at Headquarters even before the war, while in the country the number of volunteers both in the local authority organizations for air raid precautions and in the Women's Voluntary Service grew rapidly. By the time war broke out almost every adult in the country had been equipped with a gas mask.

In September 1939 the lord privy seal with all his civil defence responsibilities became the minister of home security and the Air Raid Precautions Department and his co-ordinating staff formed the new Ministry. The post of minister of home security and that of secretary of state for home affairs were throughout the war always held by the same person and the Home Office continued to provide some common services for the Ministry. Close links between the two Departments were all the more necessary in that in some matters, such as fire fighting, their responsibilities were, in effect, shared. The Ministry of Home Security was responsible for the regional organization, the co-ordination of civil defence activities, including the wartime activities of the police and fire brigades, oversight of the Air Raid Precautions organizations run by the local authorities and for the related research, design, supply and finance functions. Before and throughout the war many kinds of air raid precautions expenditure by local authorities could be recovered from the Exchequer through the Home Office and the Ministry of Home Security. It must be remembered that the Ministry of Home Security never developed into a Ministry of Civil Defence with executive responsibility for all aspects of the subject. Under the civil defence organization departments retained their responsibilities in fields with which they were normally concerned, such as the Home Office in respect of police and fire services and the Ministry of Health in respect of evacuation, while the Ministry of Home Security was responsible for ensuring the co-ordination of these activities where they formed part of civil defence. This principle of co-ordination found expression throughout the war in the overall control of civil defence by the Civil Defence Committee of the War Cabinet with the minister of home security as chairman, together with a small Executive sub-committee which was formally established in September 1940. The administration of the air raid precautions services was similarly left in the hands of the local authorities though operational control was exercised by the Ministry through the regional system and it was also responsible both for the administrative policy of air raid precautions in such matters as establishments and pay and for securing an adequate allocation of manpower to be distributed among all civil defence activities.

The Ministry had, in addition to the minister, a parliamentary secretary with responsibility for its Air Raid Precautions Department and in 1940 another parliamentary secretary was appointed to deal with shelter policy. At the beginning of the war two joint secretaries headed the permanent staff but the Ministry soon reverted to the more normal arrangement of a single secretary. Under him the structure consisted at the end of 1939 of four main Divisions of which the first was responsible for finance and establishment, schemes of air raid precautions controlled by local authorities, shelters, lighting restrictions and air raid warnings, and supply, the second for fire and police services, the third for the regional organization and Home Security War Room, and the fourth for public relations and civil defence personnel. An inspector-general toured the Regions and was responsible for training standards and reporting on the conduct of operations. For eight months in 1940 there was also a chief of the operational staff whose responsibility it was to develop organization and training in civil defence so that it should be able to work effectively under attack. Regular contact was also maintained with the chief civil staff officer to the commander-in-chief Home Forces and with the Home Defence and Home Security Executives.

The Warden and Rescue Services that constituted air raid precautions remained, as has been shown, under the control of local authorities for administrative purposes and local employment but in May 1940 the power of direction of local authorities in their civil defence function was conferred on the minister and by him delegated to the regional commissioners. They were thus enabled to secure co-operation between local authorities and between Regions. The duties of the Rescue Services, including first aid, are self-explanatory. They began the war as separate Rescue and First Aid Parties but were combined into a single Civil Defence Rescue Service in May 1942. The air raid wardens were responsible, among other things, for the distribution and testing of civilian gas masks, for the enforcement, in conjunction with the police, of lighting regulations, for the reporting of incidents and, above all, for the accumulation of the local knowledge which was invaluable in emergencies. When compulsory fire-watching was generally instituted in January 1941 the wardens played some part in its organization and later in that year the Wardens' Service was made responsible for a more elaborate system of fire guards, but these guards were detached from the Wardens' Service in England and Wales in 1943. The Wardens' Service also provided some incident officers who were responsible for general control at the scene of an attack and bomb reconnaissance officers whose duty it was to trace unexploded bombs. Personnel difficulties in air raid precautions led to a 'freezing order' in July 1940 preventing members of First Aid and Rescue Parties from leaving their employment. In January of the following year conscripts under the National Service Act were allowed to opt for the First Aid Parties and in April compulsion was introduced for the Civil Defence Reserve. In practice few recruits were obtained by these methods for air raid precautions, which continued to be largely staffed by volunteers, many of whom were unpaid. In December 1941 the Ministry of Labour and National Service was empowered to direct men and women into civil defence and other services as an alternative to industrial employment.

The Ministry's responsibility for shelters included their design, which was the field of the chief engineer, and the financing of their construction, which was generally in the hands of local authorities or industrial concerns, as well as planning their total supply and distribution. Many shelters were distributed free to households for both indoor and outdoor construction. The division of responsibility for public shelters between the Ministries of Home Security and Health was settled late in 1940 when it was agreed that the Ministry of Home Security should be responsible for their number, location and construction, while their internal management should be the province of the Ministry of Health. The appropriate branch of the Shelters Department was transferred to the Ministry of Health. An associated body was the Tube Shelter Committee which was set up towards the end of 1941 jointly by the Ministry of Home Security and the Ministry of Health to be responsible for the preparation and management of deep underground shelters in the London Region.

The Research and Experiment Branch which was stationed at Princes Risborough during the war acquired the status of a department in June 1940. It was advised by a Civil Defence Research Committee of eminent scientists who conducted their work through a large number of sub-committees and panels. The Department arranged for the conduct of experiments for the Ministry by many research institutions (some of them under the Department of Scientific and Industrial Research), and was itself organized in technical sections or divisions such as the Fire Research Division. Other subjects studied were lighting restrictions, blast and armaments, while an extra-mural unit at Oxford conducted operational research. The Technical Intelligence Section collected and circulated information associated with these activities such as the details of bomb construction, the resistance of types of building and the efficacy of fire-fighting methods. The Department's Field Organization in conjunction with the Air Ministry conducted the Bomb Census, collecting on Bomb Census Forms completed locally details about the type, weight and distribution of bombs, while in some cases it supplemented such information by its own detailed examination and recording of bombed buildings. For research into camouflage there was a Civil Defence Camouflage Establishment at Leamington which at the end of 1940 was amalgamated with the related Headquarters Division to become a directorate. Detailed instructions were issued by it for the concealment of potential targets. Concealment was also practised by the restrictions on lighting known as the 'black-out' and the Ministry was responsible for advising on policy and the direction of enforcement. Early in the war a War Cabinet Interdepartmental Lighting Committee was established which considered specific industrial establishments, and in 1941 and again in 1943 War Cabinet Interdepartmental Committees on Black-out Restrictions were set up to consider the problem.

The Ministry of Home Security occupied at first an intermediate position with respect to the giving of air raid warnings. The issue of warnings was in the hands of the Fighter Command of the Royal Air Force, while their signalling to the public was in the hands of the police. As this was a war function of the police, general responsibility for it lay with the Ministry but in 1943 to this was added the responsibility for issuing warnings formerly held by the Air Ministry. In addition to the public warnings telephone warnings were sent to various government installations and industrial concerns.

The creation of a whole new apparatus of civil defence involved a considerable training problem which was accentuated by the fact that many of the personnel were part-time volunteers. Reference has already been made to the work of the inspector-general and the chief of the operational staff. The Ministry was also responsible for two training schools. Much of the output of these schools consisted of instructors who could carry out further training in their own districts and this method was developed to the ultimate by making the wardens available for the instruction of the general public.

As in other fields the effective conduct of civil defence operations was at an early stage seen to be dependent on reliable intelligence. Before the war the Intelligence Branch of the Air Raid Precautions Department collected information on civil defence organization, methods and financing in other countries. After the outbreak of war the emphasis switched to operational intelligence which was centralized in the Home Security War Room. Here reports were received from the Regions, each of which had its own War Room to receive information from Group and Control Centres, and these reports were digested into twice-daily summaries and weekly appreciations of raids and damage for the use of the Ministry, the Regions and other departments. In addition the Intelligence Section, by means of its links with intelligence correspondents in the Regions and with other departments, was able to compile reports on the morale of the nation for the Ministry of Information. The Key Points Intelligence Branch collected and distributed information about damage at particularly important locations.

The Regional Organization

The structure of government in this country has developed in such a way that in normal times there is no longer a place for full-scale local representatives of the central power. In the emergency such representatives had to be created and they lasted no longer than the emergency itself. The primary purpose of the regional commissioners was the assumption of full civil power in place of the government if communications between the government and the Regions broke down. This never came about but the commissioners developed useful functions at their level parallel to the co-ordinating functions of the minister and were also well placed to exercise operational control of civil defence in a way that was neither necessary nor possible at the centre with the exception of the Home Office Fire Control.

In May 1940 regional commissioners were empowered to issue orders in and control entry to any Defence Area either in order to hinder enemy attack or for the protection of persons and property. All parts of the country were shortly prescribed as Defence Areas, though it was not until the following spring that a full statement of the powers of regional commissioners in the event of a breakdown in communications could be compiled.

When local authorities were being encouraged before the war to undertake air raid precautions schemes they were instructed to appoint air raid precautions controllers, who were generally the clerks to the authorities or chief constables, and small Emergency Committees of councillors. The position of the latter caused some difficulty when the Regional Authorities were given civil defence powers and the authority of the commissioners over controllers had to be confirmed. Regional commissioners were responsible for the switching of civil defence resources between districts and Regions and their services were particularly valuable in the aftermath of heavy raids when resources of all kinds, medicines, food and transport as well as civil defence, had to be concentrated at speed. In 1941 Regions were encouraged to establish mobile reserves from their air raid precautions resources and these became known as Regional Columns.

The variety of tasks undertaken at Regional Headquarters is well exemplified by the number of specialist regional officers, not all of whom were responsible to the minister of home security. There were regional technical intelligence officers, for example, and regional salvage officers, though the Ministry of Home Security did not run a centralized salvage organization. Representing other departments there were, among others, regional information officers of the Ministry of Information, regional works advisers responsible to the Ministry of Works and military liaison officers through whom troops might be obtained for help in civil defence or requests come for the control of civilians in some area for military purposes. The constitutional position of the regional commissioners gave rise to discussions early in the war. Although the minister of home security was primarily responsible and the Regional Organization Division of the Ministry interested itself closely in the conduct of Regional business, other ministers might devolve duties to them, for example, the minister of health in respect of shelters or evacuation, and the commissioners were then responsible for those duties to those ministers.

The Records

AY 1   Fire Research Station: Reports and Papers
        Fire statistics notes, 1944 to 1945.
HO 186 Ministry of Home Security: Air Raid Precautions (ARP GEN) Registered Files
        Files relating to the administration of air raid precautions and civil defence and the organization of civil defence regions under regional commissioners. Many of the files originated in the 700,000 file series of the Home Office and in the Lord Privy Seal's Office. A few came from the Air Ministry. A parallel regional series will be found in HO 207. For related Home Office files see HO 45.
HO 191 Ministry of Home Security: Research and Experiments Department, Unregistered Papers
HO 192 Ministry of Home Security: Research and Experiments Department, Registered Papers
HO 193 Ministry of Home Security: Research and Experiments Department, Bomb Census Maps
HO 194 Ministry of Home Security and Home Office: Finance Divisions: Civil Defence Grants: Registered Files
        Files of the Ministry of Home Security and, after May 1945, the Home Office, relating to matters

of policy, procedure, calculation, etc, in connection with grants to local authorities for civil defence expenditure.

HO 195 Ministry of Home Security: Research and Experiments Department, Civil Defence Research Committee

HO 196 Ministry of Home Security: Research and Experiments Department, Notes

HO 197 Ministry of Home Security: Chief Engineer's Department, Registered Files
Papers concerning air raid protection measures, notably the provision of shelters, and also reports of bomb damage.

HO 198 Ministry of Home Security: Research and Experiments Department, Bomb Census Papers

HO 199 Ministry of Home Security: Intelligence Branch, Registered Files

HO 200 Ministry of Home Security: Tube Shelter Committee, Registered Files

HO 201 Ministry of Home Security: Key Points Intelligence Directorate, Daily Reports

HO 202 Ministry of Home Security: Home Security War Room Reports

HO 203 Ministry of Home Security: Home Security Daily Intelligence Reports

HO 204 Ministry of Home Security: Regional Circulars
Continued in HO 312.

HO 205 Ministry of Home Security: 'O' Division, Correspondence and Papers
These concern the provision of air raid shelters and related matters. There are a number of files concerning the Bethnal Green tube disaster.

HO 206 Ministry of Home Security: Regional Technical Adviser's and Regional Works Adviser's Registered Files
Files concerning air raid shelter provision and engineering works in the London Region.

HO 207 Home Office and Ministry of Home Security: Civil Defence Regions, Headquarters and Regional Files
See also HO 186.

HO 208 Home Office and Ministry of Home Security: Air Raid Precautions and Home Security Circulars
Continued in HO 312.

HO 209 Ministry of Home Security: Fire Services, London Region

HO 210 Ministry of Home Security: Research and Experiments Department, Factory Passive Air Defence Committee

HO 211 Home Office: Air Raid Precautions Department, Committee on Structural Precautions against Air Attack: Minutes and Papers

HO 212 Ministry of Home Security: Research and Experiments Department, Experiments Assessment Committee: Minutes and Reports

HO 216 Home Office and Ministry of Home Security: Air Raid Precautions and Research and Experiments Departments, Miscellaneous Committees: Records

HO 217 Ministry of Home Security: Research and Experiments Department, Camouflage Committee: Minutes and Papers

HO 315 Ministry of Home Security: Key Points Intelligence Branch, Bomb Damage Map Tracings

HO 333 Home Office and Ministry of Home Security: Internal Notices

Ministry of Information

Name	Date of appointment
Minister	
Lord MacMillan	4 Sept 1939
Sir J C W Reith, MP	5 Jan 1940
A Duff Cooper, MP	12 May 1940
Brendan Bracken, MP	20 July 1941
(later Lord Bracken)	
Parliamentary secretary	
Sir E W M Grigg, MP	19 Sept 1939
(later Lord Altrincham) (office vacant 3 Apr 1940)	

Harold G Nicolson, MP	17 May 1940
Ernest Thurtle, MP	20 July 1941

Director-general and secretary

Sir Kenneth Lee	1939

Director-general

Sir Walter Monckton	1941
C J Radcliffe	1941
(later Lord Radcliffe)	
E St. J Bamford	1945
(later Sir Eric Bamford)	

Deputy director-general

Lt Col N G Scorgie	1940
E St. J Bamford	1941

Joint directors of postal and telegraph censorship

Edwin S Herbert	1 Apr 1940
F S Towle	1 Apr 1940

Director of postal and telegraph censorship

Edwin S Herbert	16 Jan 1941

Director-general of postal and telegraph censorship department

Sir Edwin S Herbert	5 Apr 1943

The creation of a Ministry of Information in time of war was planned in the Committee of Imperial Defence Organization and the first steps had been taken before the war, the Home Office being designated the parent department. Officers in various home departments were reserved for the proposed Ministry and in June 1939 a Foreign Publicity Department in addition to the News Department was created in the Foreign Office to be transferred to the Ministry on the outbreak of war. The functions of the News Department of the Foreign Office were thus limited to providing information to correspondents in London, where it operated from the Headquarters of the Ministry. Certain powers of control over the British Broadcasting Corporation formerly exercised by the postmaster general were transferred to the new Ministry. The object of the Ministry was not only the planning of general government information policy but also the provision of common services for the public relations activities of other departments, who remained directly in control of their own information policy; its functions developed from censorship and dissemination of information on behalf of departments and the government generally to the collection of intelligence for distribution to them.

As with other wartime creations the structure of the Ministry of Information underwent a succession of changes. There was always a number of divisions but only a proportion of them was present from beginning to end and at different stages of the war they were formed into various groups. For example, in February 1940 after a particularly rapid series of changes the Ministry's divisions were organized into two groups. One of these under the deputy director-general contained what might be called the 'operating' divisions; the other, under the deputy secretary, dealt with the British Broadcasting Corporation, the Ministry's regional structure, Intelligence, Finance and Establishments. In overall control, subject to the minister, was the director-general and secretary. In later years, to support the director-general and his deputy, there were four controllers responsible for Censorship and News, Production, Overseas and Home Publicity.

The divisions of the Ministry included a Films Division which arranged the production of a large number of films by both outside agencies and the Crown Film Unit. This had begun as the Empire Marketing Board Film Unit, became the Post Office Film Unit, passed into the control of the Ministry of Information in April 1940 and acquired its final title at the end of that year. A selection of these films is held on behalf of the Public Record Office by the National Film Archive. Similar divisions were the Photographs Division, the Campaigns Division for the organization of publicity campaigns, the Display and Exhibitions Division and the Publications or Literary and Editorial Division which produced a wide range of books and booklets about the war. The Broadcasting, Radio Relations, Communications and Broadcasting, and Radio and Communications Divisions were at different times responsible for the Ministry's communications as well as its relations with the British Broadcasting Corporation. The Religions Division was the only one of its kind in that it dealt not with a particular technique or a particular area but with a particular subject. It confined its activities to the main western religions and was responsible for the production of weekly religious newspapers, the provision of material for other newspapers, the distribution of photographs and for arranging tours by ecclesiastical personages. It came to serve as a link between government and religious bodies.

Overseas publicity was organized by areas, there being Divisions for the Empire, America, Latin America, Soviet Relations, Far East, Middle East and Europe. Their operations were confined to neutral and Allied countries, enemy and enemy-occupied countries being the province of the Political Warfare Executive, but in the later stages of the war the Executive's work in those territories was gradually passed to the Ministry. Co-ordination inside the Ministry was provided by a General Division and a Planning Secretariat. The Commercial Relations Division mobilized British business communities overseas for information purposes and distributed information to British and Allied merchant seamen. In all these activities the Ministry collaborated closely with the News Department of the Foreign Office and received much information from our representatives abroad. It also had its own offices in the Middle East and India.

The Ministry's activities at home were similarly co-ordinated by the Home Planning Division. After the arrival of American troops in large numbers in this country an American Forces Liaison Division was established. This Division, as its name implies, had duties beyond the information field and was in fact responsible for liaison policy. Much of its work was conducted through the Ministry's regional structure which corresponded, in a sense, to the Overseas Divisions. The regions, which were coterminous with the Civil Defence Regions of the Ministry of Home Security, were administered from Headquarters by the Regional Administration or Home Division. In each of them there was a regional information officer with responsibilities to the regional commissioner as well as to the Ministry of Information's Headquarters. Regional duties covered the whole range of Ministry activities including press relations and censorship, the organization of meetings and film shows, the provision of post-raid information to Headquarters, counter-propaganda, exhibitions, campaigns and intelligence. Regional information officers were also responsible for the provision of information to the local public from Regional Headquarters in the event of air raids and were supported by a number of local Information Committees who organized meetings and shows and distributed pamphlets. They were also to provide regional information officers with evidence of the public's need for information of particular kinds. Emergency information officers were designated to operate in the event of an invasion and plans were made for the distribution of reliable information in such conditions.

The Home Intelligence Division had two distinct functions. Its Home Intelligence Unit was responsible for the preparation of reports on the morale of the civilian population, which were found to be essential not only in planning the Ministry's home publicity but also for the activities of other departments such as the Ministry of Home Security. From May to September 1940 these reports were produced daily and from October they appeared weekly. In June 1941, following a successful experiment in London, panels of correspondents were recruited by the new intelligence officers in the Regions to make reports on the state of public opinion. These were successively digested by the intelligence officers and the Home Intelligence Division to produce the distributed reports. Arrangements were made both at regional and departmental level for action to be taken at once when these reports revealed specific grievances. The other part of the Division was responsible for the Social Survey which had been instituted as part of an attempt to assess the effect of the Ministry's posters by making direct inquiries about morale. This attempt led to Press attacks and the Survey itself thereafter concentrated on market research operations, mainly as a service for other departments such as the Board of Trade and the Ministry of Food which needed information on consumer reactions, though the Mass Observation Organization continued to be used for morale investigations until it was superseded by the panels.

The Ministry's general responsibility for Press relations included censorship as well as the provision of news and facilities to the Press. The Press at home was encouraged to submit material for censorship by the provision that articles published with Ministry authority avoided the possibility of prosecution under Defence Regulations. Censorship was compulsory for material which was to be transmitted overseas. In May 1940 to this responsibility was added that for the administration of postal and telegraph censorship previously exercised by the War Office. General policy in this field was controlled by the Standing Interdepartmental Committee on Censorship. The Postal and Telegraph Censorship Department was responsible not only for the imposition of censorship on communications from the United Kingdom but also for its co-ordination throughout the Empire and with our allies and this aspect of censorship closely involved other departments, particularly the Foreign Office. The censoring of communications provided much useful intelligence as well as preventing information from reaching the enemy. The Postal and Telegraph Censorship Department became independent of the Ministry in April 1943 but the minister of information continued to be the responsible minister. For an account of the Ministry's activities see *This is your War* (HMSO, 1983).

The Records

DEFE 1   Postal and Telegraph Censorship Department
Papers selected to illustrate the organization and work on postal and telegraph censorship during the War of 1939-1945 by the Directorate of Military Intelligence at the War Office and by the Postal and Telegraph Censorship Department. The class also contains papers relating to the compilation of the official history of the Postal and Telegraph Censorship Department. Closed for 50 years.

FO 930   Ministry of Information: Foreign Publicity Files

HO 262   Ministry of Information: Home Intelligence Division (HI) Files
Papers concerning public attitudes and morale.

INF 1   Ministry of Information: Files of Correspondence
These contain the more important papers of the Ministry and are representative of the eleven series of files formerly kept by its divisions or branches. They include material relating to the immediate pre-war period, when the Ministry's forerunner was a department of the Home Office with connections with the Foreign Office.

INF 2   Guard Books and Related Unregistered Papers
These books constitute a complete set of publicity material issued by the Ministry.

INF 3   Ministry of Information: Original Art Work
Original paintings and drawings produced for, and retained by, the Ministry for propaganda and publicity purposes during the war. Copies of most of the publications in which this art work was reproduced are included in INF 2.

INF 5   Crown Film Unit Files
Files of the Establishment and Organization Division, the Films and Television Division, extra-divisional files relating to the Unit Planning Committees, studio files concerned with the

production of various films, and personal studio files of London contact officers. They relate to the production of films by government financed film units. See also INF 1.

INF 6   Central Office of Information and predecessors: Film Production Documents
The National Film Archive or the Imperial War Museum hold a copy of most of the films involved.

INF 11   British Council Photographic Collection
For records of British Council generally see Foreign Office section (pp 86-7).

INF 13   Posters and Publications
Includes many posters produced in connection with wartime publicity campaigns. Some appear in *Images of War: British Posters 1939-1945* (HMSO, 1989).

INF 14   Publications Division: Photographic Prints
Includes photographs of wartime scenes, aircraft, personalities, etc.

RG 23   Social Survey: Reports and Papers
This class contains reports carried out by the Social Survey largely on behalf of other government departments. The surveys were concerned with a variety of wartime problems, including public morale, rationing, and shortage of consumer goods.

RG 40   Social Survey: Registered Files
This class contains a few files of the wartime period concerning survey questionnaires, instructions, etc.

Board of Inland Revenue

Name	*Date of appointment*
Chairman	
Sir Gerald Bain Conny	1938
Sir Cornelius Joseph Gregg	1942

The Records

IR 15   Commissioners of Inland Revenue: Reports

IR 40   Stamps and Taxes Division: Registered Files
Includes papers concerning post-war credits, enemy debts, excess profits tax, war damage contributions, etc.

IR 63   Budget and Finance Bill Papers
Includes papers concerning war damage and pay-as-you-earn legislation.

IR 64   Statistics and Intelligence Division: Correspondence and Papers

IR 75   Private Office Papers: Committee Papers
The Departmental War Book is included in this class.

IR 76   Accountant and Comptroller General's Office: Registered Files
Many of the files relate to the pay-as-you-earn scheme.

IR 78   Notices, Instructions, Circulars, etc
Include a few posters concerning income tax.

IR 80   Office of Director of Stamping: Registered Files

IR 82   Chief Inspector of Taxes Branch: Registered Files

IR 83   Miscellanea
These relate mainly to the Income Tax Act 1945.

IR 87   Accounting Officers Briefs for Public Accounts Committee
Closed for 75 years.

IR 98   Office of the Solicitor: Law Officers' and Counsels' Opinions

IR 99   Solicitor's Opinions and Reports

IR 112   Special Commissioners of Income Tax and Surtax Office: Super-Tax and Surtax Instructions
Closed for 75 years apart from one piece.

Irish Sailors and Soldiers Land Trust

Name	Date of appointment
Chairman Sir James Bennett Brunyate	1927

The Records

AP 2	Irish Sailors and Soldiers Land Trust: Northern Ireland: Correspondence Files Include some papers concerning air raid damage to Trust properties.
AP 4	Irish Sailors and Soldiers Land Trust: Minutes, Agendas and Related Correspondence and Papers

Ministry of Labour and National Service

Name	Date of appointment
Minister	
Ernest Brown, MP	3 Sept 1939
Ernest Bevin, MP	13 May 1940
Parliamentary secretary	
R Assheton, MP	6 Sept 1939
G Tomlinson, MP	8 Feb 1941
M McCorquodale, MP	4 Feb 1942
Permanent secretary	
Sir Thomas W Phillips	3 Sept 1939
Sir Godfrey H Ince	18 Nov 1944
Deputy secretary	
F N Tribe	24 Jan 1940
Sir Frederick W Leggett	23 June 1942
G H Ince (acting)	23 June 1942
Chief industrial commissioner	
Sir Frederick W Leggett	25 May 1940
[Chief adviser to the minister	
on industrial relations since 24 January 1940]	
H C Emmerson	23 June 1942
R N Gould	21 Dec 1942

Director-general of manpower
G H Ince   9 June 1941

The National Service responsibilities that were added to the normal functions of the Ministry of Labour on the outbreak of war consisted essentially of the selective recruitment of volunteers and the operation of compulsory recruitment under the National Service (Armed Forces) Act. Under the Schedule of Reserved Occupations men in certain trades were ineligible for recruitment above specified ages or might be accepted in the Services only in their trade capacity. The Ministry's existing local offices, grouped in 12 divisions coterminous with the Civil Defence Regions, each group under a controller, were used for the execution of the Act. Two of the divisions were later amalgamated. In May 1940 these controllers became chairmen of the Area Boards which had been established by the Ministry of Supply and remained so until the Boards as Regional Boards were placed under the regional controllers of the Ministry of Production.

As the war proceeded and the Ministry directed more and more of the available manpower into the war effort manpower came to be recognized as the limiting factor and the manpower budget as one of the basic tools of strategy. The Ministry thus came to concern itself in ever greater detail with all aspects of the employment of labour such as wage rates, welfare facilities, number of hours worked and efficient utilization at the same time as it grappled with the problems of overall manpower distribution. To assist him the minister called for advice on various bodies of which the most important was the National Joint Advisory Council set up towards the end of 1939 and containing representatives of both employers and workers. The Council, which soon appointed a Joint Consultative Committee, was concerned at a general level with wage rates, hours of work, holidays and restoration of pre-war trade practices. A Women's Consultative Committee was appointed by the minister in March 1941 to advise him on policy respecting women.

The Ministry of Labour and National Service was organized into a number of departments. The deputy secretary and the under-secretary, both of whom reported to the permanent secretary, were each responsible for a group of these departments. From June 1941 each group was in the charge of a deputy secretary and one of these was known as director-general of manpower. The allocation of departments between these groups varied during the course of the war and is here described as it was in 1942.

The director-general of manpower was at that time responsible for the National Service Department, the Manpower Statistics and Intelligence Department, the Military Recruitment Department, three Labour Supply Departments, the Training Department, and the Appointments Department. The function of the National Service Department was to ensure that the available manpower was properly distributed between the Armed Forces, Civil Defence and industry. The manpower subject to the direction of the minister was increased to the limit by successive Acts and statutory instruments and, at the same time, the Ministry steadily increased control over the utilization of civilian manpower. The placing of occupations on the Schedule of Reserved Occupations together with the determination of the ages at which the reservations should apply was in the hands of a sub-committee of the War Cabinet. Individual deferments of military service could be sought for men who were engaged on work of national importance but were not covered by the Schedule. In April 1941 conscription was extended to the Civil Defence Services but in February of the following year steps were taken to transfer men from Civil Defence to the Armed Forces. Under the National Service (No 2) Act of December 1941 not only were the age limits for conscription in the Armed Forces extended but a statutory obligation was imposed on all persons aged between 18 and 60 to perform some national service, while conscription was extended to the Women's Services. At the same time the system of reservations from conscription for whole occupations under the Schedule of Reserved Occupations was changed to one of deferment solely of individuals. These measures reflected the increasing stringency of the manpower shortage.

Instead of supplying labour to meet stated requirements the situation became one of calculating available manpower and planning its distribution strategically.

The manpower situation of the munitions industries had been examined by the Wolfe Committee at the beginning of 1940 and in August the Production Council (see pp 136-7) appointed a Manpower Requirements Committee to investigate the whole field. This Committee was absorbed into the official Manpower Committee of the Production Executive and the Ministry of Production which, together with the Ministry of Labour and National Service, was responsible for the preparation of manpower budgets and their presentation to the Ministerial Manpower Committee.

The detailed execution of the National Service Acts was carried out locally through national service officers under the guidance of the Military Recruitment Department. The functions involved were the registration of men (and later women) liable for conscription, which was done in the employment exchanges and other employment offices, their medical examination, the issue of directions to the appropriate service of those required and the registration of objectors on grounds of conscience or hardship. Objections were heard by Local and Appellate Tribunals. The Military Recruitment Department was also responsible for dealing with cases of refusal by employers to reinstate those who had completed military service. In addition to registrations under the National Service Acts the local offices conducted registrations under the Industrial Registration Order of August 1940 of certain tradesmen and under the Registration for Employment Order of March 1941 of all employable persons not covered by the Acts. They were also responsible for the subsequent direction of such persons to employment if required. From December 1941 individuals could be directed into the Civil Defence Services. The National Service Co-ordinating Committee at the Ministry's Headquarters, which first met in January 1942, was responsible for the preparation of rulings on detailed points for the local offices. The National Registration system in the charge of the General Register Office was used to assist the Ministry in the execution of these duties.

The supply of labour to industry was at the beginning of the war in the hands of the Ministry's Employment Department. In May 1940 after it was agreed that the distribution of that supply to the munitions industries was properly the responsibility of the Ministry of Labour and National Service, four labour supply directors were appointed who constituted, under the chairmanship of the minister, the Labour Supply Board. Later in that year the Employment Department was split into three Labour Supply Departments, each responsible for a group of industries. The Labour Supply Board was replaced in March 1941 by the Labour Co-ordinating Committee of the Production Executive containing representatives of labour-using departments under the chairmanship of the permanent secretary to the Ministry of Labour and National Service. As the war proceeded the instruments of regulation were progressively strengthened. In September 1939 the Control of Employment Act set out to give the minister powers to encourage labour into approved occupations but was ineffective. In May 1940 the Emergency Powers (Defence) Act gave him power to direct persons to perform any service and to compel managements to operate in conformity with government directions. Under the Undertakings (Restriction on Engagement) Order of June 1940 all engagements in engineering, building and civil engineering had to be made through employment exchanges or trade unions approved for the purpose and advertisements for such employment were prohibited. This restriction was extended later in the year to coal mining and agriculture. In March 1941 the Essential Work (General Provisions) Order empowered the minister to designate undertakings as essential and in such undertakings employees could neither be dismissed nor leave their employment without the permission of the local national service officer. The application of the Essential Work Orders was the particular province of the Labour Co-ordinating Committee, and included the establishment of a National Dock Labour Corporation to employ all registered dockers in British ports with the exception of Merseyside and Clydeside, which were under the direct control of the Ministry of War Transport (see p 165). The Control of Engagements Order of January 1942 compelled women aged between 20 and 30, with certain exceptions, to obtain their employment through the exchanges or recognized agencies. The labour channelled in these ways to the exchanges was at first directed to employment on the basis of a system of priorities, but in the autumn of 1941 this was replaced by a system of preferences under the control of a Preference Committee containing representatives of the labour-using departments. This Committee, which itself came under the Labour Co-ordinating Committee, assigned preferential status for the filling of vacancies to particular industrial establishments, and its work was supplemented by that of Regional Preference Committees, who were able to accord preference of a lower status. To assist in overcoming the effects of maldistribution of labour non-essential industries were encouraged by the Board of Trade to concentrate their activities in areas where labour was more plentiful, while the Ministry of Labour and National Service undertook to assist in maintaining the labour supply to these concentrated 'nucleus' firms. Such firms would also be included in the Register of Protected Establishments in which employees had the benefit of eligibility for reserved occupations status at a lower age than elsewhere. Exceptional measures were necessary to secure labour supply in the case of the coal industry and when a system of options to conscripts failed to produce enough men conscripts became liable in October 1943 to direction to the mines.

The local organization for labour supply consisted not only of the local offices of the pre-war Ministry of Labour but, from May 1940, also of teams of labour supply inspectors. The inspectors were ultimately responsible to the Labour Supply Board at Headquarters via a chief inspector as well as to the divisional controllers via divisional inspectors. It was the inspectors' duty to visit firms, investigate the utilization of skilled labour and, if necessary, make recommendations to the divisional controller. In industrial areas local labour supply committees were established but were replaced in 1942 by District Manpower Boards when District Manpower Offices were established to handle the new individual deferments procedure. These Boards consisted of the senior district officers under the district manpower officer. Some changes were made in them in 1943 when their responsibilities for supplying labour were extended.

In the first part of the war shortages were particularly noticeable in the supply of skilled labour, though later unskilled labour also became scarce, and the Ministry was responsible for the production of skilled and semi-skilled labour in Government Training Centres. Employers were also encouraged to provide training under approved Training Schemes and Training Advisory Committees were appointed by the minister in the divisions. At the beginning of 1942, with fewer recruits coming forward, it was decided to close some of these centres.

It had been recognized before the war that there would be a need to organize the employment of very highly qualified persons, many of whom had volunteered their services during the Munich crisis. A Central Register was therefore established with the help of professional and technical institutions to provide a record of persons with particular qualifications. The Central Register provided the Secretariat for the Technical Personnel Committee set up in August 1941 to consider questions relating to the supply and demand of such personnel. A Supplementary Register was established in December 1941 for less highly qualified persons and this was used to a greater extent as a means of finding employment for those requiring it. In March 1942 an Appointments Department was established half of which consisted of the Central Register organization. The other half was concerned with the administration of the Appointments Register which now replaced the Supplementary Register and operated through thirty-one Appointments Offices throughout the country.

The Appointments Offices, like the Employment Offices, also came to play a part in the arrangements for the absorption into civilian life of men demobilized from the Services. The Ministry was here again concerned with a type of manpower budgeting for it was necessary to consider the most useful employment of demobilized men as well as to provide replacements for them by the existing conscription machinery. Certain kinds of worker were therefore given priority releases which were determined by an Interdepartmental Committee on Release from the Forces and Civil Defence. The Committee was also generally responsible for the co-ordination of preparations for applying the release scheme and keeping under review the prospective numbers for release. Training schemes were prepared to assist the demobilized and the Ministry of Labour and National Service undertook a general responsibility in the field of resettlement, including that of the disabled.

The departments under the control of the other deputy secretary were Factory and Welfare, Industrial Relations, Trade Boards, Unemployment Insurance, Statistics, Juveniles and Overseas. Much of the business of this group derived from the peacetime functions of the Ministry of Labour but the Factory and Welfare Department, in particular, was largely a fresh venture. In June 1940 the administration of the Factories Acts and control of the Factories Inspectorate were transferred from the Home Office to the Ministry of Labour and National Service. A Factory and Welfare Advisory Board was created to assist the new Factory and Welfare Department and the availability of facilities such as canteens became a condition for the application of certain measures, such as Essential Work Orders, to factories. Other welfare arrangements were pressed forward by the Ministry and, in particular, the provision of hostels for workers away from home. In May 1941 a National Service Hostels Corporation was created to run such hostels with a grant from the Ministry. The Ministry was also concerned with the provision of workers' transport and arranged for the Entertainments National Service Association to extend its activities from the Armed Forces to the factories.

In industrial conciliation the Ministry was able to secure the agreement of the Joint Advisory Council to the creation of a National Arbitration Tribunal to which all disputes that could not be settled by the existing machinery were to be referred. The awards of the Tribunal were to be binding and in July 1940 an Order was made compelling arbitration and forbidding strikes and lock-outs. Some extension of the Trade Board system for settling minimum wages was brought about and a Catering Wages Commission was established under the Catering Wages Act 1943. The Ministry also encouraged the establishment of Joint Production Committees of management and workers in the factories. Duties in this field were the responsibility of the General Department under a chief industrial commissioner in the first part of the war and came to be divided between the Industrial Relations and Trade Boards Departments. The Ministry's responsibilities for unemployment insurance were passed to the Ministry of National Insurance in 1945.

The Overseas Department was concerned both with recruiting in the United Kingdom for work overseas in connection with the war effort and with bringing men from overseas for the Services and for industry. It was responsible to the Overseas Manpower Committee which began in September 1941 as a sub-committee of the Manpower Committee to co-ordinate demands on the Dominions and later extended its scope.

The Records

BK 1   National Dock Labour Corporation Limited: Registered Files, Circulars and Minutes of Meetings
        Papers arising from the operation of certain docks from 1941 by the Corporation under the Essential Work (Dock Labour) Order 1941. Four files concern arrangements and agreements relating to preparation for the Allied invasion of France. See also BK 2 and MT 63.
BK 2   National Dock Labour Board: Head Office Registered Files
        Contains a few files overlapping with and continuing those in BK 1.
BK 9   National Dock Labour Board: Cumbria Dock Labour Board: Registered Files.
        A small number of files in this class contain wartime papers.
BK 11   National Dock Labour Board: South Coast Dock Labour Board: Registered Files
        This class includes a few files which commence in the wartime period.
BK 13   National Dock Labour Corporation and National Dock Labour Board: Newspaper Cuttings.

BK 15	National Dock Labour Corporation Limited and National Dock Labour Board: Manuscript Minute Books
	The first volume in this class includes minutes of the Corporation from 1943.
BK 19	National Dock Labour Board:London Dock Labour Board: Definition of Dock Work Files
	There are a few papers of the wartime period in this class.
BK 25	National Dock Labour Board: Maps and Plans of Docks and Harbours
	Includes some of the wartime period for Ardrossan, Holyhead, Irvine, King's Lynn, Plymouth and Weymouth.
BK 29	Dock Labour Reports and Inquiries
	This class includes reports on inquiries in 1943 into the workings of the dock labour scheme at Middlesborough and at London cold storage undertakings.
BK 32	National Dock Labour Corporation and National Dock Labour Board: Miscellanea
	This class includes a memorandum and articles of association of the Corporation and printed papers concerning wartime dock labour schemes.
BK 34	National Dock Labour Corporation and National Dock Labour Board: Grimsby and Immingham Dock Labour Board: Minutes of Meetings
	The first piece in this class contains minutes from 1942.
BK 35	National Dock Labour Board: London Docks Labour Board: Record Cards and Dossiers of Registered Dock Workers
	Includes a few documents concerning dockers first engaged during the wartime period.
LAB 3	Arbitration Tribunals
	Files concerning awards made by the Industrial Court, the National Arbitration Tribunal and the Railway Staff National Tribunal. Also includes correspondence and papers of the Tramways Tribunal, 1924 to 1945, and lists of members of the Coal Mines National Industrial Board.
LAB 6	Ministry of Labour and National Service and Ministry of Labour: Military Recruitment: Registered Files
	Files of the Military Recruitment Department dealing with deferments, conscientious objectors, control of medical manpower; files of the Military Training (Hardship) Committee and the Medical Advisory Committee; and records of the War Cabinet Manpower Priority Committee and its sub-committee on the schedule of reserved occupations. See also CAB 92.
LAB 8	Employment
	Files and a complete set of forms relating to manpower and various aspects of employment, including papers relating to port and dock labour, registrations for employment in technical, professional and scientific fields, files concerned with the employment of aliens (including prisoners of war) and special wartime arrangements and records of, or relating to, various wartime committees dealing with employment questions.
LAB 9	Finance
	Files of the Ministry's Finance Department.
LAB 10	Industrial Relations: General
	Files of the Industrial Relations Department including papers relating to the National Joint Advisory Council and National Joint Industrial Councils. The class also includes a complete set of forms relating to personnel management, and weekly reports of chief conciliation and industrial relations officers.
LAB 11	Industrial Relations, Trade Boards and Wages Councils
	See also LAB 35.
LAB 12	Establishments
	Files and a complete set of forms of the Establishments Department. The files deal with such matters as the official committee on the Beveridge Report, local offices, wartime organization, etc.
LAB 13	Overseas
	Files of the Overseas Department dealing mainly with the International Labour Organization, International Labour Conference and recruitment of labour overseas.
LAB 14	Safety, Health and Welfare: General
	Files relating to the administration of factory inspection. Until 1940 they are records of the Home Office.
LAB 15	HM Factory Inspectorate
	Inspectorial staff conferences, monthly circulars, arrangement of districts, etc.
LAB 16	Solicitor's Department
	Includes files concerning the National Service Acts and industrial disputes.
LAB 17	Statistics
	Files of the Statistics Department.

LAB 18	Training
	Files relating to training schemes and a complete set of forms concerning various aspects of training. For other files on training of juveniles and the disabled see LAB 19 and LAB 20 respectively.
LAB 19	Youth Employment
	Includes papers concerning the registration of boys and girls, aged 16 to 18, and the interrupted apprenticeship scheme. See also LAB 18.
LAB 20	Disabled Persons
	Files and a complete set of forms relating to the rehabilitation and employment of disabled persons. See also LAB 18.
LAB 22	National Service Hostels Corporation
	Certificates of incorporation, registers of members, minutes of the Board of Directors, etc, and specimen administrative papers of selected hostels.
LAB 25	Private Office Papers: Series I: War Emergency Measures
	These relate to the planning of wartime emergency measures, particularly in conjunction with other government departments, the preparation of the Departmental War Book, the keeping of a war diary, and to questions of manpower, national service, reserved occupations, emergency legislation and Departmental organization. The later papers relate to questions of demobilization and resettlement. See also LAB 32 and LAB 900.
LAB 26	Welfare Department
	Files relating to accommodation, clubs and recreational centres, entertainment, holidays during wartime, women war workers, etc. The class also contains monthly reports from welfare officers, minutes of meetings of the Seamen's Welfare Board, 1940 to 1944, and files concerning the Committee on Seamen's Welfare in Ports (the Graham White Committee).
LAB 29	Circulars and Codes of Instructions
LAB 30	Catering Wages Commission
	Files covering various aspects of the Commission's work, including wage regulation, training, rehabilitation, staggered holidays, etc.
LAB 32	Resettlement after Demobilization
	Papers leading up to the Reinstatement in Civil Employment Act 1944.
LAB 34	Trade Disputes: Record Books
	Analyses of returns of strikes and lock outs, 1939 to 1945.
LAB 35	Trade Boards and Wages Councils: Minutes
	See also LAB 11.
LAB 37	Annual Reports
	Printed annual reports of the Department, later published as Parliamentary Papers.
LAB 45	National Service Registration: Specimen Documents
	Includes documents concerning coal mining ballots and conscientious objectors.
LAB 56	Registers of Lead, etc, Poisoning and Anthrax Cases
LAB 62	HM Factory Inspectorate: Occupational Hygiene Laboratories
	Includes papers concerning health problems in Royal Ordnance Factories and miscellaneous wartime visits and reports on dusty factory processes.
LAB 67	HM Factory Inspectorate: Specimens of Regional Office Papers
LAB 69	Statistics Branch: Returns of Trade Unions and Employers' Associations
LAB 74	Sound Recordings
	Recordings made in 1939 prior to the introduction of conscription to encourage the public to perform national service. They feature the voices of George Arliss, Sir Malcolm Campbell, Lionel Gamlin, Amy Johnson and Syd Walker.
LAB 76	Official Histories: Correspondence and Papers
	Includes papers concerning the Beveridge Manpower Survey and minutes and memoranda of the Production Council, Production Executive and Labour Supply Board.
LAB 78	Reinstatement in Civil Employment Appeals: Umpire's Decisions
	Selected decisions under the Reinstatement in Civil Employment Act 1944.
LAB 79	Ince Papers
	Papers of Sir Godfrey Ince arising from his wartime activities concerning manpower and production.
LAB 80	Specimens of Stock Forms
LAB 83	Statistics Branch: Collective Agreements
	The class is arranged by industry or trade and gives details of basic (or standard) rates of wages, etc.
LAB 85	Statistical Returns: EDS Series
	Returns from local offices concerning employment and unemployment.
LAB 100	Port of London Registration Committee: Minutes and Agenda

LAB 900 Specimens of Classes of Documents Destroyed
         Includes specimen files dealing with work permits for nurses, registration for employment,
         training of nurses, etc, awards for further education and training and reinstatement in civil
         employment.
PIN 3   National Insurance, Pensions and Unemployment Insurance Acts, Bill Papers
PIN 16   Registered Files: I0 Series
         These arise from the responsibilities of the chief insurance officer concerning unemployment
         benefit and include papers about wartime emergency arrangements.
PIN 29   Unemployment Benefit: Umpire's Decisions

Land Registry

Name	Date of appointment
Chief land registrar	
Sir John Stewart Stewart-Wallace	1923
R M Lowe	1941

The Records

LAR 1   Land Registry: Registered Files
        Include a few files concerning wartime Acts affecting registry practice.
LAR 2   Chief Land Registrar's Reports
        Include a short account of wartime measures for safeguarding the register.

Law Officers

Name	Date of appointment
Attorney-general	
Sir Donald Somervell MP	March 1936
Solicitor-general	
Sir Terence O'Connor MP	March 1936
Sir William Jowitt MP	May 1940
Sir David Maxwell Fyfe MP	March 1942

The Records

LO 2   Law Officers' Department: Registered Files
        This class contains a few wartime papers relating to emergency legislation, parliamentary
        privilege and war crimes trials.

Lord Chancellor's Department

Name	Date of appointment
Lord chancellor	
Viscount Caldecote	3 Sept 1939
Viscount Simon	12 May 1940
Permanent secretary and clerk of the crown	
Sir Claud Schuster (later Lord Schuster)	1915
Hon Sir Albert Napier	1944

The Records [1]

LCO 2   Registered Files
The main series of registered correspondence and papers of the Lord Chancellor's Office and the Crown Office relating to the administrative, ecclesiastical, judicial and parliamentary responsibilities of the lord chancellor. Papers of particular wartime interest include those relating to emergency legislation and regulations, prize questions and enemy war crimes.

LCO 4   Establishment Files
Files relating to various establishment and accounting matters, including wartime prize questions.

LCO 6   Crown Office: Registered Files
Files relating to papers for the preparation of warrants for the issue of letters patent under the great seal for various civil, legal and military appointments, grants of honours, etc.

LCO 21   Sovereign's Speeches at the Opening and Prorogation of Parliament
Several are 'wanting'.

LCO 26   Liabilities War Time Adjustment Acts 1941 and 1944: Records of Adjustment Offices
These concern applications from persons living in or owning property in declared evacuation areas. Records have survived for Birmingham, Brighton, Bognor, Eastbourne, Folkestone and Hythe, Hastings, London, Portsmouth, Scarborough and Southampton. Certain proceedings under the Acts relating to Brighton and Lewes County Courts, formerly preserved under references AK 18 and AK 51, have been deposited in the East Sussex County Record Office.

LCO 29   Lord Chancellor's Committees: Signed Copies of Reports
Include reports concerning the effect of war damage on contracts and the giving of evidence in wartime.

LCO 33   Lord Chancellor's Department: Departmental Staff, Judiciary and Justices of the Peace: Personal and Disciplinary Files
Includes Lord Schuster's career file.

Metropolitan Police

Name	Date of appointment
Commissioner	
Air vice-marshal Sir Philip Game	1 Nov 1935
Deputy commissioner	
Col Hon Maurice Drummond	20 May 1935
(later Col Hon Sir Maurice Drummond)	

---

[1] For records of Courts of Law and Administrative Tribunals see separate section (pp 64-7)

The Metropolitan Police, like other Police Forces, added many wartime functions to their normal duties. They were responsible for the operation of sirens for air raid warnings, the enforcement of lighting restrictions and for the regulation of vehicles at the sites of bomb attacks. Much of the enforcement of Defence Regulations fell to them, including arrests of individuals to be detained under Defence Regulation 18B, and they also participated in exercises and the preparation of plans to meet invasion.

The war brought many aliens into the country, including those escaping from occupied countries, and the police were responsible for their initial reception and supervision.

In the performance of these duties liaison was maintained with, among others, London Civil Defence Region and its Air Raid Precautions Organization and with London Military District. A Central Casualty Bureau was operated by civilian staff at New Scotland Yard to ascertain and record casualties within the London area. It dealt with approximately 30,000 killed and 50,000 seriously injured persons.

It had been recognised before the war that these extensions would require greater strength and steps were taken to create an Auxiliary Police Reserve.

The Records

MEPO 2   Metropolitan Police: Office of the Commissioner: Correspondence and Papers
General correspondence and papers relating to the work of the Metropolitan Police. See also HO 341.

MEPO 3   Metropolitan Police: Office of the Commissioner: Correspondence and Papers, Special Series
Files dealing with special police duties including instructions in event of invasion, war measures, etc.

MEPO 4   Metropolitan Police: Office of the Commissioner: Miscellaneous Books and Papers
These include war diaries, attestation ledgers, annual reports of the commissioner and casualty lists compiled by the Central Casualty Bureau.

MEPO 5   Metropolitan Police: Office of the Receiver: Correspondence and Papers
General correspondence and papers relating to financial matters, buildings, the Metropolitan Police Canteen Board and war measures.

MEPO 7   Metropolitan Police: Office of the Commissioner: Police Orders
The volumes in this class contain general and confidential notices and instructions on personnel matters, including recruitment, promotions, transfers, awards, retirements, and dismissals, and other instructions or notices to be brought to the attention of all ranks.

MEPO 8   Metropolitan Police: Office of the Commissioner: Confidential Books and Instructions
Include War Reserve Official Handbook and War Duty Hints Booklet.

MEPO 10 Metropolitan Police: Office of the Commissioner: Senior Officers' Papers
Include Sir Philip Game's semi-official correspondence with the Home Office. Closed for 75 years.

MEPO 12 Metropolitan Police: Office of the Receiver: Correspondence and Papers, Special Series
Records dealing with disciplinary cases, claims against the police, etc. They are closed for 75 years.

Royal Mint

Name	Date of appointment
Deputy master and comptroller	
J H McC Craig	1938

The Records

MINT 20   Registered Files: Annual Series
          Include files concerning the striking of campaign stars and medals.
MINT 21   Registers of Correspondence
MINT 24   Designs of Coins, Medals, Seals, etc
MINT 25   Royal Mint Advisory Committee on the Design of Coins, Medals, Seals and Decorations
          Minutes of meetings.
MINT 26   Annual Reports of the Deputy Master and Comptroller

Ministry of National Insurance

Name	Date of appointment
Minister	
Sir William Jowitt MP	8 Oct 1944
(later Earl Jowitt)	
Secretary	
Sir Thomas W Phillips	November 1944
Deputy secretary	
Sir Thomas Sheepshanks	1944

The Ministry was established in 1944 as one of the steps towards post-war reconstruction. The Reconstruction Committee of the War Cabinet had set up an interdepartmental committee under Sir William Beveridge in 1941 to survey existing schemes of social insurance and its report led first to the establishment of a small interdepartmental staff and later to the creation of the new Ministry. It absorbed the Insurance Department of the Ministry of Health and the Unemployment Insurance Department of the Ministry of Labour and National Service in 1945.

The Records

PIN 4   Pensions and Insurance
         Files of the Ministry of Health continued in the Ministry of National Insurance relating to the administration of national health insurance, contributory old age, widows' and orphans' pensions and national insurance. A few files relate to the administration of, and appeals under, the non-contributory old-age pensions scheme. The class contains papers relating to the implementation of the proposals of the Beveridge Committee and the planning of the Ministry of National Insurance.
PIN 7   Labour Exchanges and Unemployment Insurance
         The class includes files of the Unemployment Insurance Division of the Ministry of National Insurance, containing correspondence and papers relating to the administration of the old unemployment insurance scheme and preparations for implementing the proposals of the Beveridge Committee.
PIN 8   Social Insurance and Allied Services (Beveridge Report)
         The first part of this class (PIN 8/1-84) contains correspondence and papers of the central staff of the Committee on Reconstruction under the paymaster general. The papers relate to the consideration and planning of administrative machinery for the implementation of the report of the Beveridge Committee.
PIN 17   Registered Files: Family Allowance Policy (London Office): FA Series
         These relate to the family allowance scheme under the Family Allowances Act 1945.

PIN 19   Registered Files: NI Series
          Files relating to the introduction and administration of social insurance schemes and allied services.
PIN 23   Registered Files: Staff and Establishment (SE Series)

National Savings Committee

Name	Date of appointment
President	
Sir Robert Kindersley	1920
(later Lord Kindersley)	
Secretary	
R Dixon Kingham	1927
(later Sir Robert Dixon Kingham)	

The National Savings Committee was established during the First World War to encourage small savings as a contribution to the war effort and, unlike other creations of that time, it was allowed to continue in existence after the war. In 1939 it was therefore ready to take up its old role and in November began the War Savings campaign which continued for the next five years, using every possible medium of publicity. It was decided at the beginning of the war that voluntary saving should be encouraged in preference to the imposition of forced saving on the people and this decision was not radically altered. The Savings Movement thus formed an important part of the Treasury machinery for guiding the country's war economy. In addition to the existing channels for saving in the Post Office Savings Bank, the Trustee Savings Banks and National Savings Certificates the Government introduced 3 per cent Defence Bonds which, like the Savings Certificates, could be purchased in Post Offices. The local Savings Committees developed street, school and industrial savings groups and in addition organized local activities in connection with the national campaigns such as War Weapons Week. Under the direct transfer scheme arrangements were made for savings by authorized deductions from pay to be made by employers and paid into savings banks.

The Records

NSC 1   National Savings Committee: Minute Books
NSC 2   National Savings Committee: Annual Reports
         Printed reports made annually to the Treasury.
NSC 3   National Savings Committee: Journals
         Printed bulletins of the Savings Movement circulated to the voluntary workers in savings groups. They contain details of schemes, campaigns, etc, and messages of encouragement from notabilities.
NSC 4   National Savings Committee for England and Wales: Campaign Circulars and News Letters
         These are bound volumes of Weekly Campaign Circulars and News Letters. They contain information about projected schemes and comments on organization, and were distributed to all key workers in the Movement.
NSC 5   National Savings Committee: Posters
         The class contains a selection of the posters used by the Movement to promote public interest in, and support for, its many savings schemes. See also NSC 25.
NSC 6   National Savings Committee for England and Wales: Leaflets

The class contains a collection of leaflets used to advertise schemes, to provide information and to assist officers of the Movement in their duties. See also NSC 42.

NSC 7   National Savings Committee: Organization and Development Files

This class contains a record of the origin, history and development of the National Savings Committee, showing particularly its regional organization and its various special campaigns. It also contains files on thrift organizations in England and Wales.

NSC 9   Post Office Savings Bank: Savings Policy Files

NSC 14   National Savings Stamps

Include papers concerning a new Victory Savings stamp and savings stamps damaged by enemy action.

NSC 16   National Savings Gift Tokens

These were introduced in 1940 in connection with the war savings campaign.

NSC 17   National Savings Committee for England and Wales: Establishment Files

Files concerning staffing, grading, pay, organization, etc, both at headquarters and in the regions. The class also includes minutes of Departmental Whitley Council meetings.

NSC 18   National Savings Committee for England and Wales: Intelligence Files

This class contains general papers concerning various forms of savings and some files relating to Office administration and practice.

NSC 21   Post Office Savings Bank and Post Office Savings Department: Departmental Policy Files

NSC 22   Post Office Savings Bank and Post Office Savings Department: Staff Branch Files

NSC 23   Post Office Savings Bank and Post Office Savings Department: Buildings Branch Files

Include papers concerning air raid precautions and damage.

NSC 25   Post Office Savings Bank and Department for National Savings: Posters

See NSC 5.

NSC 26   Post Office Savings Department and Department for National Savings: Publicity Branch Files

NSC 27   Post Office Savings Bank, Post Office Savings Department and Department for National Savings: Photographs

See also NSC 32.

NSC 28   National Savings Committee for England and Wales: HM Forces Branch

A few files containing papers relating to savings facilities for the Armed Forces, including minutes of meetings of the Army Savings Association and the Forces Savings Committee.

NSC 29   National Savings Committee for England and Wales: Finance Files

These relate mainly to accounting procedure and financial control.

NSC 30   National Savings Committee for England and Wales: SE Regional Office Records

Specimen reports and minutes of meetings of Local Savings Committees and Regional Conferences.

NSC 31   National Savings Committee for England and Wales: Staff Instructions

Information files for 1942, with a 1944 index.

NSC 32   National Savings Committee for England and Wales: Photographs

These were taken in 1940 and in 1942 to 1943 in connection with the war savings campaign. See also NSC 27.

NSC 33   National Savings Committee for England and Wales: Publicity

Scrapbooks, broadcast transcripts, press notices, etc.

NSC 34   National Savings Committee for England and Wales: Papers relating to Local Committees

A representative selection of headquarters files containing correspondence, etc, from local committees.

NSC 39   Post Office Savings Bank: Statistics

Record of daily transactions and miscellaneous statistics.

NSC 42   Post Office Savings Bank: Leaflets

Ordnance Survey

Name	Date of appointment
Director-general	
Maj-Gen Malcolm N MacLeod	1935
Maj-Gen Geoffrey Cheetham	1943

The Records

OS 1   Correspondence and Papers
        This class consists of administrative and general files. Many of the Survey's papers were
        destroyed during air raids on Southampton in 1940 and 1941.
OS 3   Miscellanea
        Includes reminiscences of the Survey in wartime, gathered for the Survey's official history.
OS 8   Office Notices and Circulars
        Chief clerk's circulars and circular memos.

Paymaster General's Office

Name	Date of appointment
Paymaster general	
Earl Winterton, MP	1939
Viscount Cranborne, MP	1940
Lord Hankey	1941
Sir William Jowitt, MP	1942
Lord Cherwell	1942
Assistant paymaster general	
L Cuthbertson	1938

The Records

PMG 74   Correspondence and Papers
         Include papers about payment of pensions in enemy and enemy-occupied territory and of damage
         to the Office by enemy action in 1940.
PMG 75   Office Notices
         This class also includes Office instructions.

Ministry of Pensions

Name	Date of appointment
Minister	
Sir Walter Womersley, MP	7 June 1939
Parliamentary secretary	
W Paling, MP	8 Feb 1941
Permanent secretary	
Sir Adair Hore	1935
A Cunnison	1941
(later Sir Alexander Cunnison)	

Deputy secretary
H Parker   1941

The Ministry was responsible for the payment to ex-servicemen and women of pensions and allowances to which they were entitled by reason of disabilities incurred during war service. Pensions were also payable to their widows, orphans and, in some cases, other dependants. Similar schemes existed for members of the Mercantile Marine and Civil Defence Forces and for civilians injured by enemy attack. Some functions were performed on an agency basis for the Ministry by the Assistance Board. The Ministry was assisted in the administration of the war pensions scheme by existing statutory War Pensions Committees in various parts of the country. As part of its responsibility for the treatment of disabled pensioners the Ministry also maintained a number of special hospitals.

The Records

MH 120	Ministry of Pensions and successor: Hospital Management Branch: Registered Files (HM Series)
	These deal with the administration of special hospitals.
PIN 9	War Pensions Committees
	Files of the Ministry of Pensions relating to the constitution, working and meetings of War Pensions Committees in selected areas. See also PIN 56.
PIN 14	Codes and Instructions
	Manuals of codes and instructions sent to local offices of the Ministry of Pensions, medical boards and War Pensions Committees relating to the detailed administration of war pensions, including copies of royal warrants governing such pensions.
PIN 15	War Pensions
	Correspondence and papers of the Ministry of Pensions relating to pensions or allowances payable to members of the Armed Forces, merchant seamen and civil defence workers injured in war and to the dependants of those dying as a result of wartime service.
PIN 40	Selected War Pensions Appeals
	For other appeals records see under section for Courts of Law and Administrative Tribunals (pp 64, 66).
PIN 41	Central Advisory Committee on War Pensions: Minutes
PIN 56	Registered Files: War Pensions Committees (WPM Series)
	These deal with the constitution and work of the Committees. See also PIN 9.
PIN 59	Registered Files: War Pensions Policy (WPP Series)
PIN 69	Registered Files: Public Relations (PR Series)
	One file containing papers arising out of the issue by the Ministry of Pensions of a Public Relations Bulletin for War Pensions Committees.

Political Warfare Executive

Name	Date of appointment
Secretary of state for foreign affairs	
R Anthony Eden, MP	Aug 1941
Minister of information	
Brendan Bracken, MP	Aug 1941

Minister of economic warfare
[On the Executive only up to March 1942]
Hugh Dalton, MP   Aug 1941
Viscount Wolmer   22 Feb 1942

Director-general
R H Bruce Lockhart   Mar 1942

The conduct of propaganda as a weapon of war underwent considerable extensions in the Second World War. In addition to the overt Ministry of Information (pp 113-17) a succession of covert organizations operated in this field and for the first half of the war were the occasion of much dispute both as to their external control and their internal division of responsibilities.

The first of these was Department EH, so called from its occupancy of Electra House on the Victoria Embankment. It was initially interested only in Germany but inevitably broadened its activities after the German occupation of much of Europe. It contained two basic divisions of which one was responsible for intelligence and the other for output of propaganda by means of leaflets, the British Broadcasting Corporation or secret radio stations. Further subdivision was by countries. It was succeeded in 1940 by Special Operations 1 of Special Operations Executive,[1] subordinate to the minister of economic warfare. The connection between covert propaganda and special operations persisted even after the supersession of Special Operations 1 in August 1941 by the Political Warfare Executive, for a short time at the ministerial level and for much longer at the operational level, especially in operations from overseas bases. The allocation of responsibilities between the two organizations led to considerable conflict.

The Political Warfare Executive was headed jointly by the foreign secretary, the minister of information and the minister of economic warfare. Beneath them an executive committee of officials was responsible for the co-ordination of propaganda policy and the Executive was constituted by an amalgamation of parts of the British Broadcasting Corporation and the Ministry of Information with Special Operations 1. The Executive was organized into two separate parts, a structure which continued until the end of the war, although there were many changes within this basic structure. On the one hand there were the Regional Directorates for separate territories, handling both intelligence and operations for those territories and controlled, for they were based at Woburn Abbey, by Country Headquarters. The central organization on the other hand, most of which was in London, was organized functionally with Liaison Sections in the Ministry of Information Special Operations Executive and the British Broadcasting Corporation, a Central Planning Committee, a Central Secretariat, a Military Wing, a Co-ordination of Intelligence Section and a British Broadcasting Corporation Section. The Political Intelligence Department of the Foreign Office (p 84) provided cover for the Executive. In March 1942 the Ministerial Committee was dissolved and the foreign secretary became responsible for policy and the minister of information for the administration of the Political Warfare Executive. The Executive Committee was also abolished in favour of a director-general, who is described in the Foreign Office List as in charge of the Co-ordination of Propaganda Department, with an advisory committee known as the Propaganda Policy Committee or the Director-General's Meeting. Thereafter the Executive was able to settle down to routine and its greater stability is, perhaps, marked by the establishment of a Training School and the use of printed file jackets for its papers.

Propaganda material was prepared by the Regions in accordance with central directives which might relate to general background or specify the line to be followed about particular events. The initial preparation of the directives, which were also used by organizations in the Middle East and the Far East, was the responsibility of the Directorate of Plans. Plans included the selection and specification of propaganda targets and the study of and advance preparation for possible long-term requirements.

---

[1] At the time of writing further records of the Special Operations Executive(SOE) are being reviewed for possible release.

By virtue of being a secret organization the Executive was able to put into circulation propaganda which it would be undesirable to attribute to the British government or, indeed, to any British source. The output included Black propaganda, distinguished from other kinds by purporting to come from official or other sources inside enemy territory. Depending on the nature of the propaganda the British Broadcasting Corporation, the Ministry of Information, secret broadcasts, leaflets or rumours spread by agents were used as media. The spreading of rumours was conducted under the control of the Underground Propaganda Committee.

Propaganda was intended to contribute to specific military operations as well as to attack the overall morale of the enemy and the Political Warfare Executive developed close links first with the Services' Directors of Plans and then, for example, with Army Commands and Supreme Headquarters Allied Expeditionary Force. The Psychological Warfare Division of Supreme Headquarters Allied Expeditionary Force submitted to Political Warfare Executive and the American Office of War Information its operational requirements for the use of their production facilities, while in turn the Executive took a close interest in the doctrine and practice of propaganda in the fighting areas. In conjunction with the Ministry of Economic Warfare it attacked economic targets. It also assisted with the propagation of operational cover plans and the re-education of enemy prisoners of war.

The intelligence side of secret propaganda was indispensable both for the initial preparation of material and for measuring its effect on its target. In the early days there was a single intelligence organization which was divided regionally in the spring of 1941. This experiment was short-lived, however, and centralization was re-introduced by degrees, resulting in both central and regional units. The central unit, which eventually became the Directorate of Political Warfare Intelligence, dealt with distribution and with supra-regional material. Political Warfare Intelligence had close links with the Political Intelligence Department of the Foreign Office.

The conduct of political warfare overseas was gradually assumed by the Executive and eventually a Directorate of Foreign Missions was created. A director of political warfare was sent to the Middle East on behalf of the Executive in October 1942 and this arrangement continued until responsibility was transferred to the Psychological Warfare Branch of the Mediterranean Supreme Command in 1944. The Mission in Washington, based on the Embassy, was sent to co-operate with the Office of War Information from its establishment in June 1942 and was mainly concerned with political warfare against Japan. Political warfare conducted in the Far East by the Ministry of Information and Special Operations Executive was supervised from March 1942 by a Foreign Office Committee known as the Political Warfare (Japan) Committee on which the Political Warfare Executive was represented, while the Executive also had, jointly with the Ministry of Information, a liaison officer in South East Asia Command. At the end of 1944 the Executive assumed direct responsibility for the conduct of political warfare operations in the Far East previously in the hands of the Ministry of Information and Special Operations Executive. Towards the end of the war publicity work in relation to enemy and enemy-occupied territories gradually passed from the Executive to the Ministry of Information, and after the collapse of Germany its residual work, including that of its Prisoner of War Division, passed to the Political Intelligence Department of the Foreign Office.

The files of the Political Warfare Executive during much of its history were handled solely by their users and not by a registry as in more routine departments. The Directorate of Political Warfare Intelligence introduced registration for its own papers and maintained both central and regional registries. In the last year of the war when much consideration was being given to the eventual destination of the papers a Central Registry was established. Many of the files consist of earlier folders placed in the registry jackets.

FO 898   Political Warfare Executive
              Papers relating to the formation, functions and activities of the Political Warfare Executive. The class includes a complete set of leaflets, etc, dropped by air over Germany, Italy and the occupied countries of Europe.

Ministry of Production

Production Council
(22 May 1940 - 19 December 1940)

Name	Date of appointment
Chairman	
Minister without portfolio	
Arthur Greenwood, MP	11 May 1940
Members	
President of the Board of Trade	
Sir Andrew Duncan, MP	12 May 1940
Oliver Lyttelton, MP	3 Oct 1940
Minister of labour and national service	
Ernest Bevin, MP	13 May 1940
Minister of supply	
Herbert Morrison, MP	12 May 1940
Sir Andrew Duncan, MP	3 Oct 1940
Minister of aircraft production	
Lord Beaverbrook	14 May 1940
First lord of the Admiralty	
Albert V Alexander, MP	11 May 1940

Production Executive
(3 January 1941 - 13 January 1942)
President
Minister of labour and national service

Ernest Bevin, MP	13 May 1940
Members	
President of the Board of Trade	
Oliver Lyttelton, MP	3 Oct 1940
Sir Andrew Duncan, MP	29 June 1941

Minister of supply
Sir Andrew Duncan, MP — 3 Oct 1940
Lord Beaverbrook — 29 June 1941

Minister of aircraft production
Lord Beaverbrook — 14 May 1940
J T C Moore-Brabazon, MP — 1 May 1941

First lord of the Admiralty
Albert V Alexander, MP — 11 May 1940

Minister of works and buildings and first commissioner of works
Lord Reith — 23 Oct 1940
[Member of the Production Executive from June 1941]

Office of the Minister of Production
(from 4 February 1942)
Minister

Lord Beaverbrook — 4 Feb 1942 - 19 Feb 1942
Oliver Lyttelton, MP — 12 Mar 1942

Ministry of Production
(from 13 July 1942)
Minister
Oliver Lyttelton, MP — 12 Mar 1942

Parliamentary secretary
G M Garro-Jones, MP — 10 Sept 1942

Chief executive
Sir Robert Sinclair — June 1943

The pre-war debate on the creation of a Ministry of Supply turned in part on the need for an executive authority which would be responsible for meeting the competitive demands for production made by the Armed Forces and would thus also co-ordinate and adjudicate between those demands. In the event such an organ was never brought fully into being but an increasing degree of centralization was achieved by a succession of bodies.

At the beginning of the war a Central Priority Department was located within the Ministry of Supply to execute the decisions of the Ministerial Priority Committee and its sub-committees. In practice it found itself more concerned with allocation, particularly of raw materials, than priority. The Ministerial Committee was succeeded in May 1940 by the Production Council whose members were the three Supply ministers, the president of the Board of Trade and the minister of labour, with a minister without portfolio as chairman. Apart from the chairman its membership was in fact similar to that of the Committee and it also operated through sub-committees and the Central

Priority Department. The execution of production programmes remained the responsibility of the Supply Departments but the Production Council issued a general priority directive and was able to balance the programmes to some extent by its powers of allocation. The Area Boards on which local representatives of the three Supply Departments and the Ministry of Labour met to co-ordinate their activities were established at the same time as the Production Council and central direction of them was exercised through its Industrial Capacity Committee. During the year criticisms continued to be made, both in Parliament and within Whitehall, of the effectiveness of the Council, particularly in respect of its lack of authority, and in December it was liquidated.

Its successor was the Production Executive, which came into existence as part of a general reshaping of the control of domestic affairs at the War Cabinet Committee level (see p 10). Its members were the three Supply ministers and the president of the Board of Trade under the chairmanship of the minister of labour. The minister of works was added in June 1941. Its function was to allocate materials, capacity and labour and to establish priorities where necessary. The Central Priority Department and the Secretariat of the Industrial Capacity Committee were combined into one Secretariat to assist it. It took over, with some adjustments, the sub-committees of the Production Council except that the Transport Priority Committee was made responsible to the minister of transport. Although the Executive was expected to exercise more authority than its predecessors difficulties continued to arise over the precise nature of its relationship to Supply Departments and at the end of 1941 it was found necessary to rule that it was not an administrative body but a clearing house. Although the Executive and its committees concerned themselves with very detailed aspects of production and were able to call for all kinds of returns it was never able to aim at the planned control of production. It did not, for example, receive the statements of Service requirements that were the starting point of production programmes and the overall control of these programmes remained firmly in the hands of the Defence Committee (Supply) (see p7).

Among the major developments of this period was the re-organization of the Area Boards in the spring of 1941. They were renamed Regional Boards and made directly responsible to the Executive. Capacity Clearing Centres, of which the first had been established at the beginning of 1941 to handle information about available capacity in an area, were now to be set up by all the Regional Boards. The Centres, however, reproduced in the regions the difficulties of the relationship between the Production Executive and the Supply Departments and it was not until the following year that these difficulties were resolved.

The entry of the United States into the war and the prospect thus opened of combined production planning was the occasion of the final major change in British organization in this field, the appointment of a minister of production in February 1942. This was all the more necessary because the Americans had appointed a single production overlord to whom we had to provide an opposite number. The intention was that the minister should have only a small personal staff and the description 'Ministry of Production' was at first avoided in favour of 'Office of the Minister of Production' but the former soon became the generally accepted title. The minister took over the functions of the Production Executive, other than those relating to labour, together with its committees and staff and was also particularly charged with liaison with the United States. In this respect he was represented on the Combined Production Board in Washington and as the chairman of the North American Supply Committee was represented there by the chairman of the British Supply Council (see p 12). In February 1942 the Combined Munitions Assignment Board was established in Washington to control the allocation of all the munitions produced by the United Kingdom and the United States. In practice it was found necessary to have separate Boards sitting in London and Washington which might allocate munitions to each other as well as more directly to users in their own areas. The London Board came under the minister of production and included British and American Service representatives. The minister of production also shared responsibility for the Joint American Secretariat, and in 1942 took over from the Ministry of Supply responsibility for the British Central Scientific Office in Washington. The Supply Departments retained their independent status and the role of the minister of production was affirmed to be that of co-ordination, including allocation, and not direction. The controls which executed policy in respect of raw materials and machine tools remained with the Ministry of Supply.

In the planning field the Ministry of Production was able to be more active than its predecessors had been, primarily by means of the institution of the Joint War Production Staff. The idea of a general staff for production had been put forward on a number of occasions and it now took the form of a War Cabinet Committee, with both Service and civilian members, of which the minister of production was chairman. It was able to keep the production programmes under constant review and constituted a link between the Supply Departments and the Chiefs of Staff organization. It was served by the Joint War Production Planning Group consisting of the various directors of programmes from the departments involved. To support this structure a Programme and Planning Division was developed which undertook the study of requirements and programmes and conducted liaison with the Combined Production and Resources Board in respect of munitions supply. The other elements in this part of the Ministry were the Raw Materials, Production or Industrial, and Regional Divisions. The Raw Materials Division dealt with general questions relating to raw materials production, imports and requirements, including those of the Empire, and conducted liaison with the Combined Raw Materials Board via the British Raw Materials Mission. The Materials Committee with its responsibility for allocation became responsible to the minister and its Secretariat became part of the Raw Materials Division. The Division also advised the chairman of the Central Priority Committee. The Industrial and Regional Divisions were those most closely concerned with the production processes themselves and, consequently, impinged most nearly on the areas of responsibility of the Supply Departments. Following the report of the Citrine Committee on Regional Boards the minister of production appointed regional controllers who were to co-ordinate the activities of the Supply Departments' regional controllers. A Central Co-ordinating Committee was attached to the Ministry of Production.

A Non-Munitions Supply Division was established later to plan in conjunction with the Americans, via the Combined Production and Resources Board, the production of such items as textiles and agricultural machinery. The last major reorganization in the Ministry occurred in June 1943 when all these divisions were placed under the control of a new chief executive by whom their co-ordinating functions were still further co-ordinated.

The functions of the Secretariat were not affected by this change. In addition to the usual financial and establishment duties the secretary provided advice on policy, conducted the administration of the Ministry and provided the secretariat of the many committees associated with production.

As the war developed some extensions of the functions of the Ministry occurred and the establishment of the Non-Munitions Supply Division has already been noted. Questions of production for relief purposes in the liberated areas and the planning of rehabilitation in these areas became an important part of the work. The system of labour preferences which consisted essentially of giving priorities to particular industries and firms for their labour requirements expanded as the shortage of manpower became more pressing and an interdepartmental Preference Committee was established to pronounce on the relative importance of competing claimants. The Ministry of Production became responsible, in consultation with the Ministry of Labour and National Service, for deciding which products should qualify for preference.

The surviving records of these successive and inter-related organisms form two groups. The primary records of the Ministerial Committee, the Production Council and the Production Executive together with those of the Joint War Planning Staff and other committees are to be found among those of the War Cabinet. The files of the Ministry of Production include those of its predecessors and in many cases a file originally registered by the Ministry of Supply and re-registered under the Production Executive continued in action in the Ministry of Production.

AVIA 22   Ministry of Supply Registered Files
          This class includes a few files of the Central Priority Department. See T 246 below.
AVIA 42   British Central Scientific Office: Registered Files
          The Office was established in Washington in 1941. From mid-summer 1944 it merged with the
          scientific missions of Australia, New Zealand and South Africa to form the British Common-
          wealth Scientific Office.
AVIA 46   Ministry of Supply Files: Series 1 (Establishment)
          This class includes some historical material relating to the Ministry of Production.
BT 25   Supplies to Liberated Areas Secretariat
          From 1945 these are files of the Supplies to Liberated Areas Division of the Board of Trade.
BT 28   Ministry of Production: Correspondence and Papers
          Records of the Ministry of Production: including some of the Ministry of Supply, which passed
          to the Board of Trade. See also BT 87. For indexes see BT 29 and BT 30.
BT 29   Ministry of Production: Numerical Indexes to Correspondence
          These relate to BT 28.
BT 30   Ministry of Production: Subject Indexes to Correspondence
          These relate to BT 28.
BT 87   Ministry of Production: Ministers' and Officials' Papers
          Papers which accumulated in the office of the minister of production including a number dealing
          with the minister's visits to the United States.
BT 168   Ministry of Production: Regional Boards for Industry
          This class includes files concerning invasion precautions by factories and a number arising from
          the production and housing programmes.
BT 170   Regional Boards for Industry: Minutes and Circulated Papers
BT 190   National Production Advisory Council on Industry
          Minutes and papers of meetings.
CAB 92   War Cabinet Committees on Supply, Production, Priority and Manpower
CAB 109   London Munitions Assignment Board: Secretary's Files
CAB 110   Joint American Secretariat: Secretary's Files
T 188   Leith-Ross Papers
          Papers of Sir Frederick Leith-Ross.
T 246   Central Priority Department: Allocation of Raw Materials
          See also AVIA 22 above.

Department of the Director of Public Prosecutions

Name	Date of appointment
Director of Public Prosecutions	
Sir Edward H Tindal Atkinson	March 1930
Theobald Mathew	1944

The Records

DPP 2   Case Papers: New Series
         Files of case papers consisting of police and other reports; copies of depositions and exhibits;
         counsel's briefs and papers; and related correspondence. Wartime files include cases under the
         Treachery Act 1940, Defence Regulations and other emergency legislation. The records are
         closed for 75 years.
DPP 3   Registers of Cases
         Registers and card indexes of applications for advice on action and of other communications

addressed to the director by chief constables, town clerks and others, constituting a record of cases referred. There are also separate registers of miscellaneous papers, 1899 to 1946. The records are closed for 75 years.

Public Record Office

Name	Date of appointment

Deputy keeper of the public records
C T Flower   1938

For some account of the wartime work of the Office see *The Public Record Office 1838-1958* (HMSO 1991).

The Records

PRO 1   General Correspondence
            Includes papers concerning air raid precautions and evacuation of records. Registers are in PRO 46.

PRO 17   Inspecting Officers' Committee: Correspondence and Papers
            This class contains material arising from the disposal of papers of government departments under the Public Record Office Acts, and the reduction of retention periods on account of the paper shortage.

PRO 18   Repositories for Evacuated Records: War of 1939-1945
            Correspondence and papers which accumulated both at headquarters and at the seven local repositories to which parts of the public records were moved for safe custody at the beginning of the war. They relate mainly to the acquisition, preparation and maintenance of the repositories; the evacuation and return of the records; establishment matters; and the release of the premises.

PRO 30/73 Loraine Papers
            Now FO 1011 (see p 92).

PRO 30/75 Jenkinson Papers
            Include material concerning Sir Hilary Jenkinson's work as adviser to the War Office on the protection of archives in occupied enemy territory.

PRO 43   Deputy Keeper's and Keeper's Reports
            Unpublished annual reports of the deputy keeper of the records on the work of the Office 1939 to 1945.

PRO 45   Office Notices and Memoranda
            Include reports from wartime repositories and accounts of air raid precautions and incidents at Chancery Lane headquarters.

PRO 46   Registers of Correspondence
            These relate to the correspondence in PRO 1.

Public Trustee Office

Name	Date of appointment

Public trustee
Sir Ernest Fass   1939

The Records

PT 1   Public Trustee Office: Correspondence and Papers
          Files relating to the organization and procedure of the Office, accommodation, staffing and
          general establishment matters, and to the activities of the public trustee as custodian of enemy
          property.

Royal Commissions (Standing)

Royal Commission on Ancient and Historical Monuments in Wales and Monmouthshire

The Records

MONW 1   Records
          Wartime reports and memoranda, including papers concerning Army training areas and possible
          dangers to important sites and monuments.

Royal Fine Arts Commission

The Records

BP 1   Minutes of Meetings
BP 2   Correspondence and Papers
          Include a few papers concerning proposals for war memorials.

Royal Commission on Historical Manuscripts

The Records

HMC 1   Correspondence and Papers
          Includes papers concerning the protection of archives in wartime.
HMC 3   Evershed Papers
          Papers arising mainly from Lord Evershed's wartime activities as chairman of the Central Price
          Regulation Committee and as regional controller of the North Midland coal-producing region.
          There are also some papers concerning a report made on the internal organization of naval
          aviation and others which he took over from Lord Greene, his predecessor as chairman of the
          Historical Manuscripts Commission.

Royal Commission on Historical Monuments (England)

The Records

AE 1   Royal Commission on Historical Monuments (England): Minutes
          Many of the Commission's records were destroyed as a result of a fire in 1945.

The Records

EB 1   Reports
          The class includes a published report summarizing the Commission's work during the war years.

Department of Scientific and Industrial Research

Name	*Date of appointment*
Secretary	
E V Appleton	1939
(later Sir Edward V Appleton)	
Principal assistant secretary	
L S Lloyd	1935
E Barnard	1943

At the beginning of the war it was decided to maintain in existence the various establishments that came under the Department of Scientific and Industrial Research and divert them into war work as units rather than disperse their staff among the government departments primarily concerned with the prosecution of the war. All the research establishments in various degrees put aside their long-term research in order to undertake tasks on behalf of departments. A Pest Infestation Laboratory was established specifically to undertake work for the Ministry of Food and the Department of Scientific and Industrial Research was given responsibility for the atomic bomb development. In this, the most scientific of all wars to date, much research and development work was of course carried out by the Service and other departments themselves. The development of radar in particular, which had its origins in the National Physical Laboratory, was almost entirely in Service hands, as was the new study of operational research which had itself originated from the early application of radar.

As examples of the tasks undertaken within establishments of the Department of Scientific and Industrial Research the following may be noted. The Road Research Laboratory performed a wide variety of investigations including some in connection with the effect of bombs on buildings and dams, disposal of unexploded bombs and the construction of airfields. The Food Investigation Laboratories concerned themselves on behalf of the Ministry of Food mainly with dehydration. The Forest Products Research Laboratory investigated various types of timber substitution while the Fuel Research Station worked both on producer gas as a substitute motor vehicle fuel and on incendiary bomb mixtures, flame-thrower fuels and smoke camouflage. At the National Physical Laboratory the Ship Division tested equipment for Mulberry harbours for the invasion of Europe and worked on the detection and improvement of mines. The Building Research Station carried out similar work to the Road Research Laboratory on the effect of explosives and incendiaries on buildings.

Although inquiries had started earlier the first official body created to examine the possibility of an atomic bomb was the MAUD Committee, a sub-committee of the Committee for the Scientific Survey of Air Warfare in the Ministry of Aircraft Production. It was set up in April 1940 and before the end of the year the Ministry had signed contracts with certain universities and with Imperial

Chemical Industries for research and manufacture. The reports of this committee were studied by the Defence Services Panel of the Scientific Advisory Committee who recommended that the development of the bomb should proceed, and it was decided in the autumn of 1941 to place it in the hands of the Department of Scientific and Industrial Research where for security reasons it was given the cover name of the Directorate of Tube Alloys (see p 10). Although some work continued in the United Kingdom throughout the war it was recognized that full-scale manufacture could at that time be established only in the United States. There had been communication with the American government and its scientists from the early days of the project but it proved difficult to settle terms for really close collaboration. In August 1943 the Quebec Agreement provided for the establishment of a Combined Policy Committee and the full interchange of information. Upon this Agreement many of the British researchers moved to the United States. Joint research had been carried on in Canada since early 1943 and a representative of that country served on the new Combined Policy Committee. Though Anglo-American collaboration continued until after the end of the war plans for an experimental establishment and a production plant in the United Kingdom were under consideration at this time.

Included among the records below are some of the Imperial Trust, which was established in 1916 to finance research to Industrial Research Associations. It was wound up in 1956 and its property rights and liabilities were taken over by the Department.

The Records

AB 1   War of 1939-1945: Correspondence and Papers
        These concern the atomic energy project and its organization.
AB 2   Anglo-Canadian Joint Project 1939-1946: Reports
        Most pieces date from 1943, but there is one piece of 1941 concerning the preparation of uranium.
AB 3   War of 1939-1945: Clarendon Project
        Papers accumulated by the Clarendon Laboratory, University of Oxford, during its work on the gaseous diffusion method of separating uranium isotopes.
AB 4   War of 1939-1945: British Reports
        A collection of reports describing various aspects of atomic energy research and development work in Britain.
AB 5   Chalk River Project, 1942-1946: Engineering Drawings
        These relate to buildings and equipment at the Chalk River Laboratory of the Canadian National Research Council.
AVIA 43 Personal Files
        Closed for 50 or 75 years.
AY 2   Water Pollution Research Board: Reports
        See also DSIR 13.
AY 6   Fuel Research Station: Reports and Papers
        See also DSIR 8.
AY 7   Fuel Research Station: Registered Files
        See also DSIR 8.
AY 8   Torry Research Station: Registered Files
        These concern research on fish as food.
AY 18   Princes Risborough Laboratory: Reports
        These are records of the Forest Products Research Board, and include progress reports on timber and glues for aircraft production. See also DSIR 7.
DSIR 1 Minute Books
        Minutes of the Advisory Council.
DSIR 2 Advisory Council and Committees: Meetings Files
        Files preserved in this class contain complete sets of papers for the meetings of the Advisory Council, the Scientific Grants Committee and the Industrial Grants Committee. The papers include memoranda and progress reports on research projects, reports from the individual committees, reports from research associations, applications for renewal of grants, and the agenda sheets and approved minutes of each meeting.
DSIR 4 Building Research: Correspondence and Papers
        Meetings files of the Building Research Board and its committees, and general files on administration and control of building research and the Building Research Station.

DSIR 5	Chemistry Research Board

DSIR 5   Chemistry Research Board
          This class contains a few files of the Chemical Research Laboratory.
DSIR 6   Food Investigation Board
          Meetings files of the Board and its committees, and files on the administration and work of the research stations and laboratories engaged in food investigation.
DSIR 7   Forest Products Research Board and Laboratory: Files
          Meetings files of the Board; files on the administration and work of the Forest Products Research Laboratory and on various bodies concerned with the utilization of timber. See also AY 18.
DSIR 8   Fuel Research Board
          Meetings files of the Board and of various committees concerned with fuel research; and files on research projects and the work of the Fuel Research Station. See also AY 6-7.
DSIR 9   Geological Survey Board
          This class contains a few wartime papers, including a report on the desirability of a general programme of boring.
DSIR 10   National Physical Laboratory: Registered Files
          Files on the administration of the Laboratory, accommodation, staffing, finance, investigations at the Laboratory, standards, patents, and the William Froude National Tank.
DSIR 11   Radio Research Board
          Meetings files of the Radio Research Board and its committees, and files on the Radio Research Station.
DSIR 12   Road Research Board
          This class includes wartime minutes of Board meetings, papers of the Road Tar Research Committee and a number of general administrative files. See also DSIR 27 and DSIR 28.
DSIR 13   Water Pollution Research Board and Laboratory
          These files relate mainly to general research. See also AY 2.
DSIR 14   Atmospheric Pollution Research Committee
          Meetings files of the Committee and reports, etc, of the Standing Conference of Co-operating Bodies.
DSIR 15   Imperial Trust
          The class comprises minute books, files relating to the meetings and general files about investments, grants and payments, constitution and functions.
DSIR 16   Industrial Research Associations
          These files mainly concern conditions of grants to Associations.
DSIR 17   Registered Files: General Series
          Policy and procedure files relating to finance; grants to universities, institutes, research workers and students; minutes to the lord president; relations with foreign countries and other government departments and institutions; various research proposals and projects; patents; post-war research and development; publicity and trade-marks.
DSIR 18   Registered Files: Establishment Series
          Selected files dealing with several aspects of the Department's organization and staffing, including appointments to the Advisory Council.
DSIR 19   Gas Cylinders and Containers Committee
          Papers on the constitution of the Committee, and meetings files of the Committee and its sub-committee.
DSIR 21   Pest Infestation Research Committees
          Meetings files of the Committees and some papers concerning extra-mural research.
DSIR 22   Aeronautical Research Council: Minutes of Meetings
          Minutes of meetings of the Aeronautical Research Committee and its panels and sub-committees.
DSIR 23   Aeronautical Research Council: Reports and Papers
          Reports and papers in the 'T' and plain numbers series, relating to research, trials, examination of foreign work in aeronautics and administrative matters. Many of these papers have been published in the 'R' and 'M' series.
DSIR 24   Aeronautical Research Council: Correspondence
DSIR 25   Pest Infestation Research Laboratory: Papers
DSIR 27   Road Research Laboratory: Reports
          Includes reports relating to bombing research and to various investigations undertaken for the services and for government departments in relation to civil defence, airfield construction, etc. See also DSIR 12 and DSIR 28.
DSIR 28   Road Research Laboratory: Files

This class includes meetings files of the Road Research Board and associated bodies and a number of files concerning estimates and programmes. See also DSIR 12 and DSIR 27.

DSIR 36   Records Bureau Files
Includes certain technical reports concerning air raid shelters, effect of explosions and blast, etc, at one time housed in the DSIR Library.

HM Stationery Office

Name	Date of appointment
Controller	
Sir William R Codling	1919
Lt-Col Sir Norman Scorgie	1942

The Records

STAT 14   Files of Correspondence, Series II
Includes papers concerning preservation of war literature, office machinery for government departments supplied under Lend-Lease arrangements, and publication of the United Kingdom edition of 'Stars and Stripes', the US Army newspaper.

Ministry of Supply
(from 1 August 1939)

Name	Date of appointment
Minister	
Leslie Burgin, MP	14 July 1939
Herbert Morrison, MP	12 May 1940
Sir Andrew Duncan, MP	3 Oct 1940
Lord Beaverbrook	29 June 1941
Sir Andrew Duncan, MP	4 Feb 1942
Parliamentary secretaries	
John J Llewellin, MP	14 July 1939
Harold Macmillan, MP	15 May 1940 - 4 Feb 1942
Lord Portal	4 Sept 1940 - 4 Mar 1942
Ralph Assheton, MP	4 Feb 1942 - 30 Dec 1942
Charles Peat, MP	4 Mar 1942 - 22 Mar 1945
Duncan Sandys, MP	30 Dec 1942 - 21 Nov 1944

John Wilmot, MP	21 Nov 1944 - 23 May 1945
James de Rothschild, MP	22 Mar 1945 - 23 May 1945

Permanent secretary

Sir William Brown (on secondment from Board of Trade)	1940
Sir William Douglas	1942

Director general of munitions production

Eng vice-adm Sir Harold Brown	Aug 1939

Controller general of munitions production

Eng vice-adm Sir Harold Brown	July 1941
Graham Cunningham (later Sir Graham Cunningham)	1942

Director general of explosives

Viscount Weir of Eastwood	Sept 1939
John Rogers	May 1941
J W Armit	1943

Director general of tanks and transportation

Peter F Bennett, MP	Sept 1939
Geoffrey D Burton	1940

Chairman of the Armoured Fighting Vehicles Division

Commander E R Micklem [Office lapsed December 1944]	Oct 1942

Director general of programmes

Sir Walter T Layton	May 1940
Hugh T Weeks [Office lapsed June 1943]	1942

Chairman of the Committee of Controllers

Sir Andrew Duncan, MP [Office lapsed January 1940]	1939

Second secretary for raw materials

William Palmer (later Sir William Palmer)	Sept 1939

Director general of raw materials

Sir Kenneth Lee	1942

Director general of supply services

Gilbert S Szlumper	1942

Controller general of machine tools

[Sir] Percy H Mills	June 1941
Stanley F Steward	1944

Controller general of research and development

Oliver Lucas	July 1941
H J Gough	1942

Senior supply officer

Eng vice-adm Sir Harold Brown	1942

Senior military adviser

Lt-Gen Sir Maurice Taylor	1939
Lt-Gen Sir Wilfrid Lindsell	June 1941
Lt-Gen Laurence Carr	Apr 1942
Maj-Gen F J Evetts	Aug 1944

Director general of Army requirements
[Office part of the War Office]

Robert J Sinclair	Oct 1939
Maj-Gen D R D Fisher	July 1942

In the years preceding the war much consideration was given to the problem of organizing the flow of arms and other equipment to the Armed Forces and the creation of a Ministry of Supply was much canvassed. The industrial and, therefore, civilian processes of supply had to be linked to military requirements in respect both of design and of quantities, while at the same time the conflicting demands of the Services had to be co-ordinated with each other and with civilian requirements. In the event it was not found possible to divorce naval production from the Admiralty and, as a consequence, aircraft production remained initially with the Air Ministry. When, therefore, the Ministry of Supply was set up immediately before the outbreak of war its responsibilities were limited to Army supplies and certain articles in common use among the Services.

The Ministry was created by the transfer from the War Office of all the departments concerned with supply, design, inspection and research, and from the Board of Trade of the Raw Materials Department. Co-ordination between the Ministry and the War Office, its major customer, was secured by various provisions such as the seating of the director-general of Army requirements in the War Office on both the Supply and Army Councils and direct communications between the War Office Technical Directorates and their opposite numbers in the Ministry of Supply. These communications were limited to exchanges of information and did not extend to the placing of orders. Demands for supplies were submitted through the director-general of Army requirements who was also responsible for keeping the General Staff informed of progress. The staff of the Ministry included many Army officers to whom reference will be made below.

Immediately beneath the minister the Supply Council was responsible for the general policy of the Ministry. It consisted, at the beginning of the war, of the minister, the secretary, the director-general of munitions production, the director-general of explosives, the director-general of tanks and transportation, the chairman of the Committee of Controllers, the director-general of finance, the senior military adviser and the parliamentary secretary, and the director-general of Army requirements was soon added. It began by meeting weekly, but as the war proceeded its membership grew and both its meetings and papers circulated to it became fewer. In March 1941 a smaller Executive Committee consisting at first of the minister, the parliamentary secretaries, the director-general of munitions production, the director-general of programmes, and the director of explosives production was created to undertake a general review of the Ministry's work and to deal with specific items as they arose. It met much more frequently than the Council and at one time could be said to transact the day to day business of the Ministry. In February 1942 part of the Committee became the Building Executive and undertook the increasingly important duty, which had been laid upon the Committee, of controlling Ministry applications for scarce building resources.

Some aspects of the broad structure of the Ministry will appear from the titles of the officials listed in the preceding paragraphs. The organization soon became immensely complex and was subject to frequent changes in almost all its parts so that it is not possible within the present compass to provide more than the outlines. The initial structure, apart from the minister, the parliamentary secretary and the permanent secretary, provided for a director-general of munitions production, a director-general of equipment and stores, a director-general of explosives, a director-general of tanks and transportation, a director-general of finance, a second secretary of raw materials, a senior military adviser and a chairman of raw materials controllers. Directors-general and equivalent officials were each served by a number of directorates. The director-general of munitions production, for example, controlled directors of artillery, ammunition production, instrument production, ordnance factories, movements and components, machine tools, and scientific research as well as the Area Organization, while the secretary was responsible for a Contracts Directorate and Secretariat and Statistics Branches. There was thus a number of broad production groups responsible for all stages of production together with common service elements for such matters as contracts and finance. As problems arose and gaps appeared attempts were made to supply more co-ordination or attach greater importance to particular posts in the production field by elevating directors to directors-general and creating fresh posts. In the spring of 1940, for example, the growth in the number of ordnance factories led to the appointment of a director-general of ordnance factories devoted to their equipment and control, and ammunition production was also elevated to a directorate-general. Later in the year a director-general of programmes was appointed to co-ordinate the demands received from the War Office and elsewhere. He distributed them to six directors-general who placed orders via the director of contracts under the director-general of finance (from February 1940) and were responsible for chasing progress. This process of elevation led eventually, and perhaps inevitably, to the creation of a layer in the organization above the directorates-general. In July 1941 the overall charge of all the production groups was placed in the hands of a controller-general of munitions production who eventually had as many as fourteen directors-general or their equivalents responsible to him. There were in addition a director-general of supply services, responsible for such services as transportation, a controller-general of machine tools and a controller general of research and development, the latter taking charge of all research and development, which were now separated from production. In October of the following year a new post of senior supply officer was created at this level to co-ordinate the work of the Armaments Research and Design Departments and the Ordnance Board, thus taking over some of the responsibilities of the controller-general of research and development whose post was now abolished. Other aspects of his work went to the newly established post of chairman of the Armoured Fighting Vehicles Division which was created in an attempt to remedy the failures experienced in the production of tanks. At the upper level the organization continued in this form with little change to the end of the war. The other interests of the Ministry continued to be handled by the permanent secretary, the senior military adviser, and the director-general of raw materials controls.

Among the problems around which pre-war discussions of a Ministry of Supply had revolved was that of the co-ordination of demands. Before the war this was the province of the principal supply officers and their Supply Board within the Committee of Imperial Defence system, and their work was taken over by the Central Priority Department of the Ministry of Supply. Its position therein was largely a matter of administrative convenience and the Department dealt with the Production Directorates of the Ministry on the same terms as it did with the Admiralty or the Ministry of Aircraft Production, and was represented in each of these institutions by a principal priority officer. The Central Priority Department was responsible, under various War Cabinet Sub-Committees, for the allocation of materials and manufacturing capacity but not of labour which came under the Ministry of Labour and National Service. When the Production Executive was established in April 1941 the Central Priority Department was transferred to it (see p 137).

The Secretariat of the Ministry was responsible, in addition to the usual parliamentary and establishments work, for the placing of contracts, which was immediately under the director-general of finance, raw materials, labour recruitment and management, and various co-ordinating functions handled through the Production Secretariat under the second secretary (supply). This body had begun as a statistical section under the director-general of munitions production in War Office days and came to represent the Ministry of Supply in priority questions and to handle its communications with the overseas supply missions. Representatives of the Production Secretariat were attached to the Production Directorates-General and in May 1941 it took over responsibility for labour supply. During the war a considerable degree of financial control was devolved by the Treasury to the Ministry. Authorization of major expenditure was in the hands of the Treasury Inter-Service Committee, containing representatives of the Supply and Service Departments. The function of the Raw Materials Directorate was to co-ordinate and calculate the demands for raw materials and other supplies and to present them to the purchasing missions and to the Ministry of War Transport. It also had responsibility for salvage. In some cases it acted as the direct controller of the supply and distribution of a particular material, but where an appreciable amount of work of this kind was involved a separate executive control was established. These were often based on pre-war trade associations and were handled by controllers of considerable standing. The general supervision of the Raw Materials Controls was in the hands of the Raw Materials Directorate and there was for a short time a chairman of controllers and later a director-general of raw materials controls. Without depriving the Ministry of Supply of its functions an interest in raw materials was acquired, together with some officers of the Ministry of Supply, by the Ministry of Production when it was set up in July 1942.

From the beginnings of the Ministry an attempt was made to refine the control of production by the preparation of statistics. A Central Statistics Branch was established in 1939 to prepare forecasts for the War Office, to total demands, contracts, deliveries and raw material requirements. This work was pressed forward when a director-general of programmes was appointed in May 1940 to prepare longer-term programmes of production. This was done by collating and co-ordinating forecasts of the production departments and relating them to the requirements stated by the War Office. Regular forecasts of this kind were provided for the War Office, the War Cabinet and the United States, among others, and continued after the Directorate-General of Programmes had been reduced to a directorate in 1942 and placed under the second secretary (supply).

Another War Office interest in the Ministry of Supply was met by the Inspection Departments, staffed by Army officers under the senior military adviser, who was also responsible for the provision of works services at certain out-stations. The inspectors were attached to the Production Directorates and ensured that munitions met their specifications before delivery to the Services. The senior military adviser was also responsible for the Passive Air Defence of Ministry of Supply establishments.

The development of the production of tanks suffered greatly from the neglect and restrictions of the inter-war years and frequent changes were made in the organization of tank supply as the successive attempts to make good the lost years revealed fresh gaps and deficiencies. In May 1940 a Tank Board was established, to investigate the organization of tank design and production and to provide an additional link between the Ministry and War Office. In January 1941 it was recast and given more power to satisfy War Office requirements, but again had to be reconstituted in July. Meanwhile within the Ministry the director-general of tanks and transportation was relieved of responsibility for Engineering stores and transport, and his Department of Tank Design very gradually increased its authority. Even so by September 1942 the position was so unsatisfactory that a further reorganization was put in hand and a post of chairman of the Armoured Fighting Vehicles Division was created with a director-general of production subordinate to him. Shortly afterwards a director-general of research and development was also appointed. This concentration of all aspects of tank supply, separated from other munitions, continued to the end of the war.

Organization of the research and development work of the Ministry also presented its problems. It took over the War Office research and experimental establishments when it was set up, including those dealing with radar, chemical warfare, rockets and signals, and also undertook the responsibilities of the War Office in respect of interdepartmental organs such as the Ordnance Board and the Chemical Board. The importance of scientific work in the Second World War is well illustrated in the activities of the Ministry of Supply. Equally well illustrated is the difficulty created when the responsibility for the stage linking research and production, namely design and development, fell between the Ministry and its user departments. One of the measures taken to improve performance in this field was the creation of the Scientific Advisory Council to the Ministry which began work in 1940. Its object was to ensure that the Ministry took advantage of the latest scientific discoveries and the most advanced research techniques and made the best use of outside resources. The Council had power to consider and to initiate research and development proposals, to advise on scientific matters and on the selection of scientific personnel. It worked through a large number of specialist sub-committees and continued on the same broad lines throughout the war. Organization of research and development within the Ministry, on the other hand, was subject to a number of changes. At the beginning of the war the director of scientific research controlled a number of branches dealing with research subjects, patents and inventions, and took on the provision of the secretariat to the Scientific Advisory Council. He had overall control of the Ministry's scientific staff but did not control the research and experimental establishments in which the work was actually carried out. These establishments were responsible to the appropriate technical directorates and so to the production departments. This division was maintained with the creation of additional technical directorates and further uncertainty was introduced by making the director of scientific research in turn responsible to the director-general of munitions production, the permanent secretary and the director of explosives production. In August 1941 the lines of division were redrawn and all research and development was placed in the hands of a controller-general of research and development, a member of the Supply Council, with a view to tightening control over this work and to giving it a proper voice inside and outside the Ministry. The director of scientific research became the deputy controller-general of research and development. This arrangement lasted little more than a year for the criticisms continued, particularly in respect of the handling of the Research and Design Departments and their liaison with users. This led to the appointment of an interdepartmental committee under Dr H L Guy which recommended reinforcement of these departments. Shortly afterwards the post of controller-general of research and development was abolished and his department dissolved so that research and development were now redistributed among the production departments under the chairman of the Armoured Fighting Vehicles Division, with his own director-general of research and development, the newly appointed senior supply officer, with much strengthened Armaments Research and Design Departments, and the controller-general of munitions production to whom the director of scientific research, later the director-general of scientific research and development, was once more responsible. This organization carried research and development through the later years of the war when the Ministry of Supply was concerned, for example, with the development of defences against flying bombs and in the construction of artificial harbours for the invasion of Europe in conjunction with Combined Operations Headquarters.

All the Supply Departments, together with the Ministry of Labour and National Service and the Board of Trade were concerned in the local organization of Area Boards, with employer and union representation to assist them, which co-ordinated official activities at the point where the work was carried out. They were at first organized and controlled by the Ministry of Supply but later came under the Production Executive and the Ministry of Production.

Inevitably the Ministry was also concerned with overseas activities. The British Purchasing Commission in the United States was established in the early months of the war and not long afterwards a mission was sent to develop tank production in that country. In March, 1941 a British Central Scientific Office was established in Washington for purposes of scientific co-operation between Britain and America. In 1942 administration of this office passed to the Ministry of Production. There was also an Eastern Supply Group consisting of South Africa, India, Australia and New Zealand, for their production had also to be taken into account, while the Ministry extended its supply activities by playing its part in the Allied Supply Organization in Russia (see p 12).

The filing system of the Ministry of Supply was inherited from the War Office with its central registration supported by branch memoranda. The departments transferred to the Ministry of Supply naturally brought their files with them and from the beginning there was an organized central registry under whose control files were arranged in series denoted by numbers from 200 to 325. The series numbers were followed by abbreviated descriptions and sub-numbers to indicate individual files. Outstations used both centrally registered files and their own series of branch folders for their records. The distribution of Ministry of Supply functions after the war had its effect on their files which is apparent from their present arrangement. Some non-ferrous raw materials went to the Board of Trade via the Ministry of Materials and iron and steel to the Ministry of Power. The supply functions transferred from the War Office in 1939 were handed back in 1959 when the Ministry of Supply became the Ministry of Aviation. The files transferred to the War Office were distributed among its classes except for those which had been both opened and closed in the Ministry of Supply; these form a separate class. Earlier, in August 1945 the Ministry of Supply and the Ministry of Aircraft Production operated under a single minister, and in April 1946 the Ministry of Aircraft Production was dissolved and its powers passed to the Ministry of Supply.

The Records

AVIA 7   Royal Radar Establishment: Files
Includes files of the Air Defence Research and Development Establishment and the Radar Research and Development Establishment of the Ministry of Supply.

AVIA 11   Ministry of Supply: Private Office Papers
Papers of ministers and parliamentary secretaries.

AVIA 12   Ministry of Supply: Unregistered Papers
This class includes permanent secretaries' papers, committee records, reports of missions and visits, radar equipment papers, Lend-Lease, German reparations, statistics, and some papers concerning the wartime history and organization of the Ministry of Supply and its later merger with the Ministry of Aircraft Production.

AVIA 22   Ministry of Supply: Registered Files
This class consists of files of the Ministry of Supply which relate to functions not tranferred to the War Office in 1959. Files relating to functions, which were transferred to the War Office, are in WO 32 and WO 185.

AVIA 23   Signals Research and Development Establishment: Reports, Technical Notes and Memoranda
           Reports of the Signals Experimental Establishment and Signals Research and Development
           Establishment. See also AVIA 61 and AVIA 74.
AVIA 26   Royal Radar Establishment: Reports and Memoranda
           Includes reports and memoranda of the Air Defence Research and Development Establishment
           and the Radar Research and Development Establishment of the Ministry of Supply.
AVIA 33   Handbooks and Directories, etc
AVIA 38   North American Supplies
           Mainly files of the British Air Commission, the British Ministry of Supply Mission and the
           British Supply Council in the United States. See also CAB 115 and FO 115.
AVIA 40   Rocket Propulsion Establishment: German Drawings
           These were taken into custody by the Allied agencies engaged in collecting German documents
           at the end of the war.
AVIA 41   Rocket Propulsion Establishment (PDE Aberforth): Technical Reports
           These cover early work on missile technology by the former Projectile Development Establish-
           ment.
AVIA 42   British Central Scientific Office: Registered Files
           Files of the Office established in Washington in 1941 and re-styled the British Commonwealth
           Scientific Office in mid-summer 1944, when it merged with the scientific missions of Australia,
           New Zealand and South Africa.
AVIA 43   Personal Files
           Closed for 50 or 75 years.
AVIA 44   Ministry of Supply and Ministry of Aircraft Production: Scientific and Technical Monographs
AVIA 45   Tropical Testing Establishment Nigeria: Reports and Memoranda
           These relate mainly to the testing of radar and radio components under tropical conditions.
AVIA 46   Ministry of Supply Files: Series 1 (Establishment)
           Include narratives and documents bearing upon wartime events and developments.
AVIA 48   Rocket Propulsion Establishment: Files
AVIA 49   Ministry of Supply Files: Series 2 (General)
           Includes files dealing with German reparations. See also BT 211.
AVIA 53   Ministry of Supply Files: Series 6 (Contracts)
           Include papers dealing with claims concerning wartime inventions for the Armed Forces.
AVIA 55   Ministry of Supply Files: Series 8 (Production)
AVIA 57   Ministry of Supply Files: Series 12 (Disposals)
AVIA 61   Signals Research and Development Establishment: Unregistered Papers
           See also AVIA 23 and AVIA 74.
AVIA 65   Ministry of Supply and successor departments: Branch Registry Files
           A few relate to the wartime period, including some containing minutes and papers of Trades Joint
           Councils.
AVIA 74   Signals Research and Development Establishment: Registered Files
           A few papers relate to the wartime period. See also AVIA 23 and AVIA 61.
AVIA 900   Specimens of Classes of Documents Destroyed
           Includes specimen requisitions of the British Supply Mission for supplies in Canada and the
           USA.
BT 131   War Histories (1939-1945) Files
           Includes material collected in the Ministry of Supply and subsequently transferred to the Board
           of Trade for the preparation of the *History of the Second World War-The Control of Raw
           Materials.* They are mainly narratives relating to various commodities.
BT 200   Norfolk Flax Limited
           These relate to the takeover by the Admiralty on behalf of the Ministry of Supply of the Norfolk
           Flax Station as a government establishment.
BT 201   Flax Controller: Miscellaneous Papers
DEFE 15   Royal Armament Research and Development Establishment and predecessors: Technical
           Reports and other Records
           This class contains a few administrative records and a number of wartime reports and theoretical
           research memoranda.
POWE 5   Ministry of Supply: Iron and Steel Control Registered Files
           Mainly papers cited in Official Histories.
SUPP 4   Contract Record Books
           These were compiled by the Division of the under-secretary (contracts) and constitute a record
           of all contracts placed.
SUPP 5   Ordnance Establishments: Headquarters and Factory Records
           Entry books and miscellaneous records maintained by the Royal Ordnance Factories, etc, at

Woolwich, Waltham Abbey and elsewhere. See also WORK 26.

SUPP 6   Ordnance Board, etc: Proceedings, Reports and Memoranda
         Includes records of the Ordnance Board of the Ministry of Supply.

SUPP 14 Ministry of Supply: Files
         These deal mainly with the control and importation of raw materials.

SUPP 18 Joint Industrial Council: Minutes
         Minutes of meetings from its inception in 1941.

T 246   Central Priority Department: Allocation of Raw Materials
         A few files of the Department are also in AVIA 22.

WO 32   Registered Files, General Series
         Includes files opened in the War Office before 1939 and completed in the Ministry of Supply.

WO 185   Ministry of Supply: Files
         This class contains files opened and closed in the Ministry of Supply relating to functions which
         reverted to the War Office in 1959; files which were opened in the War Office before September
         1939 and whose life was completed in the Ministry of Supply are in WO 32; files on which both
         Ministry of Supply and Army matters were dealt with have been included with the rest of the
         Ministry of Supply's registered files in AVIA 22.

WO 188   Chemical Defence Experimental Establishment: Correspondence and Papers
         Include intelligence reports on development of biological warfare by the enemy.

WO 189   Chemical Defence Experimental Establishment: Reports and Technical Papers

WO 194   Fighting Vehicles Research and Development Establishment and predecessor Establishments:
         Records
         The class includes technical reports of tests of fighting vehicles by the Mechanical Warfare
         Experimental Establishment, minutes of meetings of the Mechanical Warfare Board, data books
         and photographs and drawings of vehicles.

WO 195   Scientific Advisory Council: Papers
         Reports and papers of the Advisory Council on Scientific Research and Technical Development.

WO 254   Contracts Precedent Books
         A small collection of general notebooks and notes extracted from them summarizing decisions
         on supplies contracts and related matters.

WO 278   Chemical Inspection Department
         One file relating to emergency laboratory accommodation at Cambridge University.

WO 313   Committee on Awards to Inventors
         Minutes of proceedings.

Tithe Redemption Commission

Name	Date of appointment
Secretary	
H G Richardson	1936

The Records

IR 65   Tithe Redemption Office: Registered Files
         A few deal with changes in procedure, etc, as a result of emergency legislation.

IR 89   Tithe Redemption Commission: Minutes
         Signed minutes of proceedings and documents circulated to the commissioners.

Ministry of Town and Country Planning

Name	Date of appointment
Minister	
W S Morrison, MP	Feb 1943
(minister designate 30 December 1942)	
Parliamentary secretary	
H G Strauss, MP (designate 30 December 1942)	Feb 1943
A Jenkins, MP	22 Mar 1945
Permanent secretary	
Sir Geoffrey Whiskard	1943
Deputy secretary	
L E Neal	1943

The Ministry of Town and Country Planning was established in February 1943 with the duty of 'securing consistency and continuity in the framing and execution of a national policy with respect to the use and development of land throughout England and Wales'. Planning of this kind had been based on local authorities before the war and was therefore the responsibility of the Ministry of Health. Interest in it had developed gradually, but it was the devastation caused by bombing attacks, which inevitably involved the War Damage Commission and the need to consider town and country planning interests and post-war reconstruction in authorizing repairs, that gave it special impetus. The minister of works and buildings, Lord Reith, was also interested in reconstruction, particularly from the building aspect, and in June 1942 the planning responsibilities of the Ministry of Health were transferred to his Ministry which became the Ministry of Works and Planning. In addition to setting up a Consultative Panel on Physical Reconstruction, an Inter-departmental Committee on Reconstruction and a Survey of Social Reconstruction to be undertaken by Nuffield College, he had established two committees in 1941, one on payment of compensation and recovery of betterment in respect of public control of the use of land and the other on land utilization in rural areas. These produced respectively the Uthwatt and Scott Reports which, together with the earlier Barlow Report on the distribution of the industrial population, formed the basis on which the Ministry of Town and Country Planning, when established in 1943, tackled the work of reconstruction.

This work continued to be based on the local authorities, and legislation was introduced to impose on them the duty of planning and to extend their powers. Exchequer grants were made available to assist in acquiring and clearing war-damaged areas. An Advisory Panel on the redevelopment of city centres and an Advisory Committee on estate development and management were established in 1943 and 1945 respectively in connection with redevelopment of this kind. Other planning duties concerned new towns, national parks, wildlife conservation and the preservation of ancient monuments and historic buildings.

The Records

These general planning policy and related files include some papers of the Ministry of Works and Buildings and the Ministry of Works and Planning.

HLG 79   Town and Country Planning: Local Authority Files
This class consists of files of correspondence with local authorities concerning their plans and development proposals.

HLG 80   Committee on Land Utilization in Rural Areas (Scott Committee)
This class consists of published and unpublished material submitted in evidence, papers circulated to members and minutes of meetings, together with related papers of the Ministry of Works and Buildings, the Ministry of Works and Planning and the Ministry of Town and Country Planning.

HLG 81   Expert Committee on Compensation and Betterment (Uthwatt Committee)
This class contains published and unpublished material submitted in evidence, papers circulated to members and minutes of meetings, together with related papers of the Ministry of Works and Buildings, the Ministry of Works and Planning and the Ministry of Town and Country Planning.

HLG 82   Nuffield College Social Reconstruction Survey
This class contains correspondence, reports and papers of the Ministry of Works and Buildings, the Ministry of Works and Planning and the Ministry of Town and Country Planning relating to an inquiry which the College was asked to undertake by the minister of works and buildings as part of its proposed local surveys. The subjects for the inquiry were: the redistribution of industry and population brought about by the war; the effects of war on the working of the public social services; the human effects of evacuation, industrial migration, etc; and the bearing of all these factors on the general problems of social and economic reorganization.

HLG 85   Greater London Plan 1944 (Professor Abercrombie's Correspondence)
See also HLG 104.

HLG 86   Ministry of Works and Buildings, Reconstruction of Town and Country, Advisory Panels and Committees
This class includes papers of the Interdepartmental Advisory Committee on Reconstruction (1941), the Consultative Panel on Physical Reconstruction (1941), the Advisory Committee on Reconstruction (1942), the '1940 Council' and the Reconstruction Areas Group.

HLG 88   War Damaged Areas, Advisory Bodies on Redevelopment
Minutes and reports of the Advisory Panel on Redevelopment of City Centres, 1943 to 1944, and the Central Advisory Committee on Estate Development and Management, 1945 to 1946, together with related correspondence and papers of the Ministry of Town and Country Planning.

HLG 89   Minerals
Policy files relating to the planning control of mineral workings.

HLG 90   New Towns: General and Finance Files
These concern the planning and development of new towns.

HLG 92   National Parks and Countryside, General and Finance Files
General and financial correspondence and papers relating to the planning and implementation of the national parks and access to the countryside policy.

HLG 93   National Parks Committee (Hobhouse Committee) and Wildlife Conservation Special Committee
Includes John Dower's Preliminary Report on National Parks, 1944.

HLG 103   Historic Buildings and Ancient Monuments: Files
See also WORK 14.

HLG 104   Planning and Redevelopment Files: 99200 Series
One file concerning publicity for the Greater London plan, and another regarding an Interdepartmental Committee concerning new development of factories, 1944 to 1945, set up on the suggestion of Ernest Bevin as minister of labour and national service.

HLG 107   Ministry of Housing and Local Government: Regional Files
These relate mainly to the Northern Region of the Ministry of Town and Country Planning.

HLG 124   Establishment Division: Registered Files (EST Series)
Papers concerning the setting-up and organization of the Ministry.

HLG 125   Planning Services Division: Research Files (PS3 Series)
This class includes papers on National Parks, conservation areas, rural planning and research officers' conferences.

Board of Trade

Name	Date of appointment
President	
Oliver Stanley, MP	28 May 1937
Sir Andrew Duncan, MP	5 Jan 1940
Oliver Lyttelton, MP	3 Oct 1940
Sir Andrew Duncan, MP	29 June 1941
J J Llewellin (later Lord Llewellin), MP	4 Feb 1942
Hugh Dalton, MP	22 Feb 1942
Parliamentary secretary	
Gwilym Lloyd George, MP	6 Sept 1939
Charles Waterhouse, MP	8 Feb 1941
Permanent secretary	
Sir William B Brown	1937
(Seconded as acting secretary to the Ministry of Supply, 1940-1942; as secretary to the Petroleum Division of the Ministry of Fuel and Power, 1942-1943; as secretary to the Ministry of Home Security, November 1943-1945)	
Sir Arnold Overton	1941
Chief economic adviser to his majesty's government	
Sir Frederick Leith-Ross	1932
Principal industrial adviser	
Sir William Palmer	1944

At the beginning of the war certain departments of the Board of Trade became or were transferred to new ministries. The Food (Defence Plans) Department became the Ministry of Food, the Mercantile Marine Department became the Ministry of Shipping and the Raw Materials Department formed part of the Ministry of Supply. At a later stage the Mines Department and Petroleum Department, together with that part of the Industries and Manufactures Department which dealt with gas and electricity, became the Ministry of Fuel and Power. The activities of all these departments are described in connection with the new ministries.

In addition to its continuing responsibility for the Patent Office and Industrial Property Department the functions remaining to the Board of Trade were the control of imports and exports and the oversight of production for civilian consumption other than food. In the course of the war control over consumption was steadily extended and refined and this process provided the bulk of the Board's work. As the pressure increased it became the Board's responsibility to ensure that minimum needs were met and that the goods available were distributed where they could be most useful. To identify these needs and provide the Board with the necessary intelligence, distribution officers were appointed in the Civil Defence Regions in the spring of 1941 and a Consumer Needs Branch was established at Headquarters. Surveys were made by means of panels of consumers of various types of goods and the distribution officers from time to time conducted assessments in individual towns. They were also responsible for organizing special distributions of goods to bombed areas.

The methods available for control were price regulation, concentration of production, consumer rationing and licensing of production. Price regulation was introduced at the very beginning of the war with the Prices of Goods Act. Its object was to prevent profits from rising above pre-war levels and for its administration a Central Price Regulation Committee and seventeen local committees were established. The Act came into operation with its first Order at the beginning of 1940 and it was supplemented towards the end of that year by Orders under Defence Regulations to fix maximum prices for torch batteries. In July 1941 the Goods and Services (Price Control) Act gave the Board power to fix maximum prices and margins. These powers extended to all the stages of distribution and were accompanied by provisions for enforcement. Inspectors were attached to the Local Price Regulation Committees to investigate breaches of the regulations. The first Limitation of Supplies Order was applied to textiles in April 1940. It restricted the supply of textiles by wholesalers, who were registered for this purpose, to three-quarters of the pre-war level except in the case of government orders or exports. The main object of the Order was to direct production into exports but with the intensification of the war it became clear that the prime need was to divert resources to war production. A Limitation of Supplies (Miscellaneous) Order came into force in June limiting supplies of a wide range of goods to two-thirds of the pre-war level. At the end of November levels were further reduced and an Investigation Section was established to undertake enforcement of the regulations. To ensure that the resources released by these restrictions were capable of being absorbed in war production a 'keeping step' section was established within the Board to maintain knowledge of the industrial situation in different parts of the country and to co-ordinate the operations of the Board with the plans of the Ministry of Labour and National Service and the Ministry of Supply. The success of these methods resulted in an uneconomic dispersal of the remaining work over a large number of firms and factories, which led inevitably to the policy of concentrating civilian production in some of them, thus releasing the remainder for war purposes. This scheme was announced in March 1941 and industries were encouraged to prepare their own plans of concentration. The surviving 'nucleus' factories were given preferential treatment in labour supply by the Ministry of Labour and National Service. Where industries failed to produce a concentration plan the Board could nominate nucleus firms and use the government's powers to deny raw materials and labour supply to the remainder. Concentration and re-concentration continued to be used in the following year as the problems of manpower supply became more than ever difficult. While concentration was under consideration towards the end of 1940 another form of control over industrial activity was also being planned in the shape of a controller-general of factory and storage premises responsible to the president of the Board of Trade. The first controller-general was appointed in March 1941 and his Control began operations in May with a survey of available premises. It was responsible for allocation of premises to be used by government departments for production and storage and all requests for such premises had to be channelled through it. In July 1941 the Location of Industry (Restriction) Order extended the authority of the Control to private industry by instituting a licensing system for the use of fresh premises for production or storage. The building of new factories and stores was allowed by the controller-general only if he was satisfied that no existing premises could by used.

The largest part of the Board's field of responsibility was the textile and clothing industry, and it operated a wool control scheme under a wool controller. By 1941 the effect of the controls in restricting the supply of clothing was such that rationing became necessary if injustice was not to follow, and at the beginning of June the Consumer Rationing Order was made. A 'points' scheme was employed and some children and industrial workers received extra points. Enforcement officers were appointed to seek out cases of evasion. To ensure that the ration would be honoured the Board had to influence firms to manufacture particular quantities of particular goods, and to ensure that they could do so it had to calculate the necessary amounts of cloth and demand them from the materials controls. The knowledge of consumer needs acquired through the panels was fitted into this planning. At the same time it became necessary to ensure that manufacturers did not concentrate their efforts on higher priced goods, and this was done by the scheme of utility clothing in which the cloths and articles made from them were closely specified and identified by a mark.

For other items within the Board's responsibility, such as household goods, special distribution schemes were introduced. Goods subject to such schemes could be supplied only in limited quantities to persons in specified occupations. To co-ordinate the various distribution schemes a Special Distribution Committee under the chairmanship of the parliamentary secretary was established in 1943.

For consumer goods other than clothing, steps were taken in 1942 to limit manufacture by means of licensing schemes, and Control of Manufacturing and Supply Orders made to this end replaced the Limitation of Supplies Orders for certain classes of goods. The manufacture of some goods was completely prohibited. For furniture a utility scheme was instituted which prevented manufacture except of certain approved patterns. Utility furniture could be sold only to customers with permits received from the Assistance Board. As with clothing this tight control involved the Board more closely with production planning and the securing of raw materials.

The Board was responsible for schemes of commodity, business and chattels insurance under the War Risks and War Damage Acts, which it operated in conjunction with the insurance companies. There were also schemes for free compensation in cases of need, and advance payments could be made on behalf of the Board of Trade by the Assistance Board. Compensation for damage to real property was in the hands of the War Damage Commission.

The Board's general responsibility for the country's external trade also imposed upon it a number of new duties. Immediately upon the outbreak of war the first of a number of Import Control Orders was made and by the following June so many classes of goods had been subjected to control that it was decided to place a general control on all imports. The main object of the early restrictions had been conservation of foreign exchange but it soon became one of the tools for diverting shipping and internal resources from inessentials into the war effort. An Import Licensing Committee including representatives of interested departments supervised the issuing of licences. In the export field foreign exchange was equally the object of the Board's activities and in the early stages of the war steps were taken to protect and promote production for export. In February 1940 an Export Council was established under the chairmanship of the president and industries were encouraged to form export groups. Export credit insurance was extended to meet the risks of war. On the other hand exports were controlled by licence from the outbreak of war to conserve essential materials and keep supplies from the enemy. As with imports this work was carried out in consultation with other interested departments, in particular the Ministry of Economic Warfare. Export control was extended and intensified as almost the whole of Europe came under German domination and at the same time the increasing demands of war production pressed heavily on the resources available for export. The course of events greatly reduced the value placed on exporting and early in 1941 the Export Council was enlarged to become the Industrial and Export Council with the additional duty of promoting the concentration schemes to which reference has been made. The Lend-Lease arrangement made by the United States (see p 173) gave us considerable relief from the need to export for exchange reasons and exports were henceforth primarily undertaken to help to maintain countries and industries essential for the more effective prosecution of the war. Control of exports became additionally necessary because of criticism in the United States that advantage was being taken of Lend-Lease supplies to promote them.

The organization of the Board was expanded as necessary to correspond with its wider wartime functions. The president was supported by a number of parliamentary secretaries of whom one was

158

responsible for the Department of Overseas Trade and another assisted him with Board of Trade duties. Under the permanent secretary there were a second secretary and an under-secretary who shared responsibility for the bulk of the Board's departments. Of these the Industries and Manufactures Department was divided by stages into four divisions, of which Industries and Manufactures I continued the pre-war functions and any others which were not assigned to the later created divisions. Its duties included price control and the oversight of retail facilities, while the Import Licensing Department was also attached to this Division. Industries and Manufactures II was first established in 1940 to administer the Limitation of Supplies Orders and was later given responsibility for concentration and for the clothes rationing scheme. It included the Consumer Needs Section, the Keeping Step Section and such Directorates as Civilian Clothing and Civilian Footwear. These were responsible for ensuring the necessary production. The Factory and Storage Premises Control was attached to this Division until August 1941. Industries and Manufactures III was responsible for the gas and electricity industries until they were transferred to the Ministry of Fuel and Power in 1942. By 1943 a new Industries and Manufactures III was in charge of enforcement and thus took over some aspects of the rationing scheme and the Consumer Needs Section. It also took over the Accountants Division and the Investigation Branch. In 1942 Industries and Manufactures IV was established to operate controls over production and consumption of consumer goods other than clothing and textiles. All these Divisions were responsible for the post-war reconstruction aspects of their business, but in January 1943 an Internal Reconstruction Department was established to co-ordinate this planning. It was later known as Industries and Manufactures General. The Industrial Supplies Department was established shortly after the beginning of the war to secure essential materials for the industries for which the Board was responsible and its head was the Board's principal priority officer. The responsibilities of this Department included labour supply for Board of Trade industries.

Overseas trade questions remained in the hands of Commercial Relations and Treaties Department and the Export Licensing Department was attached to it. By its control of licences the Department was able to direct exports to the most useful destinations arising from its responsibility for export surpluses and for relief for the Allies. In 1945 it took over from the Ministry of Production work in connection with supplies to liberated areas. The enforcement of the Trading with the Enemy Act was a joint responsibility of the Board and the Treasury, and was handled by Commercial Relations and Treaties Department. In 1942 the Trading with the Enemy Branch became a separate department of the Board, although still run jointly with the Treasury. The separate Department of Overseas Trade, which had particular responsibility for the work of the Imperial Institute, and the Export Credits Guarantee Department continued during the war but their functions were necessarily limited.

Outside Headquarters the Board was locally represented in various ways. The Area or Regional Boards (see p 137) included Board of Trade representatives who were mainly responsible to Industrial Supplies Department. The Factory and Storage Premises Control had its own local organization to seek out accommodation. Enforcement of Limitation of Supplies Orders was carried out by yet another such organization containing accountants and other officers responsible to Industries and Manufactures I and later to Industries and Manufactures III. Area distribution officers and Local Price Regulation Committees have already been mentioned.

In October 1945 a German Division, (later German and Japanese Division), was set up by the Board to deal particularly with questions concerning reparations. In April 1946 it formed a Central Briefing Unit as part of its Technical Intelligence Service to brief investigators being sent to Germany to assist the operation of the reparations machinery and to collect industrial intelligence. This Unit, which worked alongside the British Intelligence Objectives Sub-Committee (BIOS) under the administrative control of the War Office, was made up of staff transferred from the German Economic Department of the Control Office for Germany and Austria (see p 86) where they had been engaged upon similar work. Later that year further integration took place when the civilian staff of BIOS were also transferred to the Division. A month after the formation of the Central Briefing Unit the Board took over the Foreign Documents Unit of the Control Office, and in 1947 this Unit was merged with the Technical Intelligence Service to form a Technical Information and Documents Unit, whose job was to provide British industry with scientific and industrial information from Germany and Japan. In April 1951 this Unit was transferred to the Department of Scientific and Industrial Research.

Another post-war body was the Nazi Victims Relief Trust. This was set up to administer residual funds of £250,000, being proceeds of German enemy property, which it was not practicable to distribute to pre-war creditors of Germany. The Trust was wound up in July 1960 after the funds at its disposal had been distributed.

The Records

BT 5   Minutes
These relate to official appointments and other establishment matters.

BT 10   Import Duties Advisory Committee
Papers, minutes, etc, of the Committee. Closed for 50 years.

BT 11   Commercial Department: Correspondence and Papers
Subjects covered include exchange control and payments agreements; imperial preference; most favoured nations; customs; navigation and shipping; tariffs; merchandise and trade-marks; League of Nations; conventions, commissions, conferences and committees; and United Kingdom internal issues.

BT 13   Establishment Department: Correspondence and Papers

BT 15   Finance Department: Correspondence and Papers

BT 25   Supplies to Liberated Areas Secretariat
Files of the Supplies to Liberated Areas Secretariat of the Ministry of Production and of the Supplies to Liberated Areas Division of the Board of Trade.

BT 37   Bankruptcy Department: Correspondence and Papers

BT 58   Companies Department: Correspondence and Papers

BT 60   Department of Overseas Trade: Correspondence and Papers

BT 61   Deartment of Overseas Trade: Establishment Files

BT 64   Industries and Manufactures Department: Correspondence and Papers
The class includes files relating to merchandise marks and the cotton and film industries. See also BT 96.

BT 70   Statistical Department, etc: Correspondence and Papers
The class includes files relating to shipping statistics, trade returns, balance of payments, census and index of production, industrial development surveys and international statistical conferences and organizations.

BT 88   Post-War Commodity Policy and Relief Department
Before March 1942 these are records of the Export Surpluses Department under the minister without portfolio, and thereafter of the Post-War Commodity Policy and Relief Department of the Board of Trade.

BT 94   Central Price Regulation Committee
Agenda and minutes of meetings of the Central Price Regulation Committee and of one of the Local Price Regulation Committees (Leeds) and files of the Central Committee. Chairman's papers for 1940 to 1942 are in HMC 3.

BT 96   Industrial Supplies Department
These relate particularly to export policy, priorities, labour supply and, in the case of later files, post-war reconstruction.

BT 101 Standards Department: Correspondence and Papers

BT 103 Solicitor's Department
The class includes papers concerning the Essential Commodities Reserve Act 1938 and the Trading with the Enemy Act 1939.

BT 105 Nazi Victims Relief Trust: Correspondence and Papers
This class includes minutes of meetings and accounts.

BT 106 Factory and Storage Premises Control

BT 131 War Histories (1939-1945) Files
Copies of documents extracted from the registered files by the official historians in the course

of their work on the Board of Trade *History of the Second World War - Civil Industry and Trade*; and material collected in the Ministry of Supply and subsequently transferred to the Board of Trade, for the preparation of the *History of the Second World War - The Control of Raw Materials*. The former papers include series of minutes of meetings of departmental and interdepartmental committees; the latter are mainly narratives relating to various commodities.

BT 132   Parliamentary Branch: Correspondence and Papers
Papers concerning the Prices of Goods Act 1939.

BT 146   Committee on Company Law Amendment (Cohen Committee)

BT 175   Cotton Board and Textile Council: Minutes and Papers

BT 183   Utility Furniture Drawings

BT 190   National Production Advisory Council on Industry
Minutes and papers of meetings.

BT 204   Wool Control Papers

BT 208   Distribution of Industry Panels: Files

BT 209   Industrial Property Department
Files relating mainly to patent and design legislation, trade-marks and copyright.

BT 211   German Division Files
These relate to reparations and the procurement and dissemination of industrial and scientific knowledge obtained from Germany, together with the recruitment of key scientists and technicians from the occupied zone for employment in Britain. For some Ministry of Supply files see AVIA 49.

BT 216   History of the Administration of Enemy Property 1939-1964
Closed until 1995.

BT 222   Accountant's Division: Files

BT 228   War Damage and War Risks Insurance Schemes
Records arising from the War Risks Insurance Act 1939 and the compensation scheme for losses of, or damage to, business and personal chattels as a result of enemy action. See also IR 900 below.

BT 230   Import Licensing Branch
This class also includes a few files concerning export policy.

BT 246   Export Licensing Branch: Policy, General and Record (P, G and R) Files
These arise from the control of the export of military and strategic materials, livestock and works of art.

BT 253   Register of Business Names (Sample)
These relate to businesses registered in 1941.

BT 271   Registered Files: Trading with the Enemy and Administration of Enemy Property Departments
Policy and case files, including a number of the Censorship Section.

BT 310   Board of Trade: Establishment Department: Divisional Organization Charts
One volume for 1942.

ECG 1   Export Credits Guarantee Department: Advisory Committee and Council Minutes

ECG 2   Export Credits Guarantee Department: Executive Committee Minutes

ECG 3   Export Credits Guarantee Department: Advisory Committee and Council Papers of Sub-Committees.

ECG 4   Export Credits Guarantee Department: Miscellanea
Four pieces concerning the Export Guarantees Bill 1938-1939, proposed changes in short-term facilities, export contracts price variation and specimens of publicity literature.

ECG 5   Export Credits Guarantee Department: Secretariat and successors: Registered files
Selected policy files from the main departmental file series.

ED 26   Imperial Institute Files
These are files of the Department of Overseas Trade. Papers of the Institute concerning its wartime publicity, etc, activities are in PRO 30/76.

IR 900   Specimens of Classes of Documents Destroyed
These relate to the operation of the business and private chattels schemes under the War Damage Acts 1941 to 1943.

T 188   Leith-Ross Papers
Papers of Sir Frederick Leith-Ross relating mainly to international and economic affairs and post-war relief in Europe.

Transport Departments

Ministry of Shipping
(13 October 1939 - 1 May 1941)

Name	Date of appointment
Minister	
Sir John Gilmour, MP	13 Oct 1939
Robert Spear Hudson, MP	3 Apr 1940
Ronald Hibbert Cross, MP	14 May 1940
Parliamentary secretary	
Sir J Arthur Salter, MP	13 Oct 1939
Director-general	
Sir Cyril W Hurcomb	13 Oct 1939

Ministry of Transport
(until 1 May 1941)

Minister	
D Euan Wallace, MP	21 Apr 1939
Sir John Reith, MP	14 May 1940
(later Lord Reith)	
J T C Moore-Brabazon, MP	3 Oct 1940
(later Lord Brabazon)	
Parliamentary secretary	
Robert Hamilton Bernays, MP	14 July 1939
Frederick Montague, MP	18 May 1940

Ministry of War Transport
(1941 - 1945)

Minister	
Lord Leathers	1 May 1941
Parliamentary secretaries	
J J Llewellin, MP	1 May 1941
Sir J Arthur Salter, MP	29 June 1941
Philip J Noel-Baker, MP	4 Feb 1942

Director-general
Sir Cyril W Hurcomb   1 May 1941

Deputy directors-general
(Shipping I) Sir E Julian Foley   1 May 1941
(Inland Transport) [Sir] Reginald H Hill   1 May 1941
(Shipping II) [Sir] T Gilmour Jenkins   1 May 1941

For the major part of the war the control of British transport, other than Services transport, was in the hands of the Ministry of War Transport which was created by a merger of the then existing Ministries of Transport and Shipping in May 1941. The records series of the separate Ministries carried on without a break at that time except where functions were merged. In such cases the files were re-registered in new series in which two files from the unmerged Ministries might become the first and second parts of a single new file. On both sides of the work a notable part was played by committees of two basic kinds. On the one hand there were the committees, both advisory and executive, which linked the Ministries with the private transport interests in various fields, while on the other there were the interdepartmental committees through which the Transport Ministries sought to harmonize the long-term and short-term supply of and demand for transport. Throughout the war these committees tended to multiply with increasing refinement of government control. They often developed along Cabinet lines in organization, with many sub-committees, whose reports to the main committee would appear among its circulated papers, and brief recording of large numbers of decisions in that committee's minutes.

Ministry of Shipping

Six weeks from the outbreak of war the Ministry of Shipping was brought into being to provide and control merchant shipping to meet war needs. Its functions had been carefully planned before the war within the Mercantile Marine Department of the Board of Trade, in conjunction with the Committee of Imperial Defence. The new Ministry absorbed the Mercantile Marine Department and became responsible for its peacetime functions, including oversight of the General Register Office of Shipping and Seamen, but was itself largely staffed by recruitment from the shipping industry. After an abortive experiment with licensing the Ministry was responsible, in January and February 1940, for the requisitioning of deep-sea tramps and liners, and in October a similar scheme was applied to coasting and short-sea liners, but not to tramps. Negotiations on the detailed conditions of requisitioning were carried out with the Chamber of Shipping, while day-to-day management was left with the owners. Requisitioning could not of itself produce more tonnage and early 1940 saw the first of many attempts, on this occasion by the lord privy seal, to match the import demands as put by the responsible departments with the tonnage assessed as available by the Ministry of Shipping. Among the limitations on tonnage was the unwillingness of neutral owners to charter their vessels and this led in the summer to the institution of the ship warrant scheme by which world-wide facilities under British control were denied to vessels not engaged on approved voyages. At the same time arrangements were made for the effective transfer to Ministry control or supervision of vessels registered in countries overrun by the enemy.

A further limitation on imports was imposed by the capacity of the ports to process and the inland transport system to distribute the goods. In this field the Ministry of Shipping's Directorate of Shipping in Port, whose task was the reduction of time spent in port, dealt with the Port and Transit Division of the Ministry of Transport, which was responsible for co-ordinating the port and transport facilities. In particular Ministry of Shipping officials shared in the work of the Diversion Room of the Ministry of Transport which on the basis of information about port conditions directed incoming vessels from closed or congested to less hampered ports. At a local level the Ministry of Shipping had representatives in the ports who were able to deal there with the representatives of other departments, and these shipping representatives eventually secured a place on the Port Executive Committees for which the Ministry of Transport was primarily responsible.

Ministry of Transport

Like the Mercantile Marine Department the Ministry of Transport had been engaged before the war with the Committee of Imperial Defence in planning its wartime operations. The separate divisions of the Ministry were co-ordinated by daily meetings of the Defence (Transport) Council which included representation from the Ministry of Home Security. Interdepartmental liaison on the employment of the railways was secured by the Railway Communications Committee, which failed to function well, and on immediate priority questions by the Transport Priority Committee (or sub-committee). At the beginning of the war the minister assumed control of railway operations which he exercised through the weekly meetings of the Railway Executive Committee consisting of the general managers of the four main-line railways and the deputy chairman of the London Passenger Transport Board, under the chairmanship of Sir Ralph Wedgwood, via the railway control officer, an official of the Ministry. Discussion between the minister and the Companies about the exact nature of the financial control to be exercised extended for more than a year after the beginning of the war and this elaborate machinery was later pruned. In the difficult days of 1940 an investigating committee was set up by the Railway Executive Committee, while other enquiries instituted by the Lord President's Committee, the minister without portfolio and the Economic Policy Committee included rail transport in their objects. Yet further investigations were required in the following year.

On the roads as with the railways pre-war plans were put into operation at once, but with this more diffuse industry the same degree of control was not felt to be possible. The Emergency Road Transport Organization consisted of regional transport commissioners in the Civil Defence Regions (see pp 111-12), with large supporting staffs of whom many were drawn from the industry. Their main function was to control road haulage and road passenger transport by issuing or withholding supplementary fuel rations and they were also expected to provide a viable organization at the regional level in the event of a breakdown of communications. The regional transport commissioners met in conferences at Headquarters regularly throughout the war. A Road Haulage (Defence) Advisory Committee represented the industry in the working out of these plans and as the Ministry began to ponder moving towards closer control a Road Haulage Consultative Committee was appointed in October 1940 with similar functions.

The Ministry's Port and Transit Division has been mentioned already. At each port there was a Port Emergency Committee in existence before the war containing representatives of various interests whose function it was to control the use of the port. At the Ministry itself there were the Port and Transit Advisory Committee from the industry and the Port and Transit Standing Committee containing officials from all user and supplier departments, under whose auspices was held the daily Diversion Room meeting to allocate destinations to incoming vessels. This organization proved to be inadequate as pressure increased during 1940, particularly when in September a major diversion of shipping from the East Coast to the West was attempted as a consequence of German attacks on London and on coastal shipping. As early as the spring an attempt had been made by an interdepartmental Transport Planning sub-committee of the Standing Committee to examine the planning of transport between ports and terminals and this had resulted eventually in strengthening the position of the local movements officers of the Ministries of Supply and Food. The Port Emergency Committees were asked to increase their control of road transport and dock labour and Port Executive Committees were established to meet more frequently than the Port Emergency Committees and grip more tightly the day-to-day business of the ports. At the end of the year on the recommendation of a Ministerial sub-committee regional port directors were appointed to the Mersey and the Clyde, and a little later another to the Bristol Channel. The Port and Transit Standing and Advisory Committees were then abolished. In the ports there had been some friction over the position of the Ministry of Shipping representatives and it was eventually decided that they should be regarded as assistants to regional directors in respect of loading and discharge of commercial ships. This was not the only area in which the work of Shipping and Transport overlapped but it was the major one and the difficulties here undoubtedly played a large part in the decision to merge the Ministries into a single Ministry of War Transport in May 1941.

Ministry of War Transport

The Ministry of War Transport was set up at a time of great pressure, particularly on the shipping side, to meet a situation which less drastic methods had failed to ameliorate. By War Cabinet decision the ministers of transport and shipping, or their immediate representatives, met regularly from November 1940 in an attempt to co-ordinate their activities. In January of the following year the Import Executive, a ministerial committee, was formed to consider departmental allocations in the overall import programme. In the spring the prime minister established and took the chair at a Battle of the Atlantic Committee, of which both ministers were members. At a lower level the interdepartmental Central Transport Committee was formed in January 1941, meeting fortnightly until the end of the war, to co-ordinate the supply of and demand for inland transport. In addition the War Transport Council (later Inland Transport War Council), containing both official and transport industry members, was set up in April 1941, in the expectation that it would be able to discuss freely the larger problems affecting the nation's transport.

In the new Ministry control of the ports was vested in the Port and Transit Control which combined the relevant parts of its two predecessors. On the introduction of a dock labour scheme in 1941 the Ministry became responsible for the employment of registered dockers on Clydeside and Merseyside. Elsewhere, control was exercised by the National Dock Labour Corporation, which was established in the same year under the Essential Work (Dock Labour) Order 1941 by the Ministry of Labour and National Service. The Ministry was headed by a director-general with, at first, three deputy directors-general, two for shipping and one for inland transport, but in the following year the Ministry was reorganized under two deputy directors-general, for shipping and inland transport, who had two and one assistant directors-general respectively. Below this level the work was distributed among various divisions which, apart from the overlapping areas, were very much those that had existed in the unmerged Ministries. In May 1942 the Import Executive was superseded by an interdepartmental Shipping Committee with the duty of keeping the shipping situation as a whole under review and, in particular, of preparing forecasts of capacity. An important feature of the development of transport control throughout the war, and one with which the Statistics Division of the Ministry of War Transport was closely concerned, was the preparation of increasingly refined programmes, forecasts and budgets of shipping capacity, imports and military movements. In this field there were necessarily substantial negotiations with the Americans which often reached the highest levels, for as the Allies moved over to offensive operations the limitations imposed by the shortage of shipping pressed even harder. The Ministry therefore took part in the military planning when appropriate.

The largest single operation of the Ministry of War Transport was undoubtedly in connection with the invasion of Europe, 'Operation Overlord'. For more than a year beforehand the Ministry was closely involved in planning for this operation and the records of almost all divisions show an increasing concern with it. For communications with General Headquarters and the up to date display of information about the invasion the Ministry had its own Operations Room.

Throughout the war both sides of the Ministry were concerned with the control of rates and charges for transport.

Deputy Directorate-General of Shipping

Provision was made for the exercise of close supervision of shipping, on behalf of the minister, by means of the Shipping (Operations) Control consisting of the deputy director-general and the directors of liner, ship management, coasting and short-sea, sea transport, and port and transit divisions, under the chairmanship of Sir Vernon Thomson. The Shipping Statistics Division, later Statistics and Intelligence, has already been mentioned. It co-operated with the Central Statistical Office and with the appropriate divisions of the user departments such as Food, Trade and Supply, while within the Ministry of War Transport it maintained a close watch on the activities of the other divisions, keeping, for example, a running check on ship movements, repairs and turn-round. In turn it provided these divisions with information and calculating services. The Allocation of Tonnage Division was responsible for all requisitioning and for allocation other than that of tankers, liners, coasters and other small vessels, which were the responsibility of specialized divisions. Through its Economic and Inter-Allied Section it dealt with general economic questions affecting shipping, particularly in overseas territories, and these are referred to below. Commercial Services Division was one of those to which tonnage was allocated by Allocation of Tonnage Division, and it received further tonnage from Liner Division and the City Central Chartering Office. Its function was to receive, scrutinize and co-ordinate civil programmes and those for military imports to the United Kingdom, with a view to arranging the requisite shipping, and its area of operations eventually comprised the Empire and members of the United Nations in the Eastern hemisphere. It consequently received applications from user departments in the United Kingdom, the Colonial Office, Dominions Office and India Office, and from Economic and Inter-Allied Section on behalf of the Middle East Supply Centre and the West Africa Supply Centre. The Sea Transport Division had formed part of the pre-war Mercantile Marine Department but had close links with the Admiralty and War Office for it was responsible for the provision of shipping for the Armed Forces, both for military cargoes and personnel and including vessels to be used in operations. Parts of the organization were staffed by naval officers. It was this division that was particularly concerned with assisting in the preparation of military plans and the planning of convoys. It was also responsible for the Fleet Auxiliaries and the loading of individual vessels for the most effective discharge for immediate use. It was represented on the spot, *eg* in Russia and the Middle East, by sea transport officers, distinct from the other representatives of the Ministry of War Transport, and at home represented the Ministry, for example, on the Shipping Space Economies Committee set up in 1942, and the Military Overseas Supply Requirements Committee set up in 1943. The Ship Repair Division, established towards the end of 1942, was responsible for keeping an up-to-date picture of the repair situation throughout the world, but it must be remembered that the responsibility for merchant shipbuilding and repair in the United Kingdom had passed to the Admiralty in February 1940, so that in the United Kingdom this Division had only a liaison function. The Liner Division dealt, through the established Liner Conferences and Companies, with the employment of requisitioned liners, while the Ship Management Division exercised similar functions both directly and through owners in respect of deep-sea tramps, chartered and seized foreign vessels, and purchased new-built vessels. The City Central Chartering Office was controlled by this Division. The Coasting and Short-Sea Division, while in the Shipping half of the Ministry of War Transport, was responsible for an area overlapping to some extent with inland transport, inasmuch as coastal transport can be an alternative to road, rail or canal movements. Its control was exercised through Area Control Committees, consisting mainly of shipowners, at the principal ports, while the Ministry planned the movement of large blocks of traffic by coasters in co-ordination with the inland transport facilities it had available. The vessels controlled by this Division were also employed to assist in the port and transit field by taking cargo overside from deep-sea vessels.

Deputy Directorate-General of Inland Transport

Before the creation of the Ministry of War Transport an attempt had been made to bring the Ministry of Transport and the Railway Executive Committee more closely together by appointing the Ministry's railway control officer as a member of the Committee. It was now decided that the posts of controller of railways (replacing the railway control officer) and chairman of the Railway Executive Committee should be held by a single person so as to streamline the existing unwieldy administrative structure and bring the Railway Executive Committee under even closer Ministry control. The Controller of Railways' Conference at which Railway Executive Committee members and senior Ministry officials met fortnightly was instituted a little later. These officials served in the two Railway Divisions, Traffic and Maintenance, and were responsible to the assistant director-general and not to the controller of railways, to whom however they were available for consultations. The railways continued to be under heavy pressure to the end of the war, particularly when invasion preparations coincided with a coal crisis in the winter of 1943-1944, and along with other forms of inland transport suffered acute labour shortage in addition to *materiel* deficiencies. As the war progressed the original diversion of traffic from road to rail was gradually reversed until in February 1944 the minister was empowered to designate traffic not to be handled on the railways. This power, which supplemented the traffic allocation work of the Central Transport Committee, was exercised through the regional transport commissioners and their staffs who were enabled to divert the traffic because of the existence of the Road Haulage Organization as well as the Emergency Road Transport Organization. The Ministry had a Road Transport Division, later split into two Divisions, in addition to two Highways Divisions. The Road Haulage Organization came into existence, after much debate, as a result of the recognition that more positive control needed to be exerted over long distance haulage than was provided by the Emergency Road Transport Organization. Voluntary pools of hauliers and vehicles had previously been established under the Ministry of Transport but with only limited success. Reference has already been made to the work of the Road Haulage Consultative Committee in working towards closer control. The first step in the creation of the Organization was to take over the existing Meat Transport Pool from the Ministry of Food in March 1941. The next stage was to charter further vehicles but this could be achieved only after a vigorous debate during the course of which the Road Haulage (Operations) Advisory Committee, representing the industry, was formed in July 1941. In October the final details were announced and the new scheme began to operate in the following February. The Road Haulage Organization in the shape of area road haulage officers controlled the operations of chartered vehicles and, if required, hired additional transport for government traffic from the Hauliers' National Traffic Pool. During 1942 the limitations of these arrangements, exacerbated by a fuel shortage, became apparent, and the Ministry of War Transport therefore took operational control of all long-distance vehicles and some complete haulage concerns, which were used to exercise day to day control on behalf of the Ministry. These constituted the Unit Centres subordinate to area road haulage officers who were in turn subordinate to divisional road haulage officers, all controlled by the expanded Road Haulage Branch of the Ministry. The existing regional transport commissioners, advised by the Allocation of Traffic Committees set up in 1943, were in general control of priorities in the acceptance of traffic, and their Emergency Road Transport Organization continued to direct the use of short distance vehicles by means of the fuel ration. At the same time the commissioners were responsible for the schemes to rationalize the distributive trades and reduce vehicle use by confining them to zones, which had begun with the Food Transport Order of October 1941 and continued to develop throughout the war. Road Transport Division A in the Ministry of War Transport was responsible for the activities described above and Road Transport Division B was mainly concerned with passenger transport and maintenance and repair of vehicles. The need for passenger transport was greatly increased by the war at the same time as the facilities providing it were depleted by the growth of freight traffic on the railways, the shortage of fuel which led to the abolition of the private car ration in 1942, and the requisitioning of vehicles for defence purposes. The Ministry of War Transport acting through the regional transport commissioners placed severe restrictions on the use of road transport for recreation and endeavoured to reduce the pressure by advocating the staggering of working hours. At the same time it represented the needs of the industry, in all its branches, in securing materials such as tyres from the Ministry of Supply and recruiting conductresses through the Ministry of Labour. The Vehicle Maintenance Directorate in particular was concerned with the supply of skilled labour and materials in the absence of the normal flow of new vehicles.

The part played by canals in inland transport could be only small but it was not overlooked by the Ministry. There were Regional Canal Committees to control the maintenance and operation of canals and canal traffic, and their chairmen together with carriers' and official representatives formed the Central Canal Committee. In December 1941 the Directorate of Canals was set up in the Ministry and in June 1942 the major canals and carriers were brought under its control.

Overseas and Related Activities

Reference has already been made to the acquisition of Allied and neutral shipping for British use. The Foreign Shipping Relations Division of the Ministry was responsible for this area including the operation of agreements with foreign governments by which we secured the use of their vessels. In particular it was responsible for the Allied Tonnage Replacement Scheme by which the United Kingdom government undertook to enable Allied governments to purchase vessels built in or bought by this country in proportion to the losses of their vessels while on Ministry service. In conjunction with the Americans from early in 1942 we operated the Combined Shipping Adjustment Board, with offices in both London and Washington, to concert the use of all available shipping. This body, however, played a lesser role than the British Merchant Shipping Mission in Washington. In March 1941 Sir Arthur Salter, joint parliamentary secretary to the Ministry of Shipping, was ordered by the prime minister to proceed to the United States to present to the United States government United Kingdom shipping needs, at a time when these needs were desperate. His influence was directed towards increasing the United States shipbuilding programme and using United States shipping to release British vessels on some Pacific and West African routes. With American entry into the war the British Merchant Shipping Mission became the channel for exchange of information with the American War Shipping Administration, and was particularly concerned with the preparation of the joint shipping allocation programmes which were an important feature of Anglo-American negotiations and, indeed, differences. In the Ministry of War Transport dealings with the British Merchant Shipping Mission were channelled through the American Section of the Allocation of Tonnage Division.

The Ministry of War Transport was represented in ports all over the world and this representation was particularly important in New York where the organization, inherited as a commercial type of agency from the Ministry of Shipping, developed in a more official direction after American entry into the war. The representative function was closely linked to Port and Transit Control and there was an Oversea Port and Transit Committee from July 1941, which included representatives of the Colonial Office, War Office, Admiralty and Air Ministry. Ministry of War Transport representatives might operate British-controlled ships in their area, help to prepare local shipping programmes, and allocate cargoes to ships and ships to convoys, as well as advising on efficient port and transit operation and feeding the Ministry of War Transport with information. Where necessary, and where possible, War Transport Committees and Port Executive Committees, modelled on the Port Emergency Committees, were set up overseas under the chairmanship of the Ministry of War Transport representative to co-ordinate the various interests in ports. They differed from each other in that the former, as distinct from its members, exercised no executive powers. By 1942 there were Committees in existence in West Africa, South Africa, East Africa, the Middle East, the Persian Gulf and India.

The transport problems of the Middle East were particularly severe and as early as April 1941 the Middle East Supply Centre was established to economize in the use of shipping in its area in exactly the same way as the Ministry of Shipping in respect to the United Kingdom. It was able to do this, though many of the governments in its area were independent, because most of the shipping was under British control, and throughout the war it was able to ensure that the civil needs of the area were met despite the pressure of military operations on transport. It operated by organizing supplies from one part of its area to another, by holding central stocks in Egypt and by organizing shipping programmes in what had become the accepted manner. It dealt in London with both the Inter-Allied Supplies Committee and the Middle East Supplies Committee in the War Cabinet and with the Economic and Inter-Allied Section in the Allocation of Tonnage Division of the Ministry of War Transport on whose vote it was borne. From 1942 the Centre was subordinate to the minister of state in the Middle East (see pp 12-13) through the Supply and Transportation Sub-Committee of the Middle East Supply Council. A similar Supply Centre was later established for West Africa. The Economic and Inter-Allied Section dealt also with Russian shipments and had wide liaison functions with the Ministry of Economic Warfare and with Allied governments.

As the war proceeded it became necessary to prepare shipping programmes for the relief of liberated territories. The allocation of tonnage to relief was regarded initially as a joint responsibility of the Ministry of War Transport and War Shipping Administration, but under the agreement establishing the United Maritime Authority it became the responsibility jointly of all the contracting governments. This agreement came into effect in May 1945 to extend the control of shipping into the post-war period by continuation of the ship warrant scheme. The Authority had 18 member governments and an Executive Board with branches in both London and Washington. It dealt with programmes, allocation, and rates of hire, and continued until October 1946.

The Records

AN 2   War of 1939-1945: Railway Executive Committee: Files
        A large collection covering the entire range of the Committee's work.
AN 3   War of 1939-1945: Railway Executive Committee: Minutes and Reports
        Also includes minutes of the Goods (Ministry of Food) Liaison Committee. See also MAF 99.
BD 30   Ministry of Transport: Registered Files: Welsh Roads Division (RDW Series)
        A few of these concern war damage to highways and replanning of war damaged areas.
BT 110 Registrar General of Shipping and Seamen: Transcripts and Transactions, Series IV, Closed Registries
        Duplicates of all forms entered concerning the registry and ownership of ships removed from the British Register.
BT 150 Registrar General of Shipping and Seamen: Index of Apprentices
        An index volume for 1929 to 1946 to apprentices indentured in the merchant navy under the Merchant Seamen, etc, Act 1823.
BT 151 Registrar General of Shipping and Seamen: Apprentices' Indentures
        One volume containing copy indentures registered in July to August, 1940 as part of five-yearly sample.
BT 164 Registrar General of Shipping and Seamen: Royal Naval Reserve, Representative Records of Service
        One volume recording awards, casualties, deaths, etc, of Royal Naval Reserve officers.
BT 166 Coastguard Service: Correspondence and Papers
        These relate particularly to the coastguards' role in the war watching and life saving organizations.
BT 261 Marine Divisions: Gallantry at Sea Awards
        Registers of awards and papers concerning cases considered for awards.
FO 922 Middle East Supply Centre

Files relating to various aspects of the Centre's work, including the director-general's office, the Spears Mission to Syria and Lebanon, agriculture, transport, industrial production, etc. Other papers will be found in MT 59 below.

IR 32   Railway Assessment Authority
Records concerning the determination of the rating of railway properties and its apportionment among local authorities.

J 101   Shipping Claims Tribunal
Records concerning claims arising from the requisition of vessels under the Compensation (Defence) Act 1939.

MT 6   Railways: Correspondence and Papers
Correspondence and papers of the Ministry of Transport and the Ministry of War Transport. The papers relate to the peacetime regulation and wartime control of railways, to railway owned canals, tramways, underground railways and related services and to the central direction of wartime transport. The class includes bill papers.

MT 9   Marine: Correspondence and Papers
Correspondence and papers of the Marine Department of the Board of Trade, the Ministry of Shipping and the Ministry of War Transport. The papers relate to the drafting and administration of merchant shipping legislation, merchant shipbuilding, war risks insurance, wartime requisitioning of ships and navigation, wrecks and foreshores.

MT 26   Board of Trade Marine Department: Local Marine Boards
Minute books of the Local Marine Boards at London and Cardiff and a register of investigations, mainly by naval courts, of seamen charged with disciplinary offences.

MT 29   Railway Inspectorate: Inspectors' Reports
MT 30   Railway Inspectorate: Indexes to Inspectors' Reports
MT 33   Road Transport: Correspondence and Papers
Selected files relating to various functions of the Ministry of Transport and Ministry of War Transport in respect of road transport. The class includes bill papers. Papers relating more specifically to road traffic and safety are in MT 34.

MT 34   Road Traffic and Safety: Correspondence and Papers
A selection of files and papers dealing with traffic and safety problems including the control of motor vehicles, the Highway Code, driving licences, third party insurance, penalties for driving offences, speed limits, street playgrounds and road signs and signals. There are papers relating to road safety in wartime and the planning of post-war reconstruction.

MT 35   Road Haulage Organization
Correspondence and papers relating to the wartime control of road haulage for government purposes, the Road Haulage Organization and the Meat Transport Organization Ltd.

MT 39   Highways: Correspondence and Papers
Correspondence and papers relating to the administration of highway powers of the Ministry of Transport and the Ministry of War Transport. The class includes papers relating to war measures.

MT 40   Sea Transport: Correspondence and Papers
Files relating to the control of shipping for government purposes, particularly the transport of troops and stores. See also MT 59 and MT 60.

MT 43   Transport Advisory Council
The class includes minutes of meetings of the Council, supporting documents and reports of various committees.

MT 45   Ministry of Transport: Establishment and Organization: Correspondence and Papers
Papers concerning the organization of the Ministry of Transport and the formation of the Ministry of War Transport, including war emergency arrangements.

MT 47   Finance: Correspondence and Papers
Papers of Finance Divisions of the Ministries of Shipping, Transport and War Transport dealing with a variety of subjects, mainly the control of railways and shipping in wartime, peacetime powers over railways and nationalization of inland transport.

MT 48   Ports: Correspondence and Papers
Papers relating to docks, harbours, piers and ferries.

MT 50   Defence Planning and Emergency Transport Committees
This class contains papers relating to the preparation of defence measures before the War of 1939 to 1945 affecting road and rail transport and ports, including the setting up of regional organizations; and papers and minutes of the Defence (Transport) Council, 1938 to 1946, the Railways Workshop Capacity Committee, 1940 to 1946, the Inland Transport War Council, 1941 to 1944, the Central Transport Committee, 1941 to 1948, the Official Committee on Inland Transport, 1944, the Shipping Advisory Council, 1939 to 1945, and various Regional Transport Committees, 1943 to 1952.

MT 52   Inland Waterways: Correspondence and Papers

Papers of the Ministry of Transport, the Ministry of War Transport and various committees concerned with inland waterways, including the Canals (Defence) Advisory Committee, 1939 to 1941, and the Central Canal Committee, 1941 to 1947.

MT 55 Emergency Road Transport Organization
This class contains material embracing the entire range of the organization's activities including employment in road transport, fuel rationing, rationalization of services, road safety and vehicle production. In addition to minutes and papers of various associated committees it also includes circulars to regional transport commissioners and area road haulage officers, and minutes of regional transport commissioners' conferences.

MT 56 Rates and Charges: Correspondence and Papers
Papers arising out of ministerial control, under the Defence (General) Regulations 1939, of charges made by inland transport undertakings.

MT 59 Shipping Control and Operations: Correspondence and Papers
Files concerning the centralized direction of shipping during the Second World War, particularly regarding the programming of civil and military requirements through requisitioning, chartering and allocation of British merchant shipping. There are also some records concerning post-war shipping policy including committee papers, etc, arising from British representation on the United Maritime Authority.

MT 62 Private Office Papers
Mainly from the offices of Lord Leathers and Sir Arthur Salter. The class also includes minutes of meetings of the Shipping (Operation) Control, 1941 to 1946.

MT 63 Port and Transit: Correspondence and Papers
These relate to the control and handling of British and Allied merchant shipping and cargoes in UK and overseas ports. A number concern the work of the Shipping Diversion Room and the operation of the dock labour scheme on Clydeside and Merseyside.

MT 64 COT (Co-ordination of Transport): Files
Papers arising from the consideration by the War Cabinet of the post-war reconstruction of transport.

MT 65 Stats (Statistics): Files
Mainly concerning the availability, employment and location of British, Allied and neutral shipping.

MT 71 Goeland Company Records
Papers relating to this government-owned company's efforts to reduce as much as possible the benefits derived by Germany from Danube shipping. Other files concerning the company will be found in MT 59.

MT 78 Highways: Stopping Up Orders
Orders made under the Defence (General) Regulations, 1939.

MT 101 Establishment Division: Marine Branch
These relate to wartime questions concerning the lights service from 1942.

POWE 13 Ministry of Transport: Electricity Correspondence and Papers
The records in this class originated largely in the Ministry of Transport, but there are a few wartime papers of the Ministry of Fuel and Power.

POWE 14 Electricity Division: Correspondence and Papers
Includes some files of the Ministry of Transport.

PRO 30/92 S S Wilson Papers
Personal notes on the organization of British ports during the winter of 1940 to 1941.

Treasury

Name	Date of appointment
Chancellor of the Exchequer	
Sir John Simon, MP	28 May 1937
Sir Kingsley Wood, MP	12 May 1940
Sir John Anderson, MP	24 Sept 1943
Financial secretary	
Harry Crookshank, MP	21 Apr 1939

| R Assheton, MP | 7 Feb 1943 |
| Osbert Peake, MP | 29 Oct 1944 |

Permanent secretary and head of the Civil Service

| Sir Horace J Wilson | February 1939 |
| Sir Richard V N Hopkins | 24 Aug 1942 |

Second secretary

Sir Richard V N Hopkins	29 Mar 1932
Sir Frederick Phillips	22 July 1942
Sir Wilfred Eady	16 Aug 1942
Sir Alan Barlow	24 Aug 1942
Sir Bernard Gilbert	1 Jan 1944

Economic advisers

| H D Henderson (later Sir Hubert Henderson) | 1 Sept 1939 |
| Professor D H Robertson (later Sir Dennis Robertson) | September 1939 |

Economic adviser to the chancellor of the Exchequer

| J M Keynes (later Lord Keynes) | 1 Jan 1941 |

Financial adviser to the chancellor of the Exchequer

| Lord Catto | 25 June 1940 |

The bulk of Treasury records of the Second World War continue to appear in the classes based on the Central Registry system established in 1920. In this system the files were divided into five series, namely F, S and E for the Finance, Supply and Establishment Divisions of the Treasury; G for files not assignable to any one of those three series; and P for the files of the Superannuation Division. Within the classes the files are arranged in chronological blocks according to the date of their closure, and since the files were allowed to continue for as long as the subject was in action those appearing in the blocks of the war years may consist largely of pre-war material and many wartime papers will be found in post-war blocks (*see* T 213 to T 236 and T 248 below) even after 1948 when the registration system was revised.

The subordination of all other interests to the prosecution of the war inevitably changed the pattern of Treasury financial control over the activities of other departments. At the same time the contribution that could be made by financial measures to the direction of all available resources into the war effort and to the equitable distribution of the resulting burdens provided the Treasury with a war role of its own. One of its major targets was stabilization, *ie* the avoidance of inflation, both by subsidies, to keep down the cost-of-living index, and by taxation, designed to draw off purchasing power. At the time consideration had always to be given to the post-war effects of financial measures and to the need for post-war reconstruction.

In the field of responsibility of the Home Finance Divisions new taxes were introduced and old ones extended. An excess profits tax designed to prevent war profiteering by limiting profits to their pre-war range was introduced early in the war and in May 1940 was raised to 100 per cent. In the next year, however, it was decided for the sake of incentive that 20 per cent of the tax should be conditionally repayable after the war. This device of repayment under the name of post-war credit was also employed from 1941 in respect of the increased income tax which was then brought up to a standard rate of 10 shillings in the pound. To cope with the much larger numbers of taxpayers now brought into the income tax range, compulsory deduction by employers of tax assessed on the previous year's earnings was introduced in 1941 by the Board of Inland Revenue and was replaced in 1944 by the PAYE system of deduction based on current earnings. Taxation to restrain consumption was introduced in 1940 with the levying of purchase tax by the Board of Customs and Excise on all goods other than raw materials, foodstuffs and goods already subject to heavy taxation. The tax gradually became complicated by exemptions and the introduction of three rates. Existing taxes, such as those on alcohol and tobacco, were also heavily increased to mop up purchasing power. Apart from the extension of its borrowing activities in the market the government increased its encouragement of small savers through the National Savings Movement (see pp 129-30). The Capital Issues Committee scrutinized proposals from non-government sources for the raising of fresh capital, being mainly concerned with their effects on government borrowing.

The Overseas Finance Divisions were responsible for all aspects of our financial relations with other countries, including those whose governments were in exile, and the administration of such bodies as the Czechoslovak Financial Claims Office. The balance of payments position was held initially by the sale of foreign securities and the imposition of foreign exchange control. The Treasury took control of all supplies of gold and key foreign currencies in the hands of United Kingdom residents and the inflow of such currencies was encouraged by the invoicing of exports in them. The Sterling Area was created within which payments in sterling were free of control on the understanding that all parts of it imposed similar exchange control restrictions to those of the United Kingdom. A further aspect of control was introduced by the Trading with the Enemy Act whose application was partly the responsibility of the Treasury in conjunction with the Board of Trade. Demands on resources outside the sterling area rapidly mounted, especially after the German forces overran Europe, and towards the end of 1940 the prospect of complete disappearance of the gold and hard currency reserves led to an appeal to the American government of which the result was the Lend-Lease Act of March 1941. Under this Act the United States government was able to transfer to the United Kingdom government without money payment goods required for the prosecution of the war. The government of Canada, which was outside the sterling area, assisted in meeting the deficit by various means, including a gift of 1,000 million dollars and, later, by a Mutual Aid Agreement of which the finance was underwritten by Canada. Within the sterling area the United Kingdom was able to draw on the resources of other countries by creating sterling balances in their favour which would be drawn on at some later date.

While the war brought a difference of approach on the finance side, for the Supply and Establishments Divisions the main change was a very perceptible loosening of Treasury control. Not only were the needs of war too pressing to permit much of the traditional scrutiny, but the great growth in government business made such procedures physically impossible for lack of staff to carry them out. Much financial control was therefore devolved to departments by raising the limits within which they could sanction their own expenditure though the Treasury continued to insist on the need to practise economy and to concern itself with many detailed issues. These necessarily formed only a small proportion of the whole field, but supply and establishments files continue to contain some information about the activities of all departments in respect, for example, of their estimates and staffing. General principles for the placing of government contracts were evolved in the Contracts Co-ordinating Committee and the authorization of expenditure by the Supply and Service Departments was the business of the Treasury Inter-Service Committee. Claims for compensation formed an appreciable part of the work arising directly from the war on the supply side of the Treasury.

Among the Treasury records detailed below are a number deposited by Commissions and Committees, such as the War Works Commission, the Royal Commission on Awards to Inventors, the Royal Commission on Equal Pay and the British Committee on the Preservation and Restitution of Works of Art, Archives and other Material in Enemy Hands.

The Records

T 160	Finance Files
	See opening paragraph on p 172 above.
T 161	Supply Files
	See opening paragraph on p 172 above.
T 162	Establishment Files
	See opening paragraph on p 172 above.
T 163	General Files
	See opening paragraph on p 172 above.
T 164	Pensions and Superannuation Files
	See opening paragraph on p 172 above.
T 166	Royal Commission on Awards to Inventors (1946)
	Files, reports and transcripts of proceedings. There are also indexes to claimants and to the subject of their claims.
T 171	Chancellor of the Exchequer's Office: Budget and Finance Bill Papers
T 172	Chancellor of the Exchequer's Office: Miscellaneous Papers
	Includes memoranda on a wide variety of fiscal subjects, briefs for speeches and papers arising from deputations from both sides of industry to the chancellor.
T 175	Hopkins Papers
	Papers collected by Sir Richard Hopkins dating from 1914 to 1942. There are some other papers of Sir Richard's among the Bridges' Papers in T 273.
T 177	Private Office Papers and Private Collections: Phillips Papers
	The class includes a few of Sir Frederick's papers concerning wartime problems affecting home and overseas finance and a file arising from a memorandum of J M Keynes on war damage to property.
T 180	War Works Commission
	The class includes agenda and minutes of meetings; general policy files; case files on closures of highways and footpaths, and acquisition and retention of land; and related case papers, proceedings of private and public inquiries and reports to ministers. There is a file concerning the appointment of the Commissions's secretary in IR 39/16.
T 189	Royal Commission on Equal Pay (Asquith Commission)
	Minutes of meetings, papers, etc, 1944 to 1946.
T 196	Exchange Requirements Committee
	Minutes of meetings, reports and returns, estimates of requirements, etc, particularly in North America.
T 199	Establishment Officer's Branch: Files
	Includes Treasury war book and papers relating to civil defence, the Anglo-French Co-ordinating Committee and government organization matters.
T 208	Financial Enquiries Branch (Hawtrey) Papers
	Includes a few papers of J M Keynes and some material relating to the *Financial History of the Second World War*.
T 209	British Committee on the Preservation and Restitution of Works of Art, Archives and Other Material in Enemy Hands (Macmillan Committee) 1944-1946.
	The class includes a minute book of the Committee's meetings, correspondence files, various reports including some from American forces on German monuments, fine arts and archives, and papers concerning the publication of booklets on losses and survivals of works of art in the war.
T 210	Czechoslovak Financial Claims Office: Files
	Correspondence on various claims and registers containing details of obligations and payments under the Czecho-Slovakia (Financial Claims and Refugees) Act 1940. See also HO 294.
T 213	Defence Personnel Division: Files
T 214	Establishments (Departmental) Division: Files
T 215	Establishments (General) Division: Files
T 216	Establishments (Manning) Division: Files

T 217	Establishments (Professional, Scientific, Technical and Industrial Staff) Division: Files
T 218	Arts, Science and Lands Division: Files
T 219	Government and Allied Services Division: Files
T 220	Imperial and Foreign Division: Files
T 221	Law and Order Division: Files
T 222	Organization and Methods Division: Files
T 223	Agriculture and Food Division: Files
T 224	Agriculture, Trade and Transport Division: Files
T 225	Defence Policy and Materiel Division: Files
T 226	Land and Building Division: Files
T 227	Social Services Division: Files
T 228	Trade and Industry Division: Files
T 230	Economic Advisory Section: Files
	Includes discussion papers of the Economic Section of the Cabinet War Secretariat.
T 231	Exchange Control Division: Files
	See also CUST 115.
T 233	Home Finance Division: Files
T 236	Overseas Finance Division: Files
T 239	Register of Daily Receipts
T 243	Treasury Circulars and Minutes
T 244	Dear Establishment Officer Circulars
T 247	Keynes Papers
	These cover the whole range of economic policy particularly in relation to overseas finance, and arise from Lord Keynes' attachment to the Treasury from 1940 as a member of the chancellor of the Exchequer's Consultative Committee. See also T 177 and T 208.
T 248	Establishment (Superannuation) Division: Files
T 263	United Kingdom Commercial Corporation
	These deal mainly with the purchase and sale of goods from neutral countries, especially Turkey, Spain, Portugal and in the Middle East and Africa. See also BT 192 under Ministry of Economic Warfare section (p 73).
T 265	Treasury Inter-Service Committee
	Minutes of meetings and circulated papers relating to the authorization of defence expenditure and approval of contracts, etc.
T 266	Capital Issues Committee
	Minutes of meetings and policy and case files arising from the control of capital issues under the Defence (Finance) Regulations, 1939.
T 273	Bridges Papers
	Papers of Lord Bridges as secretary to the Cabinet 1939 to 1945. The class also incorporates some papers from Sir Horace Wilson's and Sir Richard Hopkins' periods as permanent secretary to the Treasury.
T 900	Specimens of Classes of Documents Destroyed
	Include interest free loans files and returns, etc, of requisitioned property in connection with applications by local authorities for contributions in lieu of rates.

Treasury Solicitor

Name	Date of appointment
Treasury solicitor and HM procurator general	
Sir Thomas Barnes	1934

The Records

MAF 50	Legal Department: Papers
	These relate to case work undertaken for the Forestry Commission.

TS 13   Queen's Proctor: Prize and Prize Bounty Cases, Decrees and Affidavits
These are listed alphabetically under the name of the ship concerned.

TS 26   Treasury Solicitor and HM Procurator General: War Crimes Papers
This class contains correspondence and papers of the War Crimes Branch relating to enemy war crimes. The files include copies of charges, lists of war criminals, reports of SHAEF courts of inquiry and papers of the United Nations War Crimes Commission. A few further papers will be found in TS 27.

TS 27   Registered Files: Treasury and Miscellaneous Series
Many of these relate to matters arising out of Defence Regulations including a number concerning imprisonment under Regulation 18B.

TS 28   Treasury Solicitor: Air Ministry (AM) Series Registered Files
Case files of the Treasury solicitor when handling legal business on behalf of the Air Ministry, mainly concerning patents of inventions.

TS 32   Registered Files: Admiralty Series
Case files of the Treasury solicitor arising from legal work carried out for the Admiralty.

Wallace Collection

Name	Date of appointment
Keeper, secretary and accounting officer	
James Gow Mann	1936
(later Sir James Gow Mann)	

The Records

AR 1   Wallace Collection: Correspondence and Papers
There are a few files in this class concerning the wartime evacuation of works of art.

War Damage Commission

Name	Date of appointment
Chairman	
A M Trustram Eve	27 Mar 1941
(later Sir Malcolm Trustram Eve)	
Secretary	
F P Robinson	27 Mar 1941
(later Sir Percival Robinson)	
W R Fraser	February 1943
(later Sir W Robert Fraser)	

It had been decided before the war that no scheme of insurance against war damage to real property would be feasible and that owners of damaged property should simply receive some degree of compensation at some later date. The local authorities were empowered to undertake war damage repairs or make loans for such repairs, and loans were in turn made to them by the

Ministry of Health for the purpose. Consideration continued to be given to the method and basis of compensation, especially after experience of bombing attacks, and in October 1940 the intention was announced of proceeding with a comprehensive scheme. The War Damage Act became law in March 1941 and under Part I of the Act the War Damage Commission was established with responsibility for payments in respect of physical damage to land and buildings in the United Kingdom. Part II applied to goods and was the responsibility of the Board of Trade until 1955 when it was taken over by the Commission. Contributions were collected from property owners by the Inland Revenue, whose valuation organization also assisted in assessment. There was no direct link between contributions and compensation, and the scheme was thus not one of insurance. The payments envisaged might be either compensation (to be paid at some later date) or the cost of completed repairs, and in cases of hardship limited advance payments would be made. This scheme brought to an end the Ministry of Health loans, and local authorities now applied direct to the Commission which, however, continued in close co-operation with both the Ministry of Health and the Ministry of Works in dealing with repairs to housing.

The Commission's duties included the investigation of apparent irregularities in claims. To ensure that payments were not made in respect of works which were not in conformity with town and country planning interests the Commission required works of specified types or in specified areas to have their special sanction before execution. It thus served as one of the forerunners of the Ministry of Town and Country Planning. From 1947 until 1955 it also served as a Central Land Board under the Town and Country Planning Act 1947.

Between 1941 and 1945 an appeal from a determination of the Commission under the War Damage Acts 1941 and 1943 lay to one of the panel of referees appointed under the Finance (1909-1910) Act 1910. From 1946 jurisdiction passed to a War Damage Valuation Appeals Panel and from 1950 to the Lands Tribunal.

In addition to its headquarters the Commission had regional offices in eleven of the Civil Defence Regions (see pp 111-12), one in Northern Ireland and four such offices in the London Region. Deputy commissioners, separate from the administrative organization, also served locally. Under the War Damage Act 1964 the Commission was dissolved and residual work taken over by a War Damage Office of the Board of Inland Revenue except for functions concerning public highways which passed to the Ministry of Transport in England and Wales and to the secretary of state for Scotland.

The Records

IR 33	War Damage Commission and Central Land Board: Minutes and Papers
	Minutes of meetings and papers of the War Damage Commission.
IR 34	War Damage Commission: Policy Files
IR 35	War Damage Commission: Investigation Files
	A selection of files concerning claims, etc, where irregularities were suspected. The class is closed for 75 years.
IR 36	War Damage Commission: Miscellaneous Files
	A selection of compensation case files covering various parts of the United Kingdom which, because of their importance or complexity, were handled at headquarters.
IR 37	War Damage Commission: Regional Files
	Compensation claim files concerning certain notable public buildings, cathedrals, churches, hospitals, schools and a representative cross-section of other properties.
IR 38	War Damage Commission: Instructions, Orders, etc
	This class consists mainly of instructions, etc, issued by the Commission to its regional offices and technical advisers.
IR 39	War Damage Commission: Establishment and General Files
IR 900	Specimens of Classes of Documents Destroyed

These relate to the business and private chattels scheme and originated in the Board of Trade. See also BT 228.

LT 1   War Damage (Valuation Appeals) Panel: Case Files
LT 2   War Damage (Valuation Appeals) Panel: Indexes and Registers of Cases

War Office

The Army Council

Name	Date of appointment
Secretary of state for war	
Leslie Hore-Belisha, MP	28 May 1937
Oliver F G Stanley, MP	5 Jan 1940
R Anthony Eden, MP	12 May 1940
H David R Margesson, MP	23 Dec 1940
Sir P James Grigg, MP	22 Feb 1942
Parliamentary under-secretary	
Earl of Munster	31 Jan 1939
Viscount Cobham	25 Sept 1939
(Military) Brig-Gen Lord Croft	12 May 1940 - 23 May 1945
(Civil) Lt-Col Sir Edward W M Grigg, MP	12 May 1940 - 4 Mar 1942
A Henderson, MP	4 Mar 1942 -
(This post was then discontinued)	30 Dec 1942
Chief of the imperial general staff	
Sir W Edmund Ironside	4 Sept 1939
Lt-Gen Sir John G Dill	10 June 1940
Gen (later Field Marshal) Sir Alan F Brooke	25 Dec 1941
Adjutant-general to the Forces	
Gen Sir Robert Gordon-Finlayson	1 July 1939
Lt-Gen H Colville B Wemyss	10 June 1940
Lt-Gen Sir Ronald F Adam	3 June 1941
Quarter-master-general to the Forces	
Lt-Gen Sir Walter K Venning	2 Feb 1939
Gen Sir Thomas S Riddell-Webster	14 Aug 1942
Vice-chief of the imperial general staff	
Lt-Gen Sir Robert H Haining	27 May 1940
Lt-Gen Sir Henry R Pownall	19 May 1941

Lt-Gen Archibald E Nye	5 Dec 1941
(later Sir Archibald Nye)	

Deputy chief of the imperial general staff
(not originally on Council)

Lt-Gen Ronald M Weeks	15 June 1942 -
	29 May 1945

Financial secretary to the War Office

Sir Victor A G A Warrender, MP	29 Nov 1935
Sir Edward W M Grigg, MP	3 Apr 1940
Richard K Law, MP	17 May 1940
E D Sandys, MP	21 July 1941
A Henderson, MP	7 Feb 1943

Permanent under-secretary of state for war

Sir Herbert J Creedy	3 Mar 1924
Sir P James Grigg	26 Oct 1939
{ Sir Frederick C Bovenschen	5 Mar 1942
{ Sir Eric B B Speed	

Director-general of Army requirements

[Sir] Robert J Sinclair	13 July 1940 -
(Thereafter this office not on the Council)	14 Aug 1942

Other Positions

C-in-c Home Forces

Gen Sir Walter M St G Kirke	4 Sept 1939
Field Marshal W Edmund Ironside	c. 26 May 1940
Gen Sir Alan F Brooke	20 July 1940
Gen [Sir] Bernard C T Paget	25 Dec 1941
Gen Sir Harold E Franklyn	July 1943

GOC-in-c Middle East

Gen Sir Archibald P Wavell	28 July 1939
Gen Sir Claude J E Auchinleck	5 July 1941
Gen Hon Sir Harold R G Alexander	15 Aug 1942
(Thereafter deputy Allied c-in-c, North Africa)	
Gen Sir H Maitland Wilson	16 Feb 1943 -
	18 Dec 1943
Gen Sir Bernard C T Paget	18 Dec 1943

C-in-c British Expeditionary Force (September 1939 - July 1940)
Gen Viscount Gort

Supreme Allied commander (Mediterranean)

Gen Sir H Maitland Wilson	18 Dec 1943
Gen Hon Sir Harold R G Alexander	Nov 1944

C-in-c India

Gen Sir Robert A Cassels	30 Nov 1935
Gen Sir Claude J E Auchinleck	27 Jan 1941
Gen Sir Archibald P Wavell	21 June 1941
Gen Sir Claude J E Auchinleck	20 June 1943

South East Asia

C-in-c 11th Army Group

Gen Sir George Giffard	Nov 1943 - Nov 1944

C-in-c Allied Land Forces, SEA

Lt-Gen Sir Oliver W H Leese	12 Nov 1944

Allied Expeditionary Force (1944-1945)

C-in-c British 21st Army Group

Gen (later Field Marshal) Sir Bernard L Montgomery

War Office

Control of both the War Office and the Army has in modern times been vested in the Army Council under the secretary of state and this continued to be the formal situation during the Second World War. In practice, as with other departments, supreme control over operations was exercised by the minister of defence through the Chiefs of Staff Committee so that the work of the secretary of state and Army Council was largely confined to administration of the Army.

The Army Council consisted of the secretary of state, the parliamentary under-secretary (two under-secretaries from May 1940 to February 1943), the chief of the imperial general staff, the adjutant-general, the quarter-master-general, the vice-chief of the imperial general staff (from May 1940), the deputy chief of the imperial general staff (from June 1942), the financial secretary and the permanent under-secretary (two permanent under-secretaries from February 1942 to the end of the war). Instructions to commanders were issued in the name of the Army Council and in the earlier part of the war the Council met fairly frequently and was regularly presented with information about operational matters. It was more often concerned, however, with the policy aspect of such questions as recruitment, training, pay and the award of medals, and as the war went on it met less frequently. Considerable use was made of committees of Council such as the War Committee which was attended by deputies of members and by some directors and dealt with problems at a more detailed level. The most important of these committees was the Executive Committee consisting of the permanent under-secretary, the adjutant-general, the quarter-master-general, the vice-chief of the imperial general staff and the director-general of Army requirements, the deputy chief of the imperial general staff being added later. It was established in February 1941 to relieve the Army Council by dealing finally with all matters that could properly be settled at a lower level and otherwise making agreed recommendations if possible. Closely connected with the Executive Committee was the Army Council Secretariat, which was established at about the same time on the recommendation of the Standing Committee on Army Administration to handle the secretariat business of the Army Council and all War Office Committees, including the following up of decisions. It arranged and marked the minutes and papers in the style of the War Cabinet Secretariat and serviced both standing and *ad hoc* committees, of which there were a great many. There was a Morale Committee, for example, and a Committee on Army Post-War Problems, both of which were standing committees of the Executive Committee. Committees on

Administrative Organization in the United Kingdom and Organization of the War against Japan reported to the Army Council, and others such as that on the Higher Organization of the War Office and on the Provision and Maintenance of Motor Transport reported to the Executive Committee. The Army Council Secretariat was regarded to some extent as a means towards unifying the work of the separate branches of the War Office both by servicing these committees, performing in this way a similar function to the War Cabinet Secretariat, and by maintaining direct contact with the branches in order to keep the secretary of state and the Executive Committee of the Army Council informed.

In general the command of troops was exercised not by the War Office but by commanders acting on the basis of their instructions from the Army Council. The main exceptions to this were those troops engaged on certain administrative duties (*ie* supplies, movements and similar functions) in the United Kingdom, whose control, together with the relevant War Office branches, would pass to General Headquarters, Home Forces, only in the event of invasion. As distinct from command the War Office exercised a very close scrutiny over all aspects of the Army's activities, particularly in questions of organizational structure, establishments and all kinds of expenditure. Many decisions in these fields could be taken only with War Office approval, and the records of the War Office Directorates consequently contain an immense amount of detailed information. Some decentralization was achieved in the United Kingdom in 1941 on the recommendation of the Gale Committee by the institution of command secretaries representing the civilian departments of the War Office who were able to deal with some questions relating to contracts and civil staff at Command level and to act as advisers to commanders. By 1942 a certain amount of decentralization in respect of courts martial had been achieved but the War Office always retained control of military policy, allocation of equipment, recruitment, training doctrine and emoluments. A somewhat similar command secretary was appointed to the Middle East in 1943.

The War Office was provided with a Central Registry system whereby business was conducted on files passed between its branches. Each letter arriving in the Registry would be assigned to a file and either attached to it and sent up for action or sent to the branch which was recorded as holding the file. To avoid the delays inherent in this system branches could employ temporary branch memoranda for communication, assigning to them their own reference numbers. These branch memoranda were originally intended to be placed on the registered files as the opportunity arose but the pressure of work during the war combined with the growth in War Office branches was such that this was no longer possible and branches supplemented Central Registry by maintaining small registries of their own branch memoranda. On receiving a memorandum from another branch they might add to it their own reference numbers for that subject to serve as cross-references. The reference numbers of files and letters include the letters and numbers of the branch title. Some branches had always kept by them files of papers for information rather than action, which may thus be described as a branch library rather than a branch registry. The circulated copies of telegrams, which did not pass through the Registry, found a natural home in such informational files. The papers deriving from War Office branches, as indeed from the various Headquarters, are known as 'Collation Files' or as 'Connected Papers' in that they are regarded as connected to the war diaries discussed below. They include narratives and operations and situation reports from units, while in the case of senior officers there may be semi-official correspondence of a slightly less formal kind than the official War Office communications.

Most Army formations and units were required to keep war diaries; some War Office branches also maintained their own diaries. They naturally vary according to the functions and experiences of the branch or unit concerned, but nearly all have the same basic form of a chronological section supplemented by appendixes of original documents. In some cases the diary sections consist largely of references to documents but others contain appreciable narrative elements. With the help of the diaries it is possible to establish the nature of the activities of a branch of the War Office or an Army unit at any time during the war.

Chief of the Imperial General Staff

The senior military member of the Army Council was the chief of the imperial general staff. In the system employed both in the War Office and throughout the Army the general staff was distinguished from the administrative staff, which was itself divided into two sections dealing with personnel on the one hand and supplies and movements on the other. The sections of the War Office dealing with these subjects were headed by the adjutant-general and quarter-master-general respectively and similar titles for the staff were employed throughout the Army. The chief of the imperial general staff was a member of the Chiefs of Staff Committee and as such responsible for the overall control of operations to the minister of defence (see pp 6-7). At the beginning of the war the chief of the imperial general staff had the assistance of a deputy, but in May 1940 this officer was replaced by a vice-chief of the imperial general staff who was also a member of the Army Council and of the Vice-Chiefs of Staff Committee. The post of deputy chief of the imperial general staff was re-established in 1942 when he also was placed on the Army Council. At this time the General Staff was re-organized to relieve the chief of the imperial general staff of as much day-to-day work as possible, the vice-chief of the imperial general staff being made responsible for Operations, Plans, Intelligence and Training, and the deputy chief of the imperial general staff for Organization, Equipment, Weapons Policy and the work of the new scientific adviser to the Army Council. Various numbers of assistant chiefs of the imperial general staff held office at times during the war and bore responsibility for various specific areas of work.

As the war proceeded the directorates of the General Staff as of the rest of the War Office, together with the branches of which they consisted, inexorably increased in number. The functions of each of them can generally be established from their war diaries and only a broad outline is attemped here. On the outbreak of war the Directorate of Military Operations and Intelligence was split into a Directorate of Military Operations and Plans and a Directorate of Military Intelligence. The basic organization of the Directorate of Military Operations and Plans consisted of a general branch and a number of branches with responsibility for particular areas, and it was concerned with operational policy, the preparation of plans and the provision of briefs for the chief of the imperial general staff, for which purposes it collected information about the operations of our own forces. Thus few aspects of the Army were clearly outside its brief and it amassed in its files a quantity of information from the rest of the War Office, all theatres and from other departments. One class of these, known as 'Collation Files' is arranged by broad subject groups while the other class reflects the geographical arrangements of the branches. On the planning side the Directorate was responsible for outline plans up to the appointment of a force commander who thereafter became responsible for the detailed operational plans. In this connection the War Office planners worked closely with the other joint planners. The Directorate was also responsible, with the Directorate of Military Intelligence, for the provision of information to the War Office War Room, which was itself in communication with the Cabinet War Room. The War Room contained an informational display consisting mostly of maps with some handbooks of reports. The information available in the Directorate was used for the compilation of routine reports to commanders by which they could be kept in touch with the general picture. The subordinates of the director of military operations and plans were initially a director of plans and a deputy director of military operations. By 1942 there were two deputy directors of military operations for Home and Overseas respectively and by 1944 the director of military operations and plans was replaced by an assistant chief of the imperial general staff (o) with a director of military operations, a director of plans, a director of post-hostilities plans and a director of survey subordinate to him.

While the information collected in the Directorate of Military Operations concerned our own forces and those of our Allies in close contact, that collected by the Directorate of Military Intelligence related to enemy forces, Allies beyond close contact and general information about all other countries. Distinctions of this kind could not be drawn sharply in practice and inevitably created some overlap. The branches of the Directorate of Military Intelligence were partly geographical and partly functional, *eg* concerned with censorship, military attachés or military missions. They collected and distributed historical, topographical, economic and medical information as well as military information, prisoner of war reports on both Allied and enemy personnel, and material on prominent Nazis.

The director of military training was concerned both with training establishments and with inspection of the standard of training achieved in units. There was for a time an inspector-general of training, separate from the Directorate of Training, who was responsible for some of the inspectors.

The Directorate of Staff Duties was responsible for the compilation of War Establishments, *ie* the composition by numbers and ranks of formations and units. It issued the Order of Battle and allocated formations and units for particular forces and theatres of war. This function must be distinguished from that of the military secretary to the secretary of state who was responsible for the appointment of individual officers to particular posts. Staff duties was the sole responsibility of an assistant chief of the imperial general staff for the first part of the war, but from June 1942 together with the Directorate of Home Guard, which had been established in December 1940, it was joined with the new Directorates of Air and American Liaison and Munitions under the deputy chief of the imperial general staff. Of the latter Directorates the first was concerned with the development of airborne forces and the second arose from American entry into the war. It provided the War Office link with the London Munitions Assignment Board (see p 137) and co-ordinated matters affecting the British Army Staff in Washington. Also under the deputy chief of the imperial general staff was an assistant chief of the imperial general staff supervising a Co-ordination Branch and the Directorate of the principal arms, some of which were also reorganized at this time. War Office Directorates were responsible for policy and development in respect of the Royal Artillery (formerly Anti-Aircraft and Coast Defence), Armoured Fighting Vehicles (later Royal Armoured Corps), Weapons and Vehicles (created in June 1942), Signals and Infantry. With the development of this field a Directorate of Research (later Tactical Investigation) was added to this group in January 1943. These responsibilities of the deputy chief of the imperial general staff for organization, equipment and weapons policy were further co-ordinated by the appropriate directors meeting in the Organization and Weapons Policy and Organization and Weapons Development Committees.

Adjutant-General

The adjutant-general to the forces was responsible for personnel policy and his Department also was organized in directorates and branches. The Directorate of Personal Services was mainly concerned with disciplinary and related legal questions. In 1940, with the conscription system settling down, recruiting was transferred from the Directorate of Organization to the Directorate of Mobilization, and this latter became the Directorate of Recruiting and Demobilization in the summer of 1943. As the pressure on manpower and its use began to develop a director of personnel selection was appointed in July 1941, followed by a director of manpower planning in March 1943. Separate directorates dealt with personnel questions of the Auxiliary Territorial Service and, for a short time, the Auxiliary Military Pioneer Service, while the director-general of medical services had subordinate Directorates of Hygiene, Pathology and Dental Services. The Adjutant-General's Department was responsible also for graves registration and prisoners-of-war questions. The latter included both British and enemy prisoners and close contact was maintained with the Red Cross. The Department also worked closely with the Casualty Branch, particularly as regards battle casualty statistics.

During the war considerable developments took place in the Army as elsewhere in the educational and welfare fields and this was reflected in the Adjutant-General's Department. A Directorate of

Army Education was established in 1940 and by 1942 there was a Directorate-General of Welfare and Education controlling branches for Welfare, the Army Bureau for Current Affairs and Army Education, all of which became full and independent Directorates by the following year.

Quarter-Master-General

The quarter-master-general to the forces was responsible for their equipment and movement. The Directorate of Quartering concerned itself with the provision of accommodation both at home and abroad. The Directorates of Movement and of Transportation were co-ordinated by a director-general and their respective responsibilities were control of particular movements and the provision of facilities and training. The Directorate of Supplies and Transport was concerned with catering, provisions, vehicles and their fuelling and use.

On the Ordnance side the Directorate of Ordnance Services developed quickly into the Directorate of Warlike Stores, the Directorate of Clothing and Stores and the Directorate of Mechanical Engineering. The first was responsible for the provision, storage, distribution and issue of warlike stores, and the second exercised similar functions for other Ordnance stores. The Directorate of Mechanical Engineering was responsible for technical examination of maintenance methods and their application to vehicles, armaments and other engineering equipment. In March 1941 these directorates, together with Army Kinematography, were placed under the director-general of Army equipment. Works and Fortifications were also the responsibility of the Quarter-Master-General's Department, where they had their own Directorate, and in 1941 an engineer-in-chief was also appointed for the execution of work services. Upon the abolition of the Directorate of Auxiliary Military Pioneer Services in the Adjutant-General's Department a Directorate of Labour was established in the Quarter-Master-General's Department. The director of labour was also inspector of the Pioneer Corps.

To provide a link between the Quarter-Master-General's Department, the chief of the imperial general staff and the Ministry of Supply, a director-general of Army requirements was appointed in October 1939.

In 1940 the quarter-master-general had two deputies who apportioned the directorates between them, but in the following year they were reduced to one. In 1942 the second deputy quarter-master-general reappeared and was now charged with ensuring liaison within the Department. In March 1943 the upper echelon of the Department was again reorganized. In place of the two deputy quarter-masters-general and the director-general of Army equipment a vice-quarter-master-general was appointed to deal with operations and overseas maintenance, a deputy quarter-master-general to deal with non-operational administration, and a deputy quarter-master-general (ae) to deal with the provision, storage, repair and salvage of Army equipment. All the directorates were responsible to these officers within their particular spheres, while the engineer-in-chief, director-general of Army requirements and controller of economy continued to be directly responsible to the quarter-master-general. In 1944 the vice-quarter-master-general was provided with a new Directorate of Administrative Planning to assist him and an additional deputy quarter-master-general (movements) was appointed with separate directors for personnel and freight movements.

Permanent Under-Secretary

The Department of the Permanent Under-Secretary of State for War was primarily concerned in peace with financial matters and the administration of civilian staff. The Permanent Under-Secretary's Department had financial advisers placed for audit work in Command and some Force Headquarters, but these posts were later abolished in cases where there were command secretaries. The Casualty Branch was attached to the Department and in April 1940 the Directorate of Public Relations, which had previously been immediately responsible to the secretary of state was taken over. In the same year the Directorate-General of Progress and Statistics, also previously under the secretary of state and charged with organizing a system of reports, returns, statistics and forecasts in order to present a clear view of the trends of Army requirements, was transferred to the Permanent Under-Secretary's Department as the Directorate of Investigation and Statistics. This directorate was abolished in October 1943. In October 1940 the Claims Commission was constituted to deal, with the help of representatives in the Commands, with claims made in the United Kingdom by or against the War Department and to supervise the work of similar commissions which were set up in overseas commands. From 1942 it also undertook work arising from Air Ministry and Royal Air Force road traffic accidents at home. The appointment of a second permanent under-secretary (finance) in February 1942 has already been mentioned and from May 1942 the Directorate of Army Contracts reported to him and not to the finance member of the Army Council. This was in line with the Sinclair Report of that year which recommended that the junior members of the Council should not have executive responsibilities. During the rearmament period and the war a considerable degree of financial control was devolved by the Treasury to the War Office. Authorization of major expenditure was in the hands of the Treasury Inter-Service Committee, containing representatives of the Treasury and the Supply and Service Departments.

The Directorate of Civil Affairs was formed in the Permanent Under-Secretary's Department in June 1943 to carry out the duties previously performed by a branch of the Directorate of Military Operations. The objective of Civil Affairs in the Army was the control of the civil population to prevent interference with operations against the enemy and to make the maximum use of local resources to contribute to such operations. It included the administration of occupied enemy territory and as the prospect of victories grew so did the part played by Civil Affairs both in the War Office and in the Headquarters of the various theatres and armies. The Directorate shared in planning the administration of occupied Germany with the Foreign Office. Civil affairs at Combined Headquarters were controlled by the Combined Civil Affairs Committee in Washington which had a sub-committee in London for North-West Europe.

After much discussion it was agreed that when the British elements of the Control Commission for Germany and the Allied Commission for Austria went overseas the War Office should exercise departmental responsibility. In June 1945 the Directorate established a Control Commission London Bureau in Norfolk House for that purpose. It soon became clear, however, that questions concerning the occupation went far beyond the military sphere. Accordingly, in October 1945 all work connected with control matters in London passed to a newly-established Control Office for Germany and Austria (see p 86).

Home Forces

A commander-in-chief Home Forces was appointed in September 1938 and in June 1940, as it began to appear likely that he would have to assume control of operations, his Headquarters became a General Headquarters. He was in operational control of all military forces of the United Kingdom, except Anti-Aircraft Command which was controlled by Fighter Command of the Royal Air Force, but the War Office retained a responsibility for the training of these troops and for administrative functions as previously described. The organization of General Headquarters followed the conventional lines with, in June 1941, for example, a chief of the general staff in charge of branches for Operations, Staff Duties and Training, and Intelligence and a lieutenant-general administration in charge of both adjutant-general and quarter-master-general functions, for which he had branches for Adjutant-General, Quarter-Master-General (Maintenance and Movements), Supplies and Transport, and Ordnance. There was also a chief civil staff officer with duties in connection with the Home Defence Executive (see p 7) of which the commander-in-chief was chairman, and specialist branches for the Royal Armoured Corps, Royal Artillery, Engineering, Fortresses, Chemical Warfare, Signals, Aerodrome Defence and Camouflage. On policy and technical questions they dealt with the parallel War Office Directorates but for operations they were solely responsible to the commander-in-chief.

Like the War Office, General Headquarters Home Forces commenced operating with a Central Registry, but by August 1940 it was abolished and correspondence was addressed directly to branches who maintained their own small registries. Prefixes in references of files and correspondence show whether the source is General Headquarters or Commands and suffixes indicate the branch.

The defence of the United Kingdom may be regarded as a giant combined operation in which the commander-in-chief Home Forces, with his responsibility for carrying out exercises and trials, and preparing and examining plans, needed to maintain the closest liaison both with the other Services and with civil authorities. He had a naval staff which provided information about naval dispositions and a similar arrangement with the Royal Air Force. The Army Co-operation Command provided a liaison detachment which was known as Royal Air Force General Headquarters Home Forces to distinguish it from the Air branch which as part of the Operations branch provided the commander-in-chief with advice on airborne questions. Liaison officers at Area Combined Headquarters around the country enabled the Army to co-ordinate its activities with the other Services at the local level. Liaison officers from General Headquarters attended the Home Security War Room to collect information of military value and pass it both to General Headquarters and to the civil staff officer in the Cabinet War Room. Contact was also maintained with regional commissioners (see pp 111-12) both at General Headquarters and Command levels. The Home Forces controlled by General Headquarters were organized in Commands, namely Aldershot, Eastern, Northern, Scottish, Southern and Western, and most of these were given the status of Army Headquarters with Corps Headquarters, where appropriate, subordinated to them. In February 1941 Aldershot Command was abolished, becoming an area in the new South Eastern Command of which the rest had been carved out of Eastern Command. The units of the Field Army were supplemented by the more static Home Guard, which came into existence as the Local Defence Volunteers in May 1940 and changed its title two months later. Some units were organized as Auxiliary Units, intended to operate behind enemy lines.

In May 1942 preparations were begun for the creation of a new British Expeditionary Force and the Headquarters was set up for it. The troops assigned to this Force were available for Home Forces in the event of an invasion and equally the Expeditionary Force needed to draw for administrative services on the static units of the Home Command. In March of the following year planning for the invasion of Europe began in earnest and in June 1943 Headquarters 21st Army Group was set up to train forces for the invasion. These troops remained available for Home Forces in the defensive role but Headquarters 21st Army Group was otherwise independent of General Headquarters Home Forces and dealt directly with the War Office.

British Expeditionary Force

In accordance with arrangements made before the war a British Expeditionary Force was sent to France in September 1939, where it took over part of the frontier defences. The Force came under the French High Command via its North Eastern Theatre Command, though with its own commander-in-chief having the right to appeal to the British government. Missions from its General Headquarters were sent to the Headquarters of the French North Eastern Theatre and later to the Belgian Headquarters. The British Expeditionary Force came to an end in June 1940 when a large part of it having been successfully extricated from Dunkirk, an attempt to re-establish it in North-Western France failed. As with other Commands, records of subordinate formations have been preserved alongside those of General Headquarters.

North Western Expeditionary Force

A small Expeditionary Force was sent to Norway between April and June 1940.

The Middle East

A general officer commanding-in-chief Middle East was appointed before the war to command the British forces in Egypt, Sudan, Palestine/Transjordan and Cyprus, which were then organized as Commands, and to co-operate with the commanders-in-chief of the other Services in that area by means of a Joint Planning Staff and Joint Intelligence Committee. No General Headquarters was provided at this stage and the administration of the troops continued to be directed from the War Office. At the end of 1939 it was decided that the Middle East should be built up as a base and the general officer commanding-in-chief began to assume administrative control over the forces in his command. General Headquarters was organized on the traditional lines and as expansion of the base continued it became more and more to appear as a small version of the War Office. It was able to mount training courses, for example. It included a Combined Operations Directorate (which began as the Directorate of Opposed Landings), run by a combined board, and developed a strong Civil Affairs element for the control of occupied territory. The commander-in-chief was formally responsible for this territory but handled it through a chief political officer (chief civil affairs officer from March 1943) who was able to take political advice from the minister of state resident in the Middle East (see pp 12-13). The territory taken from the Vichy French in Syria was administered by Control Commissions. Contact with the War Office was maintained by liaison officers as well as by signals.

Middle East had both a Central Registry and reference system of War Office pattern and sets of files kept by branches. These were largely of the informational type described earlier and contain situation and operations reports from formations, minutes of commander's conferences and copies of papers circulated by the subordinate Headquarters. Files from subordinate formations are also preserved.

The area of responsibility and the structure of commands varied greatly in the Middle East during the course of the war. Iraq, Aden, British Somaliland, the Persian Gulf and East Africa were shortly added and when hostilities against Italy were imminent in June 1940 a Headquarters Western Desert Force was established. Early in the following year Cyrenaica Command was established in the territory conquered from the Italians, but it lasted for only two months before we were driven from that area. At this time also it was decided to send troops to Greece, in addition to the Royal Air Force Detachment there, which was receiving its administration from the Army, and a Headquarters was therefore formed at Athens. These forces when driven from Greece were assembled in Crete during April 1941 but were forced from the island by the end of May.

The growth of the Middle East base on a scale to rival the long-established system in India presented the General Headquarters Middle East with considerable problems. This vast area, unprovided as it was with the industry and communications available in India, let alone in the United Kingdom, placed a great administrative burden on the Army. In May 1941 an intendant-general was appointed with instructions to examine military administration in the Middle East and make recommendations, but to these duties was shortly added that of relieving the commander-in-chief of administrative responsibilities in the same way as the War Office did for the commander-in-chief Home Forces. He advised the co-ordination of all administrative services, including those of the Egyptian Government, but this recommendation was overtaken by the appointment of a minister of state Middle East, under whom the intendant-general was then placed. The latter was given very wide terms of reference, but in October a principal administrative staff officer to the commander-in-chief Middle East was appointed and the intendant-general relieved of all duties in the Army sphere proper.

In March 1941 it had been agreed that if operations became necessary in Iraq they should be controlled from India, but when fighting broke out the command was transferred to the Middle East. As soon as this situation was under control command reverted to India, but towards the end of 1941 command of both Iraq and Persia was transferred to the Middle East. By the middle of 1941 the forces available to General Headquarters Middle East had grown sufficiently to make it necessary to establish two Army Headquarters, for the 8th Army in the West and for the 9th Army in the North. Egypt and Palestine/Transjordan became the Base and Lines of Communication Areas for these theatres respectively.

In September 1941 an independent East Africa Command reporting directly to the War Office was established with Headquarters at Nairobi. It had its own political officer but he was expected to keep in line with the minister of state.

In the following year a threat to Persia developed from the German advance through Russia and in order to meet this and to take some of the burden from the commander-in-chief Middle East it was decided to establish a new and separate Persia and Iraq Command. Records from this Command will be found with those of the Middle East.

The opening of a fresh front in North West Africa under Allied Force Headquarters at the end of 1942, coming shortly after the victory of El Alamein, was soon to bring about considerable changes in the Middle East. Co-operation quickly developed; for example, in the exchange of intelligence. In February 1943 control of the 8th Army was transferred from the Middle East to Allied Force Headquarters, but its supply and maintenance, as well as that of Royal Air Force Middle East, remained with Cairo, while a Base and Lines of Communication Area for the 8th Army was set up in Tripolitania. The dividing line between the North Africa and Middle East theatres had been determined at the Casablanca conference as the Tunisia/Tripolitania frontier extended to Corfu, but this boundary was abolished when General Headquarters Middle East was joined with Allied Force Headquarters in the new Mediterranean Theatre of Operations on 10 December 1943.

Allied Force Headquarters

Allied Force Headquarters, to which reference has already been made, was activated in London on 12 September 1942. As a combined Headquarters its records will be found to reflect American as well as British practices, and the following explanation is therefore given of American Staff nomenclature, though these are by no means all exact equivalents: G1 is the British adjutant-general, *ie* personnel; G2 is G S Intelligence; G3 is G S Operations and Training; G4 is quarter-master-general; G5 is Military Government and Civil Affairs. Apart from nomenclature the actual difference between British and American administrative systems was sufficient to require elements of both to be included in the Staff. Allied Force Headquarters was also a joint Headquarters with joint planners and a Joint Intelligence Committee. The records of subordinate formations are associated with it.

On 25 November 1942 the invasion of North Africa had had such success that Allied Force Headquarters could be established at Algiers, where it remained until victories on the Italian mainland enabled it to be opened at Caserta on 20 July 1944. Its Advanced Administrative Echelon had been established at Naples since October 1943, and in North Africa it left behind a District Headquarters. In combining with General Headquarters Middle East in December 1943 it became the Mediterranean Theatre of Operations, as has been explained, and in March 1944 its commander was redesignated supreme Allied commander Mediterranean.

The files of Allied Force Headquarters were referenced on the American decimal system and each element of Headquarters maintained its own series. There was a secretary, General Staff, whose office was combined with the Inter-Service and Political Secretariat in March 1945 to form the Supreme Allied Commander's Secretariat. This had the functions of ensuring prompt and co-ordinated action in policy matters in which naval, military, air and political questions were interconnected, of providing the Secretariat for Supreme Allied Commander Conferences and Supreme Allied Commander Political Conferences, and of keeping various records. Many of the records which have been preserved were transferred to this section from their originating offices. To ensure that both parties had copies of records deriving from Allied Headquarters a microfilming programme was undertaken after the war. By and large the United Kingdom received Allied Force Headquarters originals and Supreme Headquarters Allied Expeditionary Force microfilms, while the Allied Force Headquarters microfilms and Supreme Headquarters Allied Expeditionary Force originals went to the United States.

Command of the forces operating in North West Africa under Allied Force Headquarters had at first been difficult to organize, but by February 1943 it became possible to put all forces in Tunisia into 18th Army Group whose Headquarters included a naval adviser and also accommodated the air officer commanding tactical air force. Operations in Sicily and Italy were controlled from May 1943 by Headquarters Allied Armies in Italy. This became 15th Army Group in July 1943 and this in turn became Allied Central Mediterranean Force in January 1944. In March it was redesignated Allied Armies in Italy and by the end of the year it had reverted to 15th Army Group.

Apart from its military functions Allied Force Headquarters was much concerned with political (including psychological warfare) and economic questions of the area, in connection with which high-level political advisers were attached to it (see p 85). For the consideration of such questions the supreme Allied commander had a Political Committee which later became the Supreme Allied Commander's Conference (Political), thus distinguished from the Supreme Allied Commander's Conference (Operational). The North African Economic Board, begun at the end of 1942, was concerned with the provision of food, clothing and shelter for North Africa and was taken over in 1944 by the North Africa Joint Economic Mission, which was not responsible to Allied Force Headquarters. Similarly a Central Economic Committee was set up in Naples in 1943 to determine minimum requirements, control and allocate local resources, fix prices and wages and co-ordinate transport. Shipping Boards were also established for North Africa and Italy.

In Sicily and Italy as the front moved forward administration of the liberated areas was at first in the hands of Allied Military government and later transferred to the Allied Control Commission, while later still some functions were transferred to the Italian government. Records of the Control Commission survive as well as those of G5 Division of Allied Force Headquarters, which was, of course, concerned with other areas in addition to Italy. For the Balkans, where there were no military governments formed, relief and allied questions were in the hands of Allied Military Liaison Headquarters, advising the supreme Allied commander Mediterranean, with subordinate Headquarters for Greece, Yugoslavia and Albania.

Supreme Headquarters Allied Expeditionary Force

The decision was made in January 1943 to appoint a chief of staff to the supreme Allied commander, himself yet unappointed, to plan the cross-Channel invasion of Europe. The organization of the British element of the invasion forces was entrusted in July to Headquarters 21st Army Group, to which reference has already been made in connection with the responsibilities of the commander-in-chief Home Forces. The records of both the chief of staff and the Army Group appear among those of Supreme Headquarters Allied Expeditionary Force.

The organization of the chief of staff was a combined establishment from the beginning and American elements appear in its organization, nomenclature and records in the same manner as has been described for Allied Force Headquarters. In addition to the military elements provision was made for Political and Civil Affairs and for naval and air association with the planning. Most of the staff were taken over into Supreme Headquarters Allied Expeditionary Force when that body was set up in January 1944 to continue preparation of the now expanded plans for invasion. It continued the previous arrangement of five numbered divisions of the General Staff, reinforced by Special Staff Divisions for Engineering, Signals, Air Defence, Medical Services, Psychological Warfare and Public Relations. The divisions kept their own records on American lines and there was a secretary, General Staff, under the adjutant-general who was otherwise concerned only with United States personnel.

The Headquarters of 21st Army Group formed the tactical Headquarters for the cross-Channel and the immediately succeeding land operations and moved across the Channel immediately after D-Day. By September 1944 Supreme Headquarters itself was established in France, and the supreme commander took over direct control of land operations from the commander of 21st Army Group. On 15 September Supreme Headquarters took over command of the American 6th Army Group which had come up from the South of France.

Relations with the liberated countries were handled by Missions. These were in the first place Military Missions to Supreme Headquarters from the governments of these countries, who worked, however, not at Supreme Headquarters but in the territory concerned. When, following liberation, the national government was able to take over control such a Mission would be replaced by a Supreme Headquarters Mission to it.

India and Far East

India, as befitted an important base, had always a sizeable General Headquarters organized very much in the manner of the War Office into directorates, which corresponded regularly with their opposite numbers in London. The country itself was divided into geographical commands, which under the threat of invasion were supported by Joint Planning and Intelligence Staffs. There was also a director of combined operations responsible both for training establishments and some experimentation.

A General Headquarters Far East based at Singapore had been established before the Japanese attack and operational control of Burma was shuttled between this General Headquarters and those of India and American-British-Dutch-Australian Command until our forces were driven from that country. Operations in the area of the Indo-Burmese frontier naturally fell to General Headquarters India, and a Headquarters Indian Expeditionary Force was established there in March 1943 for the eventual reconquest of Burma. Shortly afterwards a need was felt to divorce the command of operations against the Japanese in this area from control of the India base and it was agreed that the new Far East Headquarters should be a Supreme Command to include the American forces in South East Asia. Headquarters South East Asia Command opened in New Delhi on 16 November 1943. Command of operations was vested in various commanders-in-chief, among whom the deputy supreme Allied commander commanded United States forces in the area and the Chinese forces operating in Burma. Naval and air interests were represented at Headquarters South East Asia Command by assistant deputy chiefs of staff and the staff was organized in divisions for Operations, Plans, Intelligence, Special Operations (P), Deception, Airborne Operations, Stores, Signals, Survey, Operational Research, Combined Operations and Civil Affairs. There was in addition an engineer-in-chief, a principal administrative officer, a comptroller and, later, a chief political adviser. A Secretariat managed the Supreme Allied Commander's Conference, the Principal Staff Officers Committee and Supreme Allied Commander's Staff meetings, circulating papers in the manner of the War Cabinet Secretariat. Headquarters South East Asia Command moved to Kandy in April 1944, but land and air Headquarters were effectively at Calcutta during the rest of the period. Apart from the American and Chinese forces mentioned above land operations in the Command were under the command of Headquarters 11th Army Group at Delhi and the forces concerned were both those in Burma and those in Ceylon. The arrangement whereby there were separate operational commands in Burma caused considerable difficulties over a long period and in November 1944 Allied Land Forces South East Asia was formed. American staff
190

were added to Headquarters 11th Army Group to provide the new Headquarters, of which the advanced part was established at Calcutta while the main Headquarters was moved from Delhi to Kandy at the same time as Air Command South East Asia. To relieve the 14th Army of administrative detail a Lines of Communication Command was then set up in North East India with Headquarters at Comilla.

South East Asia Command, India and Allied Land Forces South East Asia continued in constant communication with each other and much information was exchanged at staff level, for example, about plans and operational research. The latter included on the spot research into jungle operations, while for the former a Joint Planning Staff was established at Calcutta in January 1945 to deal with operations, leaving the joint planners at Kandy to deal with strategy. The records of Allied Land Forces South East Asia include those of previous and subordinate Headquarters.

Missions

During the course of the war Military Missions were sent to various countries either from London or from Headquarters such as South East Asia Command. They included missions to France, China, Greece and Yugoslavia, but the most important was that in Washington, which formed part of the British Joint Staff Mission. Up to July 1941 there was a number of separate missions in the United States but in that month they were amalgamated into the British Army Staff. This was organized in five branches for General Staff, Army Requirements, Quarter-Master-General, Public Relations and Miscellaneous.

The Records

ADM 202	Royal Marines War Diaries
	This class includes war diaries of the Royal Marine Division, Special Service and Commando Units, Mobile Naval Base Defence Organizations, etc, and despatches, letters and reports and files on operations. See also DEFE 2 under the section concerning Combined Operations Headquarters, p 60.
AVIA 45	Tropical Testing Establishment, Nigeria: Reports and Memoranda
AVIA 46	Ministry of Supply Files: Series 1 (Establishment)
	Includes material concerning War Office research establishments.
AVIA 53	Ministry of Supply Files: Series 6 (Contracts)
	Includes papers dealing with claims concerning wartime inventions for the Army.
CM 4	Directorate of Defence Services I (Army): Graves and Cemeteries Files
	These relate to the maintenance of UK graves and cemeteries at home and overseas.
DEFE 1	Postal and Telegraph Censorship Department
	This class includes some records from the period when postal and telegraph censorship was the concern of the Directorate of Military Intelligence. The class is closed for 50 years.
DEFE 3	War of 1939-1945: Intelligence from Enemy Radio Communications
	These signals known as ULTRA consist of intercepts which were decrypted, translated and sent from the German Naval Section of the Admiralty's Naval Intelligence Division at Bletchley Park to the Division's Operational Intelligence Centre in the Admiralty; and intelligence summaries derived from such signals sent to the War Office, Air Ministry and overseas commands. See also ADM 223/36.
FO 945	Control Office: General Department
	This class includes some War Office files taken over by the Control Office for Germany and Austria. Other Control Office classes are listed under records of the Foreign Office, pp 91-2.
FO 1015	Foreign Office Administration of African Territories
	This class relates to the British administration of the former Italian colonies in Africa. From 1941 until 1949 the files are those of the War Office.
WO 24	Establishments
	Includes minutes of meetings of the War Establishments Committee.
WO 32	Registered Files: General Series
	Documents selected for permanent preservation from the series of registered files at the War

Office. They relate to all aspects of War Office business and include files opened in the War Office and continued in the Ministry of Supply after 1939. See also WO 141.

WO 33 O and A Papers
A collection of printed reports, memoranda, etc. See also WO 279 and WO 287.

WO 70 Volunteer and Territorial Records
Precedent books and indexes to property and to miscellaneous subjects.

WO 71 Judge Advocate General's Office: Courts Martial Proceedings.
Records mostly closed for 50 or 75 years.

WO 73 Monthly Returns, Distribution of the Army
These show the distribution of the Army month by month (a) by divisions and stations and (b) by regiments in numerical order. They give the station of each battalion or company, the numbers of officers and rank and file present or absent and other statistical information.

WO 78 Maps and Plans
These relate to the United Kingdom and overseas. See also WORK 43.

WO 81 Judge Advocate General's Office: Letter Books
Closed for 75 years.

WO 82 Judge Advocate General's Office: Day Books
Closed for 75 years.

WO 83 Judge Advocate General's Office: Minute Books
These contain the decisions and rulings of the Judge Advocate General. Records closed for 75 years.

WO 84 Judge Advocate General's Office: Charge Books
Out-letters from the Judge Advocate General's Office relating to the preparation of charges for trial by courts martial. Records closed for 75 years.

WO 86 Judge Advocate General's Office: District Courts Martial
Registers from the Judge Advocate General's Office of charges, giving the name, rank and regiment of each prisoner, place of trial, nature of the charge and sentence. Records closed for 75 years.

WO 88 Judge Advocate General's Office: District Courts Martial, India
Similar register to those in WO 86. Closed for 75 years.

WO 90 Judge Advocate General's Office: General Courts Martial Abroad
Similar registers to those in WO 86. Records closed for 75 years.

WO 92 Judge Advocate General's Office: General Courts Martial Registers
Records closed for 75 years.

WO 93 Judge Advocate General's Office: Miscellaneous Records
Include some general correspondence and progress reports concerning war trials.

WO 94 Tower of London Constable's Office
Two pieces concerning prisoners of war and an execution of a German for espionage.

WO 98 Victoria Cross
List of recipients.

WO 102 Long Service and Good Conduct Awards
One register of the West African Frontier Force.

WO 103 War Office and Associated Departments: Submissions for Royal Approval
Documents authorizing awards, etc.

WO 106 Directorate of Military Operations and Intelligence
For the wartime period these are records of the Directorate of Military Operations only. See also WO 193 and WO 208.

WO 107 Quarter Master General
Papers concerning the movement of troops and supplies in connection with various exercises and expeditions including 'Operation Overlord'.

WO 113 Finance Department: Precedent Books
These relate mainly to pay.

WO 115 Directorate of Medical Services Reports, Returns and Summaries
These consist of annual statistical returns of the director of medical services by commands, at home and abroad, of admissions to hospital, deaths, discharges from the Army and periods of treatment; and annual reports of the deputy directors of medical services on the health of troops, the prevalence of disease and work of military hospitals.

WO 123 War Office and Associated Departments: Army Circulars, Memoranda, Orders and Regulations

WO 138 Selected Personal Files
Including papers concerning the appointment of Dame Lesley Whateley as director of the Auxiliary Territorial Service.

WO 141 Registered Papers: Special Series
Documents formerly in WO 32 but subject to closure for 100 years.

WO 151   Royal Military College, Sandhurst, Registers of Cadets
          The series of registers in this class covers the separate existence of the Royal Military College, Sandhurst, up to 1939, and the period 1939 to 1946 when it, together with the Royal Military Academy, Woolwich, formed the Officer Cadets Training Unit, Sandhurst. The class is held at the Royal Military Academy, Sandhurst.

WO 156   Registers of Baptisms and Banns of Marriage
          One register from the garrison at Dover and three from Palestine Command.

WO 162   Adjutant General
          The class includes statistical returns of battle casualties.

WO 163   War Office Council and Army Council Records
          Minutes of meetings, committee reports, secretariat papers, etc. of the Army Council.

WO 165   War of 1939 to 1945, War Diaries, War Office Directorates
          Daily records of various branches of War Office directorates functioning during the war years and up to 1947. WO 165-179 are closed for 75 or 100 years except to those prepared to sign an undertaking agreeing to specified restrictions on use. Applications to be made to officer-in-charge of Search Room for form of undertaking and copies of lists.

WO 166   War of 1939 to 1945, War Diaries, Home Forces
          Daily record of events, reports on operations, intelligence summaries, etc, of formation or headquarters, divisional, regimental and other unit commanders. For access see WO 165.

WO 167   War of 1939 to 1945, War Diaries, British Expeditionary Force
          Daily records of events, reports on operations, intelligence summaries, etc, of formation or headquarters, divisional, regimental and other unit commanders of the British Expeditionary Force in France from September 1939 to June 1940. For access see WO 165.

WO 168   War of 1939 to 1945, War Diaries, North West Expeditionary Force (Norway)
          Daily record of events, reports on operations, etc, for headquarters and various unit formations during the Norwegian campaign. For access see WO 165.

WO 169   War of 1939 to 1945, War Diaries, Middle East Forces
          Day by day records of operations by units on the ground. For access see WO 165.

WO 170   War of 1939 to 1945, War Diaries, Central Mediterranean Forces
          These are records of the British element of the Allied Force which invaded Sicily and Italy in 1943 also of British units in the Balkans and Greece and of British occupation forces in Austria. They contain daily records of events, reports on operations, intelligence summaries of headquarters, formation and unit commanders. For access see WO 165.

WO 171   War of 1939 to 1945, War Diaries, North West Europe.
          These records of the British element of the Allied Expeditionary Force which invaded North West Europe in the summer of 1944 contain the daily record of events, reports on operations, intelligence summaries, etc, of Supreme Headquarters Allied Expeditionary Force and of headquarters, formation and unit commanders. For access see WO 165.

WO 172   War of 1939 to 1945, War Diaries, South East Asia Command and Allied Land Forces, South East Asia
          Daily records of events, reports on operations, intelligence summaries, etc, of formations and units of British Forces, including East and West African Forces, which served in Burma, Ceylon, Hong Kong, India and Malaya.
          For access see WO 165.

WO 173   War of 1939 to 1945, War Diaries, West Africa
          Daily records of events, reports on operations, intelligence summaries, etc, of commanders of headquarters, formations and units of the British Army and West African Forces serving in West African Command. For access see WO 165.

WO 174   War of 1939 to 1945, War Diaries, Madagascar
          Daily records of events, reports on operations, intelligence summaries, etc. For access see WO 165.

WO 175   War of 1939 to 1945, War Diaries, British North Africa Forces
          Daily records of events, reports on operations, intelligence summaries, etc, of headquarters, formation and unit commanders of the British element of the Allied Force which landed in Algiers in November 1942. The class also contains war diaries of the forces which dealt with planning and training from July 1941. The military headquarters papers of the North African campaign of 1942 to 1943 are in WO 204. War diaries of units engaged in the earlier North African campaigns are in WO 169. For access see WO 165.

WO 176   War of 1939 to 1945, War Diaries, Various Smaller Theatres
          Daily records of events, reports on operations, intelligence summaries, etc, of commanders of headquarters, garrisons and units of the British Army overseas in commands other than the main theatres. For access see WO 165.

WO 177	War of 1939 to 1945, War Diaries, Medical Services
	For access see WO 165.
WO 178	War of 1939 to 1945, War Diaries, Military Missions
	Diaries of commanders appointed to liaise with Allied Forces on military matters, supply of aid, etc. Mostly open but for access to certain pieces see WO 165.
WO 179	War of 1939 to 1945, War Diaries, Dominion Forces
	Daily records of events, reports on operations and intelligence summaries etc. For access see WO 165.
WO 181	Directorate of Military Survey
	Unregistered branch files of the Geographical Section, General Staff, including papers concerning ordnance survey recruitment and training and air survey research.
WO 186	Proof and Experimental Establishments
	Reports of the Trials Establishment Royal Artillery, Ty Croes.
WO 190	Appreciation Files
	Reports on the military situation in Germany and adjacent countries prepared in the Directorate of Military Intelligence.
WO 192	Fort Record Books
	The official records of the operation, administration and history of forts at home and abroad.
WO 193	Directorate of Military Operations: Collation Files
	These give general information on a world-wide basis of military planning, operations, intelligence, statistics, etc. See also WO 106 and p 181 above.
WO 196	Director of Artillery
	Reports and appreciations on the defence of coasts and fortresses at home and overseas, prepared for the Director.
WO 197	War of 1939 to 1945, Military Headquarters Papers: British Expeditionary Force
	This class consists of the surviving files of the British Expeditionary Force in France from 1939 to 1940 plus various narratives, notes and summaries of operations written by the officers concerned after the evacuation from Dunkirk in May 1940.
WO 198	War of 1939 to 1945, Military Headquarters Papers: NW Expeditionary Force
	These relate to the combined expedition to Norway, April to June 1940.
WO 199	War of 1939 to 1945, Military Headquarters Papers: Home Forces
	There are also files for the first Armoured Division and the Home Guard and some material on preparation for the invasion of Europe and other operations abroad.
WO 201	War of 1939 to 1945, Military Headquarters Papers: Middle East Forces
	These cover operations of the British, Dominion and Allied Forces in the Middle East theatre including the Balkans.
WO 202	War of 1939 to 1945, Military Headquarters Papers: Military Missions
	These include the Spears Mission to Syria and Lebanon (see also FO 226), the mission to Yugoslavia and SHAEF Missions to Western Europe.
WO 203	War of 1939 to 1945, Military Headquarters Papers: Far East Forces
	Papers of the joint Anglo-American Command, known as South East Asia Command (SEAC), including those of Allied Land Forces, South East Asia, formerly British Operational Command under SEAC.
WO 204	War of 1939 to 1945, Military Headquarters Papers: Allied Force Headquarters
	These papers deal with operations in the Mediterranean theatre, and cover the campaigns in North Africa, Sicily and Italy, military aid to the Balkans and Greece and military government of occupied territories. The records are essentially only those of combined Anglo-American units; records of units which were not integrated were for the most part treated separately after the war and are not included. American ones were returned to the United States. Detailed information is given in the Analytical Guide (WO 204/10096) prepared when the records were microfilmed prior to their distribution between the allied authorities. See also pp 188-9 above.
WO 205	War of 1939 to 1945, Military Headquarters Papers: 21 Army Group
	Papers of the British operational group under Supreme Headquarters Allied Expeditionary Force (SHAEF). See WO 219.
WO 208	Directorate of Military Intelligence
	In addition to files arranged under geographical headings there are papers from various sources including the Allied Translation and Interpretation Service and the Combined Services Detailed Interrogation Centre. The class includes files on individual prisoners of war, both Allied and enemy, and on prominent Nazis. There is also a transcript, WO 208/5019, of a conversation after the war at Farm Hall, Cambridge of a group of German nuclear scientists who were interned there. See also WO 106 and WO 190.
WO 212	War of 1939 to 1945: Orders of Battle and Organization Tables
	This class contains the orders of battle and organization tables of all headquarters, formations

and units of the British Army serving at home and overseas during the war period.

WO 213   Judge Advocate General's Office: Field General Courts Martial and Military Courts Registers
Registers of the Judge Advocate General's Office of charges giving the name, rank and regiment of each prisoner, place of trial, nature of the charge and sentence. The class is closed for 75 years.

WO 214   Alexander Papers
Official and semi-official correspondence of Earl Alexander of Tunis, supreme Allied commander Mediterranean Theatre, 1944 to 1945.

WO 215   War of 1939 to 1945, GHQ Liaison Regiment: War Diaries and Papers.
A collection especially made up by the Regiment, formerly No 1 GHQ Reconnaissance Unit, and known also as Phantom.

WO 216   Chief of the (Imperial) General Staff Papers
Include correspondence with the prime minister, high-ranking officers and other notable persons.

WO 217   War of 1939 to 1945: Private War Diaries
Accounts by various officers of actions in which they were engaged while serving with the British Expeditionary Force in France from 1939 to 1940 and with the Middle East Forces from 1940.

WO 218   War of 1939 to 1945: War Diaries: Special Services
These were compiled by Commando Brigades, Long Range Desert Groups, Special Air Service Units, etc. The class also includes reports on particular operations.

WO 219   War of 1939 to 1945, Military Headquarters Papers: SHAEF
These concern the invasion of Northern Europe, 1944-1945, and are copies of the originals held in Washington. For headquarters papers of the British 21st Army Group which formed the tactical command for the Normandy operations see WO 205. For papers after the collapse of Germany see FO 1030 among records of the Control Commission (p 62).

WO 220   Directorate of Civil Affairs
Files, reports, handbooks, etc, concerning the administration of territories formerly occupied by the enemy.

WO 221   Inter-Departmental Contracts and Procurement Committees and Sub-Committees
Minutes and agenda of the Contracts Co-ordinating Committee and its sub-committees. The class includes files concerning the constitution of the committees, 1942 to 1944, which have been cited by the official historian.

WO 222   War of 1939 to 1945: Medical Historian Papers
Papers collected for use in compiling the Army contribution to the UK Medical Series of the History of the Second World War. See also WO 347.

WO 223   Staff College Camberley 1947 Course: Notes on D-Day Landings and Ensuing Campaigns
See also WO 277.

WO 224   War of 1939 to 1945: Enemy Prisoner of War Camps: Reports of International Red Cross and Protecting Powers
See also FO 916.

WO 226   Committee on Detention Barracks
Minutes, evidence, report, etc, of the Committee set up in 1943, under the chairmanship of Sir Roland Oliver, to inquire into the treatment of men under sentence in naval and military detention barracks.

WO 227   Engineer in Chief Papers
These records concern planning and operations at home and abroad carried out by the Royal Engineers, including the construction of airfields, minefields and pipelines.

WO 230   British Military Administration of African Territories
Papers of the East Africa and Middle East Commands arising from the occupation of Italy's African Territories.

WO 231   Directorate of Military Training: Papers
These are mainly reports on operations.

WO 232   Directorate of Tactical Investigation: Papers
These include papers concerning British arms and services, German Armed Forces and the organization, etc, of the war against Japan.

WO 233   Directorate of Air: Papers
Policy and organization papers concerning air support for army operations, dating from 1941.

WO 234   War of 1939 to 1945, Military Headquarters Papers: North African and Mediterranean Theatres, Maps
Some maps are of German or Italian origin.

WO 235   Judge Advocate General's Office: War of 1939-1945: War Crimes Papers
Case files of persons tried for war crimes before British military courts. The class also includes a few cases tried before Canadian military courts, and files of the deputy judge advocate general

issued from the headquarters of the British Army of the Rhine. See also WO 238, WO 309-311, WO 325, WO 331 and TS 26.

WO 236   Erskine Papers

These papers of General Sir George Erskine relate to operations in North Africa.

WO 237   War Office Committee Lists

Membership, terms of reference, etc, of War Office Committees or Committees on which it was represented.

WO 238   Judge Advocate General's Office: Sound Recordings: Trial of Field Marshal von Manstein

Von Manstein was accused of committing war crimes in Poland and Russia between 1939 and 1944. No equipment survives upon which these sound recordings can presently be played.

WO 240   Mulberry Harbour Photographs

The harbour was used to provide port facilities for the Allied forces invading Europe in June 1944. Copies can be obtained from the Imperial War Museum where a descriptive catalogue and a collection of negatives are held. The photographs show various stages of the harbour under construction and while being towed across the Channel.

WO 241   Directorate of Army Psychiatry: Reports

These concern the psychological effects of war on troops and the psychological basis of enemy morale.

WO 244   Directorate of Signals: Papers

Unregistered papers, mostly concerning particular operations, including Operation Overlord and the crossing of the Rhine. Also contain material relating to communications matters in various territories.

WO 253   Directorate of Labour: Papers

These relate mainly to the activities of the Pioneer Corps.

WO 255   Daly Papers

Private and semi-official papers of Brigadier T D Daly concerning German armed forces and military strategy at the outbreak of war; and notes, etc, arising from his service as area commander, North Caribbean from 1942 to 1944.

WO 257   War of 1939 to 1945: War Diaries: Ship Signal Section

Daily records of events, reports on operations, etc, by officers commanding various ship signal sections between 1942 and 1945.

WO 258   Private Office Papers: Permanent Under-Secretary
WO 259   Private Office Papers: Secretary of State
WO 260   Directorate of Staff Duties: Papers

These relate to war establishments and concern the composition organization, etc, of formations and units.

WO 268   Quarterly Historical Reports: Far East Land Forces

Includes some of the teams investigating Japanese war crimes.

WO 272   Directorate of Supplies and Transport: Papers

These relate mainly to fuel and lubricant supplies and date from 1942.

WO 276   East Africa Command: Papers

This class includes a few files of the Second World War period concerning war establishments, operations, etc.

WO 277   War Office: Department of the Permanent Under-Secretary of State: C3 Branch: Historical Monographs

These were produced after the war for use within the War Office and by students at Staff Colleges. See also WO 223 and WO 366.

WO 279   Confidential Print

Handbooks, manuals and memoranda printed for use within the War Office or by the Army. See also WO 33 and WO 287.

WO 282   Dill Papers

One file containing personal and official correspondence from August 1939 until November 1941. Other papers of Field Marshal Sir John Dill are to be found at the Liddell Hart Centre for Military Archives at King's College London.

WO 283   Inter-services Security Board: Minutes of Meetings
WO 284   Gibraltar Garrison Orders

These were issued from the Town Major's Office and deal largely with administrative matters.

WO 285   Dempsey Papers

Papers of General M C Dempsey mainly concerning his command of the 2nd Army in France and Germany between 1944 and 1945.

WO 287   B Papers

Confidential reports and handbooks printed for internal circulation within the War Office and the Army. They are related to 'A' Papers in WO 33. See also WO 279.

WO 290	War Department Industrial Council: Minutes
WO 291	Military Operational Research
	Reports, memoranda and notes on test and operational performance of military equipment.
WO 293	Army Council Instructions
	Formal orders issued by the Council.
WO 296	Department of the Permanent Under Secretary of State: Central Department (C2): Legal and Parliamentary
	Notebooks containing precedents, decisions and policy.
WO 304	War of 1939 to 1945: Roll of Honour
	This class consists of a list of army servicemen and women who died during the war. Personal details of rank, regiment, place of birth and domicile, and theatre or country where fatal wound was sustained or death occurred may be found by reference to a key which precedes the class list.
WO 305	Unit Historical Records and Reports
	Most date from 1950, but a few relate to the war years.
WO 306	Claims Commission: Minutes of Meetings and other Records
	These concern claims against the War Office for accidents, theft or damage caused by troops.
WO 307	War of 1939 to 1945: Prisoners of War Information Bureau
	These relate to enemy personnel held as prisoners of war.
WO 309	War of 1939 to 1945: HQ BAOR: War Crimes Group (NWE): Files
	See also WO 235, WO 238, WO 310 - WO 311, WO 325, WO 331 and TS 26.
WO 310	War of 1939 to 1945: Rear HQ British Troops Austria: War Crimes Group (SEE): Case Files
	See also WO 235, WO 309, WO 311, WO 331 and TS 26.
WO 311	War of 1939 to 1945: Military Deputy, Judge Advocate General: War Crimes Files
	See also WO 235, WO 238, WO 309 - WO 310, WO 325,WO 331 and TS 26.
WO 315	Army Records Centre (Polish Section): Polish Records, 1939-1950
	These deal with Polish service during the war and its aftermath. See also AST 18 and ED 128.
WO 325	War of 1939 to 1945: War Crimes, South East Asia: Files
	See also WO 235 and TS 26.
WO 328	War of 1939 to 1945: Allied Forces Headquarters (Central Mediterranean Forces): Statements by Former Political Prisoners
	These concern statements from individual prisoners upon their release from Nazi captivity.
WO 331	War of 1939 to 1945: H Q Allied Land Forces Norway: War Crimes Investigation Branch Files
	See also WO 235, WO 309, WO 311, WO 353-WO 355, and TS 26.
WO 333	War of 1939 to 1945: War Diaries: Southern Rhodesia Forces
	Daily records of events, reports on operations, etc, in Africa, Europe and South East Asia.
WO 343	War of 1939 to 1945: South East Asia Command: British Army Aid Group Papers: Microfiche copies
	These are papers of Lt-Col Lindsay Tasman Ride CBE. The originals were donated by his widow to the Australian War Memorial, who presented these microfiche copies to the Ministry of Defence by whom they are at present retained. The Aid Group acted as a military escape and evasion organization in China, primarily to organize escape routes from prisoner of war camps in Hong Kong.
WO 344	Directorate of Military Intelligence: Liberated Prisoners of War Interrogation Questionnaires Retained by Department.
WO 345	War of 1939 to 1945: Japanese Index Cards of Allied Prisoners of War and Internees
WO 347	War of 1939 to 1945: Allied POW Hospital Records: South East Asia
	This class, which is closed for 75 years, except to those who agree to specified restrictions on use, consists mainly of admission and discharge registers, sick registers and death registers, kept by prisoners of war at Nong Pladock Camp and its Ubon satellite in Thailand. There is also an unofficial war diary and death register of Tanbaya Hospital Camp in Burma, including a brief account of the move from Singapore to Thailand. See also WO 222.
WO 353	War of 1939 to 1945: Military Deputy Judge Advocate General: War Crimes, Europe: Card Indexes
WO 354	War of 1939 to 1945: Judge Advocate General: War Crimes, Europe: Card Indexes
WO 355	War of 1939 to 1945: War Crimes, Europe: Card index of persons passed to or wanted by various allied authorities
WO 356	War of 1939 to 1945: Military Deputy Judge Advocate General: War Crimes, South East Asia: Card Indexes.
WO 357	War of 1939 to 1945: War Crimes, South East Asia: Record Cards
WO 366	War Office: Department of the Permanent Under-Secretary of State: C3 Branch: Branch Memoranda on Historical Monographs
	These deal with the organization and control of the overall programme as well as of the individual texts. See also WO 277.

WO 373   War Office and Ministry of Defence: Honours and Awards for Gallant and Distinguished Service: Citations
WO 379   War Office: Disposition and Movement of Regiments (Regimental Records)
          There is one volume for the wartime period concerning Territorial Army Drill Stations 1936 to 1939, and reorganization of Home Forces, locations, 1944.
WO 380   War Office: Designation, Establishments and Stations of Regiments (Regimental Series I-IV)
WO 389   War Office and Ministry of Defence: Military Secretary's Department: Distinguished Service Order and Military Cross Record Books
WO 900   Specimens of Classes of Documents Destroyed
          These include flying log-books of Royal Air Force pilots serving with the Glider Pilot Regiment and forms of personal particulars of captured high-ranking German officers. There is also a daily report book of a battalion of the Home Guard.
WORK 43 Maps and Plans: Army Establishments
WORK 52 War Office Directorate of Contracts: Works Contract Precedent Books

Works Departments

Office of Works

Name	Date of appointment
First commissioner of works and public buildings	
Herwald Ramsbotham, MP	7 June 1939
(later Viscount Soulbury)	
Earl de la Warr	3 Apr 1940
Lord Tryon	18 May 1940
Secretary	
Sir Patrick Duff	1933

Ministry of Works and Buildings
(October 1940 - June 1942)

Minister	
Lord Reith	3 Oct 1940
Lord Portal	22 Feb 1942
Parliamentary secretary	
George Hicks, MP	19 Nov 1940
Secretary	
Sir Patrick Duff	1933
Sir Geoffrey Whiskard	May 1941
Director-general, works and buildings	
Hugh E C Beaver	Apr 1941

Deputy secretary
W Leitch   1941
(Acted as secretary from May to November
1941, until Sir Geoffrey Whiskard returned
from Australia)

Ministry of Works and Planning
(June 1942 - February 1943)

Minister
Lord Portal   22 Feb 1942

Joint parliamentary secretaries
George Hicks, MP (Works)   19 Nov 1940
H G Strauss (later Lord Conesford) (Planning)   4 Mar 1942

Secretary
Sir Geoffrey Whiskard   1941

Director-general, works and buildings
Hugh E C Beaver   Apr 1941

Deputy secretary
W Leitch (later Sir William Leitch)   1941

Ministry of Works
(February 1943 - 3 July 1962)

Minister
Lord Portal   22 Feb 1942
Duncan Sandys, MP   21 Nov 1944

Parliamentary secretary
George Hicks, MP   19 Nov 1940

Secretary
Sir Percival Robinson   1943

Director-general
Hugh E C Beaver (later Sir Hugh Beaver)   Apr 1941

The description 'Ministry of Works' is here used to denote the organization which began the war as the Office of Works, became the Ministry of Works and Buildings in October 1940, the Ministry of Works and Planning in June 1942 and the Ministry of Works in February 1943. The Ministry was created primarily because of the need to impose a centralized control over building and civil engineering activity, to prevent wasteful competition between departments and to curtail the expenditure of effort on works not essential to the prosecution of the war. The execution of work by departments, particularly the Service departments, was largely left untouched by this measure, but the Ministry came to exercise a close control over the allocation of building resources both within and outside government.

In addition to the permanent secretary the Ministry of Works had from May 1941 a director-general with whom the administration of the Ministry, apart from finance, was shared. At the same time the Central Council for Works and Buildings was created to advise the minister. It consisted mainly of representatives of employers and labour but they were nominated by the minister and were not delegated by those interests.

Control of building was exercised according to the direction of the Works and Building Priority Committee under the Production Council and, later, the Production Executive. It operated in the first instance by according priorities by means of certificates to particular works. In common with other production controls priorities were abandoned as a method of building control in 1941 in favour of allocations. Allocations were at first made to departments in terms of the value of works but the allocation of labour was later found to be a more effective method of control and the Ministry established a statistical organization to keep track of labour supply and use. A director of programmes was appointed with a Works and Building Programme Directorate under him to operate the control and for a time in 1941 there was a Building Programmes Board. Other senior officers were the director of allocation of materials, the chief statistical officer, the director of constructional design and the director of plant. During 1941 the minister was given further powers to prohibit the starting of new works in certain areas and a general curtailment of construction programmes was undertaken with a view to releasing manpower for the Forces. Further pressure was imposed after American entry into the war by the need to provide buildings for the American forces to be based in the United Kingdom, and in 1942 the Ministry reverted to a system of priorities for contracts in place of labour allocation to departments. Building labour and plant were pooled so far as possible and assigned to contracts according to their priority. To determine priorities two ministerial directorates were established under the chairmanship of the minister of works, together with parallel official committees. The Service and associated departments, together with the Ministry of Labour and National Service and the Ministry of War Transport, formed the high priority Directorate and the remaining departments the other. They operated under the overall control of the minister of production. In January 1943 a system of labour ceilings was reintroduced in place of priorities.

Various other methods of control were available to the Ministry. Essential Work Orders of the Ministry of Labour and National Service could be applied to particular jobs, and all civil building works of any size that were not carried out under the authority of a government department required a licence from the Ministry. This measure was intended to stop all inessential private building and to ensure the most economical use of labour and materials. A controller of building materials was appointed in October 1940 with directors for cement, bricks and roofing materials, and when the controller became the director-general in April 1941 co-ordination was achieved by a Buildings Materials Board. A Directorate of Construction (Economy) Design scrutinized designs submitted by departments and prepared standard designs.

Private builders were registered in October 1941 and this measure served to provide information about the industry as well as a means of control of hours, wages and conditions. After considerable discussion builders in England and Wales were grouped in 1941 into a Works and Building Emergency Organization which was advised in the Regions by the Ministry's assistant directors of emergency works. The object of the Organization was the allocation of work on a fair and economical basis and provision of building resources for emergency work in bombed or invaded areas. Regional and local advisory committees were appointed by the minister.

A major duty of the Ministry of Works, which was inherited from the Office of Works, was the provision of accommodation for government departments, either by building or in other ways. The construction and maintenance of buildings were the province of the Directorate of Works, and building undertaken by the Ministry included factories and stores as well as office space for the swollen ranks of civil servants. The Ministry had been responsible from before the war for a central registry of premises earmarked for possible use in the event of hostilities and was actively involved in their requisitioning on the outbreak of war, particularly in respect of accommodating evacuated government offices.

It was also concerned with the building aspects of air raid precautions and civil defence measures and with the consequences of air attacks in which it worked closely with the War Damage Commission. A Directorate of Emergency Repairs, later Emergency Works and Recovery, was established in February 1941 to co-ordinate this work with other departments and with local authorities and to control stocks of materials. The Directorate appointed assistant directors in each Region and emergency works officers in each town that was a potential target. To deal with the effects of heavy raids Emergency Repairs Committees consisting of Departmental representatives and local authorities might be established. In the flying bomb attack on London a Repairs Executive was established with representatives from the War Damage Commission, the Ministry of Labour and National Service and the Ministry of Health, and large numbers of men were brought into London to carry out repairs. Another responsibility of this Directorate was the recovery of salvage.

The supplies function inherited from the Office of Works was continued throughout the war by the Ministry's Supplies Division and was called upon to provide a great variety of items. For a short time the Ministry had planning functions, particularly in connection with post-war development, but in 1943 these passed to the Ministry of Town and Country Planning (see p154). A Directorate of Post-War Building remained, however, which was responsible for the preparation of sites and the manufacture of pre-fabricated houses.

The Records

HLG 71 Ministry of Town and Country Planning and successors: Registered Files
This series contains a few earlier papers of Works Departments, including minutes of the Planning Board.

HLG 79 Town and Country Planning: Local Authority Files

HLG 80 Committee on Land Utilization in Rural Areas: (Scott Committee)
This class consists of published and unpublished material submitted in evidence, papers circulated to members and minutes of meetings, together with related papers of the Works Departments and the Ministry of Town and Country Planning.

HLG 81 Expert Committee on Compensation and Betterment (Uthwatt Committee)
This class contains published and unpublished material submitted in evidence, papers circulated to members and minutes of meetings, together with related papers of Works Departments and the Ministry of Town and Country Planning.

HLG 82 Nuffield College Social Reconstruction Survey
This class contains correspondence, reports and papers of the Works Departments and the Ministry of Town and Country Planning relating to an inquiry which the Nuffield College Social Reconstruction Survey was asked to undertake by the minister of works and buildings as part of its proposed local surveys. The subjects for the inquiry were: the redistribution of industry and population brought about by the war; the effects of war on the working of the public social services; the human effects of evacuation, industrial migration, etc; and the bearing of all these factors on the general problems of social and economic reorganization.

HLG 86 Ministry of Works and Buildings, Reconstruction of Town and Country, Advisory Panels and Committees
This class includes papers of the Interdepartmental Committee on Reconstruction (1941), the Consultative Panel on Physical Reconstruction (1941), the Advisory Committee on Reconstruc-

tion (1942), the '1940 Council' and the Reconstruction Areas Group.

HLG 94 Interdepartmental Committee on House Construction
This class consists of minutes of meetings, reports, circulated papers and suggestions from various bodies and members of the public.

HLG 126 Registered Files: Ancient Monuments and Historic Buildings
See also WORK 14 below.

WORK 6 Miscellanea
This class contains volumes and papers relating to a wide range of services of the Office of Works and its successors. A few files relate to the maintenance of a central register of accommodation suitable for government offices during the War of 1939-1945.

WORK 10 Public Buildings Overseas
Correspondence and papers relating to the acquisition of sites or existing buildings for embassies, consulates and other establishments overseas; the construction and conversion of the individual buildings; their equipment and furnishing; and their subsequent maintenance or disposal. Some files relate to wartime arrangements and war damage.

WORK 11 Office of Works and successors: Houses of Parliament: Correspondence and Papers
These relate to the maintenance of the Houses of Parliament, including wartime emergency measures and the demolition and rebuilding of the war-damaged House of Commons, 1944 to 1952.

WORK 12 Public Buildings: England and Wales:
Correspondence and papers (including a few plans) relating to government offices, courts of law and other public buildings. They cover the whole field of the acquisition and disposal of sites and properties; and the design, erection and maintenance of the various buildings, including in the case of certain buildings wartime evacuation and air-raid precaution measures.

WORK 14 Ancient Monuments and Historic Buildings
Correspondence and papers relating to the maintenance and protection of ancient monuments and historic buildings. Some of the papers reflect wartime damage resulting from defence measures and enemy action. Records concerning ancient and historical monuments in Wales and Monmouthshire are in MONW 1 and minutes of the Royal Commission on Historical Monuments in England are in AE 1. See also HLG 126 above and HLG 103 under the Ministry of Town and Country Planning section (p 155).

WORK 15 Osborne Estate
Includes papers concerning proposed conversion of Osborne House to Ministry of Health or War Office local hospital.

WORK 16 Royal Parks and Pleasure Gardens
This class contains a few files relating to the use of royal parks for civil defence reviews, emergency horticulture, temporary housing and emergency water supplies for fire fighting.

WORK 17 Art and Science Buildings
This class contains a few files relating to schemes for the dispersal and protection of national art treasures.

WORK 19 Royal Palaces
This class includes a few files relating to war damage to royal palaces and to the protection and dispersal of paintings and furniture.

WORK 20 Statues and Memorials
Files of the wartime period include papers relating to the protection or removal to places of safety of statues and memorials. A few papers of the Royal Fine Arts Commission concerning proposals for war memorials will be found in BP 2.

WORK 21 Ceremonial
Papers concerning victory celebrations and Remembrance Day procedures.

WORK 22 Administration (General) and Establishment
Correspondence and papers of the general Administrative Divisions or Sections and the Directorate of Establishments of the Ministry of Works and its predecessors. The papers relate to general policy matters concerning the Executive Divisions, including Contracts, Finance and Supplies, and to the whole range of the work of organization and establishment. Some files relate to war damage functions, requisitioning, war works and emergency accommodation.

WORK 26 Royal Ordnance Factories
Correspondence and papers relating to contracts for the construction of emergency ordnance filling factories and ancillary buildings. See also SUPP 5 under Ministry of Supply section (pp 152-3).

WORK 28 Air Raid Precautions and Civil Defence
Correspondence and papers relating to the construction of shelters for government offices and the public, structural precautions, public buildings, lighting restrictions and other civil defence measures.

WORK 45 Construction Industry and Building Materials
Files of correspondence and papers relating to wartime control and peacetime sponsorship of the building and civil engineering industries by the government, with particular reference to legislation, licensing and collection of statistics. The class includes minutes and papers of the following bodies: the Building Programme Joint Committee of the Advisory Council of the Building and Civil Engineering Industries, 1942 to 1945; the Central Council for Works and Buildings, 1941 to 1945; the Committee on the Brick Industry, 1941 to 1942; and the National Brick Advisory Council, 1942 to 1951.

WORK 46 Official History of the Second World War, Works and Buildings, Unpublished Sources
This class contains the unpublished papers used by the official historian in writing the relevant volume of the Official History of the Second World War: C M Kohan, *Works and Buildings* (1952).

WORK 50 Government Property Registers
Requisition, compensation and settlement registers for premises in Berks, Bucks, Hants, Oxon, Isle of Wight and Surrey, and derequisitioned property register for Cambridge 2 district (Hertfordshire). These particular registers were known as 'Blue Books'.

WORK 54 Picture Files
Papers concerning acquisition of pictures executed by Second World War artists and disposition of pictures in time of war. The acquisitions file is retained by the Department.

Key to Colonial Office and Foreign Office Geographical Record Classes

(1) Colonial Office records (pp 55-8)

	Correspondence, etc	Registers, etc	Confidential Print
Aden	CO 725	CO 773	-
Africa	CO 847	CO 917	CO 879
Bahamas	CO 23	CO 333	-
Barbados	CO 28	CO 565	-
Bermuda	CO 37	CO 334	-
British Guiana	CO 111	CO 345	-
British Honduras	CO 123	CO 348	-
British North	CO 531	CO 777	-
Borneo	CO 874	-	-
(see also North Borneo, Brunei and Sarawak)			
Ceylon	CO 54	CO 337	-
Cyprus	CO 67	CO 512	-
East Africa	CO 822	CO 869	-
	CO 962	-	-
Eastern	CO 825	CO 872	CO 882
Falkland Islands	CO 78	CO 339	-
Far Eastern	CO 865	CO 975	-
Federated Malay States	CO 717	CO 786	-
Fiji	CO 83	CO 419	-
Gambia	CO 87	CO 341	-
Gibraltar	CO 91	CO 342	-
Gold Coast	CO 96	CO 343	-
Hong Kong	CO 129	CO 349	-
Jamaica	CO 137	CO 351	-
Kenya	CO 533	CO 628	-
Leeward Islands	CO 152	CO 354	-
Malta	CO 158	CO 355	-
Mauritius	CO 167	CO 356	-
Mediterranean	CO 926	-	-
Middle East	CO 732	CO 788	CO 935
Nigeria	CO 583	CO 763	-
North Borneo, Brunei and Sarawak (see also British North Borneo)	-	CO 992	-
Northern Rhodesia	CO 795	CO 796	-
Nyasaland	CO 525	CO 703	-
Palestine	CO 733	CO 793	-
St Helena	CO 247	CO 366	-
Seychelles	CO 530	CO 712	-

Sierra Leone	CO 267	CO 368	-
Somaliland	CO 535	CO 713	-
Straits Settlements	CO 273	CO 426	-
Tanganyika	CO 691	CO 746	-
Transjordan	CO 831	CO 870	-
Trinidad	CO 295	CO 372	-
Uganda	CO 536	CO 682	-
West Africa	CO 554	CO 555	-
West Indies	CO 318	CO 375	CO 884
	CO 971	CO 972	-
Western Pacific	CO 225	CO 492	-
Windward Islands	CO 321	CO 376	-
Zanzibar	CO 618	CO 772	-

(2) Foreign Office records (pp 86-92)

	Embassy & Consular records	Confidential print
Abyssinia	FO 984	FO 401
(Ethiopia)	-	FO 403
Afghanistan	-	FO 402
		FO 406
Africa and North West Africa	-	FO 403
		FO 413
Albania	-	FO 421
		FO 434
Algeria (Algiers)	FO 111	FO 403
America see Canada; Central America; South America; United States of America		
Arabia	-	FO 406
Argentine Republic	FO 118	-
	FO 446	
Asia see South East Asia		
Austria*	-	FO 404
		FO 408
Baltic States	-	FO 419
		FO 490
Belgium	FO 123	FO 425
	FO 606	FO 432
Brazil	FO 128	-
	FO 743	
Bulgaria	FO 388	FO 421
	-	FO 434
Burma	FO 643	-
Canada	-	FO 414
		FO 461

*For records of Control Office for Germany and Austria and Allied Commission for Austria see pp 63-4, 91-2.

Central America	-	FO 420
		FO 461
Chile	FO 132	-
China	FO 233	FO 436
	FO 671	-
	FO 676	-
Colombia	FO 135	-
	FO 854	
Czechoslovakia	FO 817	FO 404
	-	FO 417
Denmark	FO 211	FO 419
	FO 321	FO 490
	FO 649	
	FO 749	
Egypt	FO 141	FO 403
	FO 847	FO 407
	FO 891	
	FO 963	
Estonia	-	FO 419
Ethiopia see Abyssinia		
Finland	FO 511	FO 419
	FO 753	FO 490
France	FO 146	FO 425
	FO 561	FO 432
	FO 684	
	FO 698	
	FO 708	
	FO 710	
	FO 859	
	FO 892	
	FO 912	
	FO 969	
Germany*	-	FO 404
		FO 408
Greece	FO 286	FO 421
	FO 996	FO 434
Guatemala	FO 252	-
Holland (Netherlands)	FO 238	FO 425
	FO 242	FO 432
Honduras	FO 252	-
Hungary	-	FO 404
		FO 417
Iceland	FO 321	FO 419
	FO 962	FO 490
Iran (Persia)	FO 248	FO 406
	FO 799	FO 416
Iraq	FO 624	FO 406
	FO 838	

---

*For records of Control Office for Germany and Austria and Control Commission for Germany see pp 61-3, 91-2.

Italy	FO 170	FO 421
	FO 593	FO 434
	FO 762	
	FO 970	
	FO 995	
Japan	FO 262	FO 436
	FO 345	
	FO 908	
Latvia	-	FO 419
Levant, the	-	FO 406
Liberia	FO 458	-
Libya (Tripoli)	FO 160	-
Lithuania	-	FO 419
Luxemburg	-	FO 425
		FO 432
Madagascar	-	FO 403
Mexico	FO 204	FO 420
	FO 723	
Morocco	FO 174	FO 403
	FO 443	FO 413
	FO 835	
	FO 836	
	FO 981	
Nepal	FO 766	FO 436
Netherlands see		
Holland		
Nicaragua	FO 252	-
Norway	FO 337	FO 419
	FO 952	FO 490
Palestine	-	FO 406
Panama	FO 288	-
Persia see Iran		
Peru	FO 177	-
Poland	FO 688	FO 404
		FO 417
Portugal	FO 173	FO 425
	FO 179	
	FO 641	
Roumania	FO 770	FO 421
		FO 434
Russia (USSR)	FO 181	FO 418
	FO 447	FO 490
	FO 448	
Salvador	FO 252	-
Siam (Thailand)	FO 628	FO 436
South America	-	FO 420
		FO 461
South East Asia	-	FO 436
Soviet Union see		
Russia		

Country		
Spain	FO 185	FO 425
	FO 332	
	FO 773	
	FO 889	
	FO 927	
Sudan	FO 867	FO 407
Suez Canal	-	FO 403
		FO 423
Sweden	FO 188	FO 419
	FO 818	FO 490
Switzerland	FO 778	FO 425
Syria	-	FO 406
Thailand see Siam		
Tripoli see Libya		
Tunisia	-	FO 403
Turkey	FO 195	FO 421
	FO 198	FO 424
	FO 226	
	FO 784	
United States of America	FO 115	FO 414
	FO 700	FO 461
Uruguay	FO 505	-
USSR see Russia		
Vatican City	FO 380	FO 421
		FO 434
Yugoslavia	FO 536	FO 421
		FO 434

War Crimes of the Second World War: Documents in the Public Record Office

[These are housed at Kew apart from those of the Treasury solicitor which at the time of printing are held at Chancery Lane and may only be seen there]

United Nations War Crimes Commission

At a meeting of representatives of seventeen of the Allied nations in October 1943, the United Nations War Crimes Commission (UNWCC) was established. Its purpose was to collect, record and investigate evidence of war crimes and their perpetrators, to liaise with national governments to this end, and, at a later stage, to advise governments on the legal procedures to be adopted in bringing suspects to trial. It was the responsibility of the national governments concerned to act upon the evidence supplied to them by the Commission. The first official meeting of the UNWCC was held in January 1944, and the organization continued to be active until 1948. The Soviet Union declined to participate.

The records of the UNWCC, its sub-commissions and committees, are housed in the United Nations Archives in New York. Documentation on all aspects of the UNWCC's work occurs in the General Correspondence of the Foreign Office, mainly in that of the Political Departments (FO 371). Relevant files are listed in the *Index to General Correspondence of the Foreign Office, 1920- 1951,* under the general heading of 'War Criminals'. Minutes of UNWCC meetings, bulletins, circulars, general correspondence and lists of suspects occur in the papers of the War Crimes Branch of the Treasury Solicitor's Department in TS 26.

Central Registry of War Criminals and Security Suspects

To assist the UNWCC and Allied governments to trace ex-enemy nationals suspected of committing war crimes or atrocities in Europe, a Central Registry of War Criminals and Security Suspects (CROWCASS) was set up by the Supreme Headquarters Allied Expeditionary Force in the spring of 1945. The object of CROWCASS was to provide a pool of information on persons in Allied detention and those wanted on war crimes charges, on which national governments could draw and to which they were encouraged to contribute. CROWCASS published lists of detainees and wanted persons, similar in format to those produced by the UNWCC.

Documentation on the initial functions and organizations of CROWCASS will be found in FO 945/343 (Control Office for Germany and Austria General Department). Miscellaneous corre- spondence and papers concerning the creation, control and organization of the Central Registry exist in WO 309/1425 to WO 309/1427; related papers are in WO 32/12200. Further material of an administrative nature will be found in FO 1032/787, FO 1032/2206 and in WO 311/618 to WO 311/622. Documentation on the financing of CROWCASS is among records of the Control Office for Germany and Austria's Finance Division (FO 944/733 and FO 944/965).

For other references to CROWCASS material the *Index to General Correspondence of the Foreign Office* should be consulted. There are references to several lists of wanted persons issued by CROWCASS in the 1945 volume under the general heading 'War Criminals'. Such lists will also be found in WO 311/60 and WO 309/1703 to WO 309/1706.

The Investigation of War Crimes in Europe

In the immediate post-war period, responsibility for collecting evidence of war crimes rested with a variety of units attached to the Headquarters of the Allied Forces in Europe. In Germany, several investigation teams operated with the 21 Army Group (later British Army of the Rhine). In Austria, investigations were conducted by the British Military Police and, subsequently, by a War Crimes Section of the Judge Advocate General's Branch, British Troops in Austria. Several War Crimes Investigation Teams were active in Norway; they were responsible to the HQ Allied Land Forces Norway.

It was not long before the administrative machinery was consolidated and simplified. In Germany, the various units operating with HQ British Army of the Rhine were merged to form the War Crimes Group (North West Europe). In Austria, a War Crimes Group (South East Europe) was created in 1947 to deal with investigations both in Austria and in Italy.

Case files of the War Crimes Group (NWE) are in WO 309, and cover both individual cases and general procedural policy. A few Quarterly Historical Reports of the Group and of its War Crimes Investigation Unit will be found in WO 267/600 to WO 267/602. Case Files of the War Crimes Group (SEE) are in WO 310. Most of these files concern investigations in Austria and Italy, although a few deal with Bulgaria, Greece, Roumania and Yugoslavia. Related documentation occurs among the Headquarters and Regional Files of the Allied Commission for Austria (FO 1020). Files of the War Crimes Investigation Branch, HQ Allied Land Forces Norway are in WO 331.

Overall responsibility for war crimes policy and related legal procedures lay with the Military Department of the Judge Advocate General's Office (renamed after 1948 the Directorate of Army Legal Services). The war crimes files of this body, dealing with the investigation and prosecution of war criminals for offences committed in all military theatres of World War Two, are in WO 311. Card indexes relating to files in this record class have been preserved in WO 353. Card indexes of the Judge Advocate General are in WO 354. Card indexes of persons passed to or wanted by various Allied authorities constitute the class WO 355.

Diverse material on war crimes policy in Europe, including numerous individual cases, occurs among the Military Headquarters Papers, Allied Force Headquarters, in WO 204. Policy papers, mainly concerning crimes committed by or against Italians, are to be found in WO 204/2189 to WO 204/2193 (WO 204/2189 is closed for 75 years). Documentation on the investigation of war crimes in South East Europe is in WO 204/2194 to WO 204/2200.

Reports of Supreme Headquarters Allied Expeditionary Force (SHAEF) courts of inquiry into alleged atrocities committed against Allied prisoners of war by the German Armed Forces have the references WO 219/5045 to WO 219/5054. These files are closed for 75 years.

A sample of lists of charges prepared against Germans and Italians in connection with war crimes investigations occurs among the war crimes papers of the Treasury Solicitor's Department in TS 26/176 to TS 26/802.

For further documentation on war crimes investigations, etc, readers are advised to search classes of records containing general correspondence of the departments concerned such as the Admiralty, Air Ministry, Foreign Office, Lord Chancellor's Office and the War Office, particularly the following:

ADM 1	Admiralty and Secretariat Papers	)Subject code
		)19 relates to
ADM 116	Admiralty and Secretariat Cases	)Civil Power
		)and Legal
		)Matters

AIR 2	Air Ministry: Registered Files	)Subject code)89 relates to
AIR 20	Unregistered Papers	)Prisoners of)War
FO 371	Foreign Office: General Correspondence; Political. Refer to the *Index to the General Correspondence of the Foreign Office, 1920-1951*	
FO 1060	Control Commission for Germany: Legal Division	
LCO 2	Registered Files (See LCO 2/2972 - LCO 2/3003 under the Lord Chancellor's Office's miscellaneous files)	
WO 32	Registered Files: General Series (Subject code 94(A) relates to War Criminals: General)	
WO 208	Directorate of Military Intelligence	

War Crimes Trials in Europe

There was considerable variation in the procedures adopted by the Allies for trying those accused of war crimes in Europe and the Far East. In Europe, most cases were dealt with by Allied military courts, although in Germany itself the occupying authorities set up a number of different courts to try alleged war criminals.

Records of proceedings in British military courts, involving both members of enemy armed forces and civilians charged with committing war crimes against British and Allied nationals, are to be found among the war crimes papers of the Judge Advocate General's Office (WO 235). Records of European trials in this class are arranged as follows:

WO 235/1 to WO 235/594:	Trial proceedings, exhibits, extracted papers, etc
WO 235/595 to WO 235/602:	Canadian Military Court proceedings, war crimes trials at Aurich
WO 235/603 to WO 235/812:	Deputy Judge Advocate General files and pending files. There is a nominal index at the beginning of the class list.

The International Military Tribunal (IMT) at Nuremberg declared many organizations of the National Socialist period in Germany to be criminal. These organizations included the SS, the SA and the Party leadership corps. Under the provisions of Military Government Ordinance No 69 of 31 December 1946, former members of such organizations were liable to trial before German tribunals and various other courts set up by the occupying powers. This major operation was code-named 'Old Lace'.

The most comprehensive accumulation of papers on 'Old Lace' is to be found among the records of the Control Commission for Germany's Legal Division (FO 1060/1195 to FO 1060/1230). Further papers are in FO 1060/139 to FO 1060/142, FO 1060/1023, FO 1060/1038 to FO 1060/1040 and FO 1060/1078 to FO 1060/1086. The legal background and technical procedures of the operation are documented in FO 945/356. Reports on 'Old Lace' trials, including the first trial at Recklinghausen in June 1947, occur in FO 937/150, in FO 1005/1810 to FO 1005/1814, and in FO 1032/2205. These files also contain progress reports and other miscellaneous papers.

Between 1945 and 1949, the British and US governments undertook to try a number of senior German military figures on war crimes charges. The British trial of Erich von Manstein, which took place in Hamburg in 1949, is extensively documented. A record of proceedings and documents in evidence may be found under the reference FO 1060/1288 to FO 1060/1358. Other Manstein trial documents have the references WO 235/589 to WO 235/594. Correspondence and papers concerning Manstein, Brauchitsch, Rundstedt and Strauss, all of whom were in British custody after the war, are contained in FO 1032/1948, FO 1032/2215, and in PREM 8/1112.

Daily transcripts of proceedings and other documents relating to the trial in Venice of Albert Kesselring are held by the Imperial War Museum (formerly PRO reference FO 647; the same class also contains records of the Falkenhausen and Roechling trials). Correspondence and other papers on Kesselring, mostly concerning his imprisonment, are in FO 1005/1900 and FO 1060/493 to FO 1060/501. Churchill's reaction to the sentence imposed on Kesselring is documented in PREM 8/707.

Apart from the Four-Power IMT, Nuremberg was also the venue for a succession of United States military tribunals. Among the various cases heard before these tribunals were the German High Command Case, the 'Ministries Case' (von Weizsaecker *et al*) and the 'Industrialists Cases' (Krupp, Flick and I G Farben). Microfilmed records of proceedings and related documentation are housed in the National Archives, Washington DC. Excerpts from these proceedings have been published as *Trials of War Criminals before the Nuremberg Military Tribunals under Control Council Law No 10* (15 vols, Washington DC: GPO, 1949-50). The Imperial War Museum currently holds transcripts of proceedings, etc, of the twelve trials (formerly PRO reference FO 646).

Some documentation concerning the US military tribunals is contained in the records of the Control Commission for Germany (BE) Legal Division. Papers relating to the German High Command trial are in FO 1060/1377, and include summaries of charges, evidence, and the legal background to the trial. Transcripts of documents in evidence at the trial of Weizsaecker and Neurath are in FO 1060/1359 to FO 1060/1371; miscellaneous correspondence concerning Neurath's imprisonment in Spandau occurs in FO 1060/517 and FO 1060/518. Reports of the British observer at the trials of Friedrich Flick and Alfried Krupp are to be found among the records of the Control Office for Germany and Austria's Legal Division (FO 937/124 and FO 937/143). Correspondence on the bringing to trial of Krupp and associates is in PREM 8/391.

Other documentation on war crimes trials is to be found in the General Correspondence of the Foreign Office (Political), in FO 371. Information on the composition, terms of reference and other details of Allied Courts in Germany can be gleaned from documents contained in the records of the Control Commission for Germany (BE) Legal Division (FO 1060) and the Control Office for Germany and Austria's Legal and General Departments (respectively FO 937 and FO 945).

Documentation on the prosecution of war criminals occurs also in the Military Headquarters Papers, Allied Force Headquarters, in WO 204/11112 to WO 204/11132 and WO 204/11315 to WO 204/11326. Most of these are closed for 75 years.

International Military Tribunal, Nuremberg

The IMT Nuremberg was set up on the basis of the London Agreement of 8 August 1945, by which the Allied Powers undertook to prosecute and punish the major war criminals of the European Axis. The IMT tried the leaders of the German government, National Socialist Party and Armed Forces, and others whose actions were deemed to transcend any specific geographical location. This proceeded separately from, but in tandem with, the war crimes investigations and trials previously outlined.

The trial records of the IMT have been transferred to the Imperial War Museum (formerly PRO reference FO 645). These consist of daily transcripts of proceedings, exhibits, judgments, briefs, etc. Transcripts of proceedings and documents in evidence have been published as *Trial of the Major War Criminals before the International Military Tribunal* (42 vols, Nuremberg: IMT, 1947-1949). Transcript minutes of proceedings can be found in the General Correspondence of the

Foreign Office (Political) for 1946, in FO 371/57435 to FO 371/57517. There is no detailed index to these records.

Miscellaneous correspondence and papers relating to the IMT Nuremberg are in FO 1019. This class includes correspondence of the British War Crimes Executive (BWCE: the British prosecution team led by Sir David Maxwell-Fyfe) and of the Court Contact Committee, together with applications for witnesses, documents submitted on behalf of defendants, and correspondence from the public. Further correspondence of the BWCE on various aspects of the trial is among the records of the Control Commission for Germany (BE) Political Division, in FO 1049/425 to FO 1049/428, together with other correspondence on the progress of the trial. Similar documentation will be found in FO 945/332, FO 945/345, FO 945/346; FO 1032/2203, FO 1032/2209, FO 1032/2445, FO 1032/2446; and in FO 1060/95 and FO 1060/1378 to FO 1060/1389.

For Foreign Office correspondence on the Nuremberg trial readers should consult the *Index to General Correspondence of the Foreign Office, 1920-1951*. Documents are listed under the heading 'War Crimes: German (Nuremberg Trials)'; most of those that survive will be found in FO 371.

The Nuremberg Trial is documented also in records of the Prime Minister's Office and of the Cabinet Office. Readers should consult the class lists and (in the case of Cabinet records) the subject indexes for the following:

PREM 4	Confidential Papers.
	Pre-1946 policy discussions on the setting up
	of a Four-Power Tribunal in PREM 4/100/10,
	PREM 4/100/12 and PREM 4/100/13.
PREM 8	Correspondence and Papers, 1945-1951
CAB 65)	Cabinet Office, War Cabinet Minutes and
CAB 66)	Memoranda, 1939-1945
CAB 128)	Cabinet Minutes and Memoranda from 1945
CAB 129)	

Minutes of the first meeting of the ad hoc Committee on Appeals Against Sentences at the Nuremberg Trial of War Criminals are in CAB 130/13.

War Crimes Investigation and Trials in the Far East

The majority of Japanese who were brought to trial on war crimes charges, and who did not appear before the International Military Tribunal (IMT) in Tokyo were tried by military commissions of the 8 US Army at Yokohama. Responsibility for the investigation and bringing to trial of persons accused of crimes against British nationals devolved upon General Headquarters, Allied Land Forces South East Asia (ALFSEA) whose files are in WO 325.

For files of the Judge Advocate General's Military Department concerning South East Asia see particularly WO 311/538 to WO 311/565. Card indexes and record cards concerning investigations and trials in South East Asia form the classes WO 356 and WO 357.

Files on policy and numerous individual cases are scattered throughout the Military Headquarters Papers, Far East Forces, in WO 203. The principal references are: WO 203/2080, WO 203/4571A, WO 203/4571B, WO 203/4926A, WO 203/4926B, WO 203/4927A, WO 203/4927B, WO 203/5592 to WO 203/5596, WO 203/6086 and WO 203/6087. Some are closed for 75 years. Quarterly Historical Reports of Far East Land Forces Investigation teams, 1946-1947, are in WO 268/102 to WO 268/104. Documentation on crimes committed against Allied prisoners of war is scattered throughout the records of the War Office's Directorate of Military Intelligence (WO 208).

Transcripts of proceedings in British Military Courts in the Far East are among the war crimes papers of the Judge Advocate General's Office in WO 235/813 to WO 235/1117. Samples of charge sheets filed against individuals accused of war crimes, including charges brought by Australia, may be found in TS 26/803 to TS 26/847.

Transcript records of the IMT in Tokyo are currently deposited at the Imperial War Museum (formerly PRO reference FO 648). This set is incomplete, but the full series is available in Tokyo and Washington. See the *Tokyo War Crimes Trials. The Complete Transcripts of the Proceedings of the International Military Tribunal for the Far East*, ed R J Pritchard and S M Zaide (22 vols, New York: Garland, 1981). Foreign Office correspondence on the setting up of the IMT Tokyo is in FO 371/57422 to FO 371/57429. These and other files on war crimes trials and investigations are listed in the *Index to General Correspondence of the Foreign Office, 1920-1951*, under the headings 'War Criminals' and 'War Criminals: Japanese'.

Imperial War Museum

Readers wishing to consult war crimes trial records held by the Imperial War Museum, should enquire at the following address:

Department of Documents
Imperial War Museum
Lambeth Road
London
SE1 6HZ

Official Histories of the Second World War

[For details of Official Histories still in print reference should be made to 'History in Print' (Sectional list No 60) obtainable from Publicity Department, HMSO Books, St Crispin's, Duke Street, Norwich NR3 1PD.]

A number of classes of records in the PRO contain material concerning the preparation of Official Histories, notably:

Admiralty
ADM 261   War of 1939-1945: Material used for Official Medical History

Air Ministry
AIR 41   Air Historical Branch: Narratives and Monographs
AIR 49   History of RAF Medical Services

Cabinet Office
CAB 44   Historical Section, Official War Histories, Narratives (Military)
CAB 101   Official War Histories (1939-1945): Military
CAB 102   Official War Histories (1939-1945): Civil
CAB 103   Historical Section: Registered Files
CAB 106   Historical Section: Archivist and Librarian Files (AL Series)
CAB 140   Official Historians' Correspondence
CAB 146   Historical Section, Enemy Documents Section: Files and Papers

Education and Arts Departments
ED 138   History of Education in the War 1939-1945: Drafts, etc.

Ministry of Food
MAF 152   Ministry of Food: War History Papers

Ministry of Labour and National Service
LAB 76   Official Histories: Correspondence and Papers

Board of Trade
BT 131   War Histories (1939-1945) Files
BT 216   History of the Administration of Enemy Property 1939-1964

Treasury
T 208   Financial Enquiries Branch (Hawtrey) Papers

War Office
WO 222   War of 1939-1945: Medical Historian Papers

Ministry of Works

WORK 46   Official History of the Second World War, Works and Buildings, Unpublished
           Sources

United Kingdom Military Histories

Grand Strategy

Vol I   1933 to September 1939. By NH Gibbs
Vol II   September 1939 - June 1941. By JRM Butler
Vol III   June 1941 - August 1942. By JMA Gwyer and JRM Butler
Vol IV   August 1942 - August 1943. By Michael Howard
Vol V   August 1943 - September 1944. By John Ehrman
Vol VI   October 1944 - August 1945. By John Ehrman

British intelligence in the Second World War: its influence on strategy and operations.

Vol 1   1939 - Summer 1941. By FH Hinsley *et al*
Vol 2   Mid 1941 - Mid 1943. By FH Hinsley *et al*
Vol 3   Part 1 June 1943 - June 1944. By FH Hinsley *et al*
Vol 3   Part 2 June 1944 - VE Day. By FH Hinsley *et al*
Vol 4   Security and counter-intelligence. By FH Hinsley *et al*
Vol 5   Strategic deception. By Sir Michael Howard

Campaigns

The Campaign in Norway. By TK Derry
France and Flanders, 1939-1940. By Major LF Ellis
The Mediterranean and Middle East. (6 Vols) By Major-General ISO Playfair, with
            Commander GMS Stitt, RN (Vol I)
            Captain FC Flynn, RN (Vols II - VI)
            Brigadier CJC Molony (Vols I - VI)
            Air Vice-Marshal SE Toomer (Vols I and II)
            Group-Captain TP Gleave (Vols III - VI)
            Major-General HL Davies (Vols V and VI)
            General Sir William Jackson (Vol VI)

The War Against Japan. (5 Vols) By Major-General SW Kirby, with
            Captain CT Addis, RN (Vols I - III)
            Colonel JF Meiklejohn (Vols I and II)
            Brigadier MR Roberts (Vols II - V)
            Colonel GT Wards (Vols I - V)
            Air Vice-Marshal NL Desoer (Vols I - V)

Victory in the West. (2 Vols) By Major LF Ellis, with
            Captain GRG Allen, RN (Vol I)
            Lieutenant-Colonel AE Warhurst
            Air Chief Marshal Sir James M Robb (Vol I)

The Defence of the United Kingdom. By Basil Collier
The War at Sea. (3 Vols) By Captain SW Roskill, RN
The Strategic Air Offensive. (4 Vols) By Sir Charles Webster and Noble Frankland

Civil Affairs and Military Government

Civil Affairs and Military Government Central Organization and Planning. By FSV Donnison
North-West Europe. By FSV Donnison
Allied Military Administration of Italy (1943-1945). By CRS Harris
British Military Administration in the Far East (1943-1946). By FSV Donnison

Orders of Battle 1939-1945. (2 Vols) Compiled by Lieut-Colonel HF Joslen and based on official documents
British Foreign Policy in the Second World War. By Sir Llewellyn Woodward. This is a single-volume abridgement of the following work
British Foreign Policy in the Second World War. (5 Vols) By Sir Llewellyn Woodward
SOE in France. By MRD Foot

United Kingdom Civil Series

Introductory

British War Economy. By WK Hancock and MM Gowing
British War Production. By MM Postan
Problems of Social Policy. By RM Titmuss
Statistical Digest of the War. Prepared in the Central Statistical Office

General Series

Food. By RJ Hammond
   Vol I   The Growth of Policy
   Vols II and III   Studies in Administration and Control
Economic Blockade. By WN Medlicott
   Vol I   (1939-1941)
   Vol II   (1941-1945)
Merchant Shipping and the Demands of War. By CBA Behrens
Coal. By WHB Court
Manpower. By HMD Parker
Financial Policy, 1939-1945. By RS Sayers
Civil Defence. By TH O'Brien
Oil. By DJ Payton-Smith
Works and Buildings. By CM Kohan
Agriculture. By Keith AH Murray
Civil Industry and Trade. By EL Hargreaves and MM Gowing
Inland Transport. By CI Savage
Studies in the Social Services. By SM Ferguson and H Fitzgerald

War Production Series

The Control of Raw Materials. By J Hurtsfield
Labour in the Munitions Industries. By P Inman
Factories and Plant. By William Hornby
Administration of War Production. By JD Scott and Richard Hughes
Contracts and Finance. By W Ashworth
North American Supply. By H Duncan Hall
Studies of Overseas Supply. By H Duncan Hall and CC Wrigley
Design and Development of Weapons. By MM Postan, D Hay and JD Scott

United Kingdom Medical Series

Clinical Volumes
[Incorporating the experience of the Fighting and the Civilian Services]

Medicine and Pathology. Edited by Sir Zachary Cope
Surgery. Edited by Sir Zachary Cope
Casualties and Medical Statistics. Edited by W Franklin Mellor

Volumes Relating to the Fighting Services

Royal Navy. Edited by JLS Coulter
 The Royal Naval Medical Services (Administration)
 The Royal Naval Medical Services (Operations)

Army. Edited by FAE Crew
 The Army Medical Services (Administration). Vols I and II
 The Army Medical Services (Campaigns). Vols I, II, III, IV and V

Royal Air Force. Edited by SC Rexford-Welch
 The Royal Air Force Medical Services (Administration)
 The Royal Air Force Medical Services (Commands)
 The Royal Air Force Medical Services (Campaigns)

The following book has been compiled by the British and Commonwealth Medical Historians
 Medical Services in War: Lessons Learnt

Volumes Relating to the Civilian Services

The Emergency Medical Services. Vols I and II. Edited by CL Dunn
The Civilian Health and Medical Services. Vols I and II. Edited by Sir Arthur S MacNalty
Medical Research. Edited by FHK Green and Major-General Sir Gordon Covell

INDEX